# THE UNSINKABLE AIRCRAFT CARRIER

*By the same author*

BIG BROTHER IS LISTENING
WAR PLAN UK

# THE UNSINKABLE AIRCRAFT CARRIER

## *American Military Power in Britain*

DUNCAN CAMPBELL



MICHAEL JOSEPH
LONDON

First published in Great Britain by Michael Joseph Ltd
44 Bedford Square, London WC1
1984



ISBN 0 7181 2289 5 (hardcover)
ISBN 0 7181 2350 6 (trade paperback)

Photoset by Rowland Phototypesetting Limited
Bury St Edmunds, Suffolk.
Printed and bound in Great Britain by
Billing and Sons, Worcester.

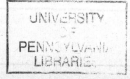

# *Contents*

# List of Figures



# List of Tables



# List of Illustrations

*Acknowledgments*

The author and publishers are most grateful to the following for permission to reproduce illustrations:
US Air Force, 3; *Leeds Other Paper*, 4; Keith Bryers, 6; Robert Moore, 7; Camera Press, 8, 9, 14, 17, 24; Michael Bennett, 10; *Sunday Times*, 12; John May, 15; Jeremy Nicholl, 20.

The maps and diagrams were supplied by David Haslam.

# *Acknowledgments*

This book began with a collaborative venture in October 1980 between the *New Statesman* and Thames Television's *TV Eye* programme. We set out, quite simply, to count the number of US bases and facilities in Britain, and to show how little was known of the scale or nature of the US military presence in Britain. We also tried to explain something of the detail of numerous, complex and interlocking American networks of intelligence, communications, navigation and so on – each with their outposts on British territory, and each of some – occasionally, great – strategic significance. We sought also to differentiate between allied activities in support of NATO, bilateral Anglo-American arrangements, and unilateral United States activities.

I am grateful for that collaboration to producer Jack Saltman, and to the many who helped then and have helped since. In particular, I am indebted to Bill Arkin, of the Washington Institute for Policy Studies, for his continual watchkeeping in the sea of information which the United States government does produce about its military affairs; and to Owen Wilkes in New Zealand, who formerly directed a worldwide project on 'Foreign Military Presence' for the Stockholm International Peace Research Institute (SIPRI). Dan Re'em and Patrick Forbes helped me unearth new documents and information in archives in London and Washington. Patrick Forbes helpfully assimilated a mountain of material on British political attitudes to the Atlantic alliance. Simon Duke provided some archive material from his own postgraduate research project. Many friends, colleagues and correspondents in Britain have been vigilant and helpful in observing defence developments: Jon Side, Malcolm Spaven, Robert Moore, John Edwards, Phil Kelly, Mark Chilvers and Harry Dean in particular. In the United States, Norman Solomon, funded by the Center for Investigative Reporting, Inc, investigated the special dangers for residents of the Clyde of Poseidon missiles. I am grateful to him and to Linda and Alistair Kirkwood, who have to live next to them in Dunoon, for help in investigating the Holy

Loch Poseidon accident. I am obliged to Keith Bryers, John May, and the Public Affairs Office of RAF Chicksands for the use of photographs. Winslow Peck, Jeff Katz and Jim Haynes helpfully provided information about US electronic intelligence activities in Britain. The US Third Air Force's Director of Public Affairs, Lieutenant Colonel Douglas Kennett, provided statistics on USAF developments in the UK.*

I am also indebted to Hugh Stephenson, the editor of the *New Statesman*, and to Jane Thomas and my other colleagues for, once again, allowing me the time and giving me the encouragement to research, write and publish this account.

DC
London, 1983

*During October 1983, the US Air Force Headquarters in Britain offered, on their own initiative, (through Colonel Kennett) to 'review (the) book for accuracy'. I gratefully accepted the offer, and initially sent tables and other data for 'review'.

This offer was later suddenly withdrawn. I infer from the previously helpful attitude of US officials that the British Ministry of Defence intervened to prohibit USAF staff confirming or correcting any details herein which would further expose the inaccurate and frequently contradictory nature of the information which the Ministry has supplied to Parliament and the public.

The partial manuscript was therefore returned by the US Air Force – after three months delay, and after the book had in fact gone to press. It was returned 'without further comment'. Some six changes or corrections, most minor, had previously been suggested (and all are included). There were still 'a number of inaccuracies' in the tables, it was then alleged to me, but 'neither the UK or US government is prepared to discuss intelligence or nuclear operations'. So what the inaccuracies might be (if any) was officially secret.

I then asked if I had been given all the corrections necessary outside these contentious areas, and was told (in January 1984) that the US Air Force could not comment at all, even on non-secret bases, unless they were included in the Ministry of Defence's inaccurate 1983 list (see pps 14 – 16). I asked if this policy also precluded confirming unclassified official testimony about the 'missing' bases by senior US Air Force and Pentagon officials to the Congress of the United States, and was told – even in respect of a 1983 statement to the Congress by the Commanding General of the US Air Force, Europe – that the USAF HQ in Britain 'had no facilities' for checking the accuracy of such information given to the US Congress.

I will not argue that the original USAF offer was not well-intentioned. But readers and users of this book may judge any subsequent official comments about alleged inaccuracies in the text in the light of the fact that such comments were diligently sought prior to publication.

# *Introduction*

Over three decades ago, Winston Churchill called on the British government of the day to heed the consequences of admitting the United States as a permanent military tenant. 'We must not forget,' he warned:

> that by creating the American atomic base in East Anglia, we have made ourselves the target, and perhaps the bull's eye of a Soviet attack.[1]

In 1950, he had cautioned Prime Minister Attlee that the power to launch an atomic attack would not remain an American monopoly, with awesome consequences for the British, as hosts to America's main forward bases:

> There is no doubt that the passage of time will place these fearful agencies of destruction effectively in Soviet hands . . . The atomic bomb . . . is only one of the factors in the military situation before us, but it is the dominant factor. If . . . Russia had 50, and we got those 50, fearful experiences far beyond anything we have ever endured, would be our lot.[2]

Churchill was accurate in his assessment. Since 1950 and 1951, when these words were uttered, the nuclear arms race has made the idea of national security ultimately meaningless. In crisis or war, there is now no defence to be had against the vengeance of an aggressor, save the threat of retaliation. In 1980, Britain's Secretary of State for Defence, Francis Pym, reminded the country that: 'the Russians, let everyone understand, can annihilate Britain easily, ten times over.'[3]

Visitors to American bases in Britain meet exhortations of similar gravity. At the Lakenheath home of the US Air Force's 48th Tactical Fighter Wing they are greeted by a disturbing slogan:

> The mission of the 48th TFW, in peace, is to train for war . . . DON'T YOU FORGET IT

This display, standing just a few yards to the side of the well-weathered and hardened concrete 'Combat Operations Center' bunker, is a chilling rephrasing of the old Latin proverb of Vegetius: 'If you wish peace, prepare for war'. Highly visible from the public roads, the sign has an abrasive quality for those who are not US Air Force employees, and who do not agree with their outlook that the only issue is *when* war will come – not *if*.

It is little wonder that visitors are discouraged from photographing this gung-ho artifact, lest further public display of the slogan lend substance to claims, by natives and dissidents of the parts, of US 'warmongering' – which is how even the Air Force's own representatives express their fears of the slogan being misunderstood. At bases like Lakenheath there is already a sufficient and highly obvious presence of the hardware of nuclear warfare – armed warplanes standing ready on quick reaction alert, weapons stores, above them high guardtowers – to focus public perception on the risks of war.

This book is intended to document and explain a major aspect of the risks of war to Britain, about which Churchill warned – the presence of substantial United States military forces in Britain. Where are they, and what do they do? Are they under British control? Would the British government really be asked before a nuclear attack was launched from British territory? Does the presence of the American bases protect Britain and its inhabitants with a nuclear umbrella and a powerful defence we could never afford for ourselves? Or are we merely providing a friendly, unquestioning, geographically convenient but expendable launching point for the projections of US military power?

If we wish for peace, we must indeed understand the machinery of war – and its origins. An historical and political appreciation of what British politicians have seen as their special relationship with the Americans, and what they have been prepared to pay for it, is more important than the mere cataloguing of military might.

The 'special relationship' between Britain and the United States has seldom been more special in the post-war era than it became in 1980. In every sphere of international affairs, from economic policy to NATO military planning, President Reagan and Mrs Thatcher seemed at first to achieve a close harmony. The compatibility of the two national leaders has not, however, created in Britain a new popular desire to draw closer to the United States; quite the contrary.

Public opinion has repeatedly shown clear and unequivocal distrust of the United States leadership, and a wavering hostility to US nuclear bases. This state of affairs perhaps owes most to European perceptions of Ronald Reagan as an unreliable and demagogic leader, in whose hands it is unsafe to place western defences. The unwillingness of his government to follow the US-Soviet *rapprochements* of the 1970s, and the start of a massive unilateral nuclear build-up by the United States had done little to dent this image.

Distrust of the United States is confirmed by the apparent paradox that, while a substantial majority in this country support continued British participation in the NATO alliance, there is also a majority against the deployment of American cruise missiles, and a majority (at times) against *any* American nuclear bases. Such hostility to the United States military presence is evidently fired in some quarters by a determined desire for nuclear disarmament and military disengagement – and in others by simple xenophobia. The hostility is clearly demonstrated by attitudes to the 'dual key' issue. Should United States forces alone have control of the firing of cruise missiles? Even before Dr David Owen of the SDP made this issue the centrepiece of his party's approach to cruise missiles, British public opinion was firmly set against sole US control: in February 1982, by 89 per cent to 4 per cent. By the summer of 1983, public opinion had stiffened against the United States, with 96 per cent saying they wanted a 'dual key'.[4]

A clear majority against cruise missiles first appeared in opinion polls towards the end of 1980. Hostility to cruise peaked early in 1983 when more than two persons out of three with an opinion on the subject were against the missiles.[5] Shortly before the June 1983 election another poll tested how British attitudes to cruise would change if there were a British veto; without a veto, there was then a majority of approximately 50 per cent to 35 per cent against cruise – but given a veto half the opposition would change their minds and accept the missiles.[6]

Public opinion about other US nuclear bases in Britain has wavered. After repeated US early warning false alarms in June 1980, there was considerable apprehension about the presence of the American bases – and a majority of almost two to one against their retention.[7] After a quieter period without these harbingers of apocalypse, however, more people were ready to express contentment with the *status quo*: by the end of 1982, the 50–60 per cent majority against the bases had eroded to 44 per cent, with 46 per cent for their retention.[8]

The opinion poll findings show that there is underlying distrust and unease about foreign military bases in British territory. The components of this unease are many – because the bases are military, because they are foreign, because they are or may be nuclear, or just because they are there. Those in favour of the bases believe that NATO, nuclear weapons and US bases have been here for more than 30 years, have not done us harm, and have kept the Russians at bay.

Whichever view is taken, it is undeniable that British government officials and ministers have shown indifference and complacency in monitoring and regulating the US presence in Britain. Since the US Air Force returned in 1948 (having left soon after the end of World War Two) there has been a *de facto* policy of 'open house'. In paying close attention to the development of US bases in Britain over the last few years, I have frequently found Ministry of Defence representatives unaware of what US forces were planning or the significance of their installations – sometimes even apparently unaware of the existence of some US military facilities in the United Kingdom.

This book aims to redress the disparities in public information, which are far more a failing of British society and government than of American. One of the ironies of US military relations with her allies is that far greater amounts of information are publicly available in Washington than are ever vouchsafed to residents around US overseas bases – or, so it often seems, to host governments. For much of the long period of entrenchment since US bases blossomed all over Britain in 1950, there has been little public information and less debate about the scale of these US deployments. But the 1980 revival of peace and disarmament movements, the upsurge in concern over the dangers of the nuclear arms race and the rebirth of CND has made the issue quite central in public opinion.

As recounted in this book, there have been many times when British defence officials have for days denied or pleaded ignorance about the situation in US bases in Britain – and then admitted the nature of new developments. On one memorable occasion (concerning the construction of a wartime-only hospital for the US Air Force), the Ministry of Defence had to obtain details of the plan from public relations officials of the US Air Force.

The record of the British government in providing information about the current military situation has been disturbingly poor. When questioned about US bases and facilities in Britain, the Ministry of Defence has provided inconsistent and uneven answers. In 1980, Labour MP Bob Cryer had to ask virtually the same question three times in order to obtain an allegedly complete list of US bases. The 'total' list Cryer obtained from the Defence Ministry at first contained just 12 bases; a second answer added 39 more; and a further 3 contained in the final answer brought the total to 54.[9]

In October that year, working almost entirely from published American sources, the author was able to compile and publish a list of approximately 103 US military bases and facilities in Britain.[10] But in subsequent private briefings for other journalists, Ministry officials ridiculed the suggestion that there were as many as 100 US bases and facilities. They seized upon mention in the article of one facility in Edgware Road, London – claimed to be a petrol pump used by US official cars, but identified in the *New Statesman* report as a 'fuel supply facility'[11] – to discount the entire report as ill-founded, and avoid debate on their earlier omissions and errors.

This theme was highlighted in May 1983 during a House of Lords debate in which Labour peer Lord Jenkins challenged that the government had been 'reluctant to reveal the growth of American nuclear and other bases'. Lord Belstead, Defence Minister of State replied that:

> I sometimes wonder whether he [Lord Jenkins of Putney] and those who think like him have first thought up the number of 100 or more and then tried to justify it. I hope that what I have said will rectify the false allegations that have been made.[12]

In the light of this ill-tempered attack, it is intriguing to discover who it was that first suggested that there were more than 100 US military bases and facilities in Britain. The figure came from the Ministry of Defence itself. In a 1977 parliamentary answer, Dr John Gilbert – Lord Belstead's predecessor in the Callaghan government – told the House of Commons that:

> Accommodation is available to the United States forces at many of more than 100 locations where they have defence facilities, and at over 30 other locations throughout the United Kingdom.[13]

By 1980, evidently, the Ministry had forgotten their own tally of more than 100 US 'defence facilities' in Britain, and some 30 additional sites used only for housing. But this figure corresponded exactly with the *New Statesman* account published in 1980.

Pressed by defence correspondents and parliamentary critics to give a more substantive account of US bases in Britain than merely sniping at the *New Statesman* list, the Ministry produced its own list to defence correspondents in April 1983. The new list enumerated 75 bases. 73 of these had been in existence at the time the Ministry had given Bob Cryer MP a 'total' list of only 54. 19 had been forgotten or ignored.

When it was pointed out to the Ministry of Defence that their 1983 list *still* omitted more than 20 military facilities and 30 housing sites (which were purported to be included), a spokesman replied that the government was not 'prepared to discuss the list or questions about specific bases in detail'. So had it been correct for them to describe the 75-base list, when they issued it, as 'definitive'? 'It is both correct and incorrect,' the spokesman replied.[14]

At the time of writing, there were 130 US military bases and facilities in Britain, ranging from tiny and almost inconsequential offices to gigantic airbases. Including housing sites, there are 160 US facilities in Britain. A complete list is given in Table 7 (pp 286–96).

The issue of British government supervision of and control over US bases and personnel on British territory is most critical on the question of the control of nuclear weapons. British control is, for practical purposes, non-existent. We clearly do not have the right to veto US operations, whatever ministers have sometimes claimed in the past. We may have a good chance of being consulted if time and circumstance permit. If hostilities commenced, as most people fear will happen by the end of the century, it is unlikely that time would permit consultation before annihilation. A 1952 statement, never superseded, defines the question as: 'a matter for joint decision . . . in the light of the circumstances prevailing at the time'.

This commentary has neither the force of a treaty nor any detailed protocol on interpretation and implementation accompanying it, as is customary in many military agreements. It is no more than a communiqué, which was quite as far as the US government has been prepared to go on the issue. It stands alone – bald, banal, and quite unconvincing. If a US President is confronting the issue of having to launch strategic nuclear weapons, possibly involving some tens of thousands of warheads from thousands of US delivery systems, are the 'circumstances prevailing at the time' likely to permit a polite call to the British Prime Minister to consult over whether the few hundred weapons based in Britain should also be released? One hardly expects so.

Nonetheless, these words alone are recited unswervingly by the British government whenever public or press enquiries about the extent of British control over US nuclear weapons – or even British-based forces in general – are raised. In contrast, a great deal that has been said on the same subject by US officials has been extremely equivocal – on the one hand trying not to embarrass the British government (by illuminating its weak situation), but on the other avoiding the wrath of the US Congress or citizenship should it be implied that any foreign power has any control over US military forces.

American war preparation alerts, both intentional and accidental, and similar unilateral actions by US commanders, have occurred sufficiently often to create a substantial impression that, in a real crisis, there would be little likelihood of US forces being responsive to substantive British disagreement over policy.

It is the issue of control and accountability, far above irritation over the presence of foreign military forces not subject to British law, that lends substance to popular fears about Britain being the 'unsinkable aircraft carrier'. The comparisons which may be drawn between the status of US forces in the UK, and some other American bilateral agreements, are not reassuring for Britons. In the most recent treaties with Spain, for example, the US has undertaken to hold neither nuclear weapons nor their components in Spanish bases, and in Turkey, current agreements provide for extensive bilateral control over US activities. One NATO ally – France, under de Gaulle – first banned US nuclear weapons from its soil when the US was not prepared to agree to a genuine 'joint decision' over the use of nuclear weapons on French territory, then, in 1966, left the NATO military structure and required the removal of all US bases and facilities. Most came to Britain.

Fully one-fifth of the US Air Force abroad is in the United Kingdom – and the numbers here are rising. We are, in the 1980s, in the middle of a USAF military build-up of personnel and equipment which – although it falls well short of the huge peak in the 1950s – is substantial. Numbers will rise even more during the deployment of the two new Tactical (cruise) Missile Squadrons, at Greenham Common and Molesworth. This huge war-making capacity quite evidently creates serious military risks for Britain. Does it provide commensurate security?

Put in simple terms, the damage that the United Kingdom may suffer in war arises in significant measure from the presence of US bases here – a feature that the British government has recognised in its own assessments of the likely pattern of nuclear warfare, such as that carried out for the 1980 civil defence exercise 'Square Leg'.[15] US nuclear bases – especially the airbases in East Anglia and central England – are among the country's prime targets. The justification for retaining the bases lies in the policy of deterrence.

It is not only in time of war that nuclear weapons have been dangerous. From both British and American governments there has been intentional dishonesty about accidental hazards to the population. The only serious nuclear weapons accident in Britain, of which details are now publicly known, was at Lakenheath in 1956 – and that was covered up for 23 years. In 1981, a determined attempt to cover up another mishap was mounted at the nuclear submarine base in the Holy Loch. During the 1950s and early 1960s, US bombers carried war-ready bombs aloft on 'alert' flights over Britain, a policy which may not have caused harm in Britain, but which led to two catastrophic accidents – when bombed-up B-52s crashed in Spain and Greenland.

In the first ten years of the Anglo-American postwar 'special relationship', US Air Force commanders were easily and informally able to capitalise on the strong ties created during the Second World War. By 1950, the constellation of airbases in eastern England had become the pivot of American atomic power and strategic war plans. There was nowhere else (given the then absence of bombers of intercontinental range) from whence the United States could mount an atomic attack on the USSR.

During this period, as declassified US strategic war plans of the time now make clear, the United Kingdom was indeed regarded at least by the planners of the US Strategic Air Command (SAC) as an expendable asset from which they could expect no more than six months' use, and perhaps as little as thirty days. If the United Kingdom is unsinkable, it is certainly not indestructible in an atomic war. From these early days on, the presence of the American airbases put Britain firmly in the nuclear front line. Although public concern and awareness declined through the 1960s, the recent deployment of cruise missiles has again reminded many that Britain is still in the nuclear firing line.

A year after victory in Europe, a US Air Force team toured RAF airbases, reviewing their potential for atomic weapons operations. Even before the first SAC bombers came to Britain during the Berlin crisis of 1947, RAF airfields had been prepared and converted so that atomic weapons could be deployed there. The SAC deployment to Britain in 1948, spoken of publicly as a 'temporary matter', became, by discreet and unannounced agreement, 'long term' and the weapon itself arrived in Britain in the summer of 1950. The European stockpile of nuclear weapons, once numbered in dozens, has long since climbed above 10,000, on both sides.

The capacity of the US Air Force in Europe for strategic nuclear warfare remains, in the 1980s, centred on the UK. Like the national nuclear forces since developed by Britain and France, the presence of these US forces causes the Soviet Union considerable discomfort. Soviet negotiators in disarmament talks have made persistent and determined attempts to have the 170 or so F-111 bombers now in Britain included in Strategic Arms Limitation Treaties. As 'forward-based' US strategic weapons, they can strike Soviet targets from their British bases. In addition, other US nuclear forces would move forward in war or crisis, and many additional RAF bases and hundreds of aircraft would be added to the present inventory of operational bases and warplanes.

Discomfort for the Soviet Union is not, of course, an undesirable objective for US and NATO planners. It has often been claimed that the presence of US nuclear forces in Europe is a concrete demonstration of US resolve to hold the 'nuclear umbrella' out over Europe. But many wish neither for the presence of US forces nor for their nuclear shield. Over the last few years, increasingly abstract and complex theories of nuclear warfare and deterrence have been developed to justify existing and new nuclear weapons in Europe. They are claimed to provide a connection ('coupling') between the defence of Europe and the American strategic nuclear arsenal, and thus ensure an effective nuclear shield.

The new cruise and Pershing missile bases currently being constructed and operated in NATO countries are intended to reinforce this coupling. That, at any rate, was how the cruise missile plan began. The issues have shifted with the nuclear weapons controversy that has raged across Europe since 1980. Now the key issue is the internal battle in most NATO states. For the moment, it is clearly as important to NATO to beat the peace movement in the streets as it is to show resolve to the Kremlin.

The 'Nuclear axis' and the highly visible presence of US military forces on British territory is only one dimension of the special relationship. At the same time as US Strategic Air Command and RAF commanders were charting out the facilities for a future nuclear war, other, less advertised, pacts were being struck. Some of the most powerful of these were the secret agreements binding together the national intelligence agencies. Beginning with bilateral ties across the Atlantic, most of these agreements soon extended to all the English-speaking nations. These WASP (ie, White Anglo-Saxon Protestant) pacts covered Australia, Canada and New Zealand.

They brought together the organisation that became the US Central Intelligence Agency and the British Secret Intelligence Service to collaborate in operations around the world – including direct attempts to overthrow or undermine governments deemed unacceptable to the post-war Atlantic axis. This might mean force of arms, covertly applied. Or it might mean the long and slow Cold War campaign for hearts and minds, a campaign on a global scale which laid heavy emphasis on using the tools of covert propaganda and disinformation. No west European country was immune from the programmes that the CIA funded, aimed at swinging the left of European politics into the centre.

In the 1980s, the trend of US interference in the domestic politics of Europe is again upwards. This time the target is less sophisticated – the bolstering only of right-wing and 'New Right' politics, and the 'destabilisation' of anti-nuclear dissent.

Anglo-American intelligence-gathering collaboration includes previously undisclosed joint spy flights over Soviet and East European territory. These deeply-secret missions began in earnest in 1950, with the urgent objective of seeking atomic bomber routes into the Russian heartland. They continued into the U-2 era which reached its zenith in 1960. In a remarkable echo of this spur to Cold War confrontation, U-2 planes are back in Britain today, in force. At the Alconbury reconnaissance base, newly-built U-2s have been cosmetically retitled TR-1s.

In the arcane field of 'Signals intelligence' (Sigint), the electronic spying, surveillance and code-breaking agencies of the WASP nations have been bound together by the closest ties of all. Britain is the junior partner in a global harvest of intelligence from the world's communications. The target of this intelligence empire is not simply the messages of Soviet forces or high military commanders, but the diplomatic, civil and commercial communications of literally every nation, and of every variety. No one is exempt, be they western, eastern, or non-aligned. Many important stations in these spy systems are on British soil, and tapped into the international network from Britain. One of the most controversial and sensitive bases doing this work – the extensive US National Security Agency (NSA) centre at Menwith Hill, near Harrogate in Yorkshire – has been described by a former Director of the Agency as 'the most important station for our mutual security in the world'.

In 1947 a secret agreement between Britain and the US, called UKUSA, formally bound the two countries together for Sigint purposes. The members of the British-led Commonwealth Sigint Organisation joined shortly after. Each member state was apportioned a region of the globe wherein it would co-ordinate surveillance.

Other treaties and operating arrangements bound together other segments of the secret world: the security agencies, like the FBI and Britain's MI5; the Joint Intelligence Committees; and more humble parts of the military intelligence machinery. There were collaborative arrangements between the 'unconventional warfare' troops each partner set up (the British SAS and the American Special Forces) which led to British SAS men serving in Vietnam although Britain was never, officially, at war. Other parts of the secret Anglo-American intelligence machinery, such as the electronic spy post in Hong Kong, also operated in direct support of the US Vietnam campaign. Secret treaties and agreements are ever the handmaidens of secret foreign policy. The requirements of the secret world and the intelligence axis have often imposed their own foreign policy on Britain and the United States.

Apart from collaborative efforts overseas, many major intelligence bases are located in Britain. They control spy satellites (and spy on other satellites), and trap and intercept vast quantities of communications. A base in Wales monitors undersea movements in the Atlantic.

These support facilities are in many ways as vital to the conduct of warfare as the aircraft and other weapons. But the presence of the vital intelligence gatherers, and their command and control infrastructure, is disguised, their mission always secret. It is extremely doubtful whether the British government is fully aware of many activities conducted from US bases in Britain.

In a nation which still makes some claim to independence and self-respect, such a situation, in addition to the inadequacies of the official line of 'joint decision-taking', is absurd and quite unacceptable.

The intelligence system is now, however, only one element of much more extensive, co-ordinated networks for the overall control of military forces. This network includes the computers which process and record military data, the electronic displays to present commanders with information, and the communications to link the whole together. This apparatus has now been entitled, by the Pentagon, $C^3I$, standing for Command, Control, Communications and Intelligence. The $C^3I$ machinery is central to new nuclear war plans, which foresee an extended nuclear conflict during which control of the battle has to be conducted by survivors, using damaged and degraded systems and communications.

Important parts of these $C^3I$ networks are in Britain, such as the computers of the Worldwide Military Command and Control System (WWMCCS or 'Wimex'), at US Naval Headquarters in central London. There is also a flight of airborne war-rooms for the US European Command – converted Boeing 707s code-named 'Silk Purse' – operating from Mildenhall, Suffolk. Additionally many British bases provide communications links in the nuclear command networks.

This intimate involvement in US war planning adds to British national risk, but is never publicly discussed. Yet much can be learned from what is available in Washington and elsewhere. Constructing a picture of Britain's pivotal role in US military planning has not been difficult for Soviet planners either. A 1980 study published in the restricted Soviet military journal *Foreign Military Review* (discussed in Chapter 11) gave extensive details of US bases in Britain, commenting that: 'the Pentagon maintains here a ramified network of bases, dumps of nuclear and conventional weapons, various headquarters, communications centres, intelligence centres and other installations.'

US forces in Britain do not provide any direct defence for these islands. All our eggs are very firmly in the deterrence basket and that alone. Indeed, it is the responsibility of the RAF to provide air defence for US bases as well as their own. No serious attempt is or can be made to defend British cities, which are left hostage to Soviet bombs and missiles. This has been British defence policy since the 1950s, echoing the despair of politicians when terror bombing was introduced in the 1920s and 1930s: 'the bomber will always get through.'

The consensus on defence policy, and in particular on the American link, broke finally during the first Thatcher government. CND's campaign encouraged and highlighted the widespread resistance to cruise missiles and the US bases. Labour party policy became unilateralist and in favour (with many qualifications) of the removal of US bases. The Conservatives, on the other hand, unswervingly backed President Reagan's policies in almost every part of the world. Their electoral victory in June 1983 was not an endorsement of US strategy, but it has postponed reconsideration of the issue.

Yet the cause of Atlanticism has never been entirely accepted by the political right. Nonetheless, there is relatively little in common between socialist or peace movement arguments, and other, right-wing views, which seem partly to be based on post-imperial resentment at the rise of the US empire. One new minister in Mrs Thatcher's government, and a former prominent member of the House of Commons defence committee, Alan Clark, wrote in 1983 that:

> Opinion in the West has to be divided between those who believe that the influence of the US is benign and protective; and those (among whom I count myself) who believe that, like the power of the 18th century monarchy, it has increased, is increasing, and ought to be diminished.[16]

The consensus on military matters has also recently divided on the western side of the Atlantic. In the United States, as in Europe, individual former senior military officers have joined campaigns on such issues as the nuclear freeze, and backed the call for reducing or removing nuclear weapons from the European theatre. One of the most outspoken of these has been Rear-Admiral Gene LaRoque, a former Pentagon strategic planner who commented brusquely on the 'limited' nuclear war idea during the original research for the article that preceded this book:

> We fought World War I in Europe, we fought World War II in Europe, and if you dummies let us, we'll fight world War III in Europe.

This may seem a cheerful overstatement of LaRoque's concern that Europeans should be loud and effective in their campaigning to cut down the nuclear arsenals, and reduce confrontation. It is chilling prophesy, but no more chilling than the USAF exhortations in Suffolk to prepare for the coming war.

This examination of the US military presence in Britain is not inspired by hostility to the United States *per se.* It is, certainly, inclined to the view that there are alternative, more generous and understanding ways of looking at the position of our chief designated 'enemy', the Soviet Union, than those which are part of the present, almost hysterical, official American ideology. If all that Europe could ever expect from America is a President and administration which recycles the scare talk of the 'Committee on the Present Danger'; if no one in Congress ever debunked the idiotic military sabre-rattling over supposed 'windows of opportunity' which more missiles must be provided to close; if there were no dissenters and dissidents in the United States fighting for nuclear freezes and disarmament in some, or any, form – then we should have to have nothing to do with them. But the United States is better than that.

It is not, however, apparent that we have all the time we may need to wait for the US (and Soviet) military and political establishments to rebuild and extend *détente.* The current US nuclear build-up will doubtless be matched by the Soviets in some years, in kind and in number. More US missiles and weapons means more roubles in their budgets for Soviet generals, greater levels of confrontation and more risks for everyone. Since the time that US bombers came back to Britain, from Moscow's viewpoint the world has looked implacably hostile and uncomfortably near. She in turn has made western Europe equally insecure and uncomfortable, holding us hostage against US good behaviour with SS-20 missiles and other weapons. Perceptions of these unpleasant risks, on both sides, are being renewed by the cruise and Pershing missiles.

There is much in the United States to admire and to seek to emulate: a plural constitution, and laws upholding personal liberty and rights in a way unknown in many Western countries, including the UK. But it is poisonous '-isms' that the United States seems to export, rather than the values from the Revolution of 1776, or the US constitution – militarisation around the world, exploitative mercantile and multinational capitalism, an imperialism more insidious than that of which it accuses the USSR, and the tacit or active support of brutal totalitarianism in too many states in the so-called 'Free World' – all wrapped in the flag of anti-communism. It is this unpleasant brew which has travelled abroad with GIs, not the US constitution.

A military and political relationship as massive, complex and (often) as carefully shrouded as that between Britain and the United States will not readily be dismantled; that is clear. Grand, Gaullist gestures will not come easily to a British political establishment which has been weaned on the idea – or delusion – of the 'special relationship' of American beneficence to the UK. The first requirement, however, is to understand the scope and structure of the relationship, so that alternative ideas of defence can be tested and examined against what we have now.

There are four parts to this book. Chapters 1 to 3 chart the historical development of the first postwar US bases in Britain, from the 1940s to the 1970s. Three thematic chapters in the second section (Chapters 4 to 6) describe special areas of collaboration between Britain and the United States: the development and manufacture of nuclear weapons, secret intelligence organisations and operations.

The third section (Chapters 7 to 10) deals with the development of contemporary US bases and facilities in Britain: command and control arrangements, the Polaris and (subsequently) Poseidon base at the Holy Loch, and US airbases and reinforcement plans.

The last chapter discusses defence policy issues affecting US bases in Britain: the myth of the 'joint decision'; the costs and benefits of the US military presence; the cruise missile debate; and the risks of war. Should the bases, or some of them, be removed? And would the United States be prepared to leave if so requested by a future British government?

## Notes

1 *Hansard*, 15 February 1951.
2 *Hansard*, 28 March 1950.
3 Interview, *TV Eye*, 30 October 1980.
4 Opinion Research Centre polls for *Weekend World*, February 1982 and May 1983.
5 61 per cent to 27 per cent; Marplan for the *Guardian*, 24 January 1983.
6 MORI for Yorkshire TV *First Tuesday*; reported in British Public Opinion, Vol V, nos 5&6, May/June 1983.
7 59 per cent to 31 per cent, and 58 per cent to 32 per cent, respectively, reported by MORI for BBC Radio 4, October 1981; and System Three for the *Glasgow Herald*, 19 December 1981.
8 Gallup for *Sanity* (CND), December 1982. Subsequent figures for early 1983 showed a trend towards acceptance of US nuclear bases.
9 *Hansard*, 18 June 1980; 7 July 1980; 8 August 1980.
10 *New Statesman*, 31 October 1980.
11 *Mea culpa.* The Edgware Road 'facility' identified in my 1980 article is indeed a humble petrol pump. Why did I identify it as a 'US military facility'? I first noted its existence during a 1979 official visit to a US Air Force base where it was one of a number of US installations marked on an office map. What was the site in Edgware Road, I asked the Base Public Affairs Officer. The reply given, 'a fuel supply facility', was an over-dignified description of a petrol pump.
12 *Hansard*, 3 May 1983.
13 *Hansard*, 20 July 1977.
14 *Observer*, 17 April 1983.
15 See Chapter 11.
16 *Guardian*, 4 April 1983.

# PART ONE
# BUILD-UP

## 1 *An Unsinkable Carrier*

Conventional history has it that United States armed forces returned to Britain in July 1948 after an absence of more than two years, for a temporary show of strength during the Berlin blockade. But this history is inaccurate. The US Air Force began planning for an atomic war against the Soviet union within a month of destroying Hiroshima and Nagasaki; in such a war, it was anticipated, British bases would play the key role.

In fact US military forces never left the UK, and a US Naval headquarters, airfield and radio station remained throughout the immediate postwar period. More importantly, the arrival of US bombers in Britain in 1948 was neither the 'temporary' mission of 'goodwill and training' announced publicly, nor was it (as widely understood) the hastily conceived political response to Soviet activities in Berlin. It was, rather, a convenient opportunity to move bombers to Britain indefinitely.

Plans for the United States to 'strike the first blow' against the USSR with atomic weapons were prepared in September 1945, just a month after the surrender of Japan, according to now-public records of the US Joint Chiefs of Staff.[1] The same official records chart how, in October 1945, the Joint Chiefs planned to 'seize and hold', if need be, airfields in the United Kingdom and the Far East, from which to mount atomic bomb raids against the USSR.

Strategic Air Command (SAC), the bomber component of the United States Air Force, was set up in March 1946. Its principal task was nuclear warfare – although at that time both atom bombs and crews and aircraft to drop them were scarce indeed. SAC was eventually to become the *de facto* centre of US nuclear policymaking for nearly two decades. Despite its well-known motto, 'Peace is our profession', SAC requirements for weapons and delivery systems were the driving force behind the nuclear build-up of the 1950s that endowed the world with the new word, 'overkill'.

In June/July 1946, shortly after the formation of SAC, US Air Force commander General Carl Spaatz visited England to obtain permission to use British bases for atomic bomb missions in emergency. Spaatz obtained the agreement of Air Chief Marshal Lord Tedder, the Royal Air Force Chief of Staff, to have five RAF bases designated and made ready for B-29 bombers. The Spaatz-Tedder agreement was struck between officials, without public discussion or political debate of the momentous issues involved. This secret administrative agreement was the first step, extremely casually taken, in the establishment of postwar US bases in Britain.

In August 1946, an official of the US 'Manhattan District' (the codename for the atomic bomb construction project), Colonel E. E. Kirkpatrick, visited England to supervise the construction of assembly buildings and loading pits at the chosen bases – Lakenheath, Mildenhall, Scampton, Marham and Bassingbourn. Atom-bomb handling facilities in Britain, and in the Mariana Islands in the Pacific, were ready by 1947.[2]

The first atom bombs were cumbersome contraptions. A team of 39 men had to work for two days to put one together. To load one into an aircraft required the use of a specially prepared pit, 8 feet deep and 14 feet wide, with a special hoist. The aircraft was rolled over the pit, and the bomb hoisted in.

These early bombs were of the 'Fat Man' variety which had wiped out Nagasaki. Nine of these 'B-3' bombs were available in July 1946. Two years later, the United States had a stockpile of 50. There were 30 B-29 Superfortress bombers, codenamed 'Silverplate', which had been converted to drop atomic weapons.

The first detailed plan for an atomic war was 'Broiler', in 1947. This 'Joint Outline Emergency War Plan' listed 24 Soviet cities for destruction, emphasising, as with Hiroshima and Nagasaki, the destruction of population rather than industrial assets or military forces. Broiler was one in a long series of continually amended and updated war plans. The last plan to be made before the Soviets themselves detonated an atomic bomb, and codenamed 'Offtackle', reflected the growth in the US nuclear arsenal. Some 220 bombs would be directed against 104 Soviet targets, all cities. Another 72 bombs would remain in reserve.

Tours to Europe by SAC bombers began in June 1947, as part of the command's 'mobility plan'. In the spring of 1948, the deepening divisions in Europe led – after the proposal to create an independent West German state – to the Soviet blockade of land routes into Berlin. As the crisis built up, the US Ambassador in London asked that three groups of heavy bombers should be allowed to come to Britain, as a temporary show of strength. On 28 June 1948, this was agreed by a small Cabinet committee – whose identity or existence, let alone its agenda or decision-taking (like all such) was quite unknown to the public.

To the British Cabinet, the move seemed a reasonable temporary gesture at a time of alarm; publicly, they invoked what were described as 'informal and longstanding arrangements between the USAF and the RAF for visits of goodwill . . .'.[3] Privately, however, the United States had long-term intentions right from the start. Access to British bases was of critical importance in fast-developing atomic warfare plans. US Defense Secretary James Forrestal wrote in his diary on the day the bombers arrived in Britain, 17 July 1948, that:

> We have the opportunity now of sending these planes, and once sent, they would become somewhat of an accepted fixture.

A cluster of RAF bases, forming the USAF Third Air Division (Provisional), came under US control on 16 July 1948. The bomb groups which then arrived at Marham, Waddington and Scampton airfields for 'operational training' were due to stay at first for just 30 days. This was soon extended to 60; and when the first bombers left, they were replaced by other groups on 'rotation', a process which was then continued in effect for 15 years. The presence of the US Air Force units was regarded, and officially described as 'temporary'. But the deployments remained, grew, and within two years had become as permanent and accepted as Secretary Forrestal had intended. With a convenient range to the Soviet Union, and facing the United States across the Atlantic, Britain was the ideal forward base; truly, an unsinkable aircraft carrier.

The first six squadrons of B-29 Superfortresses arrived in July 1958. The Superfortress, a very large four-engined bomber sprouting multiple defensive gun turrets, had first joined the US Air Force in the closing days of the war in Europe. The first squadrons of bombers which arrived in England were not 'Silverplate' models, converted to carry atomic weapons, although that fact was unknown to the public (and the British and Soviet governments) at the time. At the end of 1948, the 30 Silverplate aircraft were still at their US home base of Roswell, New Mexico. Gradually the rest of the force was converted, and the first A-bomb carriers came to England in 1949. By late 1950, all the bombers returning to Britain from the United States on 'rotational tours' had been converted.

At first, no questions were raised at the political level about the terms and conditions of the Americans' tenure, despite the aircraft's capabilities. The government did not ask the Americans whether they intended to store the atomic bomb in England – despite the fact that, at a lower level, RAF officials were in no doubt as to USAF intentions. The legacy of this casualness is with us today. The difficulty, for Britain, of later trying to put British interests in the use of the bases on a firmer footing without seeming distrustful (at a time when close and sensitive US–UK collaboration was being sought) led directly to the inadequacy and ambiguity of later agreements and statements on the use of US bases.

In August 1948, a month after it was first established, the Third Air Division at Marham was made a permanent military unit. Lord Tedder's RAF Deputy Chief of Staff, Sir William Dickson, proposed that the US bases should remain designated as Royal Air Force stations – a cosmetic disguise intended to alleviate local hostility to the presence of foreign military forces on British soil in peacetime. The proposal was accepted and, on this basis, almost all American bases in Britain are described as 'RAF' bases, and have an RAF 'commander'. These 'commanders' – Squadron leaders who are two or three ranks inferior to the US commanding officer – are in reality local liaison officers with no rights or responsibilities beyond community relations.

The newly formed US Third Air Division soon moved to a new headquarters at Bushy Park, in London's western suburbs. (This too was temporary; the eventual headquarters, until 1972, was to be a large converted factory in another suburb, South Ruislip, not far away.)

In November 1948, four months after the first B-29s landed, the US Air Force intimated to the RAF that they would like a permanent presence in Britain. This was accepted by the Air Ministry, but not, apparently, submitted to the Foreign Office for political decision until a year later. A search began for suitable sites – this time, much further inland, and thus behind defensive fighter cover. The Foreign Secretary, Ernest Bevin, accepted the new, permanent bases, but wanted safeguards on critical aspects. According to the superb history of early British atomic policy by Professor Margaret Gowing[4] (who alone has had access to many of the official papers), the conditions were twofold.

Firstly, Britain must have the right to terminate the base arrangements. Secondly, what would be the position if the United States unilaterally wished to mount military operations from British bases, when Britain was not at war; or, for that matter, if there was a disagreement on policy? Britain was a sovereign country, not a colonial annexe, and US offensive operations from bases on its soil could not, in the Foreign Office view, be tolerated without UK government consent.

It was later claimed by the Foreign Office that the US Ambassador had, in 1948, given Mr Bevin assurances that Britain would be consulted about any plans for the use of US bombers from Britain. These assurances proved somewhat ephemeral. They were not written down, nor mentioned in any negotiation up to 1952. Only a decade later, when the issue arose again, were they reported in official statements.

With the crisis in Berlin continuing to raise tension, in 1948 the US Joint Chiefs of Staff authorised the preparation of a new global war plan, codenamed 'Charioteer'. The plan supposed that the US would mount an atomic offensive to repel Soviet expansion west of the zones of influence accepted after Potsdam. The plan anticipated that the US would:

> . . . initiate strategic air operations as soon as possible after the outbreak of hostilities by launching a concerted attack employing atomic bombs against governmental, political and administrative centres, urban industrial areas and selected petroleum targets within the USSR from bases in the western hemisphere and the United Kingdom.

War plan 'Trojan', prepared at the same time, enumerated 70 Soviet targets for 133 atomic bomb raids.

The continuing blockade of Berlin brought into being the Western alliance. The North Atlantic Treaty was signed on 4 April 1949. It pledged mutual assistance between the twelve original signatories in the event of an armed attack on any. The agreement to station US bombers in Britain was one move in a joint programme to develop an 'individual and collective capacity to resist armed attack'. It was welcomed and did not seem out of place, given the tension in Europe then.

All the airfields mentioned in the Spaatz-Tedder agreement, save one – Bassingbourn near Cambridge – became B-29 bases by mid-1950. These were Lakenheath, Mildenhall, Scampton and Marham. There was the new Third Air Division HQ at South Ruislip, and a burgeoning depot complex at Burtonwood, near Warrington in Lancashire. This vast store – the 59th Air Depot – was set up to service and support the bomber force in Britain. Auxiliary bases nearby at Sealand and Squires Gate were also handed over in the next year or two. Burtonwood is still, in the 1980s, a major US depot – but now in Army hands. Additionally, a Hertfordshire airfield, Bovingdon, was provided to the Third Air Division in 1949 for light aircraft and communications.

The next stage in Strategic Air Command's expansion began early in 1950. Under a new 'Ambassador's Agreement', four new airfields were given to the USAF for full development. They were Greenham Common, Upper Heyford, Fairford and Brize Norton. All are well known today, and all are still earmarked for US use in war (although Brize Norton is primarily an RAF transport base). The Ambassador's Agreement, was so called because it was signed between the US Ambassador, Lewis Douglas, and the British Air Under-Secretary, Aidan Crawley.

The Ambassador's Agreement, like all other key documents governing the use of US bases, has been withheld from the Public Record Office, although more than 30 years old. The Ambassador's Agreement has been retained by the Foreign Office; Downing Street and the Cabinet Office have retained all other key files on the *Modus Vivendi* (p 97) and other postwar US-UK negotiations.

In June 1950 war began in Korea, and the new crisis provoked further raising of the nuclear stakes by the US supreme military command, the Joint Chiefs of Staff. During June they urged the President and the US Atomic Energy Commission now to allow the non-nuclear components of the atom bomb stockpile to be moved to the British bases. In the event of a general, world war, only the nuclear cores would need to be flown over, saving time and risk. The President agreed on 11 July 1950[5], and the bombs' components were moved in. If war came, SAC had now some 250 nuclear-capable bombers, plus the stocks to match. The US had moved one step closer to holding complete atom bombs on UK soil.

In Britain, considerable anxiety now focused on the unwelcome news, which had been received in September 1949, that the Soviet Union too had the bomb. Notwithstanding that Soviet stocks could, as yet, only be miniscule, there was no doubt as to the damage they could do. Nor was there much doubt that Britain, as the forward base for SAC, would receive the brunt of atomic retaliation. It would be extremely difficult for the Soviet Union, lacking both aircraft carriers and intercontinental bombers, to make a direct attack on North America, but they could reach Britain easily enough. American policymakers saw clearly that almost all of their nuclear capacity depended on Britain. That capacity was too important to the US to allow a decision on its use to be shared in London. The view of the Air Force Secretary, Thomas K. Finletter, was clear. The British could not be relied on to move as quickly, or act as decisively, as the US Air Force might wish. A Top Secret memorandum he wrote on 7 July 1950 to the US Secretary of Defense, declassified during the research for this book, noted:

> We are dependent at this moment almost entirely on the availability of UK bases for the launching of our strategic countermeasures.
>
> I haven't any real doubt but that the British will come along if we do get engaged in war. But the question is when. I do not like at all the fact that we are almost entirely dependent on the UK . . .
>
> I know [the British] well enough to know that sometimes they can be very slow; and this strategic countermeasure is something which cannot afford to be held up while the British cabinet is debating about things.[6]

He noted that the US and UK had, by then, diverging policies over China, where conflict threatened in Formosa. 'I do not feel happy about it,' the Air Force Secretary wrote, noting: 'It should be called to the attention of the President.'

The fears of backbench MPs that Britain might face annihilation without consultation were sharpened by the overt threat to use atomic weapons in Korea which President Truman made at a press conference on 30 November 1950. Nuclear weapons had now become an instrument of politics, and a tool of power adaptable to circumstances short of all-out warfare. (This was certainly the first occasion on which the United States publicly threatened the use of nuclear weapons as an act of policy. An earlier, but secret, threat by Truman, over a crisis in Iran, was alleged in 1980 by Senator Henry Jackson. The tours around Europe by SAC bombers from 1946 onwards were, of course, a more restrained version of the same threat.)

In December 1950, Prime Minister Attlee rushed to Washington for urgent discussions about the atomic threats. The discussions were deeply unsatisfactory to Attlee, despite a valiant window-dressing operation performed in Parliament on his return. In a private discussion with the President, Attlee understood that he had had the assurance he sought on joint decision before use of atom bombs. In subsequent conference with Truman and Secretary of State Dean Acheson, the assurance – if it had really been given in the first place – was rescinded. British officials at this meeting did record that the President had given an assurance that Britain would be consulted about the use of the bomb. But there was to be no written agreement, and no public communiqué, as US officials warned that the President could not publicly curtail his own authority.

In place of any positive public commitment, the joint communiqué then spoke only of a desire by the President to keep the Prime Minister 'at all times informed of developments' which might affect the use of the bomb. On 14 December 1950 Attlee presented this to the House of Commons as being perfectly satisfactory. He refused to divulge what 'assurances' he believed Britain had received. Nor did he tell the House that the Americans had in any case disputed the British record, disavowing any assurance from the President about consultation – not even an oral record, nor a private one.

This pattern of events had occurred before, and has been repeated as farce many times since. It may yet become tragedy. There would be little disagreement with the British Chief of the Air Staff's view in 1950 that:

> The present situation, whereby the United States could launch atomic bomb attacks on Russia making use of United Kingdom bases and facilities [without consultation] is intolerable.[7]

The Attlee statement was a considerable provocation to Winston Churchill, then leading the Conservative Opposition. It was the first occasion on which he learned that, since he had left office, Britain had given up its right under a wartime agreement (the Quebec Agreement, see Chapter 4) to jointly control all use of the atomic bomb. He entered his own demand, by letter direct to President Truman, that atomic weapons should not be used from British bases without prior agreement.

Even in those days, where the pace of international developments was much more leisurely than now, the government anticipated that in a developing crisis there might be little time to review the issues. The Korean involvement had been hurried, *ad hoc*; the Foreign Office did not want a repetition in Act One of World War III.

As the Korean War went on, the US began to change its plans for atomic warfare. The first priority in new schemes went to the destruction of targets which provided the Soviets with their own atomic power. Subsidiary targets included refineries, power stations, atomic energy industries, some chemical plant and submarine yards – and many cities.[8] Priorities slowly changed towards an emphasis on industrial targets. But SAC's atomic plans and target lists were very much a reflection of the almost mystical belief of Americans that their nuclear near-monopoly gave them the power to restore their version of world order with a single, mighty blow. No assessment was made of how Soviet society, and its capacity to make war, would be affected by the atomic onslaught from England. It was merely assumed that the Soviet Union, under a sufficient rain of atom bombs, would just collapse.

No exact SAC target lists have been published, but a description of the SAC Emergency War Plan given in the 1950–2 official history of the US Joint Chiefs of Staff outlines an attack involving 114 bombs. Bombers would start out from Britain, Labrador, Maine, the Azores and Guam. The largest raiding group, from Britain, would strike the Soviet Union from the south, after flying along the northern edge of the Mediterranean. The targets of this group were the industrial centres of the Ukraine and southern Russia, in the Volga and Donets basins.

Work began at the four new airfields – Greenham Common, Fairford, Brize Norton and Upper Heyford – almost immediately, with the construction of large new runways, dispersal pads and storage facilities to accommodate the expected new generation of jet bombers. No sooner had this begun than another vast programme was proposed for discussion. Under the Special Construction Programme, eventually agreed in February 1951, the USAF would get 26 further bases in Britain. They would provide peacetime bases for new, tactical units, and a host of extra emergency bases for SAC bombers.

The Air Force organisation also changed to reflect the new pattern: it became a major permanent British-based force, with a visiting SAC presence, never less than one bomber group. In early 1951, the Third Air Division became the Third Air Force. A new 7th Air Division was set up to support the visiting bomber units, and to 'supervise the preparation of a SAC forward operating area in the UK'.[9] Soon after this, SAC took over High Wycombe Air Station, not an airfield but an administrative headquarters in high woodland overlooking the Buckinghamshire town. Its key feature was an underground command centre which had been constructed during the war to control US strategic bombing raids in Europe. The three-storey underground bunker, well concealed, backed onto Wycombe Abbey, a girls' school,

---

OVERLEAF LEFT

**Fig 1. Arrival: US bases in Britain, January 1950**

Britain's Second World War role as the unsinkable aircraft carrier returned when five airbases were secretly designated as the bridgehead for atom bombers to come to Europe. After the Berlin blockade, the agreement was activated. The US Navy, with bases in London and Northern Ireland, never left Britain.

OVERLEAF RIGHT

**Fig 2. First growth: US bases in Britain, December 1952**

After new agreements in 1950 and 1951, the US Air Force were given first 30 and then over 70 airbases for major development. Their presence was now taken to be 'long term'.

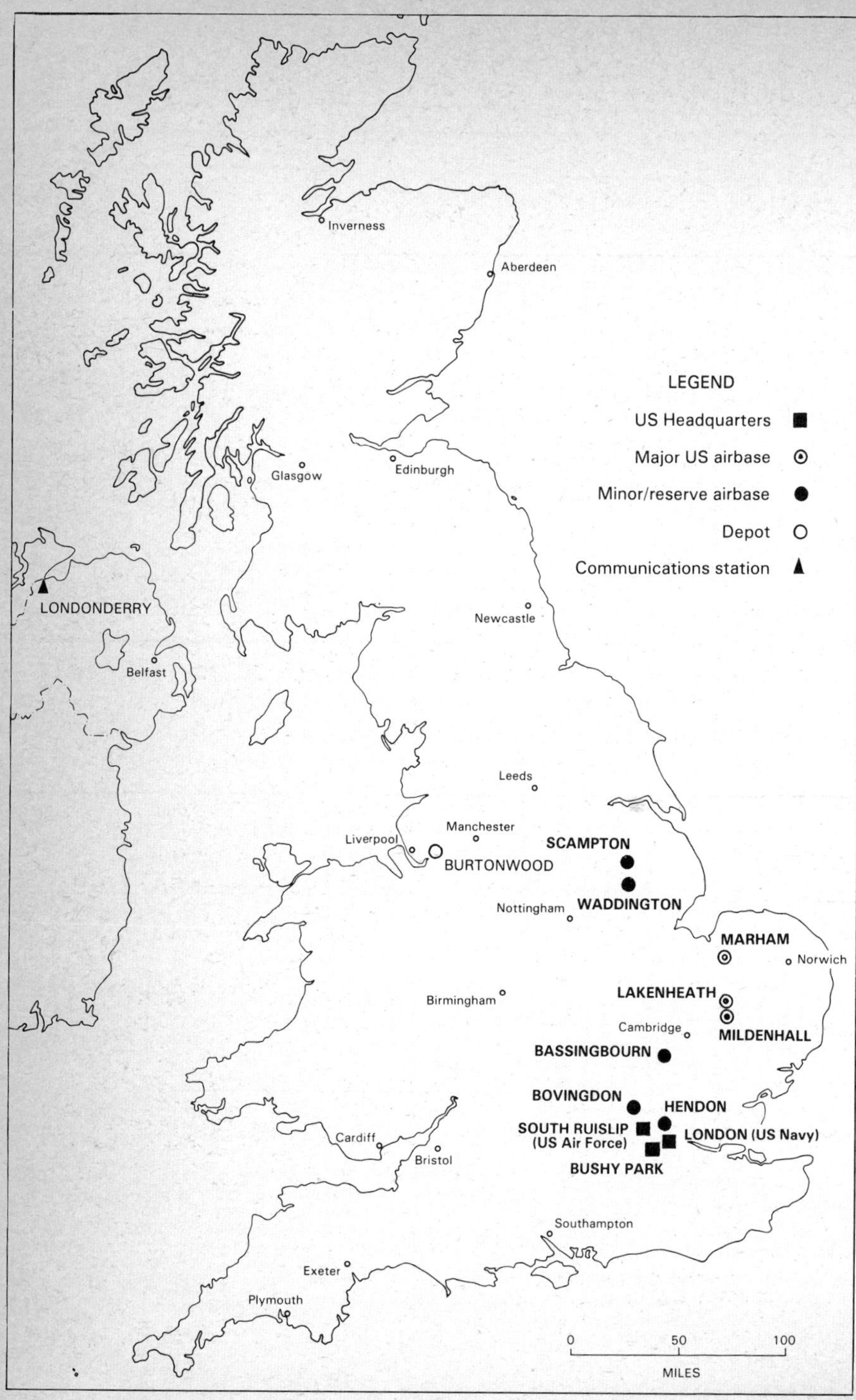


Fig 1. Arrival: US bases in Britain – January 1950

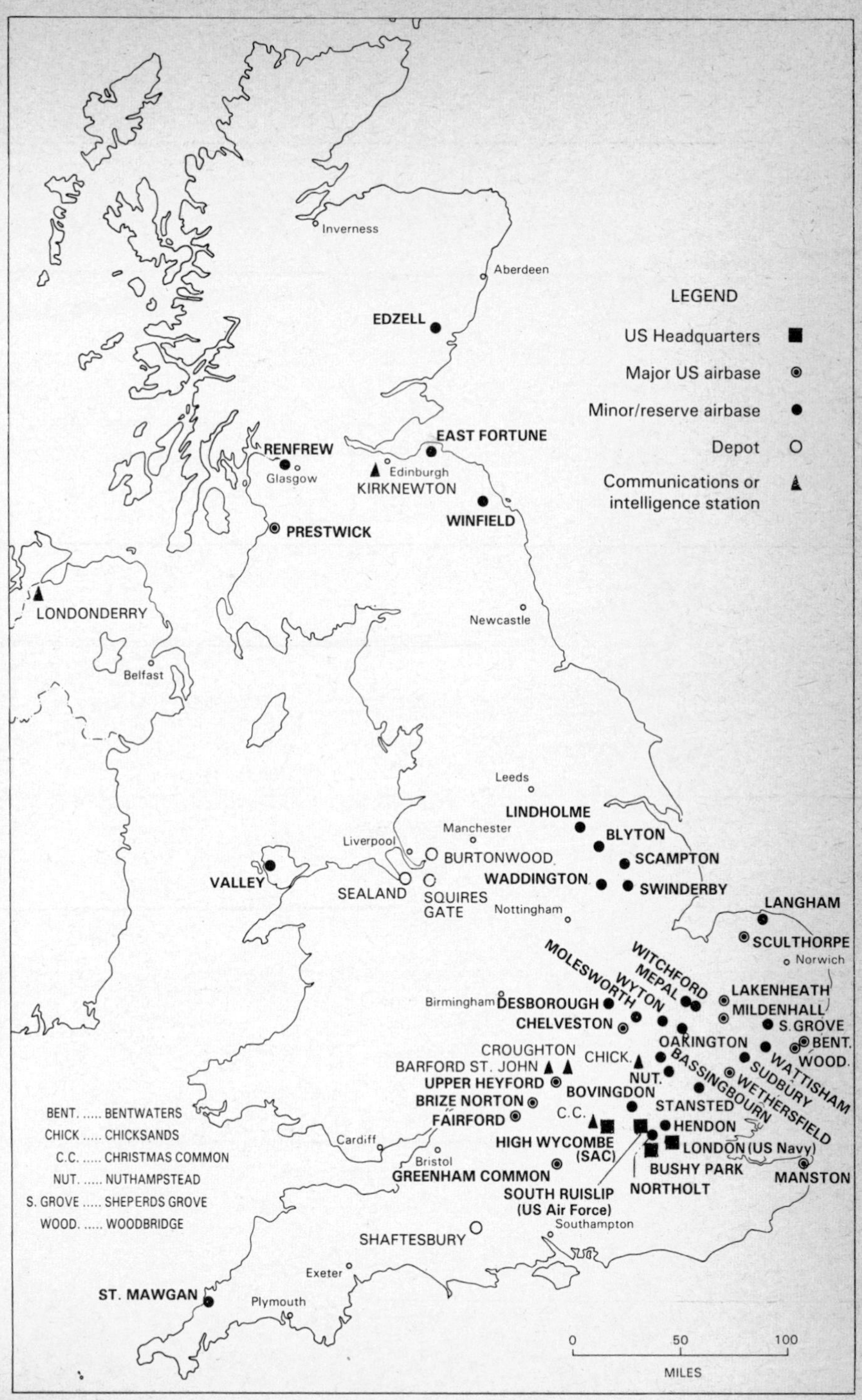


Fig 2. First Growth: US bases in Britain – December 1952

which had provided administrative offices in World War II. A few miles to the north was its RAF counterpart, then the headquarters of Britain's Bomber Command.

By the end of 1952, the total of airfields apportioned to the US Air Force grew to 43, plus a constellation of support bases. In the same year, the level of US forces in Britain rose to 45,000 – plus some 3,500 American civilians and 28,000 dependents. This strength was maintained throughout most of the 1950s.

The Ambassador's Agreement in 1950 had provided for an equal split of construction costs, but this was not a proportion Britain, still in the grip of rationing and recovery measures, was prepared to sustain. For the first two years, 1951 and 1952, the UK paid half. Subsequently, the US agreed to provide a 60 per cent stake. A March 1952 USAF memorandum noted that full 50-50 participation by the UK might not be possible 'because of the dire economic and financial status of the UK'. Eventually, the US undertook to pay all but $53 million of the $300 million-plus programme planned in 1953, for 43 major airbases. More than 2,000 aircraft, it was anticipated, could operate from the bases in war. Most of them would be bombers from Strategic Air Command.

At the same time as the new airbase programme was going ahead, the United States had submitted to its NATO allies a voluminous list of military rights and bases which it sought overseas. In Britain (see Table 1), they asked for seven main bomber bases, three fighter bases, five air transport bases, two depots, a naval headquarters, port rights and administrative sites and the right to deploy army, anti-aircraft and similar units to defend the bases.

A special section of the list dealt with navigation systems, which were critical to long-range bombing operations. The US set out a plan for a worldwide LORAN system (for LOng RAnge Navigation), a network of radio beacons. In the early 1950s, the LORAN system was extended throughout Europe; in Britain, stations were built at Angle, Pembrokeshire and in the Hebrides.

In each NATO territory, the US sought extensive military rights, including 'the right for storage and stockpiling of supplies and material including ammunition and atomic explosives'.[10] The negotiations led, in 1951, to an agreement with NATO member states on the Status of Forces in their territories. It was signed in London in June 1951. Legal provisions affecting US servicemen in Britain were given statutory force by the passing of the Visiting Forces Act of 1952, which followed the 1951 NATO agreement.

**Table 1**
**US base requirements for NATO purposes, 1950**

| | |
|---|---|
| *Main bomber bases** | |
| Brize Norton | Fairford |
| Upper Heyford | Chelveston |
| Mildenhall | Sculthorpe |
| Lakenheath | |
| *Main fighter bases* | |
| Woodbridge | Manston |
| Carnaby | |
| *Transport bases (Military Air Transport Service, or SAC)* | |
| Stornoway | Prestwick |
| Heathrow | Valley |
| Nutts Corner (Northern Ireland) | |
| *Depots* | |
| Burtonwood | Alconbury |

*Greenham Common, although omitted from the document, should have been included in the list of bomber bases required by the US in 1950.

The US construction budget in 1951 was estimated at over $100 million, shared 50-50 with Britain, after some $21 million worth of direct troop labour had been deducted. This money was spent on the 8 main SAC bomber bases and the Lancashire and Cheshire depots. The 1952 programme included a further $39 million for the development of the Burtonwood depot, and the first few dispersal bases for SAC aircraft from the main stations. These included Stansted, Essex, and Desborough, Northamptonshire. In 1953, it was expected that the cost of developing UK bases would require expenditure of a further $167 million.

After the Americans acquired some (conventional) bombing experience in the Korean War, it was realised that the bombers would fare badly without an escort of fighters to deal with Russian air defenders. So in January 1951 a Fighter Escort Wing was transferred to Manston airfield, at the eastern end of Kent. A permanent station for escorting fighters was provided soon afterwards, at Bentwaters, near Ipswich.

The US presence in Britain had quickly multiplied in scale, as a comparison between US facilities as they stood at the start of 1950 and at the end of 1952, shows (see Figures 1 and 2). The range of units included temporary as well as permanent bomber bases, and a panoply of military facilities, now often lumped together as 'infrastructure'.

A key development in this early period was the provision of intelligence-gathering facilities, which were employed in order to learn more about the military development and plans of the Soviet Union. Five years after the end of the Second World War, very little indeed was known about Soviet military forces, or indeed about Soviet industrial development and the society's recovery from the devastation wrought by the Nazis. Intelligence was sought by the US in order to assess Soviet plans and capabilities; and it was particularly sought in order to provide targets for the rapidly-growing bomber force.

There were two primary intelligence sources which required, and made use of, British bases (discussed at greater length in Chapters 4 and 5). One was electronic eavesdropping, or radio monitoring, of Soviet and East European radio signals. Electronic monitoring bases like Chicksands near Bedford and Kirknewton near Edinburgh were opened in this period. Closer in to the USSR, electronic intelligence stations in Turkey and Germany detected radar and missile signals.

But more important than these, for the moment, was a growing programme of clandestine intelligence gathering, involving secret overflights of Soviet or Soviet-controlled territory, to obtain photographs of targets or approach routes. Radar mapping of possible target areas was critical, as this had become the major means of bomb-aiming as the aircraft approached its target. The first reconnaissance aircraft arrived early in 1950. This aerial reconnaissance became another facet of secret Anglo-American intelligence co-operation as, during the following decade, the RAF and the British Secret Intelligence Service became intimately involved in the U-2 spy plane programme.

The growing foreign military presence provoked mixed reactions in Britain. The phrase with which some had disdainfully and unkindly greeted the US Air Force in the 1940s – 'overpaid, over-sexed, and over here' – had not been forgotten. Press reporting included both hostility, and the simple jingoism of the farmer whose field ended at the fence of one of the largest atom bomb stores in Europe, and who was more concerned that the Air Ministry might requisition some further acres of barley fields than about the weight of nuclear bombs planted in earth-covered 'igloos' where the barley stopped growing: 'I realise fully, like everyone else, why they are here – and I am glad that they are'.[11]

There was much concern about community relations around the expanding bases, and a great deal of bemused comment on the American Way, which was even to export to their far-off British bases most of the food which servicemen and their families would buy and eat.

These commodities go on sale in an institution called the 'PX' – Post Exchange. In British bases, as in most other countries, these goods are brought in duty free – including drink and tobacco. When Americans first arrived, price differentials and scarcity led to a repeated series of black-market scandals as goods were smuggled out from the PXs. The world outside these oases of the American Way, the PX and the Commissariat, is known to the Americans as the local economy, or just the 'economy'.

The massive runway building and expansion of the major bases at Greenham Common, Fairford, Brize Norton and Upper Heyford caused particular local grievance. Houses and pubs were levelled – and at Greenham acres of ancient common land was taken over – roads were closed, and farmers dispossessed. With local residents also fearing the noise the jet bombers would make when they arrived, feelings sometimes ran high enough for American servicemen to be advised to stay inside their bases.

At first, security on many of the bases was quite lax. In September 1950, a *Daily Express* reporter embarrassed the USAF and the Air Ministry by strolling on to Lakenheath airbase and examining in detail a half-dozen B-50 atomic bombers parked on its runway surrounds.[12] (The B-50 was a more recent version of the B-29 Superfortress. It had more powerful engines, and other modifications.) An embarrassed Air Ministry promised that better defences against enemy saboteurs (or curious pressmen) would immediately be applied.

Soon, however, the scene was very different. At the major SAC bases, continuous armoured-car patrols by US Air Force Security Police covered the perimeter. They were accompanied by dog patrols – organised in so-called 'K-9' units. Anti-aircraft batteries were positioned around the perimeters, and fully manned. In a remote corner of each airfield was constructed an area of extremely high security, in which the base's supply of nuclear weapons was to be held.

These areas, called 'Special Ammunition Stores', were (and are) dedicated to holding only the nuclear stockpile and a few other very special items (for example, nerve gas bombs). Each store was surrounded at least by a high, double fence in which guard dogs would be let free. At each corner of the perimeter was a guard tower, with searchlights and gun positions. The perimeter was floodlit at night. Inside were the 'igloos': storage hangars of thick concrete with earth piled up the sides and over their tops (the primary purpose of which was to prevent any accidental explosion or fire spreading from one igloo to another).

Few more horrific acts of God are conceivable than that an accidental lightning strike should detonate a nuclear weapon. So the igloos were protected by a network of lightning conductor spikes, with more protective cables slung between them. These arrays were placed around any building in which the weapons were to be assembled or maintained, for each bomb contains large quantities of conventional explosive with which the nuclear reaction is started, and which could be ignited by a lightning bolt.

Most of the original Special Ammunition Stores constructed in the 50s are now out of use, or used only to hold conventional explosives. At Greenham Common, however, where such a store had been derelict for almost two decades, that site was selected to become the home of the new cruise missiles. At the time of writing, the old watchtowers at Greenham still stand, rusty and forlorn, as the outer sentinels of the new cruise missile complex.

The new stores did not stand empty long. The first atom bombs which came to Britain, in July 1950, were probably MkIIIs: replicas of 'Fat Man', as used over Nagasaki. They were replaced fairly quickly by a MkIV bomb, similar but slightly smaller. The main difference, however, was that MkIV was in mass production. But it still required a complex and careful assembly procedure, including the insertion of a nuclear core, called a 'pit', not yet stored in the UK.

Non-nuclear components of the weapons were shipped out of US depots. In 1952, the US Joint Chiefs of Staff asked for a substantial increase in overseas storage; more weapons went to the British bases, and others to aircraft carriers, to Guam in the Pacific, and to Labrador in Canada.

A year later, in June 1953, the new President, Eisenhower, agreed that the US armed forces might take over the custody of complete nuclear weapons, and store them at their overseas bases. Gradually, most of the stockpile, which up to that point had been in the civilian custody of the Atomic Energy Commission, was handed over. New storage sites were sought and constructed in France and Germany. The stockpile size, by this time, was well into thousands.

The old, piston-engined Superfortresses were replaced by jet bombers, B-47 Stratojets, with a crew of 3 (instead of 11). The first Stratojets came to Fairford in June 1953, as part of the rotation of the SAC bomber groups doing 'operational training' in Britain. The continuing pattern of swapping bomber groups between the United States and the UK went on at three-monthly intervals. Under normal conditions there would be one bomber group in the UK at any one time. In emergency, of course, hundreds more aircraft would cross the Atlantic to fill all the airfield space the old carrier could provide.

The key objectives of US war plans of the period can be glimpsed in documents which have now been declassified and made available in the US National Archives. Early plans, like Broiler, were replaced by more extensive designs for a general atomic war which might begin four, or even seven, years later. In 1949 a long-range plan for a general war in 1957 – 'Dropshot'[13] – was prepared by the Joint Chiefs of Staff. Then, in 1950, a new series of plans, for a war starting in July 1954, were distributed to give the 'basic strategic guidance for mobilisation, budgetary, NATO and Mutual Defense Assistance Programme planning'.[14]

The new plan at first bore the grim title of 'Reaper'. This changed to 'Groundwork', and then, continuing the scarcely buried *motif* of the series, to 'headstone'. Headstone defined holding the United Kingdom as one of the three critical defensive tasks for the Western side. The first strategic objective in each version of the plan was 'to impose the war objectives of the United States upon the USSR by destroying the Soviet will to resist'. This stern objective tempered only slightly with time.

The Joint Chiefs' assessment of what Britain then faced was not pleasant:

> It is estimated that the principal threat to the United Kingdom beginning on D-Day, would be an assault by the Soviet Long Range Air Force. It is considered that initially two or three hundred bomber or mining sorties and an equal number of fighter sorties daily could be expected.

In this onslaught:

> Perhaps 30–40 atomic bombs would be allocated for use against the United Kingdom. The establishment of bases in Western Europe [ie, by the USSR] . . . would permit an intensification of the scale of attack . . . Soviet saboteurs would probably make a strong effort to assist the overall plan of operations against the United Kingdom . . . Loss of the United Kingdom . . . would greatly augment the military and possibly the industrial potential available to the Soviets . . .

Nonetheless:

> The security of the United Kingdom must of necessity be primarily a British responsibility.

The planning staff estimated that 40 atom bombs would cripple the UK. 120 would utterly destroy the country. In a general war, SAC did not expect more than 60 days use out of Britain and its forward airbases.

New governments took power – Eisenhower's in the United States and Churchill's in Britain. But the old arguments and concerns about the control of the airbases did not change. Indeed, for Winston Churchill, it was a matter of some urgency for him to see what might be recovered of the *entente* he had enjoyed with the United States during the war, when Britain had been allowed joint mastery of the projected superweapons.

The struggle waged by Attlee and Foreign Secretary Herbert Morrison to get a definitive agreement with the Americans, during the period of headlong expansion before Churchill took office, had failed utterly. The Americans continued to refuse to give formal assurances, and tried to change the argument. They maintained, in 1951[15], that neither politically nor legally could the US President curtail his right to direct United States forces in the use of nuclear weapons.

Gowing reports that a meeting held between General Omar Bradley, the Chairman of the US Joint Chiefs of Staff, and British Ambassador Sir Oliver Franks on 14 September 1951 produced, finally, an agreement that prior discussion with the British was necessary before the United States launched an atomic attack from Britain. In October 1951, a General Election was called in Britain, and Franks – sensing that this contentious issue might surface during the election campaign – asked the US National Security Council to agree a draft statement, to be made public if Britain so required in future. The critical passage promised that the use of the airbases and facilities in Britain:

> . . . naturally remains a matter for joint decision in the light of the circumstances at the time . . .

Early in 1952, Churchill visited Washington to discuss these and other matters with President Truman. They met on the presidential yacht, *Williamsburg*, and on 9 January 1952, issued a communiqué which remains the sole and fundamental source document referring to any right the British government may have to control the use of US bases in emergency.

The communiqué stated:

> Under arrangements made for the common defence, the United States has the use of certain bases in the United Kingdom. We reaffirm the understanding that the use of these bases in an emergency would be a matter for joint decision by Her Majesty's government and the United States government in the light of the circumstances prevailing at the time.

For thirty years since then this communiqué, which has not the status of treaty, agreement or contract, has been referred to by both governments on any occasion that the matter has been raised. We have been told in the 1980s by Mrs Thatcher, and by Defence Secretary Michael Heseltine, that successive Presidents and Prime Ministers solemnly proceed to reaffirm the ageing understanding on taking office – to what new purpose, it is not clear.

This arrangement has been questioned again and again in the history of the US presence in Britain. On occasions when British policy in international conflict appeared to diverge from the American, or new issues have been raised, the old communiqué has been recited in Parliament. This happened in 1954, again in 1957, and yet again in 1960. Although it is claimed that it has been adapted to take account of changed circumstances, such as the stationing of Polaris submarines at the Holy Loch in the 1960s, the substance of the 'joint decision' principle has not been modified. Its ambiguities and unsatisfactory nature are defended only with considerable difficulty. As discussed in the final chapter, it has the diplomatic merit of having no clear meaning and thus allowing the British government to promise the British people an assurance which it knows the US government likely would not or could not deliver, and certainly would never guarantee.

The British stake and risk in the military gamble later codified as 'nuclear deterrence' would soon arise. By the end of the 1950s involvement with the Americans, begun by Attlee's Labour government and continued with approval by Churchill, Eden and Macmillan, would include permanently aloft nuclear-armed bombers – whose idea of unarmed exercise, it seemed, was to rehearse nuclear bombing runs across London and Paris. There would be ballistic missiles in England, submarine missiles in Scotland, and a string of accidents and incidents that continued to remind the public of the hair trigger on which the whole system appeared balanced.

## Notes

1 Joint Chiefs of Staff documents JCS1496/3 and JCS1518, 19 September 1945; in JCS files CCS373.11; and JCS1477/1, 30 October 1945 (at US National Archives, Washington DC).

2 From General Spaatz's papers in the US National Archives; quoted in John T. Greenwood, 'The emergence of the postwar strategic Air Force, 1945–53', *Air power and warfare*, Proceedings of the Eighth Military History Symposium, USAF Academy, 1978.

3 *Hansard*, 26 July 1948.

4 Margaret Gowing, assisted by Lorna Arnold, *Independence and deterrence, Volumes 1* and *2*, Macmillan, 1974; *see* especially Vol 1, pp 309–21.

5 Richard G. Hewlett and Francis Duncan, *Atomic Shield: A History of the United States Atomic Energy Commission*, Volume 2, p 521; WASH 1215; US AEC, 1972.
6 Records from the US National Archives, Modern Military Branch: Secretary of Defense records, file 092.2 (UK)(1950).
7 Gowing, *op cit*, Vol 1, p 315.
8 David Alan Rosenberg, 'The Origins of Overkill', *International Security*, Spring 1983, pp 3–71.
9 John Robertson, 'Looking back at SAC-UK', *Air Britain Digest*, July 1968.
10 'List of US requirements for military rights within NATO countries and their territories, 26 December 1950.' In US National Archives, OSD Papers section, 092.2 (Saudi Arabia).
11 'Atom bomb village', *Daily Express*, 13 December 1954.
12 *Daily Express*, 14 and 15 September 1952.
13 Much of the full Dropshot plan was republished as *Operation: World War III*, edited by Anthony Cave Brown, Arms and Armour Press, 1978.
14 US National Archives, Joint Chiefs of Staff File CCS 381, Headstone.
15 Gowing, *op cit*, Vol 1, p 317.

# 2 *Crises and Consolidation*

*They would bomb London perhaps twice a week. The* B-47 *Stratojets flew the attack run over London at 40,000 feet. The target was the* EMI *electronics factory at Hayes, Middlesex. Not far away were a group of hangars, whose characteristics produced an excellent, bright, clear return on the bomb-aiming radar screen. The bomb-aiming system was automated to the extent that the aircraft could be flown, and its hydrogen bomb dropped, using an 'offset', which allowed the bombardier to align his bombing to some clearly identifiable landmark.*

*They had already bombed Edinburgh and Paris. At Edinburgh, they had aimed for Leith docks, alongside the Firth of Forth. Over Paris, the twists of the River Seine showed prominently on the bomb-aiming scope; the pinpoint target was the town hall of one* arrondisement *boasting a ball tower decoration which made a particularly suitable electronic landmark for an atom bomber . . .*

These exercises were the main activity of the Strategic Air Command bomber wings, which came to the Command's eight main British bases for 'rotational' 90-day tours throughout the 1950s. From bases such as Brize Norton, Upper Heyford or Fairford, the bombers would fly long, triangular courses over Britain and France, using dummy target material and rehearsing the atomic destruction of several European capitals. There were many 'alert' flights during which the aircraft would carry complete nuclear weapons, ready for arming. On these highly-dangerous occasions, it was later claimed, it was not the practice of the US Air Force to allow its crews to idly rehearse removing London and Paris from the maps. Usually, when 'bombing' these capitals, they would fly either empty, or with their bellies filled with concrete replicas of the bomb – as they called it, 'The Beast'.

A description of such SAC activities in England, which included an eyewitness account, appeared in print in the *New York Times* magazine in 1958.[1] It caused, as might be imagined, a considerable stir, including several rows in Parliament. The Air Minister assured Parliament in July that when the Americans flew the 'practice radar exercises . . . they did not carry these bombs'. One doughty and independent Tory protagonist was moved to warn, with characteristic British understatement, that an accident would not go down well:

> The advantage of flying over towns must be very small set against the disastrous consequences that could follow from any mishap.[2]

But there were accidents in England in this period, including at least one serious enough to merit inclusion in the Pentagon's top accident category, known by the codename 'Broken Arrow'. That accident, at Lakenheath, was on 26 July 1956, but was not known to the public – nor for that matter, probably known to the Ministry of Defence – until 1979, when a former USAF General and others from Strategic Air Command vouchsafed their opinion to the Omaha, Nebraska, local newspaper that: 'it is possible that a part of eastern England would have become a desert'.

The secret accident was only one in a long string of incidents which demonstrated that United States military activities in Britain had long since passed far beyond the active or effective political control of the British government. US officials, from Secretary of State John Foster Dulles downwards, had repeatedly repudiated the British belief that they had a 'veto' on the use of the American bases. On almost half a dozen occasions, the Prime Minister or Defence Minister had to acknowledge to the House of Commons that they were not consulted about critical activities at the bases. The government did not know about practice bomb runs over British cities until after the fact[3]; they did not know that SAC bombers in Britain were on regular airborne alert, carrying complete nuclear weapons. Nor did they have prior knowledge of major alerts and atomic war rehearsals at the bases.

Strategic Air Command reached its maximum strength in Britain in the summer of 1955. At that time, more than 11,000 UK-based servicemen worked for SAC alone, maintaining the major bases and the other dispersed centres to which the bulk of SAC bombers would come in war. Britain was no longer the only forward-basing area for SAC's long-range bombers; the command had bases in Libya and Morocco, and the right to move bomber groups into Iceland, Cyprus and Turkey in time of crisis. In the Pacific theatre, there were bases such as Guam, Hawaii, and the Philippines. Britain, however, was the backbone of the network, as unsinkable as ever. It was also home to the Joint Co-ordination

Center, Europe, set up after 1952 to 'co-ordinate atomic operations' for the US Joint Chiefs of Staff. There was only one other Joint Co-ordination Center, that for the Pacific, located in Hawaii. The British centre was undoubtedly located underground in the well-concealed bunker at Daws Hill, High Wycombe, which had been established in 1952 as the operations centre for the SAC Seventh Air Division.

The Joint Co-ordination Center, Europe was intended not so much to plan and launch an atomic war, as to keep it going. Its chief function was to receive reports of which atomic targets had been struck, and determine where the bombers had failed to reach their targets. Reserve forces could then theoretically be brought into play – although, as described later, the US atomic war plans of the 1950s centred on the total commitment of forces to a single, massive punch which would leave the Soviet Union 'a smoking, radiating ruin'.

The 'co-ordination' the centres were intended to provide would come *post-strike*, after the bombs had dropped. A first SAC exercise of this kind – codenamed 'Open Mind' – was held in Britain in February 1955.

The JCCs were in direct contact with the two citadels which were the highest levels of American military command: the Pentagon War Room, and its secret backup, Site R. Site R was ostensibly an army camp, Camp Ritchie, near Hagerstown in Maryland, 75 miles north-west of Washington. But tunnelled into the adjacent 1,500-foot Raven Rock mountain is a 600-foot underground command post, the Alternative National Military Command Center (ANMCC) – at the time of the 1955 exercise it was called the Alternative Joint Communications Center. This is the underground Pentagon, then regarded as virtually invulnerable to nuclear attack. In a Maryland valley and screened on three sides by large mountains, it stood a very good chance of survival, even if its existence and importance were known. It cost over $30 million to build in 1950.

Such citadels have long since been regarded as insecure, given the advent of large hydrogen bombs and increasingly accurate missiles with which to deliver them. The key command centres now take to the air in time of war, such as US European Command (USEUCOM), with a flight of airborne war rooms at Mildenhall, Suffolk. Codenamed 'Silk Purse', they were first established in November 1965.

After the post-strike exercise Open Mind, the pattern of SAC bomber operations in Britain began to change. The extensive flying programmes were scaled down, and the regular three-monthly migrations of whole units back and forth across the Atlantic wound down. This was partly because of embarrassment and complaints in Britain occasioned by the heavy flying schedules and practices of the bombers, partly because the B-47s were soon going to crack up under the strain, partly because the cost of transporting between one and two thousand people and their supplies to support each deployment was enormous, and partly because Britain offered an inclement training climate.

These manoeuvres were replaced by nuclear alert aircraft ready for take-off on each runway. Instead of a whole 40–50 strong wing, gathered on one base, smaller groups were scattered around – normally on the four main bases, Greenham, Brize Norton, Upper Heyford and Fairford. The new system, called 'Reflex Alert', was gradually introduced between 1957 and 1959. At the same time, in the United States, SAC began its 'airborne alerts', involving squadrons of aircraft being permanently aloft with their H-bomb loads. It was a policy that was to lead to many unpleasant accidents.

Reflex was the British bases' contribution to this programme. Although it was the stated policy that the aircraft coming to Britain would remain on static, not airborne alert, it was later confirmed that for alerts, exercises and other purposes, H-bomb-loaded aircraft were indeed frequently in the skies over the UK.

As SAC requirements decreased, so its massive 1953 allocation of 43 major airfields was scaled down. More than a dozen airfields were handed back to British control. By 1958, there were eight main SAC bomber bases and four fighter or fighter-bomber bases under separate command. The anti-aircraft gun sites operated both by the Americans and by British forces had also been disbanded after 1955 – the guns were not held to be of much use against high-speed jet bombers, which by then were in the inventory of the Soviet Long Range Air Force.

Each of the Reflex Alert crews was required to be on continuous alert for two of the three weeks of their visit to Britain. The aircraft and its nuclear weapons were kept at constant readiness by ground crew, the air crew eating and sleeping in an adjacent hut. Up to 20 aircraft at each base had to be airborne 15 minutes after an alert was given – the first crew had to be ready for take-off in less than 5 minutes.

Despite the risks of Reflex Alert, Britain's first – and only publicly admitted – nuclear weapons accident, of the category that the Pentagon calls Broken Arrow, occurred on the ground at Lakenheath airbase in the summer of 1956.

Broken Arrow is defined by the US Army as:

> Any unplanned occurrence involving loss or destruction of, or serious damage to, nuclear weapons or their pertinent components, nuclear reactors or facilities, or other nuclear or radioactive material, which results in an actual or potential hazard to life or property.

Similar Navy and Air Force regulations refer to a variety of contingencies:

> – Nuclear detonation (other than in war).
> – Non-nuclear detonation or burning of a nuclear weapon.
> – Seizure, theft or loss of a nuclear weapon or nuclear component.
> – An occurrence from any cause leading to radioactive contamination of sufficient magnitude to affect the community, adversely.[4]

Less serious than a Broken Arrow is a Bent Spear, a nuclear 'incident'. A more minor category of unwelcome events with the Bomb, continuing the same idiom, is categorised as a Blunt Sword.

Official regulations require any of these events to be reported to the highest authorities immediately, and such messages receive virtually untrammelled precedence on the military communications networks. There is no doubt that these American authorities, in Britain and the United States, were aware of what took place at Lakenheath. The public were not told; the local police were not told; and it seems probable that the British authorities were not told. Even after the Pentagon had released a list of Broken Arrows referring to and identifying the Lakenheath accident, the Defence Ministry lied in a public brochure distributed in 1980 at the prospective cruise missile deployment sites of Greenham Common and Molesworth, near Northampton.

The glossy and colourful brochure and information pack featured a cardboard cutout of a cruise missile launcher, and a series of questions about cruise missiles, nuclear weapons, and strategy. One question asked: Are nuclear weapons safe? What happens if there is an accident? The reply was:

> Nuclear weapons have been stored in this country for many years. There has never been any accident or radiation leakage. Nuclear weapons are designed to the very highest safety standards . . .

This was, and is, a lie, which casts considerable doubt on other statements which have been made from time to time about nuclear weapons accidents in Britain. After their error, the Ministry has modified its claims and say only that there have been no 'accidents *involving* radiation leakage'.

The details of the Lakenheath accident were first published in the Omaha *World-Herald* in 1980, and later confirmed in part by the Pentagon.[5] A B-47 Stratojet, itself unarmed, had been practising 'roller' landings on one of Lakenheath's two main runways. It went out of control, slid and crashed among the earth-covered igloos of the nuclear weapons store, which directly abuts the west end of both runways. Atom bombs were held there in quantity because of Lakenheath's role as one of the four main SAC bases.

As the bomber crashed, its fuel spilled out and ignited, causing a vigorous fire. According to the official account: 'the ensuing fire enveloped a storage igloo containing several nuclear weapons in storage configuration . . .'.

There then occurred, 'not just a panic but a stampede out of Lakenheath'. Witnesses to this stampede included the British divisional fire officer at nearby Bury St Edmunds, whose appliances were called to the base to provide a stand-by service for the US crews who were attending the crash. As they travelled towards Lakenheath, they encountered en route 'a convoy of American cars full up with women and children. They were obviously panicking, simply trying to get away. It was a pretty amazing sight . . .'.

A local garage and taxi proprietor recalled that at Brandon, 3–4 miles from Lakenheath, 'there was a stream of traffic through Brandon in the middle of the afternoon.' He recalled one American airman dashing from the gates of the base, hailing a taxi with the instructions: 'Go anywhere – just get away from here.'

At the crash, the US fire crew chief had a difficult and painful decision to make about the use of his fire teams. He ordered that the fire-suppressing foam should be directed not at the burning aircraft where four crew were burned to death but on to the storage igloo which was covered in flames. It may have been a very well-advised decision. The igloo contained three 'B-6' atom bombs, slimmed down and improved versions of the Fat Man plutonium bomb. Each had an atomic yield of about 40 kilotons. Altogether they would have contained perhaps 60 kilogrammes of plutonium, and several tonnes of TNT-type high explosive.

When the fire was extinguished and the nuclear storage igloo cooled, it was discovered that the bombs, with the high explosive inside, had burned and been damaged. In the 'storage configuration', the plutonium nuclear capsule or 'pit' was stored separately, and a full-scale atomic explosion was not therefore possible, as the official account of the accident asserts. But it fails to note that the plutonium was in the same igloos and would have been widely and disastrously dispersed by an explosion of about 10,000 lb of high explosive.

This was the major fear of the US Air Force officers who gave details of the accident in 1979. The simultaneous fire meant that the radioactive debris of the explosion would rise high into the atmosphere and carry plutonium contamination across a considerable distance. A senior officer told the Omaha paper that the consequent plutonium contamination could indeed have created a 'desert'.

US Air Force officials lied about the reasons for the evacuation from Lakenheath and nearby Mildenhall. They were instructed to say that there had been a hazard from live 0.50 machine-gun ammunition in the blazing plane. The editor of a local newspaper in nearby Thetford confirmed that this was indeed the fabrication fed to their reporter.

More than 25 years later, with Lakenheath a major nuclear strike base once again, the nuclear storage area has not been moved; it is positioned beside the orthodox explosives store, at the western end of the runways. Barely a mile away are the houses of Lakenheath village itself. In contrast, the US family housing area on Lakenheath base is two miles to the south. Although they were warned to evacuate during the 1956 accident, no notice at all was given to the villagers, either directly, or indirectly through the police.

The nearby airbase at Mildenhall, with an extensive housing area nearly five miles distant *was*, reportedly, also evacuated. Villagers at Brandon, 3½ miles away, were not warned.

Had the news of the accident become public at the time, it is not unreasonable to suggest that its effect on British history would have been considerable. In the five years that were to follow, there were many more rows and uncertainties occasioned by activities at the US bases. There was also to be the new reshaping of the nuclear relationship with the United States, Skybolt missiles to come and Polaris submarines to be bought. Had the grotesquely cynical behaviour of the US commanders at Lakenheath and the manner in which American dependents were evacuated whilst those Britons at greater risk were left in ignorance come to light, it would have told heavily against the US. But all references to the involvement of nuclear weapons in the accident were ordered expunged from official records.

During subsequent controversies, the statements of the US Department of Defense contrived to omit any mention of the Lakenheath accident. Nuclear accidents became a topic of widespread concern after two highly publicised B-52 bomber crashes, in 1966 and 1968. The bombers had each been carrying four 1-Megaton H-bombs. On these occasions, according to the official lists, these were nuclear accidents numbers 14 and 15. Critics in 1966 suggested that there had perhaps been two or three more, but an official list given to the *New York Times*[6] put the 1968 crash at Thule, Greenland, at number 15. However, by 1980, the official list put the Thule accident in 26th place! Eleven more accidents had been 'discovered'.

Only then, after the accident had been revealed by the 1979 Omaha reports, was Lakenheath included. Even this new list was manifestly incomplete, since the US Army and Navy listed no accidents. The 1980 list was stated not to be 'complete . . . due to differences in record-keeping among the services'. Summaries were unavailable for 10 accidents, for 'political and national security reasons'.

Amongst those listed were some at unidentified overseas bases that are highly likely to have been British – but so far the secret of the bases' identity has been kept. On 31 January 1958, a B-47 at an 'overseas base' was taking off with one weapon in the ready-to-be-armed 'strike configuration'. A wheel failed, the tail hit the runway, a fuel tank ruptured, and the plane caught fire. Fire crews were called, then withdrawn abruptly after 10 minutes. The plane burned for seven hours but, fortunately, no explosion occurred:

> there was some residual contamination in the immediate area of the crash

Runway asphalt had to be removed. At this time, SAC's Reflex Alerts in Britain were at their height, with wings of B-47s active at Greenham Common, Mildenhall and Brize Norton. The whole B-47 alert system was temporarily suspended after the accident.

Had these statistics on nuclear accidents, now admitted, been known in Britain in the 1950s and 60s, they would have made a significant impact on public opinion. Between 1947 and 1964, when the SAC bombers left Britain, there were 21 admitted nuclear weapons accidents. At least 15 bombs were aboard aircraft that crashed; four were deliberately dropped from aircraft which were out of control; and at least two were dropped accidentally. Eleven of the accidents involved B-29, B-50 or B-47 bombers, the predominant types in Britain. On at least eight occasions the high explosive detonated. On seven occasions radioactive contamination is specifically admitted. It is likely that the real list of accidents is twice as long, even, as SIPRI has estimated (see footnote on p 68) almost five times as long as that offered by the

Pentagon. In 1981 five new accidents were 'discovered' by Pentagon officials.[7]

In a series of parliamentary exchanges between 1957 and 1961, concerning nuclear weapons accidents and related issues, it rapidly became clear that little heed was paid by the American commanders to the principle of 'joint decision' on the use of the bases, discussed by Attlee and Truman in 1951.

There had been no joint decision about the SAC order to begin the nuclear-armed Reflex Alert operations – even though, as was subsequently pointed out in Parliament, if so little time was available in an emergency that bombers were required to be on airborne nuclear-armed alert, then there was not going to be time for the British government to be consulted and deliberate. Indeed, if the bombers were already airborne, armed, and away from their bases, no joint decision on the emergency use of bases could arise. The Reflex Alerts, if they were necessary, annulled the whole arrangement.

The *Sunday Times* commented in its editorial[8] that:

> the public . . . still need to be convinced that if there were time for the neccessary Allied consultations in an emergency, there would not be time for a bomb-carrying aircraft to return to its base to load the genuine nuclear article. If nuclear bombs were delivered from bases in the islands, it would presumably be we who would suffer the inevitable retaliation. That . . . is the price we pay . . . But it is a risk we ought to incur only by our own responsible decision.

Other events at the same time undermined public confidence that US activities were under supervision:

- No arrangement had been made to notify the Prime Minister or any minister or official about real or practice alerts ordered for the US bases – even if the alert was a DEFCON (Defence Readiness Condition) 1[9]. Also known by the codename 'Cocked Pistol', this level of defence readiness would only be ordered in imminent anticipation of war.
- The US Secretary of State made it emphatically clear that Britain did not have any veto over the use of US bases.
- Representations about 'consultations' were made by the government when, just days after the Soviet shooting down of Gary Powers' U-2 spy flight, an RB-47 from Brize Norton was shot down on a spy mission over the Barents sea.

In November 1957, the SAC commander, General Powers, revealed at a NATO conference that airborne alerts had been flown since the beginning of October. In Parliament, Foreign Secretary Selwyn Lloyd appeared uninterested; it was, he said, 'a matter for the United States Strategic Command' (*sic*) what they did with their aircraft. The statement by General Powers, he noted, might well be accurate: 'I am not disputing it. It may very well be so.' But, he affirmed, there was 'no danger of nuclear weapons exploding' in a crash or accident.

The same month, US Secretary of State John Foster Dulles announced what Denis Healey suggested was a 'unilateral repudiation of the Anglo-American agreement on the use of American nuclear bases'[10]. Dulles had said that:

> There can be no question of a veto on the use of nuclear weapons being exercised by other countries . . . No government could legally cast a veto against a decision of another country taken in its own defence.

This statement, and the new SAC alerts, were the subject of repeated questions to Macmillan, and his ministers. Their answers in Parliament lacked substance.

Questioned about the Reflex Alerts, for example, Sandys told the House of Commons that the government wasn't concerned[11]:

> This is a matter for [SAC] . . . We have a firm promise from the United States that they would not use the bases for military operations except in agreement with us. We trust them . . .
>
> They do what they please about their state of readiness, training and flying . . .

Soon after, the Prime Minister did confirm that nuclear weapons were on patrol aircraft in Britain[12]. The aircraft which carried nuclear weapons also had, he said, 'the apparatus for arming them. I have the assurance of the US government that pilots have specific instructions not to arm the weapons until they are directly ordered to do so in order to carry out an operation of war. Such an order would be given after agreement between the two governments.'

'Apparatus' is perhaps an over-dignified description for a small wrench resembling an Allen key which the bombardier would carry on a chain around his neck.

In March 1958, news of a Broken Arrow nuclear weapon accident in the United States leaked out. A B-47 from Georgia took off for Europe with nuclear weapons aboard. It accidentally dropped one six miles from a South Carolina town. The bomb exploded. There was 'property damage but no injuries' caused by the high-explosive detonation – but five of six nuclear safety interlocks had failed.

The British government now confirmed that nuclear weapons were carried aloft by US Air Force bombers, for, it was stated, special operational and training exercises. Sometimes the bombs were dummies; on other occasions they were real, in 'strike configuration', and ready to be armed for dropping. It may well be imagined that public concern was not then reassured by the publication, two months later, of details of the practice bomb runs described earlier in this chapter.

The row erupted again after two separate events on 1 May 1960. Around the world, the Joint Chiefs of Staff began a 'global atomic co-ordination exercise', codenamed 'Black Rock'. It would last through the month, involving the British-based atomic Joint Co-ordination Center in a rehearsal of the complete US nuclear war plans. On at least two occasions, on 15 May and 1 June, British bases were ordered into war readiness condition. No joint decisions were taken.

When Labour MP William Warbey wrote to the Prime Minister protesting about the alerts, and suggesting that they might have been intended to influence the May 1960 US-Soviet summit meeting. Macmillan was publicly soothing, but privately rattled. He replied that the alerts involved merely testing 'communications and readiness', and 'there was no question of an error of judgment which might plunge the world into nuclear war'.

But privately, Macmillan instructed Defence Minister Harold Watkinson of his alarm about the Black Rock alerts. Britain had not been notified of the simulated raising of the atomic stakes, and should have been, in the Prime Minister's view. Secret US documents, now declassified in the National Archives[13], show that Watkinson wrote immediately to the US Secretary of Defense. His reply made it clear that there had not been, up to that point, any arrangement to warn Britain of alerts at British bases 'during periods of increased world tension, and for exercise purposes', nor any arrangement to consult before small-scale 'readiness drills' were called by local US commanders. He promised:

> I am happy to ensure that you are notified of any decision to alert US forces in the United Kingdom, and its territories.

So, late in July 1960, a completely new instruction was given by the Joint Chiefs of Staff. Details of any alert at British bases would be passed on from the Pentagon to the US Navy Commander in London; he would pass the message on to the Minister of Defence.

It was a surprisingly informal arrangement, especially considering that a DEFCON 1 order would bring US forces in Britain to the brink of war. A real DEFCON 1 would imply a state of great emergency, with an attack perhaps imminent on the United States or one of its allies. War orders to US forces could be anticipated very quickly, and much of the British-based bomber force would already have taken off from their bases or dispersed, armed, at lower readiness states than DEFCON 1. Yet until July 1960 no procedure evidently existed for such alerts to be notified, let alone discussed or agreed with the British.

Also on Mayday 1960, at Peshawar in Pakistan, CIA U-2 pilot Gary Powers took off on his ill-fated espionage mission across the Ural Mountains (see pp 129–32). As the story gradually unfolded in the United States, the US Senate discovered that Lakenheath had been used for U-2 operations. Macmillan was expected to answer parliamentary questions about the incident on 12 July. The night before he received a protest note from the Soviet government about the use of another British base for a new spy flight.

On 1 July, an RB-47 reconnaissance mission over the Barents Sea had been mounted from Brize Norton and shot down in Soviet airspace. Did Britain know about these new spy flights? Had there been a joint decision? The answer, it appeared, was yes and no. After the Soviet protest note, a Defence Ministry statement was issued on the Press Association news tapes. This asserted that the flight was perfectly legal, for 'scientific purposes', and that both its object and flight plan were known to the ministry.

Seventeen minutes later, the statement was cancelled – made 'inoperative', in the vocabulary later employed by Richard Nixon's press aide Ronald Ziegler. When Macmillan was asked to clarify this cancellation of the statement in the House of Commons the same afternoon, he declined. Asked to explain the earlier activities of the U-2s (which is described in detail in Chapter 5), he refused to respond:

> These questions have a bearing on either the scope of intelligence activities, or the way in which they are conducted and controlled. It has never been the practice to discuss such matters in the House, and I have come to the conclusion that it would be contrary to the public interest for me to depart from precedent on this occasion.[14]

The issues of control and consultation were evaded again. However, privately, the UK government had had quite enough embarrassment. Discussion on the terms of the Attlee–Truman understanding were initiated by the British Embassy in Washington the same day and followed up two weeks later with a visit to Washington by a delegation led by the Foreign Office Deputy Under-Secretary, Sir Patrick Deane. No record of these discussions is yet available, but it is apparent that the terms agreed between Attlee and Truman were not varied.

The Americans did not appear overconcerned about British anxiety, the State Department's official spokesman commenting offhandedly that:

> we are not aware of any operating problems which have required high level attention recently . . . certainly we are always prepared to give them such attention when necessary . . .

Another spokesman told *The Times* that nothing, in effect, would change:

> The talks are expected to proceed smoothly towards an understanding which will probably involve no actual change in the 1951 agreement[15]

Through the 1950s, US military power in Britain had been consolidated by the construction of ammunition dumps, intelligence facilities (described in Chapter 5), and new communications networks to support Strategic Air Command in its wartime activities. Amongst these facilities was Croughton near Banbury in Oxfordshire, which opened in 1952 as a USAF long-range radio station. One of its tasks, then as now, was to provide the radio links over which airborne alert or scrambled bomber crews would receive the coded 'Go' message from the underground control centre at High Wycombe.

The system is codenamed 'Giant Talk', and is operated by a chain of 16 stations[16] around the world. It is regularly used by spy planes as well as B-52 bombers. SAC's official handbook describes Giant Talk as:

> the means for positive control of the SAC airborne force. Its prime function is transmission of executive instructions to SAC aircraft launched under positive control. Giant Talk also provides positive control communications for day-to-day control of aircraft reconnaissance operations.[17]

The Croughton site is split between a receiver centre, now equipped with specialised satellite communications equipment, and a 'transmitter annexe' at the disused airfield of Barford St John, a few miles to the west. Both sites are the source of sufficiently powerful radio transmission for aircraft charts to identify their locations as potentially hazardous to navigation.

In operation since the early 1950s, the Croughton/Barford St John communications complex provides SAC with 'positive control' by a continuous and eerie series of 'Foxtrot' broadcasts with which radio amateurs monitoring the high-frequency bands are familiar. Every fifteen minutes, a Foxtrot broadcast from these control stations goes out to airborne-alert and other SAC aircraft. Routine information may be indistinguishable from war messages.

The Giant Talk stations also support a VIP emergency communications network codenamed 'Mystic Star'. This system is intended to provide continuous worldwide contact between the President of the United States and the White House (codenamed 'Crown'), wherever the President may be. Crown, in turn, communicates with the National Military Command Center in the Pentagon, where the Joint Chiefs of Staff are located. Mystic Star, like Giant Talk, uses high-frequency radio signals.

One of the most critical, but often forgotten, requirements for offensive bomber operations is as accurate weather forecasting as possible, so that crews may know the conditions expected to be encountered en route, and adjust their instruments and flight plans accordingly. In 1956, Croughton became one of four centres in the US Air Force Automated Weather Network (the others were in Texas, Japan and the Philippines). From then on, Croughton became critical to US Air Force operations as the centre through which all the details of weather conditions in Europe and Eurasia, Africa and the Atlantic were collected and distributed to forecasters.

Before the first transatlantic telephone cables entered service (1956) intercontinental high-frequency radio was the only reliable means for orders to be sent to the British bases. Croughton was by 1961 one of ten key automated communications centres in the USAF Aerospace Communications Complex, AIRCOM, linked to Andrews Air Force Base, near Washington, as well as to Germany, Iceland, the Azores, Spain and Libya.

The US Navy has also had long-established radio communications systems in Britain. A naval station, with the call-sign GXH, was set up at Londonderry in Northern Ireland in 1941, during the Second World War, to help co-ordinate Atlantic convoys. It was upgraded to become a major link in the US Navy's worldwide communications system twenty years later. The requirement to make Londonderry a major Naval Communications Station, arose from the sudden importance of the north-east Atlantic and Norwegian sea areas to the US Navy, as primary deployment areas for their Polaris missile-carrying submarines (see also Chapter 8).

US Naval Headquarters in London, a naval air facility at Hendon and the radio station in Londonderry are the only US bases in Britain known to have operated continuously from the end of the Second World War. The Naval Headquarters had been set up in London in 1942, and has remained since. When the Londonderry station closed in July 1977 the US commander, Admiral Richard Rumble, revealed that the first Americans had come undercover to Derry in 1941. It had been the first American base in Europe, having been set up six months *before* the United States had joined the war.

Throughout the disturbances and troubles in Northern Ireland, the base, at Clooney Park in the Protestant Waterside district, remained unfortified and its personnel unmolested. The reason was an active posture of neutrality by the Americans, complemented by the considerable sensitivity Irish Republicans felt towards the United States.

In the late 1960s, the communications network from Derry was augmented by the construction of new low-frequency transmitters on Benbradagh – one of the Sperrin Mountain peaks south of Dungiven. This facility lasted only a decade, after which, like Derry itself, it was closed. Their functions were eventually taken over by the auxiliary naval radio station at Thurso, in the extreme north of Scotland.

Croughton and Barford St John were linked to the High Wycombe command and atomic control centre by a microwave communications network constructed by the United States Air Force between 1956 and 1962. All the main airbases were linked together by this means, making the US military network completely independent on the British Post Office. At each base was built a high tower, fitted with mirror-like reflectors at its apex and microwave beam transmitters at the ground. The system provided 60 or more separate and virtually uninterruptible and unjammable communications channels.

Although the security of communications provided by this system may have been valued by the US Air Force commanders, it is not clear why they wanted – or were granted permission – to operate their own network. At the time the system was built, the British Post Office were engaged in the construction of an extensive national microwave network of their own, substantially for defence purposes. Indeed, this system appears to have been adapted for the intelligence gathering purposes of the US National Security Agency (see pp 164–7). However, the USAF communications system in Britain certainly served to preserve its independence of action.

In order to construct the new microwave communications system, the US acquired further small British facilities to connect airbases for which no direct microwave beam path was possible. Such stations were built at Christmas Common, on the edge of the Chiltern Hills near High Wycombe, Daventry, Bovingdon, Barkway in Hertfordshire, Great Bromley and High Garrett in Essex. Soon, this central nexus was joined to France and Germany, and later to Belgium, the Netherlands, Spain and then to the United States itself. The first chain involved new relay stations between High Wycombe and Dover, at Hillingdon in West London, and a chain along the North Downs of Surrey and Kent, at Botley Hill, Coldblow Lane, Dunkirk (Kent), and then Dover itself.

From a site at Swingate in Dover, high on the celebrated chalk cliffs and overlooking the busy harbour and medieval castle, US Air Force transmitters beamed signals towards their counterpart networks run by the US Army and Air Force in France. This link ran on to US bases at Orleans and Bordeaux. A second connection to the Continent was made in March 1962, when a new communications station, at Martlesham Heath near Ipswich in Suffolk, was linked to Flobecq in Belgium. In 1963, a longer-range link direct to Spain was built at Ringstead Bay, near Weymouth in Dorset. The link operated across hundreds of miles to Gorramendi, near Elizondo, in the Spanish Pyrenees.

Using massive billboard-style reflectors to direct enormous amounts of radio energy into the troposphere, novel 'tropospheric scatter' communications networks were being built all over the world. With aerials 150 feet high, the Ringstead Bay proposal occasioned considerable local controversy, and the Air Ministry was legally challenged on whether they had the right to compulsorily purchase British land for American defence purposes. Amongst the objectors to the powerful new station was the Royal Navy, one of whose officers pointed out that it would cause 'serious interference' to the many RN radio stations operating around nearby Portland Bill. However, the station was built, but it was closed down by 1970 and dismantled in 1974.

The Ringstead-Gorramendi link provided the High Wycombe atomic Joint Co-ordination Centre with a direct connection to US nuclear forces straddling the Mediterranean in Spain itself, Morocco, at Wheelus Field near Tripoli in Libya, and further east. In order to provide the necessary microwave link relay stations, the US Air Force obtained four more facilities at Golden Pot, near Alton, Hants, Dean Hill near Salisbury, Bulbarrow Hill near Shaftesbury, and on Portland Bill.

A final link, constructed between 1961 and 1963, connected the USAF chain – notably the High Wycombe headquarters and the Chicksands

Sigint base – to Fylingdales, the site of the Ballistic Missile Early Warning System (BMEWS) station. This was the access point for the ambitious troposcatter network to the United States itself, the North Atlantic Relay System (NARS). (BMEWS and NARS are fully described in Chapter 3). The link stations were at Crowland, Spitalgate near Grantham, Kirton-in-Lindsey near Scunthorpe, and Garroby Hill, near Stamford Bridge in Yorkshire. By acquiring these links, the USAF had added 21 new sites to its inventory of bases and facilities in Britain.

Other support services for the US Air Force were consolidated during the decade. The massive Burtonwood Air Depot, which at one time had housed some 10,000 people, was run down from 1954 onwards, after it was decided that most supplies should be shipped to US bases in Europe directly from the United States.

The burgeoning USAF ammunition storage requirements led to the opening of another storage centre in 1955, at Welford, north of Newbury and close to the SAC base of Greenham Common. Welford became the main supply point for the Third Air Force units in Britain. The US Air Force also acquired many other sites near main operating bases, for housing or as storage annexes.

By 1960, there were many tactical nuclear bases in England besides the main SAC centres. The (tactical) Third Air Force had built up reconnaissance and transport units, support bases and medium-range fighter-bombers squadrons. Their main bases were Sculthorpe, Wethersfield, Woodbridge, Bentwaters and Alconbury. The latter three are still major bases; the others remain in US hands for 'standby' purposes. Table 2 identifies tactical USAF units in Britain in 1960.

These units had first come to England in 1951 and 1952, as relatively short-range fighter-bomber squadrons. Both Voodoos and Super Sabres were nuclear strike aircraft (as well as having a possible conventional role). Since May 1954 these units had been formally committed to NATO, and would in war become part of the 4th Allied Tactical Air Force (4ATAF), one of two NATO air forces which combine both offensive and defensive units for operations in central Europe.

In 1960, there were no US air defence fighters in Britain, and none have now been based in Britain for 25 years. One fighter-interceptor wing was established at Manston in Kent with F-86 Sabre fighters. But these aircraft were returned to the States in 1958 and Manston closed as a US base – ending, with it, any US Air Force commitment to provide resources for or assistance to Britain's general air defences.

**Table 2**
**US Third Air Force Units in 1960**

| Base | Units |
|---|---|
| Bentwaters | 81st Tactical Fighter Wing<br>F-101 Voodoo fighter-bombers – medium-range, 'tactical' bombers allocated to NATO command |
| Woodbridge | 78th Tactical Fighter Squadron (part of 81 TFW at Bentwaters)<br>F-101 Voodoo fighter-bombers |
| Wethersfield | 20th Tactical Fighter Wing<br>F-100 Super Sabre fighter-bombers |
| Sculthorpe | 47th Bomb Wing<br>B-66B Destroyer medium bombers<br>420th Air Refuelling Squadron<br>KB-29 and KB-50 tankers to refuel bombers and fighters |
| Alconbury | 10th Tactical Reconnaissance Wing<br>B-66B and RB-66B reconnaissance aircraft – Sigint, jamming and photographic reconnaissance |
| Bruntingthorpe | 19th Tactical Reconnaissance Squadron (part of 10 TRW at Alconbury)<br>RB-66 Destroyer reconnaissance aircraft |
| Chelveston | 32nd Tactical Reconnaissance Squadron (part of 10 TRW at Alconbury)<br>RB-66 Destroyer reconnaissance aircraft |

In 1960, the SAC strategic arsenal in Britain was shortly to run down following the advent of B-52 bombers which could operate directly from US bases. But the 'tactical' nuclear arsenal was growing dramatically, augmented by the forced transfer of US nuclear forces in France. As described in the next chapter, yet more American units were to transfer from France after being evicted by General de Gaulle.

The distinction made between strategic and tactical nuclear weapons and bombers is one that might easily be missed by those living near target areas. But it is a distinction that was reflected strongly in the organisation and equipment of the US Air Force. Strategic Air Command and its long-range nuclear forces were primarily targeted on three types of Soviet objective, codenamed 'Bravo', 'Romeo' and 'Delta'.

- 'Bravo' (B) targets were concerned with the 'blunting' of any Soviet atomic attack, and the Soviet military atomic industry. This was the top priority.
- 'Romeo' (R) targets were transport facilities, troop concentrations, and depots whose destruction would 'retard' the advance of Soviet forces in the field. This was the second priority.
- 'Delta' (D) targets involved the simple 'destruction' of the Soviet urban-industrial base, starting with basic war-sustaining industries such as oil and steel. These targets need not be attacked immediately.

Tactical nuclear units, such as the fighter-bombers at Woodbridge/Bentwaters, Wethersfield, and later at Lakenheath, were concerned only with nuclear attacks which would have a rapid impact on the battle in Europe. In contrast, SAC focused on the destruction of any Soviet atomic threat to the United States, and ultimately on the destruction of Soviet society and civilisation. But SAC's war plans had to be co-ordinated with those of the theatre commanders and the US Navy in order to avoid conflicting multiple attacks on the same target.

Overlaps and conflicts did not disappear, however, until after August 1960, when the Department of Defense set up the Joint Strategic Target Planning Staff, and gave them the job of producing a Single Integrated Operational Plan for strategic nuclear attack (the SIOP, pronounced 'sy-op'). The tactical target list for use in Europe was contained in the SACEUR (Supreme Allied Commander, Europe) Nuclear Support Plan (NSP).

Secret details of US plans for both strategic and tactical nuclear warfare in Europe, obtained by a spy, were leaked in 1970, and again in 1980. Amongst the leaked plans were the US Air Force Europe 1962 nuclear targeting manual, entitled *Nuclear Yield Requirements*, and sections of US major European Command plans.[18]

Major European Command plans of the time were identified as Operational Plan – or 'Oplan' – number 100–1, 100–2 and so on. Oplan 100–1 was the well-understood general plan for US forces to combine with other NATO forces to resist a Soviet attack. Oplan 100–2 was the plan for the European Command to give logistic and administrative support to US forces committed to NATO, and to conduct some unilateral (ie, non-NATO) war operations. Oplan 100–6 had a rather different tone, however. This was a plan for the United States and some of its allies to start a pre-emptive nuclear attack, and then conquer parts of eastern Europe. The plan anticipated that NATO would break up in the face of such a proposal, and that some NATO allies might even 'deny the use of existing NATO infrastructure' to the United States.

US 'pre-emption' was defined in Oplan 100–6 as an attack:

> Launched in response to unequivocal strategic warning of impending major Sino-Soviet bloc attack upon the US or its allies, with US forces worldwide being in a state of advanced readiness.

The attack would begin with a nuclear strike from the SIOP forces. There were two 'pre-emptive US Attack Options' in the 1962 SIOP:

> Attack Option I, in which the objective is the destruction or neutralisation of the Sino-Soviet bloc strategic nuclear delivery forces posing a threat to the US and its allies and to US and allied forces overseas; and . . .
>
> Attack Option II, in which the objective is that of Option I plus the destruction or neutralisation of other elements of Sino-Soviet bloc military forces and military resources in being.

According to Oplan 100–6, US European Command would carry out 'early offensive operations . . . in co-ordination with and [in] exploitation of US pre-emptive attack'. The US forces' objective was then to go on the offensive and 'penetrate . . . certain European satellite areas'. They planned to invade East Germany and Czechoslovakia, liberating them from Soviet forces by:

> Operations . . . envisaged as airborne penetrations to capital cities, followed by link-ups, rather than frontal assault . . . USEUCOM forces . . . will undertake penetration to Berlin (US and West German forces) and Prague (predominantly US forces). Maximum mobility, including air drop, will be exploited in order to exploit the shock effect of the pre-emptive attack.

Although East Germany and Czechoslovakia would therefore be spared nuclear attack as far as practicable, it was nevertheless expected that:

> The nuclear exchange will result in extensive damage to many municipalities and industrial areas, and [this] will require substantial assistance to restore the economic viability in these areas.

Although the United States did not expect NATO to survive as a political entity if America launched a *de facto* nuclear first strike, they assumed that:

> If all of NATO does not join in the pre-emptive attacks and subsequent offensive operations, as a minimum, the United Kingdom, Italy, Greece and Turkey will participate.

Since only the UK amongst northern European nations was expected to agree to a Western first strike, it was envisaged that 'a new allied command' would be formed excluding the non-participating NATO members.

These countries would be expected to join the US Air Force Europe in delivering nuclear attacks 'in support of Attack Option II of the SIOP and the Scheduled and Regional programs of SACEUR's [Nuclear Support Plan]', and also on 'important targets in [the NSP] which are not struck because allies elect not to support the pre-emptive attack'.

These targets were among thousands listed in *Nuclear Yield Requirements*, the leaked targeting manual. The 146-page manual – of which only 40 pages have been published – appears to have included nearly 3,000 targets, many of them airfields. As well as Warsaw-pact airfields, target details had been prepared and were listed for similar targets in neutral countries and even NATO nations which might have been overrun. Examples include 18 airfields in Finland, Kiel, Lubeck and Flensburg in West Germany, and railway junctions in Austria. In case Soviet forces moved around NATO's flanks into the Middle East, target data had also been prepared for at least 60 airfields and other sites in Iran, Iraq, Syria and Egypt.

For each target, exact dimensions had been calculated from spy plane photographs, and the vulnerability to different levels of nuclear attack assessed. A suitable nuclear yield could be selected using bombs with powers ranging from 2.5 kT to 1.1 MT (about 80 times the power of the Hiroshima bomb), burst on the air – or on the ground, if the 'bonus' of cratering and fallout was desired. There were a dozen major target categories: airfields, railway bridges, road bridges, railway facilities, headquarters and camps, ports, waterways, missile sites, highway intersections, troop concentrations, and ammunition and nuclear weapons stores.

No heed was paid, however, to what is now called 'collateral damage'. No attempt was made to assess how close cities and civilian populations were to the targets. In some cases an attack on a bridge, port or airport would be indistinguishable in terms of civilian casualties from a direct attack on the city of which it was part. Assessments of collateral slaughter caused by tactical nuclear attacks are now, however, standard in NATO nuclear plans.

The British-based Voodoos and Super Sabres would play a major role in the execution of this comprehensive catalogue of destruction. The vast extent of the devastation to be wrought by the full execution of the SACEUR Nuclear Support Plan is a chilling reminder of how the simple notion of deterrence – threatening an adversary with an assured level of destruction – had been ditched by US planners at the very start of the nuclear arms race.

These 1962 documents revealed that there were then in existence plans unequivocally aimed at nuclear war-fighting, embracing the possibility of limited regional nuclear warfare in Europe. But they were not for NATO eyes. The target list was marked 'Special handling required. Not releasable to foreign nationals. TOP SECRET'.

## Notes

1 It was reprinted in the British *Evening News* and in *The Times*, on 8 and 9 May 1958, respectively.
2 *Hansard*, 17 July 1958.
3 John Robertson, *Looking back at* SAC-UK, *Air-Britain Digest*, July 1968. The article was written with the assistance of, and clearance from, official US Air Force and SAC historians.
4 For a more detailed description of the types of accidents, and a history see 'Accidents of nuclear weapons systems', Chapter 3 of SIPRI *Yearbook of World Armaments and Disarmament, 1977*; SIPRI, Stockholm.
5 Omaha, Nebraska *World-Herald*, 5 November 1979; further details were reported in the *Guardian*, 6 November 1979. The Pentagon's official list of Broken Arrows was published as the Department of Defense *Summary of accidents involving nuclear weapons, 1950–1980 (interim)*, released in December 1980. The bulk of the document was published in the New York *Nation*, 7 February 1981, and again in *Flight International* (UK), 4 July 1981.
6 *New York Times*, 23 January 1968.
7 *New York Times*, 23 May 1981.
8 *Sunday Times*, 1 December 1957.
9 *The Times*, 19 November 1957.
10 *Hansard*, 21 November 1957.
11 *Hansard*, 12 December 1957.
12 *Hansard*, 3 December 1957.
13 Joint Chiefs of Staff files, Section CCS3180, Emergency Readiness Plans.
14 *The Times*, 13 July 1960.
15 *The Times*, 15 July 1960.
16 Besides Croughton, a second Giant Talk base is on British territory in Ascension Island in the South Atlantic. The other 14 stations are in the Philippines; Guam; Hawaii; Yokota, Japan; Elmendorf, Alaska; Thule, Greenland; Incirclik, Turkey; Lajes in the Azores; the Panama Canal Zone; and five US sites in California, Illinois, Maryland, Maine, and Florida.
17 'Positive control' meant that bombers had to receive a final authorisation before they entered Soviet territory.
18 The European Command plans referred to in this and other sections are classified US documents deliberately leaked by (one presumes) persons acting for the Soviet Union. The US government does not dispute their authenticity, and they are not

cited amongst the list of forged Soviet simulations of US documents cited in recent CIA reports to Congress. There is no secret about where the Soviets obtained their copies: a spy, Sergeant Robert Johnson, photographed them while they were in his custody in the Armed Forces Courier Center in Paris during 1962 and 1963. He was caught and convicted.

In June 1980, photocopies of many of Sergeant Johnson's clandestine photographs were sent to nine MPs and five newspapers, including the *News Statesman* (27 June 1980). Many documents were the same as had been sent to and published by the West German magazine, *Stern*, in 1970. Mr Jim Dobbins, the US Embassy in London's Political Secretary, told the author in 1980 that while the US government was not prepared to comment in detail on the leaked plans, they did not dispute that the material was genuine. 'Nothing would indicate otherwise,' the Embassy official said.

Some parts of the US European Command war plans of the early 1960s are now declassified in the US National Archives, Washington. The declassified material includes plans for unconventional warfare and nuclear support, and confirms and corroborates many aspects of the leaked documents. In particular, the words used in Oplan 100–6 to define the circumstances for a US pre-emptive attack are to be found in declassified US documents, confirming that such plans existed.

# 3 *Warheads and Warning*

*A single switch controlled the arming of the Thor intermediate-range ballistic missile. The bottom setting was marked 'Peace'; the top, 'War'. The switch allowed the 1-Megaton hydrogen warhead on the missile to be armed, and its key was always held by an American officer. There was another key held by his British counterpart, which triggered the missile through each of its five launch phases. These two switches symbolise the slender thread on which existence hung in the missile age. From peace to war was a 90-degree turn of a single key.*

The two keys of the Thor missile not only symbolised, but gave concrete reality to the 'dual control' agreement for the control of the missiles. Clearly each partner, USAF and RAF, did have an absolute veto on firing. In this unique case of an American weapons system on British territory, there was no doubt that the much-vaunted but normally meaningless 'joint decision' promise had substance. In contrast, the entire process of arming and launching cruise missiles is under US control, and there is no possibility of direct British physical intervention, either to authorise launching or to prohibit it (short of an armed attack on US forces by their RAF Regiment 'guards').

The network of 20 Thor missile bases was the first part of an early 1960s wave of new US nuclear facilities in Britain. Shortly after the Thor missiles came into service, an agreement for the Clyde Polaris base was signed. As this came into effect, US nuclear-capable units (and others) in France were ordered out by General de Gaulle and came to Britain.

Thor and Polaris brought 220 more missiles to British territory, on land and in submarine. The redeployed forces from France added another 75 'tactical' nuclear aircraft and their weapons to the British-based arsenal. But the balance would shift again when, in June 1964, SAC finally withdrew its forces from Britain, and handed back its bases. Nevertheless, even without SAC, the US Third Air Force in Britain was the most powerful air force in Western Europe.

The Thor was a first generation IRBM (intermediate-range ballistic missile). It had Soviet counterparts, the SS-4 and SS-5 missiles, which were still deployed in limited numbers in the western Soviet Union in 1983. Both Thor and its Soviet equivalents had to operate from a fixed location. Each Thor had to have its own protective shelter to resist conventional bombing or near misses, and automated equipment to remove the shelter covers, raise the missile and fuel and arm it.

The missiles were liquid-fuelled, which required a careful and often unreliable fuelling operation prior to launch. Fuel and refrigerated liquid oxygen (LOX) had to be pumped into the missile tanks, raising dense clouds of vapour from the sudden cooling as the LOX entered the missile tanks.

It was officially claimed that the launch sequence would take 15 minutes, although in practice it would have taken a much longer time[1]. The Soviet SS-4 and SS-5 missiles reputedly take several hours preparation. These vulnerable and wholly obsolete weapons have only been kept in service by the Soviet Union to serve as a counter to be bargained away in talks with the United States.

The time from launch to impact of a Thor missile was less than half an hour, providing the United States and the UK with a powerful and rapid means of nuclear destruction. It was claimed to have a range of some 1,500 miles, enabling it to strike targets in the western USSR, perhaps reaching just short of Moscow. However, this seems likely to have been a highly optimistic figure.

The US–UK Thor agreement was signed at a summit conference between Macmillan (who had recently replaced Anthony Eden as Prime Minister after the Suez fiasco) and President Eisenhower, at Bermuda in January 1957[2]. The theory of the 'missile gap' (between US and Soviet capabilities), later determined to be false, was secretly evolving at this time. Intermediate-range missiles in Europe (and to a lesser extent in the Pacific) would therefore give the United States an opportunity to mount pre-emptive attacks on targets such as Russian missile bases.

That was the theory, or some of it. But the reliability of the first missiles was poor, and their typical accuracy may have been as low as one mile. This was partially compensated for by the high yield of the one megaton H-bomb warhead.

Eisenhower was eager to persuade all the NATO allies to agree to the new missile bases. The situation closely paralleled the 1979 cruise missile deployment, in that collective agreement for each country to provide IRBM bases was advocated as a useful token and demonstration of Western solidarity. This proposal was put to the NATO council in December 1957. However only the UK, Turkey and Italy accepted the proposals. Jupiter missiles went to Turkey and Italy, Britain alone receiving Thor.

The NATO commander, General Lauris Norstad, continued vigorously to pursue the possibility of further medium-range missiles for Europe, asking for 300 missiles by 1963. The missiles would be used, as with Pershing and cruise, to attack targets directly related to war in Europe, rather than missile bases or similar centres posing a 'strategic' threat; ie, a threat to the United States or its forces. These were the tactical, or 'theatre' targets.

The proposal by Norstad for extensive new NATO missile forces never came to fruition as an 'independent', or multilateral NATO nuclear force, although it led to the assignment to SACEUR of Britain's Polaris force, some of the V bombers, and eventually some 400 warheads from the US Polaris submarine force.

The first Thor nuclear missile bases in Britain became operational in 1958. The maintenance of the missiles, other than the warheads, was the responsibility of the RAF. The 60 missiles, assigned to 20 Strategic Missile Squadrons, were divided into four wings of 15 missiles each. Each squadron had three missiles, and was stationed on a separate airfield. Figure 4 (p 83) shows the locations of these Thor bases.

Each wing had one central base, and four more dispersed around this headquarters, all on former wartime airfields. The missile bases were spread across a wide area of Yorkshire, Lincolnshire and parts of East Anglia. The headquarters were at Driffield, Yorkshire; Hemswell, Lincolnshire; North Luffenham, Leicestershire; and Feltwell, close to Lakenheath in Suffolk. The latter four were working airfields, to which a massive 1,000 flight airlift brought the missiles and other essential components in 1958 and 1959. All 60 missiles were in service by May 1960.

The United States gave the missiles to Britain under the US Mutual Defense Assistance Program, so that they became RAF property, without charge. Britain paid for the construction of the operating bases. Maintenance was carried out at each wing headquarters, where a US detachment from the SAC Munitions Support Squadron was located – responsible also for custody of the warheads. These US teams took their orders direct from the Strategic Air Command, via the 7th Air Division headquarters at High Wycombe. Both that headquarters, and the RAF Bomber Command HQ, which was responsible for giving the firing order to RAF crews, had direct and permanent telephone and teleprinter links to SAC headquarters at Offutt Air Force Base in Omaha.

The threat posed by the IRBMs to the Soviet Union and its allies provoked a well-known response two years later. The Soviet Union attempted to instal similar missiles in Cuba, providing them with a rapid means of attacking key US centres in the south and on the eastern seaboard. During the celebrated crisis, from 20–28 October 1962, SAC forces in Britain and around the world reached the DEFCON 2 alert state (a 'high degree' of readiness). That happened on 25 October. On this occasion the UK was informed, at least at the level of Bomber Command[3]. The crisis ended on 28 October, after the American naval blockade had won from Khrushchev an agreement for their withdrawal.

The Thor missiles did not, however, last much longer than the Soviet IRBMs in Cuba. The first Thor missiles were withdrawn from service, their obsolescence recognised, in January 1963. The warheads were removed from the remainder some four months later. The entire force was stood down in August 1963, after being deployed less than four years.

Operation 'Red Richard' was the next event which built up US nuclear forces in Britain. This was the codename for the operation to remove all nuclear weapons and aircraft with nuclear-weapon capabilities from France. The move began in 1959, after de Gaulle had asked the Americans to grant him the rights the British pretended they had always had; control over the use of nuclear weapons from national territory.

The French position was that all atomic stockpiles on her territory must be subject to a joint decision before they were used – meaning a French veto in case of disagreement. In July 1959, the British government agreed that they should come to Britain. Although British ministers have from time to time claimed that Britain had such a veto from the 1951 Attlee-Truman understanding, they have not been upheld in this interpretation by the United States. That the US Air Force should move to Britain when France demanded a veto is strong evidence that US military commanders, like Secretary of State Dulles (p 56), did not consider that the British had a veto at all.

Two new wings joined the Third Air Division in England: the 10th Tactical Reconnaissance Wing at Alconbury, and the 48th Tactical Fighter Wing at Lakenheath. To fit these aircraft into existing bases required SAC to move out of four of its eight main bases; Bruntingthorpe, Chelveston, Lakenheath and Mildenhall were handed over. The gradual buildup of B-52s in the United States was in any case slowly diminishing SAC's need for major overseas bases, so the transfer of these airfields from SAC to a Tactical Air Command (TAC) unit imposed no hardship on the strategic warriors.

There were 75 new bombers in the 48th Tactical Fighter Wing, which came to Lakenheath – bringing, it was widely reported, their bombs with them. In fact, the bombs were transported separately, and brought to the new base by transport flights. At Chaumont the Wing, which had seen some wartime service in the liberation of France from the Nazis, had gained the ceremonial title of the 'Statue of Liberty Wing'.

The Third Air Division became, in 1963, the Third Air Force again, and came under the multi-layered NATO and US command and control arrangements (further discussed in Chapter 6). In general, under the US Commander-in-Chief, Europe, come the main Navy, Air Force, and Army commands. The Third Air Force is part of the US Air Force, Europe (USAFE); its commander, based at Ramstein, near Frankfurt, doubles as the NATO Commander of Allied Air Forces Central Europe (AAFCE), which is in turn part of Allied Forces Central Europe (AFCENT). Operational orders come to the Third Air Force from another, subordinate force (if the reader can bear with the NATO alphabet soup of military commands and their acronyms), 4 Allied Tactical Air Force (4ATAF).

Soon after the Third Air Force reformed, its UK bases were individually linked by radio to the 4ATAF wartime headquarters. This was underground in a southern German bunker at Kinsbach, colloquially referred to in NATO documents as 'The Cave'. The Third Air Force's headquarters remained in the old factory complex at South Ruislip until 1972, when the command moved out to Mildenhall.

For the first few years of the 1960s, and despite the arrival of new nuclear units from France, the British airbase network began to decline. In June 1961, a massive closure programme was announced – some of it prematurely. Nevertheless, the Burtonwood depot and other facilities were totally run down. Alconbury, Bruntingthorpe, Chelveston and Sculthorpe were intended to be closed rapidly.

The B-66 Destroyer bomber wing which had been at Sculthorpe since 1952 was disbanded and its bombers returned to the United States. Some 7,000 airmen and dependants went back with them. An Air Refuelling squadron also based at Sculthorpe went back a year later. It remains a 'Standby Operating Base', officially reduced to 'mothball' status.

Three of the four surviving SAC bases – Brize Norton, Fairford, and

Greenham Common – were handed back to the RAF in 1964 and 1965, after the B-47 Stratojets finally became too long in the tooth to remain a reliable part of the US nuclear inventory. B-47 strategic bases in Morocco were also closed. SAC was pulling back to the US where the newly-installed Titan and Minuteman missiles, and the long-range B-52 bombers became the backbone of its forces, as they remain today.

SAC finally ceased operating from Britain in July 1965 and the Air Division at High Wycombe was disbanded. But SAC detachments continued to be stationed there. They also retained Upper Heyford as a toehold in the UK, and for the rest of the sixties it was a stopping-off point for refuelling tankers and reconnaissance aircraft. Another less well known unit which closed at the same time was the nuclear weapons custodial and maintenance unit at RAF Marham. The Marham detachments had looked after US H-bombs provided to the RAF. The implication of the closure is that by July 1965 the RAF had been supplied with enough British-made A-bombs and H-bombs for the entire V bomber force then operating.

As noted in Chapter 5, U-2 missions had begun again in 1962 from Upper Heyford. It was officially claimed, as was customary, that they were engaged in nothing more malign than 'weather research and atmosphere sampling'. These were interesting tasks, but a very partial description of the photographic, electronic, and other more esoteric forms of surveillance undertaken by the high-flying spy plane.

These planes, like their successors now at Mildenhall, came on detachment from the United States – in this case, from the SAC 98th Strategic Reconnaissance Wing. Their first job, as the SAC label implied, was to gather intelligence to find targets for bombers and missiles, and to identify the obstacles in their attack path, such as surface-to-air missiles and radar stations.

SAC also retained the right to return in an emergency to some of its former British bases, and this right has been maintained. Although the

---

OVERLEAF

**Fig 3. Consolidation: US bases in Britain, 1962**

US nuclear power in Britain reached a peak with the establishment of Thor missiles, the Polaris submarine base, and the Ballistic Missile Early Warning System. New nuclear bomber squadrons arrived from France. At bases like Marham and Waddington, US detachments controlled the hydrogen bombs for the RAF which were publicly claimed to be part of an 'independent' deterrent.

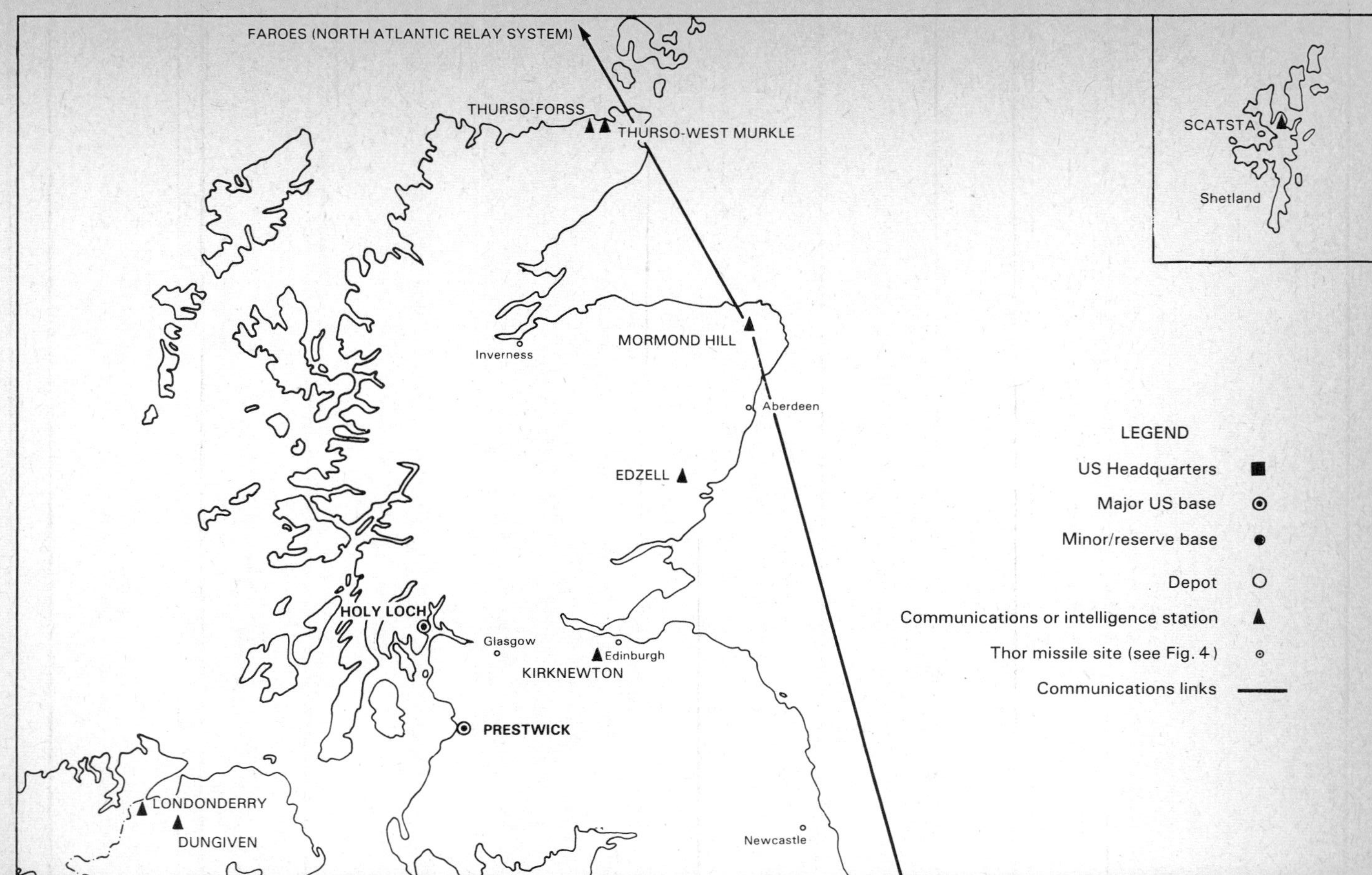
FAROES (NORTH ATLANTIC RELAY SYSTEM)
THURSO-FORSS
THURSO-WEST MURKLE
SCATSTA
Shetland
MORMOND HILL
Inverness
Aberdeen
EDZELL
HOLY LOCH
Glasgow
Edinburgh
KIRKNEWTON
PRESTWICK
LONDONDERRY
DUNGIVEN
Newcastle
LEGEND
US Headquarters
Major US base
Minor/reserve base
Depot
Communications or intelligence station
Thor missile site (see Fig. 4)
Communications links

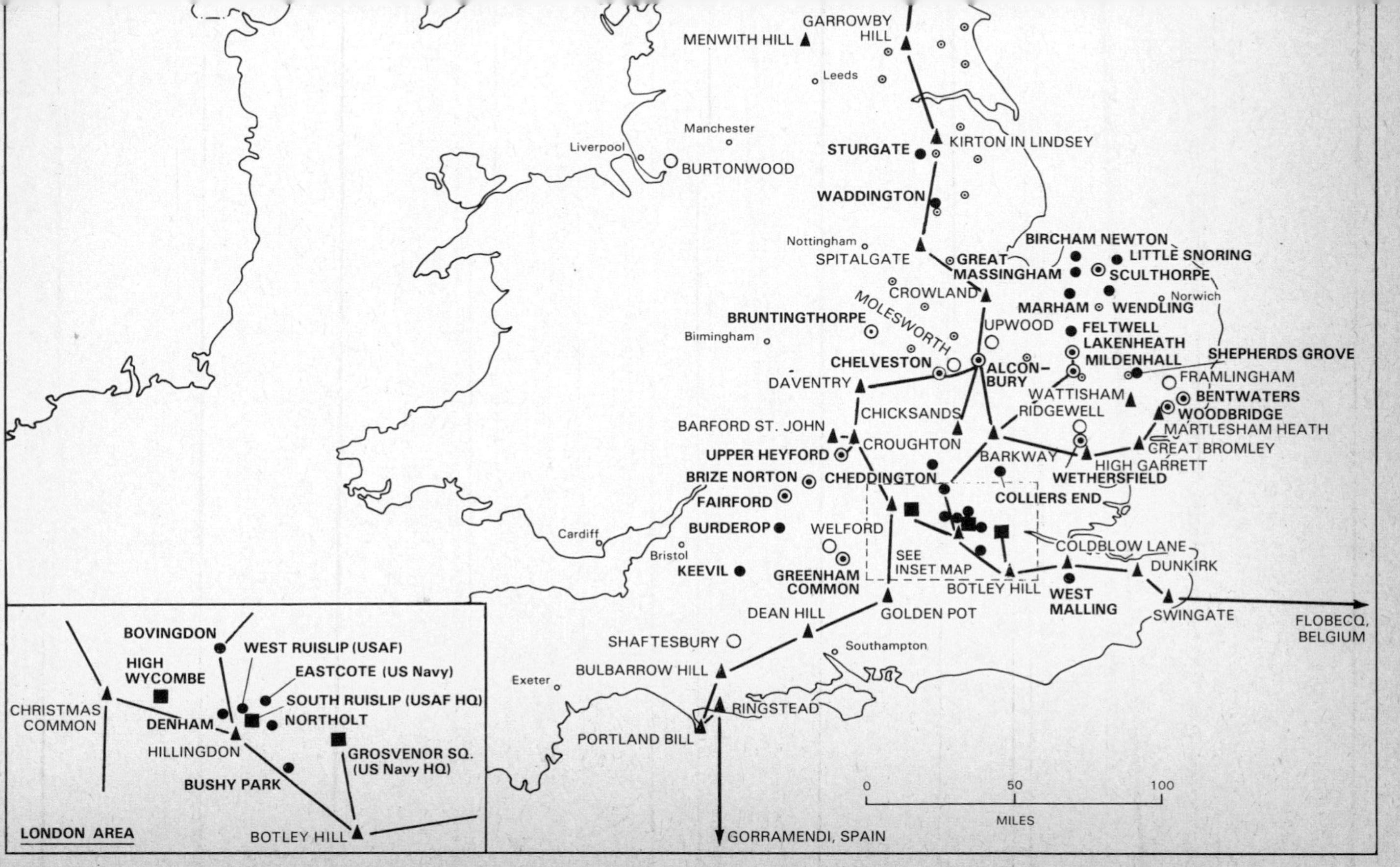


Fig 3. Consolidation: US bases in Britain – 1962

British Ministry of Defence refuses to specify which bases are included, information from the United States Department of Defense, plus observations by aircraft spotters on the intermittent B-52 and FB-111 deployments which take place, confirm that Brize Norton, Fairford (now back in US hands), and Marham are specifically allocated as SAC 'Forward Operating Bases'. Upper Heyford, which has always been a US base, is also used for forward-basing B-52 bombers.

The final closure of the Burtonwood air depot was announced in 1964, along with the demise of other, more obscure facilities such as the USAF's hospital at Burderop, near Swindon. By 1966, the extent of US Air Force real estate in Britain had significantly diminished from the 1950s peak. In that year, there were three bomber wings and one reconnaissance wing based in England. The bomber wings were at Lakenheath (the 48th), Wethersfield (the 20th), and Bentwaters (the 81st, with a squadron at Woodbridge, adjacent). The 10th TRW was at Alconbury. Between 1965 and 1971, these bomber and reconnaissance wings were re-equipped with Phantom (F-4) fighter-bombers, replacing the ageing F-100 Super Sabres and RB-66 reconnaissance craft.

Particularly significant amongst the minor units then (and still) in Britain was the 7120th (now the 10th) Airborne Command and Control Squadron, who provide airborne war rooms for the US European Command. This unit was set up in 1965. The aircraft provide emergency reserve headquarters for the US European Command HQ, then at Paris but now in Vaihingen, a suburb of Stuttgart in southern Germany.

Although the Air Force was running down a little in the mid-1960s (nevertheless deploying around 300 aircraft, the vast majority intended for nuclear missions), other US military activities, including Polaris and its support facilities, the BMEWS station at Fylingdales and new Sigint installations, were proliferating.

The Air Force build-up in Britain began afresh when President de Gaulle decided to withdraw France entirely from the unified military structure of NATO, and to expel US bases and NATO headquarters and facilities. The US European Command was then in Paris, along with NATO. Throughout France, the US had constructed the same sort of network of airbases, communications sites, and military stockpiles as were in Britain. All had to go, and did so in Operation Freloc (French relocation).

France had been central to US military strategy as providing the principal channel for supplying ammunition, fuel, food, reinforcements and other requirements to front-line forces. In military terminology, French territory supplied the Lines of Communication (or 'communication zone') between the 'rear' area (in this case, ultimately the United States) and the battleground – Germany and the central front. Some of the military depots and headquarters moved forward into Germany; some units were disbanded, or moved back to the United States; the remainder, and most of the aircraft, came to Britain. The new influx – of about 8,000 airmen – began in the autumn of 1966.

Two non-nuclear roles had been left to the US Air Force in France after the Red Richard transfer in 1959–60 – transport and reconnaissance. Transport aircraft formerly based at Evreux in Normandy and Toul-Rosieres, Lorraine were moved to Mildenhall. The 513th Troop Carrier Wing, soon afterwards renamed the 'Tactical Airlift Wing', had a number of specialised wartime responsibilities apart from orthodox troop movements. One of these was to airlift sabotage teams and supplies for partisan forces which would be organised by the CIA in eastern Europe (p 142). From Laon airbase came three squadrons of Voodoo and Phantom reconnaissance aircraft, which went to Alconbury and Upper Heyford. In 1969, however, the new Upper Heyford unit, the 66th Tactical Reconnaissance Wing, was disbanded, presumably because the previously existing wing at Alconbury met Air Force requirements. A headquarters for the Military Airlift Command, which supervised long-range air transport, was transferred from Chateauroux in central France to High Wycombe.

In effect, the military Lines of Communication which would have channelled airlifted supplies into France, or shipped them to Bordeaux and St Nazaire, had moved into Britain. The US Army, which previously had had no significant presence in Britain, repositioned weapons, ammunition and other stocks here, as did the Army Marine Fleet some years later. The move initially involved a network of five new British depots for the US Army.

At Burtonwood, near Warrington, the old USAF depot was taken over. An old British Army depot at Ditton Priors near Bridgenorth in Shropshire was also taken over as a storage site. Weapons and ammunition went to three new US bases: Fauld, near Burton-on-Trent in Staffordshire; Bramshall, near Uttoxeter, also in Staffordshire; and Caerwent in Monmouthshire (now Gwent).

At Caerwent the US Army took over a former Royal Navy Propellant Factory, where cordite had been manufactured until 1962. Its particular advantages included very close proximity to the M4 at the western end of the Severn Bridge, allowing rapid transport to the ports facing the continent. Some 232 buildings were built or converted as explosives stores, and a maintenance facility was added in 1971. The site attracted considerable local opposition, and became a focus of CND and anti-Vietnam war protests. Ludicrously overestimated promises of local employment at the depot were made to civic leaders in this depressed area. ('More than 800' jobs were promised by the Ministry of Defence in 1967; the Americans took on 50 and stopped recruiting in July 1968!)

There was continual local concern that the depot might be in use for the storage of nuclear, chemical or biological weapons. Unusually, this was firmly denied by the American commander, who nevertheless refused to allow local councillors access to the site. (Officials in both the UK and the US normally neither confirm nor deny the presence of nuclear weapons.) There was, he said, 'an agreement between our two governments limiting us to conventional weapons. That is all we have'.[4] He told the local Cwmbran council, in terms since repeated by successive commanding officers, that 'I cannot see that we have anything to discuss'. The first 12,000 tons of explosives were brought in via the nearby docks at Barry early in 1968. Local councillors, however, continued to publicise reports from workers inside the base that certain areas had specially restricted access. They claimed that in July 1969 'unconventional' weapons were secretly removed from the base.

At Fauld, the US Army took over a large underground mine store then recently vacated by the RAF. The old gypsum mine, converted for use before the Second World War, had been the site of Britain's largest-ever explosion in 1944, when an estimated 3,500 tons of high-explosive bombs accidentally detonated. The explosion, larger than would result from contemporary small atom bombs, lifted a million tons of earth and debris into the air in a mushroom-shaped cloud, destroying buildings within a radius of more than a mile as it fell to the ground.

Despite the 80-foot crater, the RAF had continued using Fauld, and the depot was able to accommodate some 40,000 tons of US war material removed from France. It remained in use until 1973. By that time, Caerwent had been modernised and extended by over 150,000 square feet of ammunition storage. It thereafter accommodated all the French stocks initially sent to Fauld, Ditton Priors, and Bramshall.

In the 1980s, Burtonwood continues as a major United States Army base, holding permanent stocks sufficient to equip the US Army divisions which would be sent to Europe for emergency reinforcement. Burtonwood is one of a network of nine such army depots; the other eight are in West Germany. Each has to support about 50 military units in war.

The 'pre-positioned' military stocks are held at Burtonwood in vast warehouses constructed previously for the Air Force, covering an area of more than 50 acres. Very little ammunition or explosives is held at Burtonwood, as that is the role of the much higher security storage in Caerwent, Wales. There over 400 bunkers, protected from each other by earth walls, are spread across the ammunition storage site. The bunkers provide over 30 acres of internal storage. The two sites, Burtonwood and Caerwent, together are estimated to be worth over £30 million, and are provided without charge to the US government.

The depot network is known as POMCUS – 'Pre-positioned military core unit stocks'. The theory of POMCUS is that everything from tanks and trucks to rations and medical kits are held together in one place. Then the units which will use them merely have to be shipped into Liverpool, collect their equipment at Burtonwood, and set off for the Humber ports and the European battleground. In practice, congressional investigations during the 1970s revealed that lack of maintenance, pilferage, and diversion of the war material for other purposes had at that stage made the POMCUS organisation seem extremely unreliable.

A US Senate investigating team found in 1975 that some ammunition was useable only in emergency, and that hundreds of vehicles were rendered unuseable by rust, broken parts and faulty or non-existent maintenance. Radios and radar sets had gone missing; some equipment had been supplied to the Middle East during the Yom Kippur war. $15 million worth had been 'lost'.

Although the British ammunition and storage depots at Fauld, Ditton Priors and Bramshall were handed back, the munitions stockpile in Britain has expanded rather than contracted since Operation Freloc. New depots have been obtained by the US Army on lease from the UK. These include a British Royal Navy depot operated for the US Navy at Broughton Moor in Cumbria, an Air Force depot at Bicester, near Oxford (where there is also an extensive British depot), and another at Bramley, near Basingstoke. In the 1930s, Bramley had held virtually all the British Army's ammunition stockpile. Since April 1978 it has been leased in its entirety to the US Army, one of a network of six new depots which were part of that year's US Army expansion. (The others are in Belgium and Germany.)

The units which would come to Britain and Europe in war rehearse this manoeuvre regularly in an expensive series of exercises called 'Reforger', each costing at least £10 million to organise and run. The unit which would come to Britain to collect their supplies from Burtonwood is believed to be the 1st Mechanised Infantry Division, whose normal base is at Fort Riley, Kansas.

The movements of supplies and troops through British bases and ports would be a major target for attack if war began. Ports like Liverpool, Newport, Hull, Grimsby, and Harwich would present as inviting a nuclear target to the strategic planners in Moscow as does a fully-fledged airbase.

Besides Thor missiles and the arrival of displaced US Army and Air Force units from France, two events marked the development of US military power in Britain during the 1960s. These were Polaris, and the construction of the Ballistic Missile Early Warning System station at Fylingdales Moor.

Fylingdales was the third and final site built in the BMEWS chain; like its partners in central Alaska (Clear) and western Greenland (Thule), Fylingdales' primary purpose is to detect ballistic missiles launched from the Soviet Union towards the United States. Secondarily, it searches for and tracks ballistic or submarine-launched missiles aimed at the United Kingdom or US forces in Europe. It fills a slight gap in radar coverage of missile sites which might be constructed in the western provinces of the USSR. A third major role, and one always underplayed in official publicity, is Fylingdales' part in the US space intelligence system, SPADATS (Space Data and Tracking System).

This role now gives Fylingdales some importance in new United States plans for war in space; the 'Star Wars' proposals made by President Reagan in 1983 will require extensive development of a worldwide network of elaborate devices for monitoring space, from 20 miles above the earth's surface to beyond 22,000.

After launch, a ballistic missile goes through a 'boost phase' during which the rocket motor delivers the final part of its energy before loosing the missile as a free, unpowered body on a trajectory toward its target. As the missile goes through this phase, it rises sufficiently high above the horizon to be scanned directly by the BMEWS radar stations 3,000 miles away. When a missile comes into view of the radar scanners,

---

OPPOSITE

**Fig 4. Thor missile bases, 1959–63**

Sixty Thor missiles were hastily deployed at twenty bases in Lincolnshire and East Anglia as a response to a feared Soviet-American 'missile gap'. The missiles were, uniquely, under 'dual key' control of the RAF and USAF.

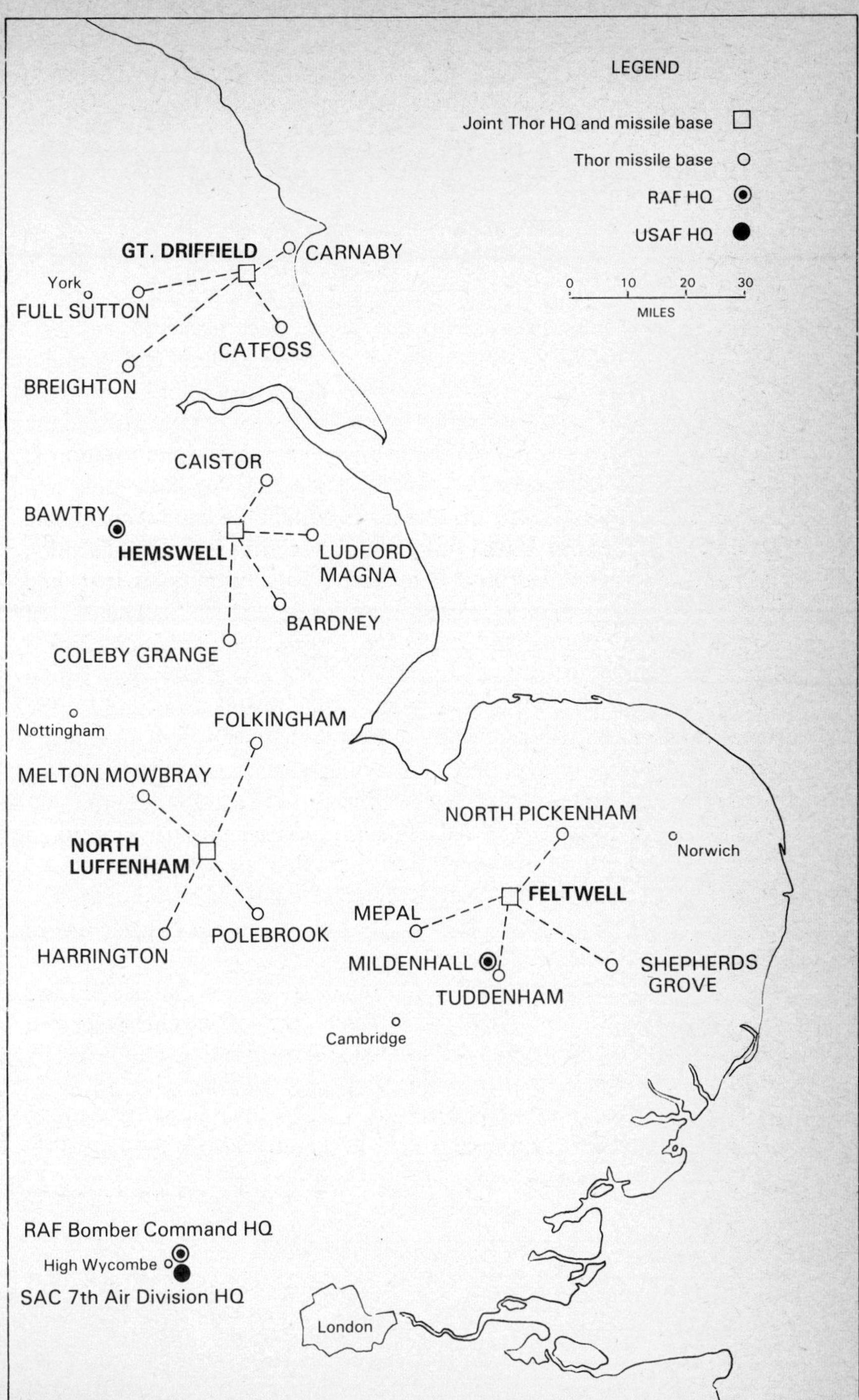
LEGEND
Joint Thor HQ and missile base
Thor missile base
RAF HQ
USAF HQ
0
10
20
30
MILES
GT. DRIFFIELD
CARNABY
York
FULL SUTTON
CATFOSS
BREIGHTON
CAISTOR
BAWTRY
HEMSWELL
LUDFORD
MAGNA
BARDNEY
COLEBY GRANGE
Nottingham
FOLKINGHAM
MELTON MOWBRAY
NORTH
LUFFENHAM
POLEBROOK
HARRINGTON
NORTH PICKENHAM
Norwich
FELTWELL
MEPAL
MILDENHALL
TUDDENHAM
SHEPHERDS
GROVE
Cambridge
RAF Bomber Command HQ
High Wycombe
SAC 7th Air Division HQ
London

Fig 4. Thor missile bases, 1959-63

its path is measured as accurately as possible. Its direction is important; a missile fired towards the North Pole is a possible attack on the United States or Canada; a missile heading towards the Pacific is probably a test launch. Some may be satellites; these will usually be launched towards the east, since in so doing they gain extra energy from the earth's rotation.

Detecting and tracking missiles heading towards the United Kingdom, or Europe, is a different and slightly more difficult task. Missiles directed at the United States or Canada, following great circle routes, will pass over the Arctic rather than Europe or the Atlantic. Missiles aimed at the UK will pass over Europe.

Fylingdales is celebrated as the source of the 'four-minute warning'. This is something of an overestimate; the current (but unpublished) Home Office training manual for civil defence scientific advisers stresses that 'no particular warning time can be guaranteed', but that it is hoped to get 'not less than three minutes' warning of attack. Britain benefits from the early warning system by a link from Fylingdales to RAF headquarters at High Wycombe. There, a Home Office official of the Warning and Monitoring Organisation is able to operate the air-raid warning siren network.

BMEWS was the second of two electronic barriers built around the United States and Canada in the late 1950s, as fear grew of a Soviet nuclear aircraft and missile threat. The 3,400 mile-long DEW-line (Distant Early Warning), which started operating in 1958, has 31 radar stations running from the Aleutian Islands, across northern Alaska and Canada to Greenland. Although not formally described as part of the DEW-line, additional and similarly powerful radar stations were built at Langanes and Keflavik in Iceland and on the Danish-run Faroes, between Iceland and Scotland.

The DEW-line was effectively extended all the way to Scotland to prevent a 'sneak attack' by bombers which might attempt to pass around the ends of the radar screen. Linking communications are believed to have been provided between the farthest north of Britain's radar stations, Saxa Vord (in the Shetland Islands) and the DEW-line, as a final defence against a flanking attack. These may have utilised NATO communications to the Faroes and Iceland, or the special and secret undersea cables which ran north from the Saxa Vord RAF station – if these were not part of a SOSUS underwater detection system (see p 171). The US Navy also operated radar picket vessels to act as early warning sentries in this area of the North Atlantic. The vessels were given port rights in Scotland.

In 1961, Defence Minister Harold Watkinson announced a new agreement with the US to supplement the DEW-line.[5] The agreement was to:

> provide facilities in connection with the Distant Early Warning Line. A small communications station will be established by the United States Navy near Thurso to supplement the facilities already available at the United States station at Londonderry. In addition, certain radar picket escort vessels will make use of existing naval facilities at Rosyth and commercial facilities on the Clyde.

Parts of this account seem disingenuous; not least because the manner in which this news was given to Parliament was the manoeuvre of the planted question, which is the customary way of discreetly and selectively announcing some controversial development. The controversial item may have been the Thurso naval communications station which was more likely to have been connected with the arrival of Polaris submarines, but the drafting of the announcement disguised its purpose as benign and defensive.

Construction of the Ballistic Missile Early Warning System began in 1958, and the first two sites, Clear and Thule, were operational three years later. A search began in 1959 for a suitable third site, and US Air Force planners at first concentrated their efforts near Prestwick, then a US Air Force base for the military air transport service. Several criteria were important – a high location with an unobstructed view to the horizon, but in a local depression and away from the sea to avoid the risk that shipborne jammers or submarine-landed saboteurs might sabotage the system at a critical moment. (Shortly after the main station was built, a new and much smaller 'golfball' radar detector was added to the Fylingdales installation. Its purpose was to receive, directly, any jamming signals which might be aimed into the three Fylingdales antennae and counter them by changing frequencies.)

To these selection criteria the British government, sensitive to the steadily-growing CND campaign against nuclear weapons, added another. A missile early warning station would surely become the very first nuclear target in hostilities, and make it difficult to win acceptance for the new US base. A 1959 report in the American magazine, *Aviation Week*[6], noted that the State Department had negotiated with the Foreign Office for rights to build the BMEWS station, but as yet unsuccessfully:

> The British are reluctant to allow it. The reason is that it would make the area a prime target in time of war.

Prestwick was rejected. An agreement was signed in London in February 1960, selecting instead a site in eastern England – Fylingdales. East of Whitby and Scarborough on the Yorkshire coast, it was remote indeed from habitation, and thus avoided the political difficulty of planting a prime nuclear target in any MP or protest group's backyard.

The BMEWS agreement specified that the US Air Force would own and supply all the radar, computer equipment and communications systems at Fylingdales. The UK had to provide the site, power and housing, as well as its own communications requirements. The UK pays for most of the maintenance and operation of the station, which is contracted out to the US electronics corporation, RCA. Fylingdales initially cost £45 million, and started operating in 1963.

The heart of Fylingdales is the jointly operated Tactical Operations Room where US Air Force and RAF personnel run eight display consoles coupled to the three tracking radars – 84-foot diameter dishes, inside Fylingdales' celebrated duck-egg blue golfball domes. These dishes direct radar beams of considerable power across the horizon in order to detect the faint echoes from relatively tiny and very distant targets. The power is such that spillage of even a small part of the radar energy would be dangerous to health, so the base is entered by tunnels, and the equipment and working areas are protected by metal screens.

Fylingdales was originally linked to the United States by the North Atlantic Radio System, NARS – the radio relay network spanning across Iceland and Greenland to Canada and the United States. Ordinary, high-frequency radio connections were unreliable and relatively easily jammed. On routes across the north Atlantic, in particular, they would be seriously disrupted by nuclear explosions. Troposcatter radio relay, used for NARS, provided a more reliable connection.

The NARS system was publicly demonstrated in July 1963 in a phone call from Washington to a US Air Force officer in London. The relay connections ran from Goose Bay in Labrador, and across Canada and Greenland on the DEW-line network. Then from Kulusuk in Greenland NARS relay stations passed the signal to Keflavik and Langanes, major US bases in Iceland. The relay chain then ran via the Faroes to Mormond Hill, a solitary high outcrop in the north east of Aberdeenshire overlooking Peterhead, and on to Fylingdales. From Fylingdales (see Map 4), US Air Force microwave relay stations ran across England to the airbases and headquarters and then on to the Continent. With the opening of NARS, the United States had created a global military communications system that spanned from Alaska in the west to Turkey in the east – all under its sole control.

In the late 1960s, NARS was expanded and provided with a further, direct troposcatter link to the communications base at Martlesham Heath, near Ipswich. This link was intended to provide a direct connection between NARS and the 99-station strong US communications system in the Mediterranean. It is still in operation, endowed with the endearing codename of Project Tea Bag!

NARS was not intended to service the missile early-warning station alone. Rather, it was a multi-purpose network and the backbone of several electronic systems in the north Atlantic, which would reflect the sudden growth in the strategic significance of the area. Map 9 (p 227) shows the network of radar stations, electronic listening posts and underwater surveillance that was set up in the early 1960s.

The north Atlantic, around the Greenland–Iceland–UK gap, and in the Norwegian and Barents sea areas, was important as a primary deployment area for Polaris submarines, and their defenders. That required new navigation networks (including a LORAN-C station in the Shetlands), new communications stations (such as Thurso), underwater surveillance (from Iceland), and electronic listening stations. These were built at Edzell near Dundee, Keflavik in Iceland, and at Bremerhaven in Germany. The north Atlantic was important also as the end-stop on the DEW line. And the Soviet Navy, although still dwarfed by the capabilities of US and NATO navies, was expanding; the US wished to be able to block naval or submarine movements into, or through the north Atlantic.

NARS provided 72 separate radio link channels between Britain (and Europe) and the United States. Declassified US documents show that NARS was particularly important to the US Navy because of the imminent extension of its underwater surveillance system, SOSUS; a memorandum to the US Assistant Secretary of Defense in 1957[7] noted that the US Navy had extensive demands to make of NARS, when it was installed. The note reveals that a north Atlantic chain of underwater listening stations was then being planned:

> The Navy circuit requirements for the North Atlantic scatter system [are for] the Seaward extension of the Distant Early Warning (DEW) line and Sound Surveillance System (SOSUS) . . . in the North Atlantic area. The imminence of implementation of a SOSUS system in this area increases the sense of urgency . . . the Navy [also] has requirements to support the High Frequency direction finder system and certain communications . . . in the North Atlantic area.

The same source indicates that an ostensibly civil telephone cable laid between Canada, Greenland, Iceland, and Scotland had originated as a military project to provide a cable alternative to the NARS radio system. Codenamed 'Deep Freeze', the cable was to have been laid by the American Cable & Radio Corporation, with links at the British end provided by the Post Office.

Deep Freeze seems eventually to have come to life as two 'civil' cables – SCOTICE, and ICECAN, both laid in 1962. ICECAN was installed first, and linked Montreal and Reykjavik, with a connection in Greenland to the US military base at Thule. SCOTICE linked Reykjavik to Gareloch, in the west of Scotland. Despite being operated by civil agencies, much of the cables' capacity was permanently leased to military agencies. This was also the case with the first two transatlantic telephone cables to Britain, TAT1 (1956) and CANTAT (1961). Both cables came ashore near Oban. Until 1978, TAT1 also provided the USA–USSR 'hot line' connection between the White House and the Kremlin.

The close inter-relation between NARS and SCOTICE/ICECAN was effectively demonstrated when the Icelandic cable terminal at Vestmannaeyjar was destroyed by volcanic activity in March 1973. The US Air Force was able to provide four NARS circuits between Iceland and Britain while the undersea cable was being repaired.

After the first decade of BMEWS operation, there was considerable speculation about the future of the stations. Their main role, detecting missile launches, was supplanted by satellites in fixed orbits, with long-range infra-red telescopes to detect the sudden, intense heat of a missile launch. At the same time, the United States began experimenting with a new form of long-range surveillance radar, 'over the horizon' (OTH). An OTH station built at Orfordness in England (see p 201) in 1970 was one of a series of semi-experimental sites. By using the ionosphere as a natural mirror to reflect radio waves downwards onto a remote target area, OTH radar did indeed see thousands of miles over the horizon. Although the system had the potential to observe right down 'on the trans-Siberian railway', as was claimed, it did not prove a practical successor to BMEWS.

In 1980, it was announced that the entire BMEWS chain would receive an extensive new lease of life. New computers would take over the Missile Impact Projector role, then still performed by very early vintage IBM computers. The tracking radars would also be renovated, rather than replaced. The heart of each centre would continue to be the Tactical Operations Room, where four modern display consoles would control all station functions. Normally, two of the tracking radars are surveilling large areas, rather than following a single target.

The news of the improvements, which imply that the BMEWS stations will probably be operating up to the year 2,000, was accompanied by the revelation that their tracking abilities had previously been somewhat overstated. Public relations statements were normally couched in terms of the ability to detect an object the size of a door, over Siberia. But the station's actual tracking specification was the ability to detect an attack 'consisting of *20 or more* missiles incoming within a 5-minute interval'.[8] The new BMEWS system would have to deal with thousands of re-entry vehicles at once.

Of neccessity, Fylingdales is in peacetime primarily an intelligence station, since its actual role of early warning will only be tested and operated under attack and in war. The rest of the time it detects and can track the launches of Soviet satellites, or missile tests. Orbiting satellites cross the horizon, and fall (or rise) into Fylingdales' view, and can be monitored for their likely functions. As a space intelligence station, Fylingdales feeds information into SPADATS (Space Data and Tracking System), which is controlled from a computer centre 1,000 feet underground in Colorado. It has thus become, and will remain, a centre of considerable importance to the developing confrontation in space, discussed in Chapter 6.

## Notes

1 Fifteen minutes was then the standard time allowed for ground-based nuclear bombers to respond to an alert, which may have been why the figure was also quoted for the Thor missiles.

2 *Exchange of notes concerning . . . intermediate range ballistic missiles*. Cmnd 366, (1957 treaty series no 14).

3 Three previous DEFCON alerts are known to have been issued to US forces in the UK, over Indo-China (Vietnam) in 1954, Hungary in 1956, and Lebanon in 1958. (Source: *Welcome to England*, a guide to the Third Air Force; USAF, undated circa 1972.)

4 *Western Mail*, 22 April 1970.

5 *Hansard*, 26 July 1961.

6 *Aviation Week*, 9 March 1959.

7 US National Archives, JCS papers section CCS 334 JCEC (CECMS), section 8.

8 *Aviation Week*, 16 June 1980.

# PART TWO
# ALLIANCE

## 4 *The Nuclear Axis*

While many of Britain's airfields were being converted to an emergency parking lot for the Strategic Air Command, fundamental aspects of British defence policy, far beyond the 1950s, were being shaped. Britain was seeking its own nuclear weapons, and developing both atom bombs and the first aircraft to deliver them – the V bombers. The development of British nuclear weapons began in total secrecy, undeclared to Parliament, public, or even most members of the Attlee government. The British policy-makers had not intended to go it alone in weaponry, but the speed with which the US Congress moved to protect American atomic secrets, and the jealousy with which they were then guarded, left the British with little choice – if they wanted a weapons programme at all.

Fundamental to the British desire to press ahead was not just the self-image of a great power, but the desire to keep abreast of the Americans so as to set the stage for as close a co-operation in atomic affairs as had existed during the war. It took more than a decade for Britain to begin to realise these goals. There is now no closer nuclear axis between two countries, in planning and co-ordinating nuclear affairs, than between Britain and the United States.

The British political leadership has often deluded itself about the 'special relationship' it believes we enjoy, based on a common language and liberal-democratic capitalist societies. American attitudes have always been ambivalent. But the deeper ruptures in the nuclear relationship have always been well-concealed – at least for a lengthy period. The leader of the A-bomb development programme in the United States, General Leslie R. Groves, wrote in 1947 a Top Secret history of the project, only made public 26 years later, in which he castigated Britain as having contributed nothing scientifically to the A-bomb project, having spied on US efforts and hoodwinked President Roosevelt into signing the 1943 Quebec Agreement, which granted Britain control over any military use of the bomb by the United States.

The first postwar decade of US–UK negotiation on nuclear matters was characterised by considerable mutual distrust, and accusations of broken promises and bad faith – on both sides. Although understandings were clarified and improved in the late 50s, the co-operation was often far less complete than public impressions and pronouncements would suggest. Were it not for the bases and military facilities which Britain provided – for SAC bombers, Thor missiles and for Polaris, both in the UK and elsewhere in British territories – American incentives for atomic co-operation would have been greatly reduced. Even when the trade-off was not explicit, from either point of view, the trusting grant by Britain of any American requirement was evidently taken to be a *sine qua non* of receiving US help in technological matters.

Despite postwar disagreements, the nuclear axis began to mature significantly in 1958. In that year, sections of a critical 1946 Act of Congress, the MacMahon Act, were repealed. The MacMahon Act had forbidden dissemination of military or industrial atomic energy information, even to close allies. A host of special agreements on the supply and exchange of materials, information and facilities followed its repeal. Britain undertook to supply plutonium for US bombs, thus underpinning the massive American nuclear build-up during the 1960s. Information on A- and H-bomb development could be exchanged, and the Atomic Weapons Research Establishment at Aldermaston was able to make rapid progress in thermonuclear weapons by copying US designs.

Subsequently, following the Partial Test Ban Treaty, Britain gained the right to use the US underground test site in Nevada for further nuclear tests. The United States also agreed to sell Britain the Skybolt missile, to be launched from RAF bombers. But the Skybolt project was cancelled by the US Air Force and, in its place, the 1962 Polaris Sales Agreement provided for Britain to buy Polaris missiles and make its own submarines. In September 1980, the Polaris agreement was adapted to allow Britain to buy Trident missiles in place of Polaris.

The Polaris Sales Agreement has thus given way to a companion compact for Trident. All the missiles and the basics of warhead design come from the United States. In return, Britain was asked to supply larger quantities of plutonium to the United States, both from the stockpile created by civil nuclear power reactors, and from the military plutonium production reactors – Chapelcross, near Dumfries, and Calder Hall, at Windscale, Cumbria. Nuclear cores for British Trident missile warheads are to be constructed in a new 'plutonium processing' complex at Aldermaston which is virtually a direct replica of the US nuclear weapons laboratory at Los Alamos, in New Mexico. The £250-million 'A90' complex will be in operation in 1986.

Nuclear weapons which are manufactured in the United States cannot lawfully be transferred out of US control, unless 'released' for wartime use. Nevertheless, accompanied by United States 'custodial detachments' (who have ultimate control over the arming of a weapon) many types of nuclear weapons are supplied to and stockpiled by Britain and other NATO partners for their use in war. Thus, the US Navy operates two nuclear storage sites in Britain (Machrihanish and St Mawgan) for nuclear depth bombs allocated to the British, Dutch and Canadian anti-submarine warfare forces, as well as their own.

In Germany, there are prolific facilities for storing missile warheads, atomic artillery, ADMs[1] and orthodox bombs. All such installations are jointly controlled, but weapons can only be handed over to the host nation after elaborate authorisation messages and codes have been passed down through US-run communications systems. Although Britain, like Germany and other states, has bought battlefield nuclear weapons – Lance nuclear missiles, atomic shells, and ADMs – from the United States, the weapons are under 'dual control'.

British nuclear weapons have, since 1960 at least, been targeted in accordance with US war plans, with RAF V bombers allocated specific target areas within the Soviet Union. The targets form part of the American strategic war plan, SIOP.

The SIOP and other target plans are prepared by a subdivision of the US Joint Chiefs of Staff, the Joint Strategic Target Planning Staff. The headquarters of these architects of holocaust are in Omaha, Nebraska, at the headquarters of the Strategic Air Command. A small British team works at Omaha, and British nuclear forces receive their data on the prescribed UK share of strike targets – identified, according to RAF pilots, not as named cities or other localities, but as 'Allied List Numbers' on a numerical target list.

This arrangement was formalised within NATO plans after a Ministerial Meeting of the North Atlantic Council at Ottawa in 1963, when British V bombers and the Polaris force were formally put under command of SACEUR, NATO's Supreme Allied Commander, Europe. British, Italian, German and (until 1968) French NATO liaison officers then joined the Joint Strategic Target Planning Staff at Omaha. They work only on the SACEUR Nuclear Operations Plan, and its 'options', rather than on the SIOP.

The co-operation, or at times, conflict in this most intimate area of government secrecy has always been an important factor in the background to decisions about the US presence in Britain. At critical times in the 1940s and 1950s, British leaders were looking for co-operation and collaboration, not independence. British nuclear forces have never been in a position, technically, where they could operate independently of all United States assistance – even if this were thought plausible, or desirable, on a political and strategic basis.

A study of the notion of British independence in deterrence for the House of Commons Select Committee on Expenditure thoroughly castigated the idea that Britain was or has been independent. The committee were examining the future of Polaris (and a possible decision to buy Trident) in 1979, and were told that the nomenclature of an 'independent' force was quite misleading:

> While there existed grounds for believing that in certain (highly improbable) circumstances it might operate as an independent force, its major function and justification was to serve as an alliance force, and operate as a dependent adjunct of United States strategic forces . . .
>
> The United Kingdom nuclear deterrent has been, from its inception, directed towards creating a specific type of linkage with the United States.[2]

In addition to seeking better atomic weaponry from the United States through the provision of bases, British policy makers were also, in effect, using the weapons supplied to help fulfil wider aspirations towards the United States.

The early history of the development of atomic weapons has been discussed in many accounts[3], and here we can only set out the critical arrangements between Britain and the United States, which both reflected perceptions of the 'special relationship', and underpinned it for the postwar period.

Early British work on the principle of atomic weapons had in 1941 triggered off the search for suitable materials and methods on both sides of the Atlantic. Co-operative relationships then followed but had an uneven history, flowing high in 1941 and into 1942, then ebbing to almost nothing for nearly a year. The leading scientists on the committee overseeing the Manhattan District project (the American codename for atomic weaponry development) and the project's director, General Leslie Groves, were unimpressed by the value of what the British might offer, and suspicious that their real motive lay in gaining free access to information which would help in the valuable postwar development of atomic energy.

In this they were both right and wrong. British representatives, including Lord Cherwell, made it fairly plain that the British did have their sights set on postwar use of the information – but for military rather than civil purposes.

The 1943 cut-off of information led to direct discussions between Churchill and Roosevelt, which culminated in the Quebec Agreement, signed by the two leaders on 19 August. This document required collective consent before use of the bomb. A Combined Policy Committee was established with US, British and Canadian representatives (Canada was also doing atomic energy research) to oversee the development of atomic energy. The Quebec Agreement referred to 'the matter of Tube Alloys', not atomic energy, using the British codename for the project.

That Britain and the United States would never use atomic weapons against each other was the first head of agreement. Subsequent clauses undertook, without apparent time limit, that Britain and the United States 'would not use it [ie, the bomb] against third parties without each other's consent'; and that 'neither of us will communicate any information about Tube Alloys to third parties except by mutual consent'.

The agreement resulted in the migration of British scientists to work on the bomb project at Los Alamos. Britain supplied materials like heavy water to the United States, together with a design for part of the plant used to separate out the vital fissile uranium isotope, $U^{235}$, needed to make a bomb. The three countries participated in a 'Combined Development Trust' whose purpose was to monopolise postwar as well as wartime supplies of uranium and thorium, the key atomic energy materials.

In the American component of the Manhattan Project, however, there were strong feelings both for and against the British. General Groves, writing his 1947 'Diplomatic History of the Manhattan Project', unequivocally regarded the Quebec Agreement as a piece of fast footwork by the British: 'as finally signed, it agreed practically *in toto* with the version presented by Sir John Anderson [in charge of the British Tube Alloys team]'.

General Groves' vituperative views are worth quoting to underline how shallow were British perceptions that their science and industry were something special in American eyes. After acknowledging that an optimistic review completed by the British in 1941 was a 'considerable factor' in the rapid build-up of the US project, he summarised the British contribution in these terms:

> The British sent over about a dozen scientists, including a few of their top nuclear men. These were definitely helpful in many cases, but it became quite evident that their primary purpose was to follow our work and to obtain information from us . . .
>
> The scientific and technical information obtained in the United Kingdom laboratories was of so little value to us as to be practically negligible. Their most important, if not their only information of value, was their discovery that a certain kind of rubber was satisfactory for seals in the diffusion plant.
>
> In general, the scientific contribution of the British was far less than is generally believed. It was in no sense vital and actually not even important. To evaluate it quantitatively at one per cent of the total would be to overestimate it. The technical and engineering contribution was practically nil. Certainly it is true that without any contribution at all from the British, the date of our final success need not have been delayed by a single day.

Groves left the project in 1947. But by that time the wartime collaboration between Britain and the United States had virtually disintegrated. In particular, Britain had sacrificed the critical provisions of the Quebec Agreement on control over the use of the bomb, in a vain attempt to obtain more extensive American collaboration.

In November 1945, President Truman and Prime Ministers Attlee and MacKenzie King (of Canada) had met in Washington to discuss atomic energy and weapons collaboration. They pledged to 'prevent the use of atomic energy for destructive purposes' and promote its utilisation for 'peaceful and humanitarian ends'. A day later, General Groves and Sir John Anderson devised a memorandum which should have replaced the wartime Quebec Agreement. The memorandum, although never agreed as drafted, set out a diluted form of control:

> The three Governments . . . will not use atomic weapons against other parties without *prior consultation* with each other (author's italics).

But the Groves-Anderson agreement was never ratified by the Combined Policy Committee of the three nations. 'Full and effective co-operation' was promised by the Americans, but was not forthcoming when British scientists asked for details of the construction of full-scale atomic plants, including the gaseous diffusion equipment necessary to separate uranium.

Confronting these problems Attlee wrote three times to President Truman – obtaining only one curt, negative reply. In an extensive, pleading letter in June 1946 Attlee asked Truman to recall that 'our three governments stand on a special relationship to one another . . . we

1. Left: Satellite tracking dishes at Menwith Hill, Yorkshire, the world's most important communications intelligence centre—run directly by the US National Security Agency.

2. Below: Menwith Hill's secretive Yanks go into town.

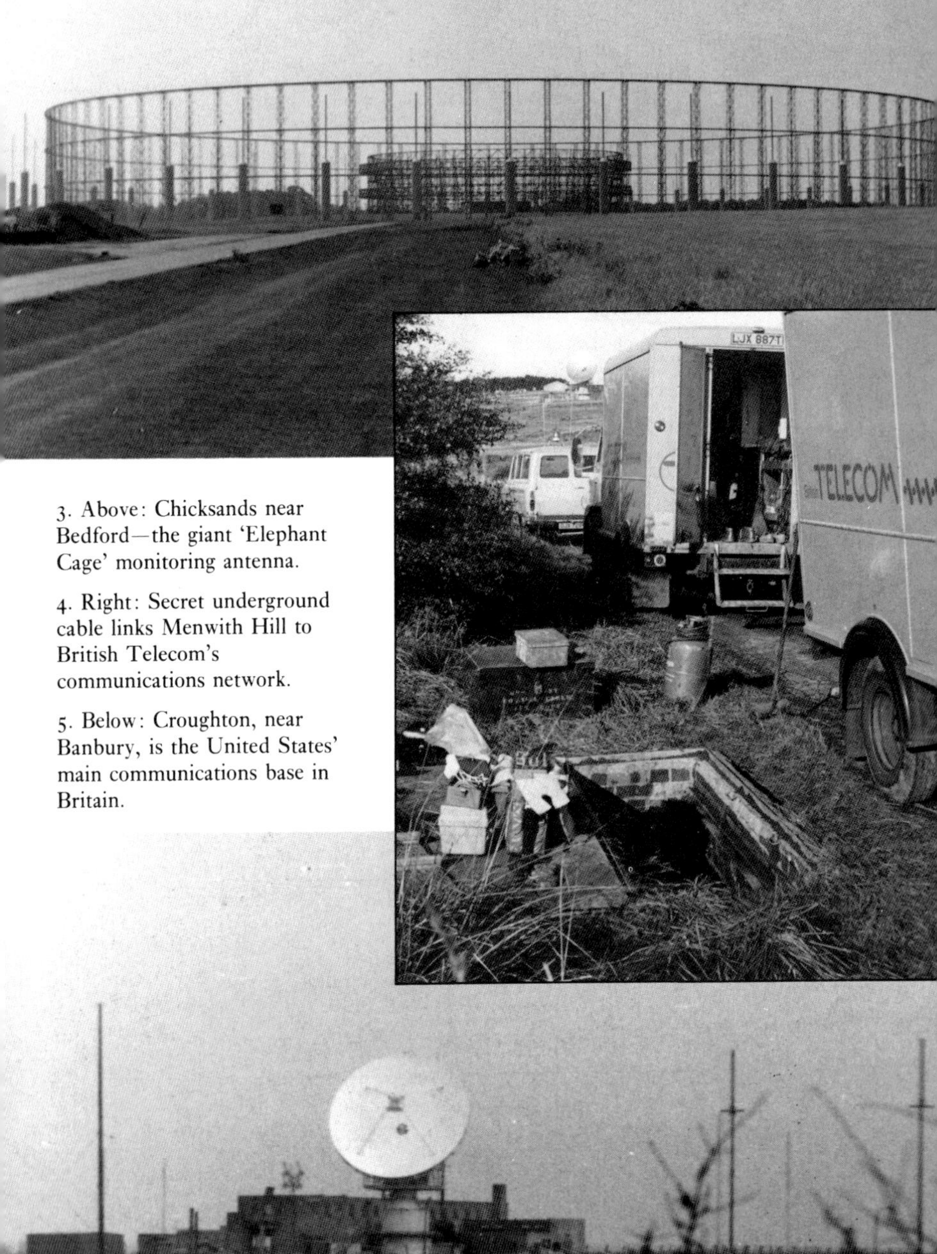


3. Above: Chicksands near Bedford—the giant 'Elephant Cage' monitoring antenna.

4. Right: Secret underground cable links Menwith Hill to British Telecom's communications network.

5. Below: Croughton, near Banbury, is the United States' main communications base in Britain.

6. US Naval Security Group at Edzell, Tayside, is an electronic monitoring centre for ocean surveillance.

7. Mormond Hill, near Peterhead, a key relay centre for transatlantic and North Sea communications, and the British ground station for the nuclear war control aircraft, 'Silk Purse'.

8 and 9. Strategic Air Command spy planes based at Mildenhall, Suffolk, are the SR-71 'Blackbird' (above) and the RC-135 Elint or 'ferret' aircraft (below).

believe we are entitled [to full information], both by the documents, and by the history of our common efforts in the past.'

But these pleas, repeated in December, remained unanswered. The US Congress had, meanwhile, passed the MacMahon Act, making it illegal for US government employees to divulge atomic information abroad. A month later, in January 1947, a secret British cabinet committee, known merely as GEN163, took the formal decision to carry British atomic weapons research on to the point of production.

The next agreement between the three allies was not achieved until January 1948, when a so-called *Modus Vivendi* was agreed. It was so-called, and it remained unsigned, because otherwise the US President would have had to tell the Congress, and if signed as an international treaty, it would have had to have been publicly registered with the United Nations. The Americans had become interested in a new agreement largely because of their desire to secure a bigger share of the scarce uranium supplies which were still apportioned and controlled by the Combined Development Trust.

The *Modus Vivendi* replaced the Quebec Agreement and subsequent exchanges. But it omitted entirely American undertakings on the control of the bomb. Margaret Gowing records how, just six months before the arrival of US bombers in England made control of the A-bomb quite critical, British officials casually threw national rights away:

> neither officials nor Ministers showed any concern or interest in the surrender of Britain's veto, or right to consultation on the use of the bomb. Uranium and other fissile supplies would in effect be bartered for US information; the end product of it all, the bomb, seemed almost forgotten. Thus ended any formal sanction that Britain might have enjoyed over the use of US atomic weapons from their new strategic bases.[4]

For the United States, this had been another important issue:

> The Joint Congressional Committee on Atomic Energy . . . had been very disturbed at this provision, and had urged most strongly that steps be taken to abrogate it. A salient objective of the negotiations [leading to the *Modus Vivendi*] was to terminate the provision concerning United Kingdom consent.[5]

A planted question in the House of Commons, in May 1948, was the Attlee government's device for announcing that Britain was developing its own atomic weapons. This news was received by US policy makers with some alarm. Britain was in their eyes a vulnerable forward zone which the Soviet Union might well eventually conquer in a general war and, in so doing, gain the materials, laboratories and industrial sites of an advanced atomic weapons' programme – if Britain proceeded. US fears were expressed in an assessment prepared that year for the National Security Council, which warned:

> Should the Soviets overrun Western Europe during 1948 . . . the probable date by which the Soviets *will have* exploded their first atomic bomb would be advanced from mid-1953 to mid-1951 . . .

Various solutions were proposed, including that Britain should not have atomic weapons at all, or that all British manufacturing centres and stockpiles should be sited in Canada. Or, Britain would supply plutonium to the United States, and get in return a supply of finished bombs. None of these ideas were taken up with enthusiasm by the British.

A slight thaw in the US–UK relationship followed the *Modus Vivendi*; the new SAC bases in East Anglia, the developing Cold War and the creation of NATO, all made for greater political collaboration. One specific, and highly ambiguous co-operative measure was the supply to Britain, in 1950, of its own force of B-29 Superfortress bombers – renamed, in RAF service, *Washingtons.* Some 70 bombers (later increased to 88) began to arrive in Britain in March 1950, to be stationed initially at Marham – which had been SAC's first base in Britain.

Opinions remain divided as to whether the bomber was ever intended to carry nuclear weapons against the Soviet Union; its capability to do so was clear, and it was indeed called an 'interim *strategic* bomber' to supplement RAF strength until the first V bombers came into service. Marham had, of course, been one of the bases at which the RAF and USAF had secretly prepared assembly areas and loading pits with which to arm B-29s with atomic bombs.

In 1951, the Atomic Energy Commission agreed to amend the 1946 MacMahon Act, in order to allow more extensive information-sharing with Britain and Canada. The amendments were passed in October; the US could then legally transfer some atomic information abroad. Intelligence details on atomic energy could also be swapped. Provision of test facilities in the United States for the first British atomic test was considered.

Soon after, however, the military desire to deploy abroad the booming US atomic stockpile began to create further pressure for liberalisation. Even after the 1952 British atomic test, the US Joint Chiefs of Staff proposed again that the British should be offered details of weapons construction in order to stop them going into full-scale production:

> Once the United Kingdom has completed its first successful atom bomb test, the matter of such exchanges will become urgent if the United Kingdom is to be dissuaded from embarking on a program for the manufacture of atomic weapons in Britain . . . there is need also for permissive legislation so that arrangements can be made in an emergency for a transfer of weapons to certain of our allies to enable them to assist us as required in delivering atomic weapons to targets.[6]

These deliberations led to a revised Atomic Energy Act, passed in 1954, and increasingly wide rein was allowed on the scope of US atomic weapons collaboration with its allies. The nuclear axis was on its way to a postwar rebirth. During the first postwar decade, Britain had given away many rights, whether justly held or not. In the second postwar decade, Anglo-Saxon nuclear collaboration would greatly increase.

Two new treaties – one dealing with information on weapons to be exchanged for 'mutual defence purposes', the other dealing with peaceful uses of atomic energy – were signed in 1955, the year after the new Atomic Energy Act. Britain was by this time well advanced in atomic weapons production facilities, and in the means to deliver them. The first V bomber squadron came into service at RAF Wittering. Their payload would be 'Blue Danube', Britain's first and cumbersome replica of 'Fat Man', the plutonium-fuelled weapon that had destroyed Nagasaki.

Although the technical prowess of the Aldermaston team was demonstrated to the world – and to the Americans in particular – when the first British test, codenamed 'Hurricane', was held at Monte Bello in May 1952, it took four more years, to 1956, before the Hurricane device had become a reliable bomb, and went into RAF service. Gowing reports that the first 'production model' of the bomb was delivered in November 1953. But this was not, evidently, in a form thought to be secure against either accidents or operational failure. In March 1955, the *Sunday Times*' Washington correspondent, Henry Brandon, drawing on the confidence of US State Department and other officials, reported that the 'US may lend us atomic bombs [providing] interim protection until we have enough of our own'.[7] Meanwhile, US stocks of weapons in Britain and in the Far East were to be built up yet again.

The 1954 Atomic Energy Act was amended in 1958 at the suggestion of President Eisenhower, leading to a new atomic treaty with Britain which is still in effect.[8] This is the 1958 Agreement 'for co-operation on the uses of Atomic Energy for mutual defence purposes'. It allowed Eisenhower:

- The power to transfer non-nuclear parts of weapons to other states.
- The power to transfer military reactors, and their fuel, including weapons-grade enriched uranium.
- The power to transfer fissile 'special nuclear material' for use in atomic weapons research and development, and construction.

The 1954 act had also allowed exchange of information on training, defence against nuclear weapons, and the evaluation of potential enemies' nuclear weapons capabilities. The new law imposed conditions that any such co-operative agreement must be with a state with which there was a mutual defence and security treaty in force, so that the transfer would promote, and not risk, US security. The prospective partner had also had to have made 'substantial progress in the development of atomic weapons', a condition clearly only applying to the United Kingdom.

When the agreement went through Congress, they were told that the new collaboration would 'permit a strengthening of our defences coupled with a conservation of the scarce talents and resources of both nations'. The US would gain by learning both of similar, and different, British solutions to atomic weapons technical problems.

The 1958 Anglo-American agreement defined three major areas for collaboration:

- A general exchange of information, equipment and materials.
- Specific information on the development of delivery systems for atomic weapons, and the weapons themselves. This exchange would last for ten years, and could then be renewed for successive five-year terms.
- Transfer to the UK of a submarine reactor, and limited quantities of fuel. This provision would expire after ten years, but could be renewed.

In July 1959, the United States made arrangements and new agreements 'for mutual defence purposes' whereby nuclear weapons could be provided for the use of other NATO allies in war: Canada, the Netherlands, Germany, Greece and Turkey. The US retained ultimate custody of the warheads, but the foreign forces could then, like the British, receive US weapons and training in their use. But the nuclear components of American weapons would remain under the control of American forces.

A major result of the 1958 agreement (which was also slightly amended in 1959) was the barter of nuclear materials. Britain supplied the United States with plutonium from its civil and military reactors, and in return received highly enriched uranium (for submarine fuel, and some weapons assemblies), tritium (the fuel for a thermonuclear – hydrogen bomb – explosion) and nuclear weapons, less their nuclear cores.

In fact, nothing in the agreement prevented the United States from supplying Britain with a virtual do-it-yourself kit for bombs. They could supply both the bomb assembly, less its special nuclear materials, plus a raw supply of nuclear material to be fabricated as required.

The Congressional Joint Atomic Energy Committee published details of the basic plutonium-for-uranium barter in 1959. The elements were traded so that the UK would receive, weight for weight, nearly double the amount of $U^{235}$ that she provided of plutonium. The exact ratio, applying to an undisclosed quantity to be traded over the following ten years, was 1.76 grammes of uranium to 1 gramme of plutonium. The United States, it was stated, would 'benefit by obtaining needed plutonium for its small-weapons programme'.

Britain has supplied at least several tonnes of plutonium to the United States, and it would be unreasonable not to believe that some, at least, of this has found its way into US nuclear weapons. This, after all, was the erstwhile purpose of the agreement, which specified that 'except as otherwise agreed . . . materials or equipment transferred shall be used by the recipient party exclusively for the preparation or implementation of defence plans'.

After 1960, these agreements became the instrument of a new dependence of Britain on the United States. Chapter 3 traced the evolution of US bases in Britain from this period. It is sufficient now to note that the effects of these agreements were to link the special relationship inextricably to all aspects of British defence policy.

There were both overt aspects and covert aspects of this cooperation. The agreement on the sale of Skybolt was an explicit 'missiles-for-bases' deal; in return, the US got a forward base for the Polaris force at Holy Loch. Without Holy Loch, the US Navy would have faced considerable difficulty in finding the necessary forward deployment site for its submarines as Norway and Denmark would not accept nuclear weapons on their territory in peacetime.

On the covert side, the evidence that can be assembled about the British nuclear weapons production programme after 1958 suggests strongly that – having first won its spurs with A- and H-bomb programmes and getting a production organisation into operation – the Atomic

## Table 3
## From Quebec to Trident – nuclear treaties with the United States

1943 Quebec Agreement on 'Tube Alloys'; Quebec, 19 August 1943. British consent was required for use of bomb against third parties.

1946 Groves-Anderson memorandum; drafted after Washington summit but not accepted. 'Consultation' replaced 'consent' over use of bomb.

1948 Anglo-American *Modus Vivendi*; Washington; neither consent nor consultation agreed.

1955 Agreement for co-operation regarding atomic information for mutual defence purposes. (UK Cmnd 9555; 1955 treaty series 52.)

1955 Agreement for co-operation on the civil uses of atomic energy; 15 June 1955. (UK Cmnd 9560; 1955 treaty series 55.)

1956 Amendment to 1955 agreement; allowed exchange of information on naval nuclear propulsion units. (UK Cmnd 9847; 1956 treaty series 35.)

1958 Agreement for co-operation on the uses of atomic energy for mutual defence purposes; Washington, 3 July 1958. Allowed transfer of nuclear weapons under US control, to allies. (UK Cmnd 537; 1958 treaty series 4.)

1959 Amendment to 1958 agreement. (UK Cmnd 859; 1959 treaty series 72.)

1963 Polaris Sales ('Nassau') Agreement. (UK Cmnd 2018, 1963 treaty series 59.)

1963 Amendment to 1955 civil atomic energy agreement. (UK Cmnd 2166, 1963 treaty series 82.)

1969 Amendment and renewal of 1958 agreement. (UK Cmnd 4119; 1969 treaty series 85.)

1970 Amendment and renewal of 1958 agreement. (UK Cmnd 4383, 1970 treaty series 46.)

1971 Amendment and renewal of 1955 civil atomic energy agreement. (UK Cmnd 4694; 1971 treaty series 31.)

1975 Amendment and renewal of 1958 agreement. (UK Cmnd 6017; 1975 treaty series 65.)

1980 Amendment and renewal of 1958 agreement (UK Cmnd 7976; 1979 treaty series 61.)

1980 Trident Sales Agreement; exchange of letters between President Carter and Prime Minister Thatcher; 10 and 14 July 1980; published as *The British strategic nuclear force.* (UK Cmnd 7979, 1980.) Terms specified to be as in the Polaris Sales Agreement in a second exchange of letters, September 1980.

Weapons Research Establishment at Aldermaston abandoned, for a period at least, original design work.

The first British A-bomb, 'Blue Danube', was in operation in 1956. The first production British H-bomb, supplied for the V bombers, was 'Red Beard', an inelegant Moloch over 15 feet long and 5 feet in diameter with a box-like tail. Red Beard's fissile core – or 'pit' in US jargon – a sphere the size of a football, was carried separately until the bomb had to be armed, when the navigator-bomber on the aircraft would lock it into the bomb after it had been slung into the bomb bay.

'Red Beard' was the product, apparently, of the British H-bomb test-programme of 1956–8. Thereafter, Britain carried out only four nuclear weapons tests until 1974, two of which must have been concerned with Polaris warhead development. None were megaton yield H-bombs; on the contrary, all were below 200-kT yield, and three were probably 20–40 kT yield, or even lower. Thus, it is unlikely that Britain ever tested an H-bomb design again after 1958.

Although a detailed analysis of UK nuclear weapons is beyond the scope of this book, it appears that after the first H-bombs were in production, all subsequent weapons (save Chevaline in the 1970s) were more or less copies of US designs. It is hard otherwise to explain the rapid miniaturisation of British H-bombs which occurred between 1960 and 1970.

By 1970, instead of the 10,000 lb or heavier Red Beard, the V bombers and other British nuclear forces, such as Buccaneers, were re-equipped with a sleek white '950MC' (950 lb, medium capacity) bomb, whose external appearance and date of arrival in the British stockpile suggests it was a copy of another standard US design.

Table 4 identifies and describes the nuclear weapons which have been developed or used by British armed forces. The analysis indicates that of 17 types of nuclear weapon which have been used by British forces, only two – the first, crude A- and H-bombs – were produced without US assistance.

After the 'Red Beard' H-bomb came into service, it was rapidly followed by another, codenamed 'Yellow Sun'. According to descriptions given by former RAF personnel, this seems likely not to have been a further product of the British test programme, but instead a copy of much more advanced US H-bombs of the same era – in particular the US B28 or B43 bombs, which by the early 1960s were routinely being carried by the B-52 intercontinental bombers of Strategic Air Command.

Although a great deal was said in the early 1960s about the supposed

**Table 4**
**US input to British nuclear weapons**

| Weapon | Year tested | Year of entry into stockpile | Comment |
|---|---|---|---|
| **British design and manufacture:** | | | |
| Blue Danube | 1952–3 | 1953 | British-designed A-bomb; prototype delivery |
| | | 1956 | Operational versions delivered |
| Red Beard | 1956–8 | About 1960 | British-designed H-bomb, weight 10,000 lb approx; MT yield; detachable nuclear core ('pit') |
| **US design, British manufacture:** | | | |
| Yellow Sun | 1957 (US) | About 1961 | Probably copy of US B28 or B43 bomb; weight 2,000–2,500 lb, yield 500 kT to 1.1 MT |
| Blue Steel | 1957(US) | 1963 | Standoff missile, probably using warhead identical to Yellow Sun bomb |
| Polaris | 1964–5 | 1968 | Direct copy of US W58 warhead for Polaris A3 missile |
| Bomb '950MC' | – | 1968–70 | 950 lb, 'medium' – sub Megaton – yield; probably copy of US B61 bomb |
| Bomb '600' Green Parrot (?) | – | 1968–70 | 600 lb, variable yield bomb, also provided British nuclear depth bomb; probably copy of US B57 depth bomb (see below) |
| **US design and manufacture:** | | | |
| Artillery shell | – | 1956 | W33 shell for 8 inch howitzer yield less than 12 kT, being replaced by W79 neutron bomb variant |
| Honest John missile | – | 1958 (UK) | W31 warhead, yield 10–60 kT |
| Thor missile | – | 1958 | W35 warhead, yield about 1 MT |
| Artillery shell | – | 1963 | W48 shell for 155-mm gun yield about 1 kT |
| Atomic demolition munition | – | 1964 | W54 'backpack' A-bomb |

| | | | |
|---|---|---|---|
| Atomic demolition munition | – | 1965 | W45 medium ADM |
| Lance missile | – | 1973 | W70 variable yield warhead |
| Nuclear depth bomb | – | 1965 (UK) | B57 used by British anti-submarine aircraft |
| **British design and manufacture of US delivery system:** | | | |
| Chevaline | 1974–81 | 1982 | Independent development of new warhead for US Polaris missile |
| Trident | 1978 on | 1988 | Independent development of warhead for US Trident missile |

British 'independent deterrent', details of the RAF's bomb supply indicate that up to a third – possibly more – of the V-bomber force at that time were wholly dependent on US weapons, and subject to a US veto on their use. This was the case at at least one major RAF base, Marham, where all the nuclear weapons in the 'Special Storage Area' (SSA) were guarded by USAF Security Police. Targets for the Valiant squadrons at Marham were allocated by SACEUR, not by the RAF.

Britain's next generation of nuclear weapons was the Polaris submarine force. The Polaris missiles were made by the Lockheed Corporation in America. While the Polaris warheads were British-made, their design was a straight copy of the American W58 warhead. It is not known whether the US supplied the non-nuclear parts, as they would have been permitted to do by the Mutual Defence Co-operation agreement, but it would have been sensible for the UK to have taken advantage of such an arrangement.

In common with other NATO countries, British forces in Europe began to re-equip for atomic warfare on land in the late 1950s. The first battlefield nuclear weapons were 8-inch artillery shells, quickly followed by short-range missiles such as 'Corporal' and 'Honest John'. Atomic land mines (ADMs) were available for use in Germany by the mid-1960s. Soon after this, nuclear depth bombs were stockpiled for British and NATO use in the UK. By 1970, there were 7,000 tactical nuclear weapons stored in Europe. In 1973, the obsolescent Honest John missiles were replaced by 'Lance'. Replacement artillery shells for the 1950s stocks, which have a built in 'neutron bomb' ('enhanced radiation') option have been in production since 1981.

Britain has been completely dependent on US manufacture and

supply for all these weapons. The actual warheads are retained in US custody, and are under dual control. British nuclear weapons production capacity at Aldermaston, and the subsidiary manufacturing plants at Burghfield and Cardiff, has been limited to producing copies or adaptations of US air-dropped bombs or missile warheads. Even in the early 1970s, Britain had apparently yet to manufacture a sufficient bomb stockpile to fulfil national strategic plans and NATO 'tactical' requirements. During this period, some RAF strike aircraft in Germany, such as at RAF Bruggen, remained dependent on US-controlled weapons.

Two lower yield tactical or 'theatre' nuclear bombs were introduced into the British stockpile in the late 1960s, according to RAF sources. One was the '950MC' variable-yield bomb, which had a sufficiently wide range of yields to be used for either strategic or tactical purposes. The second was a 600 lb low-yield bomb, also with variable yields. One of these bombs, probably the latter, has the codename 'Green Parrot'. Since there were no United Kingdom nuclear tests between 1965 and 1974, it must be concluded that any new 'British' bomb designs in this period were in fact further copies of American weapons.

The characteristics and weight of the British bombs introduced around 1970 match well those of two new US bombs of the same era. These were respectively the B61 and B57 (see Table 3). Both were supplied to US forces in Britain in the same period, for use by F-4 Phantoms and F-111 bombers. The B57 was primarily an anti-submarine nuclear depth bomb. Britain has evidently produced its own copies of this bomb for use by Royal Navy helicopters – although, curiously, not for RAF Nimrod aircraft, which rely on American supplies. The Royal Navy probably did not wish to have US custodial detachments in charge of nuclear weapons on board RN ships – whilst the RAF was satisfied with existing arrangements for getting bombs from US-controlled depots.

In the 1970s and 80s, the Aldermaston Atomic Weapons Research Establishment has concentrated on the design of new warheads for Polaris – 'Chevaline' – and began work on possible Trident warheads, some time before the political decision to buy Trident had been taken. The Chevaline and Trident projects are obviously dependent on US design information.

A similar dependence on the United States is apparent in the supply of highly-enriched uranium, which is needed to fuel Britain's nuclear-powered submarines, both Polaris and 'hunter-killer' types. The supply of submarine uranium fuel has been an American monopoly since the

1958 agreement, following which British high-enrichment facilities at Capenhurst, near Chester, were closed down.

Yet another critical commodity is tritium, a fusion fuel for thermonuclear (H-bomb) weapons. H-bombs may use two different kinds of fuel, either of which is consumed to release copious energy after the bomb is first 'triggered' by an ordinary fission explosion. Tritium is a heavy version of hydrogen and is a gas at normal temperatures and pressures. The other is a compound called lithium deuteride, formed of lithium, a light metal, in combination with another type of heavy hydrogen, deuterium. Either substance can boost the energy yield of an ordinary fission 'atomic' explosion of some tens of kilotons by a factor of one thousand or even more.

Large hydrogen bombs are believed predominantly to use lithium deuteride. Britain is not known to have any plant preparing the special form of lithium (lithium-6) which is required for this job. Weapons such as the Polaris warhead, with an estimated yield of about 150kT, are usually 'boosted' fission weapons, rather than 'true' hydrogen bombs – which have yields of the order of 1–10MT. In one design of 'boosted' bomb, a gas bottle of tritium is attached to the warhead, and injected into the explosion, greatly boosting the fission process by destroying more plutonium. Such weapons are much more easily miniaturised to fit inside a missile than an orthodox H-bomb.

Until about 1980, Britain relied exclusively on the United States for supplies of tritium, and probably also for supplies of lithium-6. This was another critical link in the nuclear axis, as tritium's relatively short lifespan before radioactive decay (a 'half life' of roughly 12 years) requires that stockpile bombs be refurbished periodically, recovering and then refreshing the tritium component.

In 1976, British Nuclear Fuels Ltd (BNFL), who operate British military plutonium production facilities, was given a Ministry of Defence contract to start tritium production inside nuclear reactors at its Chapelcross centre near Dumfries in Scotland. The award of the contract appeared to anticipate that US supplies were to be discontinued. This was probably because the US anticipated a shortage of tritium for the planned neutron bomb programme, although speculation in the UK at the time focused (wrongly) on possible non-renewal of parts of the Mutual Defence Co-operation agreement when it expired in December 1979.

Although Britain could have 'gone it alone' some distance in nuclear weaponry, it is evident that most of the British nuclear arsenal would not now exist but for US collaboration. Whatever the public rhetoric about independent deterrence, this had been Macmillan's hope in 1957 when US Secretary of State John Foster Dulles brought him the good news that the MacMahon Act was going to be amended to let Britain in on US nuclear secrets:

> We could now . . . remain a nuclear power without the apalling waste of effort involved in slowly arriving by our own efforts at the point of development which [the Americans] had already reached.[9]

After the 1958 and 1959 Agreements, Britain abandoned independent nuclear testing, and came to rely entirely on the United States for strategic nuclear weapons systems, as well as for parts, facilities and materials. Between 1958 and 1963, the RAF and USAF jointly operated Thor missiles. Thereafter, Britain has bought or attempted to buy Skybolt ballistic missiles, Polaris missiles, F-111 bombers and, most recently, Trident submarines.

After 1959, British nuclear tests were conducted underground at the US Nevada Test Site. A short series lasted from 1962 to 1965. The current series, believed to be concerned only with Chevaline (multiple independent warheads for Polaris) and Trident, began in 1974. Table 5 lists British nuclear tests in Nevada. Tests of unarmed British Polaris, Polaris-Chevaline and (ultimately) Trident missiles take place at the US Air Force Eastern Test Range in Florida.

Britain is also dependent on the United States for the maintenance of satellite and radio navigation systems, without which Polaris submarines could not accurately fix their launching points. Britain's Polaris programme began with an agreement to buy Skybolt ballistic missiles for V bombers, made during a meeting between Eisenhower and Macmillan at the Camp David Presidential retreat in Maryland, during March 1960. Under the agreement, Britain would buy 100 Skybolts and, in return, the United States were to get the Holy Loch base for their Polaris submarines. But that detail of the agreement was not made public until six months later.

In the following three years, British strategists' illusions of nuclear independence took three hard blows from the United States. First Skybolt was cancelled. Second, the RAF/USAF Thor missiles were stood down on US instructions – ostensibly because of obsolescence, although it is noteworthy that Macmillan records that he suggested (to President Kennedy) that they be dismantled as a conciliatory gesture to the Russians during the Cuban missile crisis. Third, Kennedy made it clear that he did not favour a new and independent British strategic force. If the United States was to help, he said, Britain should join a

**Table 5**
**British nuclear weapons tests conducted in the United States**

| *Test name* | *Date* | *Yield* | *Comment* |
|---|---|---|---|
| Pampas | 1 March 1962 | 'Low' | Radioactivity released onto site |
| Tendrac | 7 Dec 1962 | 'Low' | |
| Cormorant | 17 July 1964 | Less that 20kT | Radioactivity released onto site |
| Charcoal | 10 Sept 1965 | 20–200kT* | |
| Fallon | 23 May 1974 | 20–200kT | |
| Banon | 26 Aug 1976 | 20–150kT | |
| Fondutta | 11 Apr 1978 | 20–150kT | |
| Quargel | 18 Nov 1978 | 20–150kT | |
| Nessel | 29 Aug 1979 | 20–150kT | |
| Colwick | 26 Apr 1980 | 20–150kT | |
| Dutchess | 24 Oct 1980 | Less than 20kT | |
| Serpa | 17 Dec 1980 | 20–150kT | |
| Rousanne | 12 Nov 1981 | 20–150kT | |
| (unknown) | 22 Apr 1983 | Less than 20kT | |

Main Source: *Announced United States nuclear tests, July 1945 through December 1981*; US Department of Energy, January 1982, NVO-209 rev 2. The tests are conducted under the terms of the Agreement for Co-operation on the Uses of Atomic Energy for Mutual Defense Purposes, 1958.

*Other sources suggest that the yield in *Charcoal* may have been as low as 15kT.

European-wide, NATO 'multilateral' force. Meanwhile, plans for British short- and long-range nuclear missiles – 'Blue Water' and 'Blue Streak' – were cancelled.

Macmillan almost completely gave in to United States pressure to have Polaris made a NATO rather than national nuclear force. Polaris and its missiles, together with a significant part of the V-bomber force, were to be 'assigned and targeted' as part of NATO forces, in accordance with SACEUR's Nuclear Support Plan. Co-operation over targeting became quite explicit, replacing more informal links between the RAF and SAC. NATO targeting staff were assigned by SACEUR to work at Offut Air Force Base in Omaha, Nebraska, the home of Strategic Air Command. All that remained of independence was a clause allowing the emergency withdrawal of Polaris from NATO command:

> Except where Her Majesty's government may decide that supreme national interests are at stake, these British forces will be used for the purposes of international defence of the Western Alliance in all circumstances.[10]

The Polaris sales agreement negotiated four months after the Nassau meeting is still in force. It was extended to include the sale of Trident by an exchange of letters between President Carter and Mrs Thatcher in July 1980.

In return for the supply of weapons, information and materials, the United States has received military bases and facilities in Britain and abroad – as well as the benefits to its security policy that the NATO alliance and other bilateral arrangements are thought to bring.

Since 1941, the UK has provided the United States with bases in many territories. Sometimes, a weapons-for-bases deal has been quite explicit. In 1941, the United States was given bases in Jamaica and Bermuda in return for war material supplied to Britain. In the postwar period, the US has been given base rights in a succession of territories, starting with the Bahamas in July 1950, where the US wanted tracking stations for a new Long Range Guided Missile Proving Ground in Florida – which subsequently became NASA's Cape Canaveral launching centre, and is also now the US Air Force Eastern Test Range.

New sites for the missile range were annexed during the mid-1950s in St Lucia, Ascension, and Antigua. Sosus underwater listening stations were also built on a number of British Caribbean islands. In 1973, a base to launch pilotless target drones was established on the British Virgin Islands. These were relatively straightforward deals, fully recorded by treaty. Diego Garcia, a small atoll in the Indian Ocean with a superb natural harbour, was in a quite different category.

Diego Garcia, now the keystone of the US military build-up in the Indian Ocean, was secretly and forcibly depopulated by the British government between 1965 and 1971. Between one and two thousand islanders were evicted and dispatched to live in continuing poverty and misery in Mauritius and the Seychelles. Some families had been living on the island for five generations.

The islanders' rights had literally been sold off by the British Foreign Office, who in return received $14 million – worth about £5 million at then current exchange rates. In 1975, US Congressional officials discovered how this shabby financial transaction had been concealed by the two governments as part of a secret *quid pro quo* for Polaris. In order to pay for the base, the US Department of Defense set up a secret internal 'Polaris Trust Fund' to pay for base rights in the Indian Ocean.[11] Money from the 'Trust Fund' was then deducted from Britain's bills for Polaris research and development costs (which were set at five per cent of the total bill).

The US Joint Chiefs of Staff had first sought a base in the Indian Ocean territories as early as 1959[12], and thereupon persuaded the British to hive off the Chagos Archipelago prior to granting independence to Mauritius and the Seychelles. The 'British Indian Ocean Territories' were established in 1965. A year later, an Anglo-American Treaty guaranteed the United States the right for 50 years to set up bases on the islands of Diego Garcia, Aldabra, Farquhar and Desroches. The treaty agreed that:

> The Islands shall remain available to meet the possible defence needs of the two Governments for an indefinitely long period.[13]

The Americans began to move in to Diego Garcia during 1971. The first US military project was to establish a naval Sigint (signals intelligence) station to monitor radio signals in the Indian Ocean area. With limited Royal Navy participation, a US Naval Security Group monitoring station was set up in 1972. It is part of a joint British-Australian-US electronic surveillance network covering the Indian Ocean and West Pacific areas, and is now a satellite receiving terminal for ocean surveillance satellites (see Chapter 6).

Meanwhile, the last few islanders were cleared out on pain of starvation. The United States left the task of eviction to the British, who under the terms of the 1966 treaty had promised to clear out the unwanted local population. Once the US authorities had a 'requirement for use of a particular island', they would agree with the UK how long it would take for:

> those administrative measures that may be necessary to enable defense requirements to be met.[14]

The British government assigned the job to the British Indian Ocean Territories administration, who instructed the Chagos-Agalega Company, coconut exporters and the island's only employer, to resettle them elsewhere. The last few islanders left in September 1971, having been told by US officials that:

> If you don't leave, you won't be fed any longer.[15]

A second US–UK treaty in 1972 sanctioned the creation (which had in fact already begun) of the so-called 'limited naval communications facility' on the island, paving the way for full-scale military development. An airstrip and port facilities were developed to support the new base. The new treaty now restricted access to Diego Garcia to British and American military personnel only. In Congress, US military officers repeatedly referred to the islands as 'uninhabited'.

In 1976, a third treaty authorised the United States to begin construction of 'anchorage, airfield, support and supply elements and ancillary services'. Now, a massive $280-million construction programme is under way to turn the tiny island into the major base of a new United States 'Central Command', a keystone for intervention forces in the Middle East.

The 1980 Trident agreement has been discovered to embody numerous special features agreed in unpublished protocols, diplomatic exchanges and understandings. In one related deal, for example, the United States agreed to purchase British Rapier missiles to provide close-in air defence for its British bases. The RAF Regiment will operate these defences, however, at no cost to the US Air Force.

Another agreement specified that British companies could compete to supply equipment for all Trident submarines 'on the same terms as US firms for subcontracts for Trident II (D-5) weapons system components for the program as a whole'.[16] A 90-page brochure with diagrams and exploded views[17] to illustrate how Trident submarines are assembled was prepared for and circulated to potential British contractors by the US Navy's Strategic Systems Procurement Office, responsible for missile submarines.

Despite this appearance of collaboration, British companies' expectations of being able successfully to compete are minimal. A separate document obtained by the author, dealing with the restrictions on the provision of classified Trident information to the UK, shows how Britain emphatically remains the junior partner.[18] Similar restrictions were presumably applied to Polaris sales. In the case of Trident, the United States has banned Britain from getting:

- Strategic and operational planning information – this included the 'absolute values of the vulnerability of the (Polaris or Trident) systems to 'possible defensive environments' such as anti-ballistic missiles.
- Naval nuclear propulsion (ie, nuclear reactor) information, classified *or unclassified.*
- Communications doctrine, procedures – this included all details of mobile VLF (very low frequency) communications, ELF (extra low frequency) communications, and their security and effectiveness.
- Tactical doctrine . . . including command and control methods.

Not having information on the absolute probability of missiles evading Soviet defences, or the most effective ways of communicating with and sending orders to submarines will make a certain difference to the reliability of the British force. In addition, the UK was also forbidden details of 'SSBN (ie, ballistic missile submarine) acoustic or magnetic signatures' which would tell the British planners how easily enemy forces could find a submarine through its noise emissions or inbuilt magnetism. The prohibition seems the more extraordinary since, once the British had built their own Trident submarines, they would be able to measure the noise and find out!

Thus, even within a period of apparently wholesale co-operation, Britain's subordinate position and incomplete access to information – even on a submarine force she herself was to build – is clear. When questioned about the instructions prohibiting these disclosures to Britain in 1982, the Ministry of Defence said that they didn't know about the instruction[19]; and anyway:

> We haven't a copy of [the instructions]... We never felt the US was withholding information which we needed.

Exchanges of nuclear weapons information between Britain and the United States are arranged through national 'Atomic Co-ordinating Offices' which were established in December 1960. The main channel of communications is the British-run Atomic Co-ordinating Office (Washington), which forms part of the vast British Defence Staff in the Washington Embassy. Before being passed onto allies like Britain, US atomic information is vetted by the Joint Atomic Information Exchange Group, part of the US Defense Nuclear Agency.

Besides getting military bases in return for atomic information supplied to the UK, the US has also been supplied with several tonnes of plutonium, most of it suitable for use in nuclear weapons. This matter was raised by the Campaign for Nuclear Disarmament during the 1983 Sizewell nuclear power station inquiry, who sought to establish a 'plutonium connection' between British civil electric power reactors and US nuclear weapons.

The accusation that civil reactors were producing plutonium for military use is a matter of considerable sensitivity for the nuclear power industry, which faces both widespread public protest and close international scrutiny. Nuclear power utilities, such as the CEGB, have repeatedly – and unconvincingly – tried to repudiate suggestions that their activities could assist in nuclear weapons' proliferation.

Successive governments have refused to resolve contradictions in official statements. The 1959 amendment to the Mutual Defense Co-operation Agreement provided for the exchange between the two governments of 'special nuclear material' – uranium, plutonium, lithium-6, and tritium. This amendment was invoked in order to barter, between then and 1971, an unspecified quantity of British plutonium for US highly-enriched uranium. For material supplied by Britain to the United States, Article III *bis*, B specified that the UK would send the US:

> *For military purposes* such source, byproduct and special nuclear material and equipment of such types . . . prior to December 31, 1969, on such terms and conditions as may be agreed (author's emphasis).

No annulment of the condition that British materials should be received for military purposes has been published. Yet, in 1964, it was stated by the then Prime Minister Sir Alec Douglas Home that:

> The civil reactors which . . . are being brought into service in this country to produce plutonium . . . part of which will be sent to the United States under an agreement whereby uranium-235 is supplied in exchange by the United States government. I am informed by the United States government that they have no intention of using the plutonium received from us for weapons purposes.[20]

These reassurances were repeated in 1982 by Energy Department secretary John Moore, who stated that the plutonium which had been transferred had been devoted to civil uses only, such as test fast reactors. Some 200 kg had been used to refine a rare element for medical use, Californium.[21]

But in June 1983, a scientist employed by the Central Electricity Generating Board, Dr Ross Hesketh, who had written widely on his fears that British civil plutonium had found military uses, was summarily dismissed from his job. The exact quantity of plutonium sent to the US remained secret. Dr Hesketh estimated that 3–4 tonnes had been exported; in fact, at the time of the 1959 agreement, it was suggested that some 10.3 tonnes of British plutonium had been sought by the United States authorities.[22] No evidence, other than the unaltered terms of the 1959 amendment, points to a military use for the British plutonium. But several points remained unanswered:

- A separate barter agreement, or direct sale, must have governed the transfer of tritium; it is not known what the United States received in return. At least one 'Mutual Defense Co-operation Agreement' tritium transfer to the UK has been recorded, by the US Department of Energy[23], between 1975 and 1978.
- The United Kingdom has a separate military stockpile of plutonium, some of which is produced by British Nuclear Fuels Ltd's reactors at Chapelcross and Calder Hall. British government statements have scrupulously avoided making any reference to transfers from, or even the existence of, the military stockpile. In May 1983, reports alleged that at least one military reactor at Calder Hall had begun operating on a military plutonium production cycle, to meet new US requirements.[24]
- Even though British plutonium reaching the United States may have gone into a 'civil use' stockpile, that stockpile has been considered for transfer to the weapons programme. Mixing of the civil stock of plutonium with high-purity weapons grades to make acceptable bomb material was begun in 1982. Plutonium from 'foreign governments' was, US officials stated, one element of a 17.8 tonne 'civil' stockpile earmarked in 1982 to assist in nuclear weapons expansion.

A further argument is that civil plutonium supplies from the UK would free – or have freed – part of the US civil plutonium stockpile to be diverted to weapons use. If this were not available, the US civil nuclear reactor research programme might be denuded of resources with which to fuel prototype experimental fast breeder reactors. In October 1981, it was revealed that the US Department of Energy had asked to buy British civil plutonium as a commercial transaction. Britain had agreed. This was intended to enable US civil plutonium to be diverted to weapons production. However, in the face of growing congressional opposition to weapons proliferation, the proposal was abandoned five months later.

This discussion of American bases cannot be treated in isolation from the central tenets of postwar British defence policy. There is an unbalanced dependence on the United States for almost every aspect of strategic nuclear weapons: missiles, nuclear design, nuclear materials, testing facilities for warhead and weapon, launching platforms, navigation systems, target allocation and target intelligence. Thus, although British popular opinion makes a significant distinction between its desires for national nuclear weapons, and for US bases, the view from Whitehall is necessarily far more blurred.

To say goodbye to American bases and the special relationship, would seem to Whitehall to be saying goodbye also to Britain's long-term future as a strategic nuclear power. It would leave France as the only independent nuclear power in Europe, a prospect that at times civil servants seem to find more objectionable than the idea of Red Army hordes moving west.

## Notes

1 Atomic Demolition Munition, or atomic mine.
2 Dr John Simpson, 'The Anglo-American nuclear relationship and its implications for the choice of a possible successor to the current Polaris force', memorandum in the Sixth Report of the Expenditure Committee, Session 1978–9 (House of Commons Paper No 348).
3 On the British side, Margaret Gowing, *British and Atomic Energy 1939–1945*; Macmillan, 1964. On the US side, Richard G. Hewlett and Oscar E. Anderson, *The New World 1939–1946*, US Atomic Energy Commission, 1972; WASH 1214. Other accounts include Martin J. Sherman, *A world destroyed – The atomic bomb and the Grand Alliance*; Alfred A. Knopf, New York, 1975.
4 Gowing, *op cit*, Vol 1, p 251.
5 *Foreign Policy Relations of the United States*, 1950, Vol VII, p 1463.
6 US Joint Chiefs of Staff records; CCS471.6, Section 32.
7 *Sunday Times*, 6 March 1955.
8 Table 3 lists the major atomic agreements with the United States
9 Harold Macmillan, *Riding the Storm* (Vol IV of autobiography), p 323, Macmillan, 1962.
10 Joint Communiqué following meeting in the Bahamas, 18–21 December 1962, (UK Cmnd 1915), para 9.
11 *Sunday Times*, 25 January 1976.
12 Lenny Siegel, *Pacific Research*, *Vol VIII*, No 3, March–April 1977. (Pacific Studies Centre, Mountain View, California.)
13 *Availability for defence purposes of the British Indian Ocean Territory*, treaty series no 15 (1967), UK Cmnd 3231.
14 *ibid*, para 2(a).
15 *Guardian*, 10 September 1975.
16 Letter from US Defense Secretary Caspar Weinberger to his British counterpart, John Nott.
17 *Trident II (D–5) Strategic weapons system*; *Guide for potential subcontractors*, December 1982.
18 US Department of the Navy, Chief of Naval Operations, OPNAVINST 5510.48H, Part III, Chapter 10; 29 July 1981.
19 *New Statesman*, 26 March 1982.
20 *Hansard*, 21 April 1964.
21 *Hansard*, 27 July 1982.
22 *Daily Telegraph*, 19 March 1959. Statement quoted from the Chairman of the Congressional Joint Atomic Energy Committee, Senator Clinton P. Anderson.
23 *International Atomic Defense Co-operation*, Department of Energy (United States), 27

October 1978. Cited in Thomas Cochrane and Milton Hoenig, *Nuclear Weapons Databook*, Volume 2, Appendix D (to be published).

24 *Guardian*, 12 May 1983, reporting the Windscale local newspaper, *Whitehaven News*. The Ministry of Defence refused to confirm or deny the report.

# 5 *The Intelligence Axis*

By the end of the Second World War, both Britain and the United States had built up an extensive apparatus of secret warfare, with scope for overt and covert propaganda, sabotage and assassination, espionage, aerial reconnaissance, communications intelligence and counterintelligence. In common with the rest of the wartime establishment, both countries discarded or partially dismantled this clandestine warfare apparatus in the aftermath of victory in Europe and the Pacific. In Britain, where secret state agencies had a longer pedigree, the dismantlement was both slower and less complete.

During the developing US–USSR confrontation of the late 1940s, this secret apparatus was extensively restored. In both the US and UK, new and old secret warfare techniques and establishments were reincarnated to meet Cold War requirements. The secret organisations were not again to be dismantled. In succeeding years, military or political requirements would dictate new intelligence priorities. All too often, it was the other way around, as foreign policy became the handmaiden of the dictates of the secret world.

In the secret world, the Anglo-Saxon intelligence axis has been durable and powerful. No feature of the special relationship, other than the trade in nuclear weapons know-how, has been of comparable importance in binding together British and American political and military establishments. Secret pacts, whether established by treaty or merely by custom and practice, have virtually created integrated multinational intelligence agencies. Numerous security and intelligence arrangements, and plans for military research, have been established between the white Anglo-Saxon nations – Britain, Canada, Australia (with New Zealand as their junior partner) – and the United States. These sometimes informal and always secret collaborative arrangements are invariably more comfortable, mutually trusting and extensive than their equivalents formally prescribed by treaty between the NATO countries.

Many such agreements have become known, usually identified by new permutations of the countries' names: ABC, ABCAN, BRUSA, CANZAUSUKUS, UKUSA and so on. Within each, however, the Anglo-American 'special relationship' is the tightest tie of all.

In the first few postwar years, the intelligence axis seems to have reflected much more 'interdependence' than was the case in nuclear matters. At the end of 1946, the United States government had yet to establish its vast intelligence and clandestine operations troops, in the Central Intelligence Agency (CIA) and National Security Agency (NSA). The US secret intelligence service – the Office of Strategic Services – had not existed before the war and had been closed down immediately after it, having come under attack late in its short life as an 'American Gestapo'. The British Secret Intelligence Service (SIS) could, on the other hand, trace its origins to the turn of the century, and to a historical tradition of espionage and secret state agents over several centuries. Shortly before the war, the US State Department had closed down its codebreaking division, and then rebuilt from scratch. Britain's codebreakers had been at the game since before wireless came into use. For those attempting to create an extensive intelligence apparatus in the United States, there was something to learn from the transatlantic tie-up. For the British, such co-operation came naturally as part of the pricetag on the special relationship.

It did not take much more than a decade for mutual interdependence to turn around to become British dependence on the US, with disturbing consequences for British politics. By the 1960s, Britain's supply of secret foreign intelligence had come to depend substantially on the co-operation of US 'cousins'. Doubtless as usual accurately reporting the *mores* of the Whitehall secret world, the right-wing exposé journalist Chapman Pincher wrote in 1978 that 'Britain is totally dependent on the USA for intelligence . . . dependence is so great and co-operation so close that I am convinced that the security and intelligence chiefs would go to any lengths to protect the linkup, and that they would be right to do so'.[1]

It is unnecessary totally to rely on Pincher for proof of this highly reasonable assertion. In 1967, when Britain's chief of communications intelligence, Sir Leonard Hooper (the Director of Government Communications headquarters, GCHQ) sought funds for an extensive new installation in Cornwall to tap commercial communications satellites, it apparently availed him more to plead the value of the installation for the United States to the Treasury, than to assert its importance for British affairs. Elsewhere in the world, Hong Kong for example, Britain still operates extensive communications and human intelligence operations against China that have only peripheral internal security value for the soon-to-be-discarded colony, and none at all for British interests. The station's intelligence 'take' is for the United States, part of the trade-off for forms of special intelligence unachievable by the UK, such as satellite reconnaissance, and for the special relationship.

How far would British intelligence chiefs go to 'protect the linkup'? The role of the CIA in frequently violent intervention in the internal affairs the third world, from Guatemala (in 1956) on, is well known. But there is a presumption that such clandestine warfare will not be waged inside Western democracies, within allied countries – and above all that there will be no interference in the affairs of the white English-speaking partners of the special relationship. This assumption is fallacious. It is certainly the case that alliance, the English language, and the special relationship afford a high degree of immunity from the unwelcome attention of the CIA and associated agencies. But it is a relative, not an absolute, immunity.

Britain was in no way exempt from the massive Cold-War propaganda campaigns run by the CIA and its front organisations throughout western Europe. British trade unions were infiltrated by CIA agents. Student, educational and cultural organisations, news agencies and charitable foundations were annexed or established in pursuit of the aims of the secret American foreign policy. The CIA's money, backing attemps to sweep aside any ideology further left than American liberalism, may have touched the course of British political life more deeply than will ever be discovered. In a close relationship of high complexity, it may be hard to disentangle where fellow-feeling for the United States finished, and the effects of clandestine intervention in British politics began.[2]

CIA money has been directed, even in the 1970s, into initiatives to interfere in Italian elections, and to right-wing groups in Scandinavia. Several reports and leaked US government documents in the late 1970s emphasised that the US intelligence agencies had been recruiting their own agents and informants inside the intelligence services of even the most friendly countries.

Some of the leaked documents were unreliable, evidently having been tampered with in the interests of KGB-inspired 'disinformation'. One at least was not. In March 1979, a US Defense Attache Office official was ordered out of Rome under a 24-hour expulsion order by the Italian government, after a report he had prepared revealed that he was obtaining secret information from five US agents or sources inside

Italy's intelligence and anti-terrorist agencies.[3] The report was one of a series on the 'status and orientation' of the Italian agencies.

When the Iranian students seized the US Embassy in Tehran, they discovered more material of the same sort, which was later reprinted and distributed by Khomeini's supporters and embassies around the world. One of the documents thus circulated was the March 1979 Israeli volume in a secret CIA series called the 'Foreign Intelligence and Security Services survey'. It was classified SECRET/NOFORN/NOCONTRACT/ORCON. The phrases after 'SECRET' meant that no foreign agency (such as SIS), US government contractor or person not approved by the CIA might see reports in the series.

English-speaking special partners in intelligence arrangements with the United States have not necessarily fared any better. Australians continue to suspect that the hand of US intelligence and the CIA was at work in the removal of Gough Whitlam as Australian Prime Minister in 1974. This may never be proven, but ample documentation of the Australian secret world has emerged to show that the officials of the Australian Security Intelligence Organisation (ASIO) and related agencies regarded themselves as more beholden to their US counterparts than to their own government, and were so regarded by the CIA.

When in November 1975 the CIA wanted to express their distaste at the Australian Prime Minister taking an interest in what CIA employees and secret installations were actually doing in Australia, they did so not to him but to the Director-General of ASIO. A top secret message was fired off from the Langley, Virginia CIA headquarters via a telex from ASIO's liaison officer in Washington. This '*demarche* on a service-to-service link' (as the CIA itself described it) remained secret until 1977[4]. The terms in which it is cast give a rare insight into the leverage exerted by and between the intelligence agencies:

> CIA is perplexed at the point as to what all this means. Does this [an allegation by Whitlam that the CIA had financed one of his parliamentary opponents, and a subsequent row] signify some change in our bilateral intelligence security related fields [sic]?
>
> CIA cannot see how this dialogue with continued reference to CIA can do other than blow the lid off those installations in Australia where the persons concerned [whose identities had been revealed] have been working and which are vital to both of our services and countries, particularly the installation at Alice Springs . . .
>
> CIA feel that everything possible has been done on a diplomatic basis and now on an intelligence liaison link . . . if this problem cannot be

> solved they do not see how our mutually beneficial relationships are going to continue.
>
> The CIA feels grave concern as to where this type of public discussion may lead. The Director-General should be assured that CIA does not lightly adopt this attitude . . .

The terms in which the CIA berated its junior intelligence partner, demanding action against the elected government of Australia, are revealing. CIA officials also complained that the Australian row had triggered off a further enquiry into CIA activities by the US Congress, and demanded a reply indicating ASIO's course of action.

One of the Whitlam government's advisers, journalist Richard Hall, later recalled[5] how at the start of the term of office, US officials had reacted when Whitlam forbade security vetting of his personal staff. A day later, security officials were leaking abroad the threat that the US might cut off the intelligence supply. At lunch, a US Embassy official added:

> Your Prime Minister has just cut off one of his options . . .

However, in 1975, the CIA's problem just went away. A day after the secret telex message was sent, on 11 November 1975, Whitlam's government was sacked by decree of the Governor-General, a unique and controversial event. The ostensible cause was a financial crisis; however his dismissal removed an irritant for many in both Australian and American bureaucracies.

Disclosures in Australia have continued to reveal how intelligence liaison has beholden the country's security services to US interests. In 1983, Brian Toohey of the *National Times* reported how ASIO had gathered extensive and derogatory information about target Australian political figures, and had routinely supplied it to the CIA when ASIO officials had visited Washington.[6] Amongst other initiatives, ASIO's programme of gathering adverse political intelligence had included a break-in at the home of a future Prime Minister. The information came from an extremely secret report on Australian security by Justice Hope in 1976; his report perspicaciously warned the government that there was no such thing as a 'friendly intelligence service'; there were only the intelligence services of friendly governments.

Such scandals have seldom been reliably reported in Britain – simply because Britain is unique amongst the English-speaking partners in that here alone no government has either permitted or dared to mount an independent enquiry into security and intelligence services. Canada,

Australia, New Zealand and the United States have all held enquiries since 1972, and all have found – at a minimum – that their intelligence agencies indulged in domestic illegalities and improprieties similar to the Australians.

If Britain's special relationship has had an impact on local activities by the CIA, it has been only that the British Secret agencies – like their Australian counterparts – have been ready to participate in US clandestine intelligence operations.

Britain's geographical situation provides a convenient platform for US technical intelligence collection and support activities. In terms of US foreign policy considerations, the UK is regarded as an extremely suitable outpost for sensitive intelligence installations – devoid of Scandinavian political sensitivities towards the Soviet Union or international law, the mercurial attitudes of Greece or Turkey, or the political instabilities of Africa or the Middle East. The United Kingdom is a convenient piece of real estate.

But in the era of space surveillance and communications, British geography now matters far less than it did at the start of the Cold War. Nonetheless, scattered across Britain are many major and minor intelligence-related installations and agencies, whose functions go back to the postwar years. They include:

- Secret Intelligence: the CIA has a very large staff in London, liaising with SIS. The CIA formerly had arms dumps and mounted secret airborne missions from Britain. It still has a secret agent communications radio station, an overt foreign broadcast monitoring station, and a base for operations against European and African world countries.
- Communications intelligence (Comint or Sigint): the NSA and subordinate military interception services moved into Britain in 1950. The largest NSA base outside the United States, and possibly the most important, is in Yorkshire. A major NSA communications centre is in London, and the work of the British Comint agency, GCHQ, is wholly co-ordinated with NSA.
- Aerial reconnaissance: For more than a decade, the RAF collaborated with the CIA and US Air Force in repeated secret penetration flights into Soviet and Soviet-controlled territory. US spy planes have been based in and operated from US bases in Britain from 1950 to the present day.
- 'Special Operations': US Special Forces have had a base for sabotage troops in Britain since 1981. There is close liaison between US Special Forces and the British SAS. In war, Britain is likely to be the base for CIA and Special Forces operations in Europe.

- Security and intelligence co-operation: There are formal liaison links between the British Joint Intelligence Committee, and Security Service (MI5) and their US counterparts (including the Federal Bureau of Investigation, FBI).
- Satellite intelligence and communications: US military or intelligence satellites have been operated from or controlled by at least a dozen separate ground stations in Britain. Some of these stations have been operated by US or British Civilian agencies to disguise their military role.[7]
- Technical intelligence systems: operating from Britain include sites for the SPADATS (Space Data and Tracking System) space surveillance network; the SOSUS (Sound Surveillance System) underwater listening station: an Over The Horizon (OTH) radar station (for intelligence on missile tests); and seismograph centres (for detecting and monitoring nuclear tests). Similar installations have also been built in several British territories or dependencies.

Besides the intelligence installations located in Britain and overseas, the instrument of UK–US co-operation has often been the huge military staffs which have been maintained in London and Washington since 1942, when combined allied planning began. In almost every field, from textile research to intelligence on biological warfare, there are military officers and civilian specialists in the British Defence Staff Washington and their US counterparts in London sitting in (sometimes) on the relevant committees and receiving (selectively) their paperwork. With time, the relationship has become progressively more one-sided, with selectivity in what is given on the part of the United States.

Britain started supplying the United States with the intelligence estimates prepared by the Joint Intelligence Committee in 1943, and continued, willy-nilly, after the war. The United States stopped the flow after VJ day, leading to British protests only after about a year. Some of the subsequent history of US–UK intelligence and security negotiations can be traced through the public records in the US National Archives in Washington (information of this sort has generally been weeded out from British public records). Most of the secret pacts on intelligence collaboration were struck between 1947 and 1952. Of these, the most powerful is the UKUSA agreement on signals intelligence, binding the English-speaking powers into a collaborative arrangement to co-ordinate the interception of, literally, all the world's communications. UKUSA, which supplemented the similar 1943 BRUSA agreement, was in effect the plan to supply the ears and eyes of an American-led world hegemony.

In 1947, as US War Department documents reveal, Britain was still thought to have something to offer; a review of the value of turning the intelligence supply to Britain back on again stressed that:

> Since there are many areas, particularly parts of Europe, the Near East, and the Middle East where the British sources of information are superior to those of the United States, it is believed desirable that the United States JIC (Joint Intelligence Committee) continue to receive such estimates. This view is reinforced when the present world situation is considered . . .

After some deliberation, the United States Joint Chiefs of Staff only agreed, in September 1948, to the limited release of US intelligence reports to the British after 'thorough re-editing'. At about the same time, however, the United States–United Kingdom Security Agreement was signed, between the two countries military Chiefs of Staff. This still-secret agreement homogenised security regulations and the system of classifications markings[8] between the two countries. Its terms required:

> The British Chiefs of Staff will make every effort to insure that the United Kingdom will maintain the military security classifications established by the US authorities with respect to military information of US origin, and the military security classifications established by UK–US agreement with respect to military information or joint UK–US origin . . . the safeguards also apply to information developed by the US and UK jointly in collaboration with a third nation.

Later, in the wake of the spy scandals of the early 1950s, the United States successfully applied more pressure on the UK, leading *inter alia* to the creation of the 'positive vetting' system. A tripartite Security Working Group (including, on this occasion, France) to this end was set up following a secret agreement signed in Paris in March 1951.

After the return of American forces to British bases in 1948 came the need for military intelligence to prepare for confrontation and possible war. British and American intelligence estimates of the strength, whereabouts, and order of battle of Soviet Forces were at best scanty. At first, the only available source of information was returning German Nazis and other prisoners of war and refugees from the east.

This, however, was a limited intelligence source, and one whose intelligence would gradually dry up and go out of date. So the United States, with Britain and German collaborators in tow, embarked on a programme of intrusion into Soviet territory and airspace so extensive that it scarcely justifies the label 'clandestine'. Had the protagonists been reversed, and Britain and the United States experienced such a protracted assault on sovereignty with spy flights, dropped and landed agents, and the recruitment or training of thousands of 'fifth columnists', it should certainly have been held to justify starting open war.

The Soviet authorities were hardly unaware of the hundreds of agents that were infiltrated into their territory, or of the hundreds of overflights by American and British planes (often on joint operations) that went on (despite several being shot down) until the celebrated occasion when CIA pilot Gary Powers' U-2 was downed near Sverdlovsk. But their claims about Western intelligence activities were inevitably dismissed in the west as (false) propaganda.

Despite the gathering United States air power in Britain and its intended atomic potential, the US had prepared few operational plans. Maps of the Soviet Union were out of date, and unreliable for aircraft navigation. Where, in the aftermath of reconstruction after the Nazi retreat, were the key industries and military headquarters located? What research institutes might be working on the Soviet atom bomb? If war began, US Air Force navigators did not have either photographs of likely targets or intelligence on their radar and anti-aircraft defences, on which to plan their attacks.

Britain participated in three types of US operations to supply this data:

- Clandestine overflights – photographic reconnaissance, electronic 'ferret' missions or radar profiling – for navigation, and for bombardiers to line up on their targets.
- Agent infiltration – to determine industrial targets, and locate ground targets for radar navigation.
- Agent infiltration for peacetime sabotage, and to set up the nuclei of wartime 'unconventional warfare' guerrilla teams.

In Germany, the US Air Force began Project Wringer, which involved over 1,300 interrogators and thousands of refugees and ex-POWs. In Scandinavia, as a former Norwegian intelligence officer revealed in 1977, the SIS and the CIA had collaborated during the 1950s (with Norwegian assistance) to infiltrate right-wing nationalist sabotage groups into the Soviet Union, via Finland.[9] From late 1949, Frank Wisner of the CIA's covert operations 'Office of Policy Co-ordination' had begun raising a CIA task force that was supposed to be the vanguard of the liberation of eastern Europe and the USSR from communism. Arms dumps, airfields and seconded US Army teams experienced in guerrilla warfare were set up in Britain, as well as in Germany, Greece and Japan. Agents from these groups were dropped in ones and twos, from the Baltic republics to Romania. All were caught, most quite quickly.

A notable British CIA asset from this period is known. Close to Aylesbury and the famous country seat of Mentmore Towers, was the largest CIA arms dump in Europe, at RAF Cheddington. From 1956 on, the CIA had acquired and stockpiled captured and surplus weapons in bunkers at the base, intended for Wisner's war of liberation; until the war, stocks of non-US weapons could conveniently be issued to CIA clients without revealing the source of their sponsorship. Cheddington closed as a US base in 1964, and only the ammunition bunkers on the base remained in use, as the RAOC (Royal Army Ordnance Corps) Sub-Depot, Marsworth. The CIA base was revealed in 1975[10] by the former US Air Force liaison officer to the CIA, Colonel Fletcher Prouty. For clandestine flights and radio communications with agents, the CIA had the use of orthodox US Air Force facilities in Britain.

For the British-based SAC bomber force, the priority was target intelligence. Until 1950, the bombers' targets were, for want of intelligence on industrial and military targets, exclusively cities, 'selected with the primary objective of the annihilation of population, with industrial targets incidental'.[11]

In April and May 1950, President Truman and his Secretary of Defense, Louis Johnson, were briefed on military proposals to start clandestine overflights of the Soviet Union, for photographic and radar reconnaissance, and electronic intelligence purposes. By 5 May 1950, the President had authorised the secret missions.[12] This marked the effective start of the secret US spy flight programme. The RAF had participated in similar efforts for some time, flying Mosquitos from RAF Benson and Wyton, and from Germany to photograph Soviet military targets in the east. But the new American planes had much greater range, and more advanced equipment.

Following the President's approval, two spy-plane units were established in Britain between May and July 1950. The 72nd Strategic Reconnaissance Squadron, with RB-50 reconnaissance bombers (based on the four-engined and heavily armed wartime Superfortresses) arrived at Burtonwood, having initially been set up at Sculthorpe, Norfolk. A detachment of the 91st Strategic Reconnaissance Group, with RB-45 Tornados arrived at Manston airbase in Kent. Another RB-29 (similar to the RB-50) squadron was temporarily stationed at Lakenheath. Other special missions were flown by RB-36 reconnaissance bombers on detachments from the United States to British bases such as Brize Norton, and by US Navy craft based at Port Lyautey naval air station in French-controlled Morocco.

The US Navy spy planes, Privateers and Mercators, on occasion used the US Navy's British Air Facility[13] at Blackbushe airfield, Surrey. A Privateer from Port Lyautey had the unwelcome distinction of being the first US spy plane known to have been shot down, whilst flying 14 miles inland near Leyaya in Soviet Latvia, on 8 April 1950.

Elint (electronic intelligence) equipped EP-3 Orions from the same unit as was then in Morocco, Navy Squadron 'VQ-2', still operate regularly from Britain for intelligence flights in the Baltic and northern Europe. They come now from Rota airbase in southern Spain, where they fly surveillance missions in the Mediterranean. When in Britain, the VQ-2 detachment was normally based at RAF Wyton near Huntingdon – which for three decades has been the RAF's main base for spy plane operations. Recently the US Navy Orions from Rota have worked from Mildenhall instead.

British crews joined the secret Tornado reconnaissance squadron based at Sculthorpe, and flew joint photographic and radar reconnaissance penetration missions. The RAF presumably wanted a share of the action in order to get target intelligence for its own planned atom bombs and atom bombers. The Sculthorpe group specialised in high speed, high altitude penetration of hostile territory. The joint RAF and US Air Force crews marked the start of a new and still-secret collaboration which led directly to RAF pilots flying U-2 spy missions for the CIA and SIS.

At first, the aircraft appeared in US markings. But by 1954, although they were never on the official strength of the RAF, they were repainted with RAF roundels and flown by joint RAF and USAF crews. This manoeuvre was denied, but a photograph showing the mixed crew and RAF-marked USAF plane exists (see plate 11). The markings ensured that Britain, too, would have to carry the can if any were shot down. For at least four years, the Sculthorpe Tornados flew multiple long-range spy flights into Soviet territory. It was hazardous work. Just before entering Soviet territory over Germany or Greece, the Tornado would refuel from an accompanying KB-29 tanker (also from Sculthorpe), so as to have both maximum range, and to fly at top speed to outrun pursuers. In December 1950, the second US spy plane to be shot down was an RB-45 Tornado, on a spy overflight of North Korea.

One RAF pilot who flew on the joint spy missions was Squadron Leader Johnny Crampton, now an employee of British Aerospace. Like many of his colleagues, he was decorated in 1953 and 1954 with two Air Force Crosses (AFC) in recognition of the personal risk involved in the secret overflights. But discussion of the 30-year-old Anglo-American penetration flights is still impossible, he said in 1983: 'It was an exercise which is still covered by a total security blanket'.

Other ex-RAF personnel based at Sculthorpe confirmed that the Tornados 'were going across the border'. In flights lasting over 12 hours, the spy planes could have penetrated 1,300–1,600 miles into hostile territory – far enough to reach well beyond Moscow, perhaps even the Ural Moutains. None of the British/American Tornados are known to have been shot down.

Another penetrating aircraft based in Britain was the Convair RB-36 spy plane, with mixed jet and propeller engines. According to a Swedish Air Force Colonel later convicted of spying for the Soviet Union, the RB-36s simply could not be shot down. Its operating height of more than 40,000 feet then made interception difficult; the Soviet Union's first jet interceptor, the MiG-15, only entered widespread service in 1949.

RB-29s, RB-50s, RB-36s and Navy aircraft flew 'Special Airborne Electronic Search' or 'ferret' missions, flying along and over Soviet borders, to discover and analyse defensive radars and communications. They did not need to penetrate as deeply as the target-seeking photographic flights. The CIA got involved in photographic operations with its bizarre operation 'Moby Dick', sending large numbers of high-altitude balloons equipped with spy cameras to drift across from western Europe to Japan. The programme was not a great success as, when the balloons arrived and pictures were developed, it was not usually possible to say where the balloons had flown and what they had photographed.

For bomb-aiming and navigation, however, the critical information it was necessary to get was likely targets which could be identified by radar. CIA agents sent into the Soviet Union were told to identify large metal hangars and the like, which would stand out well on radar. Neutral Sweden even contributed secretly to Strategic Air Command's intelligence programme, flying DC-3 Dakota aircraft loaded with US-provided radar analysis equipment around target areas and bombing runs in the Baltic. In June 1952, one of these DC-3s was shot down, and a Catalina searching for it was attacked soon after.[14]

The first U-2 base set up by the CIA was in Britain. It was a logical progression from the earlier spy plane types, although the U-2 programme had been developed and controlled by the CIA. The CIA were interested in wider aspects of Soviet military capabilities and developments than merely charting targets for nuclear attack, and the routes to them. Ten U-2s of the 1st Weather Reconnaissance Squadron (Provisional) were deployed to Europe in May 1956, going to Lakenheath and subsequently to Wiesbaden, Germany. Before any operational missions were flown, however, a British security débâcle caused Prime Minister Anthony Eden to withdraw the CIA's permission to operate U-2s from Britain.

On 19 April 1956, a frogman working for SIS had dived in Portsmouth harbour to spy on the keel of the Soviet warship *Ordzonikidze*, which had brought Khrushchev and Bulganin to Britain on a goodwill visit. Commander 'Buster' Crabb was never seen alive again, and the Admiralty admitted his death on a fictitious 'test dive' ten days later. When the Soviet Union published a secret exchange of notes with Britain about the fatal spy trip early in May, an embarrassed Eden claimed in Parliament that SIS had acted 'without the authority or knowledge of ministers'. He did not therefore want a repetition of the affair with the first U-2 flights.

The first U-2 flight, audaciously directly over Moscow and Leningrad, took place from Wiesbaden. Other U-2 detachments were established at Incirlik near Adana, Turkey, and Atsugi near Tokyo. Bases in Peshawar, Pakistan, and Bodo, Norway were also used. Ostensibly, the U-2 pilots were civilian employees of Lockheed. At least four RAF pilots joined this arrangement and 'left' the RAF to pose as British employees of Lockheed. They trained at Laughlin Air Force Base in Texas, and then flew (along with Powers) on U-2 missions from Adana. The dark blue-black planes carried no national markings. One of the RAF pilots under training by the CIA, Squadron Leader Christopher Walker, was killed when his U-2 crashed in Texas in 1958.

Each British U-2 flight over Soviet territory was specifically authorised by Anthony Eden or his successor, Harold Macmillan. When the U-2 story eventually broke in May 1960, Eden was particularly anxious that no hint about British participation should emerge. Yet one in five of the spy missions had in fact been flown by the RAF/SIS pilots.[15] The CIA director of the U-2 project, Richard Bissell, had his own reasons for bringing the British in as they had requested. If the US President or Secretary of State Foster Dulles were nervous and slow to approve any particular flight, the British government could approve a flight with a British pilot instead. On this, as on other occasions, the multinational Anglo-Saxon intelligence axis was able to escape the national control even of the United States.

Operation Overflight (of the Soviet Union), but not the U-2 missions, ended in 1960. Deep penetration of the Soviet Union by manned aircraft was forbidden, and peripheral incursions by any aircraft but the U-2 had become too dangerous. No other territory – including eastern Europe – remained inviolate, and China was until 1971 the victim of hundreds of spy flights, latterly by pilotless drones.

In Britain, the Tornados which had penetrated so deeply in the early 1950s had been reallocated to tactical reconnaissance, and finally, in 1959, withdrawn along with the RB-29s. With advancing electronic technology giving each ferret plane a greater capacity, and ferreting confined to peripheral reconnaissance missions, fewer were needed. Converted RB-66 'Destroyer' bombers were based at Alconbury for tactical reconnaissance. Each carried four 'Ravens' – the self-applied nickname of USAF Elint specialists[16] – in front of whom were an interception receiver, panoramic displays, and two direction-finding devices.

At Brize Norton, Strategic Air Command operated converted RB-47 Stratojet bombers with similar equipment on board. In the early 1960s, each of these bases was to see one of their aircraft shot down, casualties in the continuing electronic Cold War in the air.

This secret war between the United States, Soviet Union and their allies has gone on for decades. Radar and anti-aircraft defence screens are repeatedly penetrated in order to discover how they operate – and how, in war, to defeat them. This dangerous activity has been much more extensive than is generally known. Between 1950 and the present, the United States has lost at least 32 aircraft, forced down or shot down (including at least 4 U-2s operated by the Chinese Nationalist Air Force), and seen 60 others attacked in the course of electronic or photographic reconnaissance activity.[17] At least 140 US servicemen have died in this reconnaissance programme.

Ferret missions were not infrequently intentionally provocative, so that the extensive ground-based listening station network which ringed the Soviet Union by the mid-1950s (see Figure 5) could monitor the reactions of ground controllers and air defence commanders. In 1958, two Oxford undergraduates who had worked in British Sigint stations in Germany were jailed under the Official Secrets Act for publicly describing the provocative penetration missions in a university magazine:

> Since the Russians do not always provide the required messages to monitor, they are sometimes provoked. A planes 'loses' its way; while

> behind the frontier tape recorders excitedly read the irritated messages of Russian pilots; and when sometimes the aeroplane is forced to land an international incident is created. The famous Lancaster bomber incident near Berlin was deliberately provoked in this way.[18]

Soon after this was written, there was to be a succession of similar major international incidents:

- 27 June 1958 – CIA spy plane was shot down in the Caucasus, with nine men aboard. A secret briefing to President Eisenhower about the incident was only declassified early in 1983.
- 2 September 1958 – C-130 Hercules spy plane from Germany carrying 17 National Security Agency monitors was shot down over Soviet Armenia.
- 11 May 1960 – Gary Powers' U-2 was shot down over the Urals; the famous incident.
- 1 July 1960 – an RB-47 from Brize Norton was shot down in the Barents Sea.

The Elint-equipped RB-47 was accused of having been flying over Soviet waters, and protests were made to the British and American governments. The Russian claims were rejected, as Macmillan told an agitated House of Commons shortly afterwards (see p 58). Basic common sense suggests that on this occasion, the western account of the incident was correct, as there could have been no strategic requirement for further marginal penetration missions so soon after the U-2 incident.

The remainder of eastern Europe was not exempt from overflights, however, and these continued. In March 1964, an RB-66 from Alconbury was shot down over East Germany, after experiencing 'total navigation failure'. Seen in context, this statement was clearly phoney. Between 1960 and 1965, there were 62 separate infringements of East German airspace by T-39 and RB-66 spy planes, according to a DDR statement published in 1966.[19] In central Europe, this provocative penetration was a reciprocal activity. Between 1962 and 1964, there were 90 Soviet penetrations of West German airspace.[20]

US Air Force tactical reconnaissance aircraft in Britain have progressively reduced in number since these violent and dangerous times, even after a new reconnaissance wing arrived from France in the late 1960s. The Alconbury spy plane base (where the RB-66 in the 1964 incident was based) re-equipped twice, finishing up with three squadrons of RF-4 reconnaissance Phantoms. But two of these squadrons were withdrawn to the United States in the mid 1970s. A US army intelligence unit, the 2nd Military Intelligence Battalion, has detachments at Alconbury and Mildenhall, for photographic, infra-red or radar 'imagery exploitation'.

Strategic reconnaissance aircraft have operated continuously from Britain since President Truman authorised the first electronic spy missions in 1950. The RB-36s and RB-50s of that era were replaced first by the RB-47s, and then by RC-135s – converted C-135 transport and tanker aircraft, whose design was based on the civilian Boeing 707 airliner. After leaving Brize Norton, the 98th Strategic Wing operated RC-135s and RB-47s from the SAC base at Upper Heyford until 1970, when the US spy plane centre in Britain was moved to Mildenhall – where it remains. With codenames like 'Big Safari' and 'Covered Wagon', the RC-135 carries literally tons of new electronic sensors to explore the developing electronic environment around Soviet shores.

The primary mission of the RC-135 is to document the 'electronic order of battle' of the Soviet defenders. SAC wants to know where the radar stations and anti-aircraft missile bases are, and how defences will react if the Soviet Union is penetrated by B-52 and FB-111 nuclear bombers. But often important defence systems are turned off by the Russians to prevent just such eavesdropping. Thus such spy missions continue to be accompanied by deliberate 'provocative penetration', to measure the alertness and emergency response of the defenders.

The prominent US military journal, *Aviation Week*, detailed in 1976 the character of RC-135 and Elint missions, and those of its high-flying companion, the SR-71:

> . . . peripheral intelligence missions . . . to pinpoint locations and characteristics of potentially hostile signal emitters . . . Information of this nature helps [Strategic Air Command] to develop ways of evading troublesome emitters . . .[21]

Or, more simply, they may choose just to 'destroy the [radar] sensors'. The reason for all this activity is not to check on the threat of Soviet missile tests, but is unambiguously offensive; the purpose is to analyse:

> the environment that bombers may be directed to penetrate in the event of war . . .

During a flight of up to 17 hours from Mildenhall, automatic Elint computers on the RC-135 record Soviet radar signals on reels of 1-inch magnetic tape. When the plane returns, IBM and other computers use the tapes to provide an up-to-date map of Soviet radar stations. Prominent on recent models of the RC-135 (see plate 9) are flat panels or 'cheeks' near the nose. These contain sideways-looking radar, identifying targets and ground radar reflections that may be used to help bombers and cruise missiles navigate to their goals.

The oceans have been another theatre of secret warfare. Although the United States Navy's former fleet of spy ships did not operate from Britain, Soviet spy ships, formally known as AGIs (Auxiliary Gatherers of Intelligence), but popularly called 'trawlers', are frequent visitors to British shores. Their interests are most often centred on the emissions of radar stations on the east coast, or the Clyde and the Irish Sea, where they observe the arrival and departure of Polaris and Poseidon submarines. These selfsame submarines have also been used secretly to penetrate Soviet waters. Under Project Holystone, Naval Security Group intelligence specialists working for the NSA or CIA have boarded submarines on spy missions into the Barents Sea and other hostile waters – including, on one occasion, Vladivostock harbour. Holystone submarines intercepted communications, filmed port installations and ships through their periscopes and monitored undersea sound to record the characteristic accoustic 'signatures' of naval vessels.

In the Atlantic and Mediterranean, these exceptionally dangerous missions using missile-carrying submarines were mounted from the Holy Loch. Hawaii was the Pacific Holystone base. In 1976, the US House of Representatives investigated the Holystone project, reporting that a 'highly technical US Navy submarine reconnaissance programme' had resulted in:

> at least 9 collisions with hostile vessels in the last ten years, over 110 possible detections, and at least three press exposures. Most of the submarines carry nuclear weapons[22] . . .

The Pike Committee reported that there had been 'hundreds of missions' under Holystone, whose risk the US Navy fallaciously assessed as 'low'. The committee insisted that the programme should only continue if it could be operated at 'significantly less risk'. But a few months after this comment was made, it was revealed that the US Navy was spending millions of dollars updating its submarine Sigint collection system, the WLR-6 'Waterboy'. The new system is called 'Sea Nymph'.

Intermittently, the most exotic spy planes still in the US arsenal have operated from British bases. Three U-2s arrived at Upper Heyford in August 1962 for a so-called 'high-altitude sampling programme' over the north Atlantic. But the U-2s were still spying; two months later, another U-2 was shot down over Cuba. A solo U-2 appeared briefly at RAF Kinloss in Scotland in 1969, and other sightings occurred from time to time between 1965 and 1975, when the U-2 and its successor, the SR-71, began to be deployed to Mildenhall with increasing frequency. The spy planes operating from Britain come from Beale Air Force Base in California (U-2RS and SR-71S of the 9th Strategic Reconnaissance Wing) and Offutt Air Force Base in Nebraska (RC-135s of the 55th Strategic Reconnaissance wing).

The SR-71, the near-invulnerable successor to the U-2, began life in 1959 as a CIA project, the A-12. Nothing at all is known, even now, of where the CIA flew its A-12 photographic spy planes. The first of 18 was delivered to the CIA in 1962 and, like the first U-2s, they flew from the secret base, Watertown Strip in Nevada. Six of the now retired A-12s are missing, whether through accident or combat being a matter of conjecture. SAC began operating SR-71s – a two-seater update of the A-12 – from California in 1966. No SR-71 was ever seen at a British base until 1976. It has however been claimed that even after 1960, RAF pilots continued to participate in clandestine U-2 and SR-71 spy missions.[23] U-2s based in Britain were accused of overflying Egypt to photograph SAM-3 missile sites in the late 1960s.

The A-12, although not the SR-71, was also equipped with a pilotless drone, carried piggyback, whose existence was completely unknown until the drones were retired to a stockpile in Arizona in 1976. The drones were launched in mid-air on 1,600-mile long Mach 3 supersonic flights. The nature of their use is unknown – but their use over the USSR would not have violated the US President's 1960 promise to ban manned overflights.

US officials do not deny that the RC-135, U-2 and SR-71 aircraft regularly fly along the borders of the Soviet Union with a battery of monitoring devices aboard. Besides Mildenhall, there are U-2/SR-71 detachments at RAF Akrotiri in Cyprus, Osan in Korea and Kadena in Okinawa. RC-135s are also based in Alaska, Hellenikon near Athens and Kadena. From these bases, the USAF maintains continuous electronic surveillance along the Soviet periphery, and has directed spy planes to report on conflicts such as the Middle East wars. The U-2s now in Cyprus have, *inter alia*, the more pacific task of monitoring the disengagement agreement signed between Israel and Arab states after the 1973 Yom Kippur war.

On average, the Soviet Union has four Elint planes snooping round its borders every hour of the day. When a Soviet fighter shot down a

Korean jumbo jet which had made an unauthorised crossing of the Sea of Okhotsk in September 1983, Soviet authorities blamed the controversial tragedy on mistaken identification of the plane as an RC-135. RC-135s were admitted by the United States to be continuously operating in the area as the incident occurred.

The RC-135s and US Navy EP-3s from Mildenhall regularly fly in the Baltic, where they have often been photographed along with British, German and Soviet aircraft on a spy circuit that weary Swedish Air Force officers call the 'tram run'. The US Navy spy planes spend about a week in England every month, updating their knowledge of Baltic coastal defences in anticipation of naval operations in the area.

The high-flying SR-71 respects no national boundary or legal airspace restrictions anywhere in the world, save that it avoids deep penetration of the Soviet Union (and latterly China). More than nine hundred attempts have been made to shoot down the SR-71 'Blackbird', since it began overflying hostile territory in the early 1960s – Cuba, Vietnam, China and Egypt included.[24] None have succeeded. At over 80,000 feet, it flies too high and too fast. Despite the promise to refrain from manned overflight of the Soviet Union after 1960, there is evidence that SR-71 pilots do regularly challenge Soviet fighters.

Viktor Belenko, the Soviet pilot who defected to Japan in 1976 bringing his MiG-25 with him, described in his autobiography how the SR-71s flew off the coast of Russia:

> taunting and toying with MiG-25s sent up to intercept them, scooting up to altitudes the Soviet planes could not reach and circling leisurely above them, or dashing off at speeds the Russians could not match

Mildenhall's SR-71 unit has recently been increased to two (see Chapter 10). But US spokesmen at Mildenhall say that they 'don't even acknowledge that there are any reconnaissance aircraft' on the base. Early in 1983, United States national markings were removed from the all-black planes. In nuclear war, SR-71s have the additional task of 'post-strike reconnaissance'. Flying over the holocaust that had been wrought alike in hostile and friendly countries, their sensors would report to SAC and the US 'National Command Authority' about what still existed of the resources and cities of the United States and its allies, and what had survived in the Soviet Union and eastern Europe that then remained to be struck.

The bombs that strike eastern Europe and the USSR may come from the ground, as well as from aircraft or missiles. 'Unconventional warfare' – including guerrilla atomic, biological and chemical attacks in enemy-controlled territory – is a key part of all US European Command plans for conflict in Europe. Hundreds of US Special Atomic Demolition Munitions, which can be carried by one person in a backpack, are stockpiled in readiness for partisan nuclear combat.

Some, at least, of this unconventional army will operate from Britain, probably including airlift teams to fly US Special Forces detachments and their weapons behind enemy lines. According to Top Secret 1962 US European Command war plans leaked to British newspapers[25], US Special Forces would attempt to raise guerrilla armies in eastern Europe more than 100,000 strong, to mount sabotage, subversion and psychological warfare operations against Eastern bloc governments, and help downed aircrew and other military personnel to escape or evade capture. Using atomic mines and other secret weapons supplies, the CIA and Special Forces-led guerrillas would harass and destroy Soviet or Warsaw Pact 'communications, transportation and supply systems, installations and facilities'. According to the leaked plans, their final mission would be to prepare for the vanquishment of the Soviet Union, and:

> Assist United States sponsored indigenous leaders in establishing control over Soviet Bloc political and social structures . . .

The Special Forces, or 'Green Berets', are the *corps d'elite* of the US Army, championed by John F. Kennedy at the beginning of the Vietnam War as a vanguard to combat subversion and contain communism in South-east Asia. Their motto is 'De oppresso liber' – 'To free the oppressed'. Each 12-man Special Forces detachment is supposedly capable of generating freedom fighters, US-style, at the formidable rate of a fully-trained 500-strong battalion of partisan guerrillas during each successive month of war behind the lines in Europe.

But the liberation dream quickly faded in Vietnam, and the Green Berets' reputation was sullied. Four years after Kennedy's death, his brothers Robert and Edward were leading US opposition to these commitments. But in 1983, President Reagan turned the clock back to these early days of Vietnam, championing the Special Forces as an undercover force to keep the free world free and backing a boost in their numbers.

After war begins, clandestine operations throughout Europe will be run from the wartime HQ of the Special Operations Task Force Europe (SOTFE). According to the 1962 plans, this base would have been at

Fontainebleau. Supplies would have been airlifted to the east from a 'Special Forces Operational Base' at Orleans.

After US forces were expelled from France in 1966, the 10th Special Forces Group (Airborne) – the key unit in the secret war plans – moved to Bad Tolz in West Germany, a mountainous training area in the Bavarian Alps close to Salzburg in Austria. SOTFE's planning staff moved, with the US European Command to which it is attached, to Vaihingen, near Stuttgart. According to 1976 US Congressional hearings, the SOTFE nucleus of planning staff in Stuttgart now consists of 21 officers and men. In war, however, the commander of SOTFE is responsible for directing Army and Navy Special Forces units, Air Force airlift teams, and a SOTFE (CIA) Liaison Group. Britain is involved in SOTFE operations in at least three ways:

- Before fighting starts, non-NATO parts of the US European Command HQ – which would include the Support Operations Task Force Europe Commander – will move to an underground war headquarters at High Wycombe.
- The unit responsible for flying supplies behind enemy lines, according to the plans, is the 513th Tactical Airlift Wing; this unit is now at Mildenhall, Suffolk.
- The US Navy Special Forces unit in Europe, known as SEALS, is based at Machrihanish, on the Mull of Kintyre.
- Airlifts into enemy territory would be mounted from the secret Special Forces Operational Base, established in a rear zone away from the front line – in 1962 at Orleans. Special Forces exercises, using 'covert infiltration' aircraft, are held at least once a year at Sculthorpe and/or Wethersfield airbases in England – suggesting that the rehearsals may be in preparation for using one of the bases as the Special Forces Operations Base in war.

The existence of SOTFE or the Special Forces is not secret, but all aspects of their plans are. It is one of six separately constituted forces at the disposition of the US Commander-in-Chief, Europe, in war.[26] The SOTFE chief would act in conjunction with the Commander, CIA Force Europe (COMCIAEUR), whose task would be to send in the thousands of nationalist mercenaries trained and waiting in Germany. By 1956, there were 'five thousand . . . in camps around various parts of Germany, trained and armed to start a clandestine campaign'.[27]

The secret plans for a 'CIA Force Europe' are a remarkable reminder that the CIA is basically an activist clandestine intervention organisation, rather than a passive intelligence-gathering agency. Throughout the 1950s, CIA Chief Allen Dulles and his bitterly anti-communist Director of Plans (ie, covert operations), Frank Wisner, continued to believe that it would suffice for the United States merely to light a torch, and throughout Europe oppressed hordes would arise to throw off the yoke of Soviet oppression. In war, the task of the CIA Force Europe would be 'set [occupied] Europe ablaze' – the mission that Churchill had set the CIA's forerunner in this regard, Britain's Wartime Special Operations Executive. The US European Command plans give COMCIAEUR the job of conducting:

> covert psychological warfare operations ... in support of [US] national efforts ... [and to] endeavor to assure that satellite peoples stage insurrections phased to support and to exploit opportunities growing from the ground battle scheme of maneuver ...

Some 35 Special Forces detachments would be landed in enemy territory – including Norway, Sweden, Finland, Austria, Greece and Turkey if occupied. With the help of the CIA Force Europe, they would set up 49 Guerrilla Warfare zones and 6 subversive activities zones, with which to fight for liberation. Within six months, according to detailed estimates signed by the SOTFE commander, Colonel Charles Boswell, the CIA would have raised 74,500 guerrillas to fight for the United States.

According to SOTFE's basic operations plan (Oplan 10-1), both US Special Forces and partisans might employ nuclear or chemical weapons in this conflict:

> National policy will permit, during time of war, the use of indigenous personnel to assist in the arming, employment and firing of nuclear weapons ...

The weapon they would normally use is a true mini-bomb – the W54 Special Atomic Demolition Munition. In its lightest configuration (warhead only), it weighs only 58.6 lbs. An SADM mine containing a W54 warhead is about a foot in diameter, 15 inches long, weighs less than 163 lbs, and has a nuclear yield selectable between the equivalents of 10 tons to 1 kiloton of TNT. A larger 'medium' ADM can be air-dropped to guerrilla forces, and carried by vehicle. With a yield of up to 15 kilotons, this 'medium' sabotage device is equivalent in power to the bombs which destroyed Hiroshima and Nagasaki.

Another annexe to the SOTFE plan authorises the use of 'chemical and biological munitions':

> Specific targets for the employment of chemical and biological munitions, which include defoliants, herbicides and anti-crop agents, will

> be designated as the situation and operational requirements dictate . . . If requests are approved, COMSOTFE co-ordinates details of delivery of CB munitions to operational area.

In 'Psyops' – psychological operations – Special Forces teams are directed to:

> condition the people of Soviet Bloc nations to believe that to accept and to support US Special Forces personnel is action in furtherance of their own idealistic and nationalistic aspirations; prompt the people of Soviet Bloc nations to take active measure in opposition to control by Soviet and Soviet Bloc dominated governments. Such opposition should be channeled into forms of guerilla warfare, subversion, formation of dissident groups, etc . . .

The Special Forces unit permanently in Britain, Naval Special Warfare Unit 2, is a 37-strong cadre at Machrihanish, training for covert infiltration and demolition by air, sea, or submarine. They exercise in and around the Mull of Kintyre, the southern tip of a beautiful and remote Highland peninsula – whose one-time quality of isolation from the worst of the twentieth century had been sought out by earlier residents such as Scottish novelist Naomi Mitchison, and former Beatle Paul McCartney.

The men at Machrihanish, also known as SEALS (for Sea/Air/Land operations), first undergo a gruelling 25-week training course in California. After BUD/S – the Basic Underwater Demolition/SEAL training course – they may go in groups of 20 to Machrihanish for six months further training and exercises. In war, about 1,000 US Navy SEALS would be divided between Machrihanish, and its sole sister unit, Naval Special Warfare Unit 1 at Subic Bay in the Philippines.

Naval Special Warfare Unit 2 was set up at Machrihanish in mid-1981. Gullible journalists on the *Guardian* and *Daily Mail* who learned of the unit's existence two years later were assured that it was there to combat piracy and fight terrorists operating at sea. This was ingenious and audacious misdirection by the Machrihanish commanding officer; SEALS *are* pirates and terrorists (in war). US Navy representatives officially offer only the bromide that the unit has to 'maintain readiness to conduct operations in support of NATO in times of war'.

The mission of the Naval Special Warfare Group was described to the US Congress Committee on Appropriations in February 1980:

> The special warfare group conduct clandestine and unconventional warfare. Various teams operate against targets near the water . . . [they]

> are basically a further development and advancement of what began in World War II as underwater demolition teams . . .

A new aircraft hangar was built at Machrihanish, apparently to house an MC-130 Hercules transport plane converted for special operations. Codenamed 'Combat Talon', the MC-130E's most celebrated fitting is the 'Fulton apparatus', or STARS (see p 251), with which the black-painted, low-flying plane can pluck an agent 200 feet below off the ground and spirit him or her away to safety. The Machrihanish unit also has a 36-foot 'Seafox' boat to use in operations and training around the Highland coast, including rock climbing and parachute drops. The boat is normally moored in Campbeltown harbour.

The secret Combat Talon aircraft are regular visitors to Britain, arriving periodically at Mildenhall, Sculthorpe, Wethersfield – and, latterly Machrihanish – for Special Forces exercises. One Combat Talon pilot, Lieutenant Bernard Moon, recently offered this description of his work[28]:

> Our speciality is covert infiltration and exfiltration at ultra low altitudes at night, using special avionics for terrain masking, navigation and airdrops.

Moon wrote as a member of one of the two MC-130 squadrons whose covert operations planes regularly come to Britain. These are the 7th and 8th Special Operations Squadrons, based respectively at Rhein Main airbase near Frankfurt, and Hurlburt Field Army airbase in Florida.

The 'special avionics' fitted to the transport plane does indeed permit it to fly at extremely low altitudes, terrain-following like an F-111 bomber to avoid being detected by radar. Well-suited to a major role in a James Bond[29] film, gadgets on board the MC-130 also include anti-radar paint, radar-jamming countermeasures equipment, infra-red surveillance television, and accurate navigation aids including star sights.

Every April and May since 1970, at least four or five MC-130s from these two squadrons visit Sculthorpe or Wethersfield for the major US Special Forces exercise, now codenamed 'Flintlock'. They are accompanied by many specialised supporting aircraft. In 1982 and 1983, the MC-130s were joined by EC-130 jamming and airborne control aircraft, codenamed 'Rivet Rider' and 'Comfy Levi', from US-based reserves. Of the two British airfields used for Flintlock exercises, Wethersfield – which, unlike Sculthorpe has not been earmarked for any known reserve US Air Force squadrons – is most likely to be designated the Special Forces wartime Operations Base.

At Frankfurt's Rhein Main airbase, aircrews of the Frankfurt 7th Special Operations Squadron are nevertheless on constant alert to be able to carry an agent 'deep into heavily-defended enemy territory' 48 hours after first being given the job.

Apart from Flintlock, joint exercises are held regularly with British units; in November 1981, US Special Forces exercised at the SAS's premier undercover operations training area, Pontrilas camp near Hereford. The United States in its turn provided highly unusual on-the-job training for a selected few from the SAS in the 1960s. Rumours that members of the SAS had secretly joined the US Special Forces in Vietnam were confirmed when, in June 1969, the SAS Regiment's normally discreet magazine *Mars and Minerva* printed a photograph of SAS Sergeant Dick Meadows receiving the US Silver Star for his service in Vietnam.

The United Kingdom had not, of course, been at war with Vietnam. But through the intelligence axis it had given its support through this and other parts of the secret apparatus. Both before and during B-52 raids on the cities of North Vietnam, the British/Australian Sigint station in Hong Kong, Little Sai Wan – designated UKC201 in the international Sigint network – analysed and reported the radio signals of the Vietnamese air defence units to the US Air Force. At Little Sai Wan, the station commander sought to rationalise this conflict with international law by assigning North Vietnamese interception tasks to Australian staff at the station (whose government had entered the war). But for Britain it was participation, by any other name, in the war.

CIA agents in Britain have not confined their operations to the elaborate plans for the liberation of Europe laid by SOTFE. In the last 30 years, the CIA in Britain has infiltrated and reported on trade unions, mounted major propaganda and psychological warfare campaigns, and established support facilities for operations in other parts of the world.

In April 1975, Prime Minister Harold Wilson asserted to the House of Commons that everything the CIA did in Britain was known to the government. This is perhaps a reasonable view from above; British intelligence staff are no doubt normally informed in general terms about any CIA operation which involves British facilities or personnel. But that is not the same thing as the government knowing, or knowing everything.

Within the secret world, 'unilateral' or 'US eyes only' operations are the rule, not the exception. There is ample evidence of CIA unilateral political or subversive activity in friendly, allied, and English-speaking countries – or, as mentioned above, via 'service-to-service' contacts which exclude national political authorities. But if Britain has had special treatment in these affairs, it has been because British security and intelligence services have been ready to participate alongside the CIA in political operations within the UK as well as outside.

CIA activist operations – whether intelligence gathering or major covert operations – may have political or military consequences for a host country as severe as those resulting from overt military action. Yet British control is much more tenuous than in the case of the open military bases, or even the secret Sigint stations (where an agreement, UKUSA, is known to exist). The Anglo-Saxon axis in secret intelligence is not reflected in any known treaty. It consists of a series of *ad hoc* arrangements between two clandestine agencies, one of whose key professional skills is the art of the 'plausible denial'.

Since the creation of the CIA, liaison with the British Secret Intelligence Service (SIS) has been almost as close as that of GCHQ with NSA. Inside the secret intelligence world, special in-service jargon is used by the practitioners to identify and strengthen their special relationship. SIS operatives call themselves the 'Friends'; the CIA are the 'Cousins'. CIA staff, as is well known, call the agency the 'Company'. They have a variety of names for the Brits, not all kind, but the official one is the Company's secret cryptonym – a code consisting of two letters indicating the key country concerned, and some random phrase. Britain's letters are SM; the Secret Intelligence Service is 'SMOTH'.

A large Central Intelligence Agency staff, estimated at between 50 and 70, work in London. Most are accommodated in a CIA wing on the third floor of the American Embassy in Grosvenor Square, Mayfair. The Chief of Station heads the Embassy's 'political liaison' section, a cover for the CIA team liaising with SIS. The other CIA unit within the Embassy is the Joint Reports and Research Unit, who swap intelligence assessments with Britain's Joint Intelligence Staff in the Cabinet Office. CIA staff are also responsible for all embassy telecommunications links, and run a 13-person Area Telecommunications Office for the US State Department.[30]

The Chief of Station is the CIA's ambassador to SIS; the attractive London posting has usually been held by a senior member from the covert action, rather than the intelligence, wing of the Agency. In the 1970s, the CIA has been represented in London by Cord Meyer, Jr, then Edward Proctor, and from 1980 until 1983 by Richard F. Stolz, a veteran of the Company. His previous overseas post had been as Chief of Station in Yugoslavia. Both Stolz and the National Security

Agency's SUSLO (Special US Liaison Officer), also based at Grosvenor Square, are accredited diplomats. The current SUSLO (in 1983), Dr Don C. Jackson, was formerly the NSA's Deputy Director for Management Services. Both Stolz and Jackson are disguised as 'Political Attachés' in diplomatic staff lists.

Besides SUSLO and the CIA political liaison team, the Defense Intelligence Agency (DIA), the FBI and the US Air Force National Reconnaissance Office (NRO) all have liaison and operations staff in Britain. Two FBI officers, identified only as embassy 'Legal Attachés', work with MI5, the Security Service. 'DIALL' – the Defense Intelligence Agency Liaison London – has its office inside the Ministry of Defence main building in Whitehall. The NRO – which runs US spy satellites – has a Satellite Control Facility at Oakhanger, Hampshire, and liaises with the Royal Air Force's Joint Air Reconnaissance Intelligence Centre (JARIC) at Brampton Park, Huntingdon – close to the British and US spy plane bases at Wyton, Alconbury, and Mildenhall.

CIA-originated intelligence, however, is principally the product of 'human sources' or Humint – rather than Sigint from monitoring posts, or Photographic or Imagery Intelligence ('Photint', 'Imint') from spy planes and satellites. Secret agent reports are produced and marked with codes to indicate their sensitivity, and then swapped at the rate of many thousands every year. British Humint reports sent to the CIA are called C-X reports; the CIA's return supply is marked Top Secret-Remarkable. The Australian Secret Intelligence Service, which also participates in these intelligence exchanges, classifies its agents' reports Top Secret-Oyster (a mollusc known for its ability to stay clammed shut).

Much that happened in the early days of joint subversive activities by SIS and CIA around the world has now been chronicled. In 1950, they were landing hundreds of saboteurs in Albania – all of whom died, betrayed by Kim Philby. Under Operation Ajax in 1953, SIS and the CIA successfully deposed the Iranian premier, Mohammed Mossadeq, and installed the Shah for a 26-year term in his place. There were other joint conspiracies in Syria and Iraq, and a decade later, the Colonial Office, SIS, and MI5 sat back whilst the CIA fomented a general strike and racial strife in British Guiana (now Guyana) to oust the leftist premier, Dr Cheddi Jaggan. Through the years, in Africa, the Middle East and South America, the two agencies appear often to have worked on the principle that the right to have the government of their choice installed in other nations is an Anglo-American birthright.

Western European countries have not been exempt, even recently, from covert CIA interference in their affairs. In the 1972 Italian parliamentary elections, the CIA spent $10 million backing 'political parties, affiliated organisations and 21 individual candidates'.[31] Over the previous 20 years, the US had already pumped in $65 million. But a CIA-sponsored attitude survey in 1970 concluded that more money was needed. According to the Pike Committee, which investigated CIA covert action in 1976:

> American observers concluded that another 'quick fix' was necessary to see our clients through the next vote . . . A major political party received $3.4 million; a political organisation created and supported by CIA, $3.4 million; other organisations and parties, a total of $1.3 million.[32]

Whether such subsidies have been used directly to interfere in British elections must remain a matter of conjecture.

In the 1950s and 1960s, all US military units in Britain were instructed to beat the propaganda drum in a lengthy 'Cold War Activities' campaign. According to the US Navy's 1961 Cold War Plan, cold warriors should utilise US military forces 'in appropriate ways to reinforce and support political, economic, cultural, technological, ideological and psychological measures'. But the campaign was secret:

> It is necessary for the United States to avoid the onus of perpetuating the cold war . . . Public reference to US cold war activities is to be avoided.

But actual details of the 'Cold War Activities' plans focus almost entirely on such events as band shows and baseball 'Little League' matches, which were reported by the US Air Force in Britain to have produced 'a desirable mixing of American and British youngsters of impressionable age'.

CIA agents have penetrated British trade unions. One such operative was Edwin Wilson, later a renegade who set up a terrorist training camp in Libya in the mid-1970s. On 20 December 1982, Wilson was convicted on six charges of smuggling arms and war materials to Libya. He was fined $200,000 and sentenced to 15 years in jail.

In late 1950s and early 1960s, Wilson was associated with a joint CIA/Naval Intelligence operation known as Task Force 157. The Task Force set up maritime front companies and, according to the *Wall Street Journal*, 'learned a lot by infiltrating maritime trade unions'.[33] Wilson, a full time Task Force 157 employee between 1971 and 1976, had a decade before been one of its undercover agents, according to colleagues. Starting with the American longshoremen's (dockers) union, he moved to London to infiltrate the docks branch of the Transport and General Workers Union (TGWU). Subsequently, he moved on to a similar task in the Netherlands. From there, he sent a courier regularly to Britain, carrying CIA funds with which to pay off the informers and agents he had recruited in the TGWU.

After interviewing ten former members of the Task Force in 1982, the *Journal* reported:

> Some task force members concede that they secretly broke laws in certain countries by recruiting foreign nationals who spied in part on their own governments.

The CIA's obsession with covert action was eloquently and impressively unfolded and analysed in a 1974 book which came close to blowing the whistle on the CIA's largest-known independent British operation. The book, *The CIA and the Cult of Intelligence*, by ex-CIA executive Victor Marchetti and ex-State Department intelligence specialist John Marks, became the first volume in American history to be censored before publication.

US courts permitted the CIA to excise some of the authors' revelations, and the book was published with blank spaces instead. Where the spaces were in the published version had been details of at least three CIA operations in Britain – an international news and features agency, a secret agent radio station, and a covert office, codenamed LCPIPPIT, for organising CIA operations in African and Middle Eastern countries.

The agent radio station was identified as being about a hundred miles from London, and near Banbury[34] – evidently a reference to a CIA communications team within the US Air Force radio station at Croughton, a few miles away. The station, with a 'transmitter annexe' at Barford St John, includes both military and 'civil' staff. Military staff are not permitted to visit the civil section, all of which is ostensibly part of the US Defense Communications Agency network. The civil section includes a satellite tracking dish concealed inside a white radome, which was installed in the early 1970s. Croughton may now be a ground station for CIA covert communications satellites – which enable agents or implanted electronic sensors in hostile territory to communicate to their US controllers by direct satellite link. An agent's satellite radio transmitter can be carried in a small suitcase; US covert communications links of this kind were used in 1982 by SAS teams operating in the Falklands War.

The CIA's covert London office, LCPIPPIT, is a more secure centre for briefing and debriefing agents than the US Embassy itself. But LCPIPPIT appears to be located so close by as to make little or no difference to security. The CIA team appear to have offices and a radio station in a house in Upper Brook Street, W1 – round the corner from the Embassy, and next door to the London bureau of the prestigious *Washington Post*.

But the biggest operation detailed by Marchetti and Marks was Forum World Features, a features agency. For a decade, the CIA funded Forum to produce a slanted journalism service for third-world newspapers – and ultimately, more than 30 US newspapers – that portrayed world events the way the CIA wanted.

This operation continued until April 1975, when it was abruptly closed – shortly before the London weekly *Time Out*, in a celebrated exposé, printed a 1968 CIA internal memorandum from the London Chief of Station Cord Meyer to Director Richard Helms setting out exactly what Forum was doing in London:

> Forum World Feature Ltd (FWF) is an international news feature service located in London and incorporated in Delaware, whose overt aim is to provide on a commercial basis a comprehensive weekly service covering international affairs, economics, science and medicine . . . In its first two years, FWF has provided the United States with a significant means to counter Communist prop[aganda] and has become a respected features service . . . FWF was created from the residue of Forum Service, an activity of the Congress for Cultural Freedom, from which CIA withdrew its support in 1966.[35]

Below, in manuscript, was added the note that Forum was:

> Run w[ith] the knowledge and co-operation of British Intelligence.

Indeed it had been. In 1970, Forum took over some of SIS's clandestine propaganda assets – journalists who had worked for SIS-sponsored British news agencies in Africa and the Middle East. The agencies – such as the Arab News Agency Ltd, set up during the Second World War as a barely disguised British propaganda outlet – were part of a large group which had exclusive rights to gather and distribute news for Reuters.

Four years before Forum closed, its director, right-wing activist and former *Economist* journalist Brian Crozier, set up an 'Institute for the Study of Conflict' (ISC). Just as Forum World Features was the offshoot of the CIA's Congress for Cultural Freedom, so the Institute grew out of a 'Current Affairs Research Services Center' within Forum itself. Seed money to set up ISC was provided by John Hay Whitney, the American publisher who had fronted for the CIA as the ultimate owner of Forum.

Links between the Institute and the CIA-funded Forum World Features were denied by Brian Crozier and his colleagues until late in 1975, when someone in ISC anonymously leaked photocopies of many of the Institute's key files to *Time Out.* The documents showed how the Institute – which has periodic media publicity successes with reports on such matters as 'subversion in industry' – had originated inside FWF.

## Notes

1 Chapman Pincher, *Inside Story*, p 38, Sidgwick and Jackson, 1978.
2 Richard Fletcher traced how some aspects of British social democracy were supported in the 1950s by CIA-funded cultural organisations in: Fred Hirsch and Richard Fletcher, *CIA and the Labour Movement*, Spokesman Books, 1977. The role of the CIA in international trade unions is described in Don Thomson and Rodney Larson, *Where were you, brother?*, War on Want publications, 1978.
3 *New Statesman*, 2 March 1979.
4 *Australian Financial Review*, 29 April 1977. On 5 May 1977, the then former Prime Minister Gough Whitlam read its full text into the Australian *Hansard.*
5 Richard Hall, *The Secret State*, Cassell Australia, 1978.
6 *National Times*, 6 May 1983.
7 Satellite ground stations for intelligence and other purposes and signals intelligence are described in Chapter 7.
8 In Britain, they rank upwards from RESTRICTED to CONFIDENTIAL, SECRET and TOP SECRET. Beyond TOP SECRET, other *ad hoc* agreements prescribe special codewords for specific operations, which are themselves secret.
9 *Ny Tid* (Oslo), June, July 1977; *New Statesman*, 2 June 1978.
10 Granada TV, *World in Action*, 17 June 1975.
11 Rosenberg, *op cit.*
12 *ibid.*
13 From 1942 until 1954, this Facility was at Hendon airfield in north London, and some of the spy planes operated from the Bovingdon US Air Force base. The Naval Air Facility was at Blackbushe from 1955 to 1959, and then at West Malling in Kent. In 1964, it moved to join the Air Force at Mildenhall, where it remains.
14 *Folket i Bild* (Stockholm), 19 April 1973.
15 Leonard Mosley, *Dulles*, pp 369–70, Hodder and Stoughton, 1978.
16 Most Ravens and former Ravens belong to a special intelligence society, called the 'Association of Old Crows'.
17 Most of these incidents between are listed in 'The Silent War: Electronic Spying', by John M Carroll, *Electronics* (US), 20 April 1964.
18 *Isis*, 26 February 1958.
19 E. H. Cookridge, *Gehlen – Spy of the Century*, p 315, Corgi, 1972.
20 Carroll, *op cit.*
21 *Aviation Week and Space Technology*, 10 May 1976.
22 Report of the House Select Committee on Intelligence (Pike Committee), 1976; *Village Voice* (New York), 20 September 1976. The original report was classified Top Secret.
23 *Observer*, 11 March 1979.

24 *Washington Post*, 9 January 1983.
25 See Chapter 2, note 18.
26 The other four, excluding COMCIAEUR, are the Commanders in Chief US Army, Europe; US Navy, Europe; US Air Force, Europe; and the Military Assistance and Advisory Groups attached to embassies in some countries.
27 Leonard Mosley, *Dulles*, p 325, Hodder and Stoughton, 1978.
28 *Air International* (London), October 1980.
29 The STARS apparatus was used in the James Bond film *Thunderball.*
30 *Leveller*, January 1977; see also Philip Agee and Lou Wolf (eds), *Dirty Work: the CIA in Western Europe*, Zed Press, London, and Lyle Stuart Inc, USA, 1978.
31 From the 'Pike Report', the unpublished 1976 Report of the House of Representatives Select Committee on Intelligence (see note 22); also published in the UK (as *CIA: the Pike Report*) by Spokesman Books, 1977.
32 *ibid.*
33 See *Wall Street Journal*, 11 November 1982.
34 Victor Marchetti and John D. Marks, *The CIA and the Cult of Intelligence*, Jonathan Cape, 1974 and 1975.
35 *Time Out*, 20 June 1975.

# 6 *Surveillance Centre*

Exotic military systems and weapons are, inevitably, electronic. US forces in Britain and Europe have assembled a lengthy lexicon of codenames for their computer networks and communications systems. They have also developed extremely elaborate devices with which to spy on and subvert enemy electronics.

Under the rubric of $C^3I$ – for Command, Control, Communications and Intelligence Systems – the Pentagon is now buying and deploying billions of dollars worth of electronics, the key purpose of which is to keep some lines of military communication intact under nuclear bombardment. They range from 'Night Watch' on high – the US Presidential flying command post – to 'Clarinet Pilgrim' in the depths – a link to nuclear missile submarines. Some of the names and electronic systems are rather odder than these examples. Who, for example, was the sardonic nuclear-war planner who invented 'Cemetery Net'? This is the codename for a radio link network, constructed since 1976, through which US authorities would authorise the unleashing of nuclear warfare in Europe.

US bases and facilities in Britain play an extensive role in command, control, communications and intelligence arrangements. These include a plethora of satellite terminals and communications stations, switching centres, command and control computers – some airborne – and a major network of signals intelligence (Sigint) and other surveillance and intelligence-gathering facilities.

Sigint activities conducted by US and British agencies have reached the same scale and complexity as the overhead reconnaissance operations of the US Air Force and CIA. Britain and the United States had begun collaborating extensively on Sigint during the Second World War, exchanging personnel and codebreaking information under the terms of the BRUSA (British-US) agreement signed on 17 May 1943. The subsequent, postwar agreement, UKUSA – signed in 1947 – then bound the communications intelligence agencies of the United Kingdom, the United States, Canada, Australia, and New Zealand together to collaborate on the interception and collection of foreign signals, and to share the intelligence results. There were four signatory agencies:

- Government Communications Headquarters (GCHQ), Eastcote, London (later Cheltenham) – for the United Kingdom.
- Armed Forces Security Agency (AFSA), Washington (later the National Security Agency, NSA) – for the United States of America.
- Communications Branch of the National Research Council (CBNRC), Ottawa – for Canada.
- Defence Signals Branch (later the Defence Signals Division, DSD), Melbourne – for the Commonwealth of Australia.[1]

Each of the four main participants took responsibility for co-ordinating signals intelligence in one portion of the globe, GCHQ's territory being Africa, and Europe east to the Ural Mountains. The agencies share procedures for identifying and labelling Sigint material, and have developed a unified communications network – relying, in the 1980s, extensively on satellite communications relays, including special-purpose Sigint satellites, poised 32,000 miles away in space.

Sigint has two sub-branches: Comint and Elint. Comint is defined in the NSA's fundamental directive, NSCID-6 (National Security Council Intelligence Directive 6), as 'technical and intelligence information derived from foreign communications by other than the intended recipients'. Elint is intelligence gathered from 'foreign non-communications' – such as radar signals.

Voluminous International Regulations on Sigint – IRSIG for short – prescribe security procedures, including 'indoctrination', which Sigint staff must obey. Finished Sigint material is never classified lower than Secret, and is protected by special codewords, for each of which a special clearance is required. At the very least, a contemporary Sigint report will be designated Top Secret UMBRA. Any Sigint message, even concerning personnel, is always marked 'Handle via Comint Channels Only' or HVCCO. Comint signal channels have, above all, to be invulnerable to enemy codebreaking efforts, and therefore receive the highest available level of communications security.

As international ambassadors of Sigint, each agency appoints senior officials to work as liaison staff at the others' headquarters. After the NSA was set up in 1952, the United States sent a Senior US Liaison Officer to London, and set up a Special US Liaison Office (SUSLO) and SUSLO communications centre beside the US Naval headquarters in Grosvenor Square. A large SUSLO detachment of NSA and US Navy staff, at least 60 strong, works within GCHQ's extensive Cheltenham offices. SUSLO's British communications links are provided and operated by the US Naval Communications Unit, London. The Grosvenor Square building also houses the European headquarters of the Naval Security Group – the US Navy's Sigint apparatus.

In Washington, GCHQ officials work at a corresponding UK Liaison Office. Sporting a large royal crest and the 'EIIR' legend on its door, UKLO has its own suite of offices inside the NSA headquarters, Fort Meade, between Washington and Baltimore.

Signals intelligence officials consider their work to be so valuable that all public attention should be completely prohibited. But details of the operation of the Sigint intelligence axis were accurately and damagingly revealed by two NSA defectors at a press conference in Moscow on 6 September 1960. The exactitude with which they described NSA activities was forgotten as quickly as possible in the West. Condemnation of their treachery was mingled with homosexual and other slurs heaped on their heads by security investigators in the United States, who managed to forget in their reports that the defectors – Bernon Mitchell and William Martin – had told the world what NSA was about. Their Moscow revelations were reprinted in full, however, in the *New York Times*[2]:

> The National Security Agency includes a special group, the United Kingdom Liaison Office (UKLO), which is staffed by British citizens. Likewise, in the British Communications Intelligence organisation called GCHQ, there is a corresponding NSA liaison group . . .
>
> Britain and the United States exchange information as to cryptanalytic methods and results in reading the code systems of other nations, and their respective networks of radio intercept systems supplement one another . . .
>
> We know from working at NSA [that] the United States reads the secret communications of more than forty nations, including its own allies . . .
>
> NSA keeps in operation more than 2,000 manual intercept positions . . . Both enciphered and plain text communications are monitored from almost every nation in the world, including the nations on whose soil the intercept bases are located . . .

The Second World War had left Britain and GCHQ with an extensive network of Sigint stations in operation; some fixed in Britain, others, operated by the Navy, Army or RAF now, forward in Germany and scattered across Europe from Gibraltar to Habbiniyah in Iraq. The agency continued to monitor the signals and break the codes of allies and friends, as well as of past or future belligerents.

After the signing of the UKUSA pact, a new chain of stations began operating along the boundaries of the Western sphere of influence, monitoring the signals of Soviet ground and air forces. British Sigint outposts were established on the Elbe near Hamburg, and elsewhere in the north of the Allied Zone, in Austria, and secretly in Iran. US listening posts were set up in central and southern Germany and later in Turkey, Italy and Spain. Another secret US Sigint base – Kagnew Station at Asmara in Eritrea – was taken over from the British in 1941, and later grew to become, until its closure in 1970, one of the largest intercept stations in the world.

In Sigint planning, Britain's position to the west of the USSR was far from disadvantageous. Unlike radar signals which can only be gathered by ground stations or ferret aircraft on (or over) target borders, the high frequency (HF) radio signals used for normal communications travel over the horizon, bouncing between the ground and the ionosphere. The way in which radio signals travel can often be fickle, affected strongly by weather and solar conditions. It is typical of this uncertain world that quite remote and unexpected sites could be discovered to be endowed with good and reliable qualities of radio reception.

Chicksands Priory, a medieval building and country estate near Bedford, was one such site. In 1941, hundreds of RAF wireless interception staff gradually took over the Priory, stringing dozens of aerials across the hills of the 2,000-acre estate. It was soon discovered to be a remarkably good site for intercepting German communications from Berlin, Poland, and the Eastern front. It became the most productive intercept site for the top level of German High Command signals that were deciphered nearby at GCHQ's predecessor, the Government Code and Cypher School, Bletchley Park, and sent on from there, as ULTRA intelligence, to Allied commanders and heads of states.

When the US Air Force sought their own source for the interception of strategic signals from eastern Europe, Chicksands Priory was given to them. As 'RAF Chicksands', it developed from 1950 onwards as one of the three main strategic USAF interception sites in Europe. (The others were San Vito dei Normanni, near Brindisi in Italy, and Karamursel near Istanbul in Turkey.) Chicksands still houses the 6950th Electronic Security Group of the US Air Force Electronic Security Command (at that time known as the USAF Security Service, or USAFSS).

Antennae which had plucked the signals of the Luftwaffe and the Nazi High Command from the ether were now directed towards the US Air Force's anticipated combat enemy – the Soviet Air Force. Chicksands intelligence 'tasking', as at other military intelligence stations, inevitably gave first priority to their own service's requirements, just as navy Sigint stations would primarily monitor opposing naval forces. But Chicksands tasks have expanded to embrace diplomatic and military signals of western European allies as well as those of enemies.

As the Sigint network spread its electronic tendrils across Europe, Chicksands grew in importance as a key communications and interception centre. NATO countries provided long-distance telephone lines under many guises, to link the widely-spread stations of the international network into a secure system. In 1956, Chicksands was designated as one of ten 'Comint Communications Relay Centers' (CCRCs)[3] in NSA's global communications plan. More than 40 channels linked the Chicksands relay centre (see Figure 5) both to the Sigint stations and to their intelligence clients. Chicksands' CCRC was the first of the ten to be completed, in the autumn of 1956.

Getting intelligence out to those who want it is the ultimate purpose of any intelligence operation. Besides routing intercepted signals to GCHQ in Cheltenham and NSA at Fort Meade, the Chicksands relay centre was connected to 'special security officers' at the US headquarters in London, South Ruislip, and the Strategic Air Command atomic war Joint Co-ordination Center underground at High Wycombe. Intercepted signals were received and retransmitted from Chicksands' 'torn tape' relay centre on long banks of punched paper tape printers and readers. Everything that went in and out was top secret, and enciphered. Signals could only be seen by specially Comint-cleared personnel.

Sigint was passed to Chicksands by British and American intercept stations, including RAF stations at Cheadle, Staffordshire, and Digby, Lincolnshire. US intercept centres directly linked to Chicksands included Keflavik in Iceland, and Kirknewton, west of Edinburgh, where in 1952 another USAF Security Service unit – the 6952nd Radio Squadron (Mobile) – had found a permanent home.

Other European monitoring stations relayed their Comint gatherings to and through Chicksands via three other European and Mediterranean area relay centres – at Pirmasens in south-west Germany, Karamursel in Turkey, and Port Lyautey in Morocco. The relay network was the United States' most urgent and immediate communications system, known as CRITICOMM. In principle, once a CRITIC (Critical Intelligence Communication) had been originated, it should have reached the President's desk (if that was where it was bound) in ten minutes.

By the end of 1973, the CRITICOMM torn tape relays at Chicksands had been junked and Sigint communications were integrated into the main US military telex and data communications system, the Automatic Digital Network (AUTODIN). Through these centres, such as Croughton, near Banbury, millions of words of military and intelligence information flow daily.

In 1956, a third US monitoring unit was just setting up in Britain, and was connected to the Chicksands CCRC. This was an Army Sigint team that had arrived to develop a new base at Menwith Hill, near Harrogate – now a giant American NSA 'Big Ear' on European communications.

Edzell, nestling in the foothills of the Grampian Mountains near Montrose in Scotland, soon after became the fourth NSA-controlled station in Britain. Set up in 1960, it is operated by the US Naval Security Group. Other specialised NSA-sponsored or operated facilities arrived in the late 1960s, at Orford Ness, Suffolk (an over-the-horizon radar station) and at Morwenstow, near Bude in Cornwall (commercial communications satellite interception). At Mildenhall airbase, two Electronic Security Squadrons now provide Elint operators to work in and process information from RC-135 and SR-71 spy planes.

In 1964, according to a US Defense Department weekly report to the President, Chicksands and San Vito, Italy were the first two bases to be equipped with the NSA's premier new radio interception system, Sylvania's 'Flare 9'[4] – part of a new Sigint network codenamed the 'Iron Horse' system. The Flare 9 antenna, often nicknamed the 'Elephant Cage' in recognition of its dramatic form and proportions, is now the dominant feature of the landscape around Chicksands – a giant circle of steel pillars and connecting girder and wire more than a quarter mile in diameter (see Plate 4). An underground tunnel connects the antenna array to Building 600, the heavily guarded Chicksands operations centre.

Perfect circular symmetry and the wide extent of the Flare 9 antenna system enables faint signals to be retrieved from every point of the compass, and their source direction measured. Based on a 'Wullen-

OVERLEAF

**Fig 5. Monitoring Europe; the National Security Agency network, 1956**
The bombers needed intelligence on targets. An electronic monitoring network was set up in Europe, aimed eastwards, Chicksands was one of a dozen Comint (communications intelligence) Communications Relay Centres across the world, automatically passing on intercepted signals from thousands of listening post radio operators.

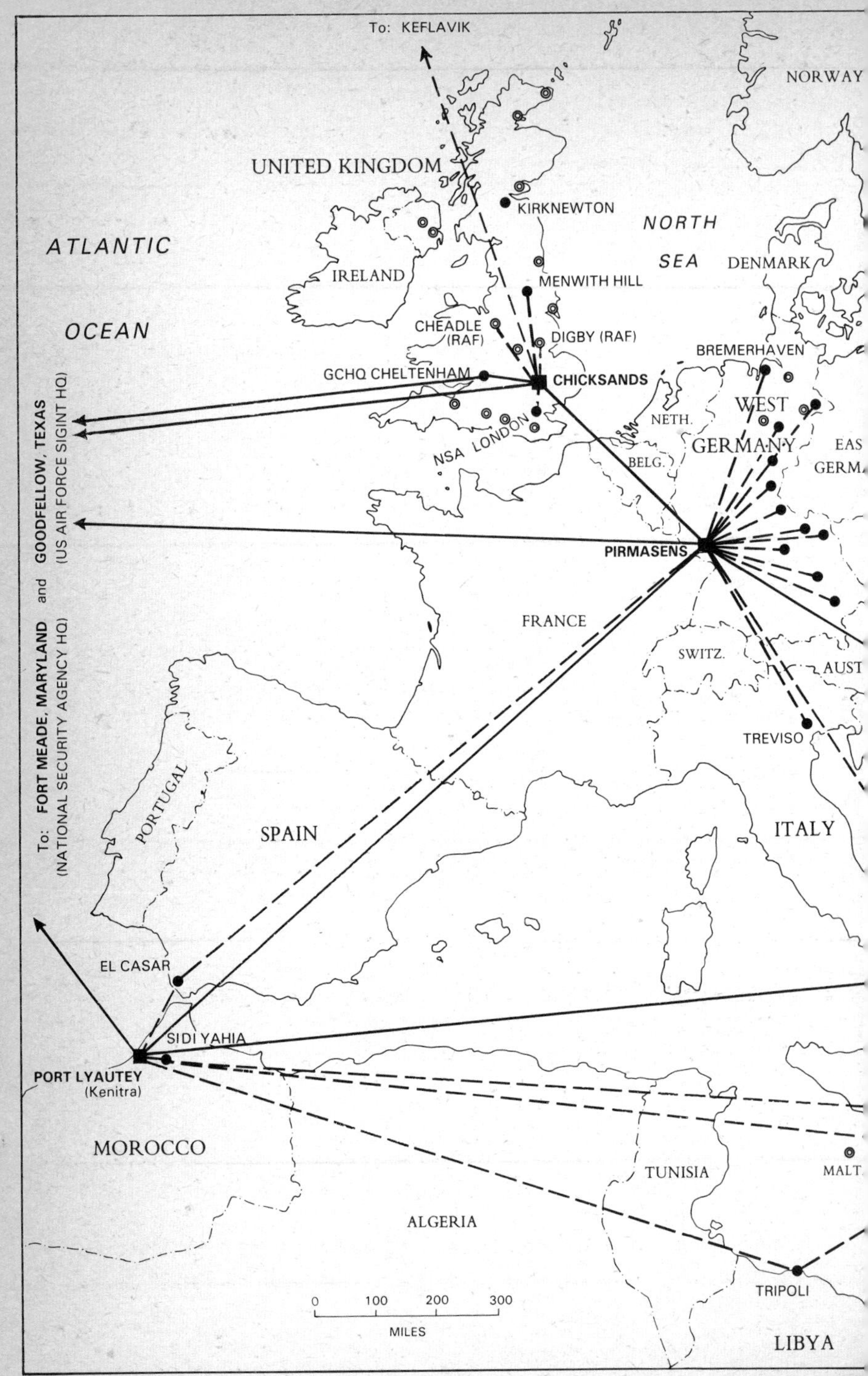


Fig 5. Monitoring Europe: the NSA network, 1956

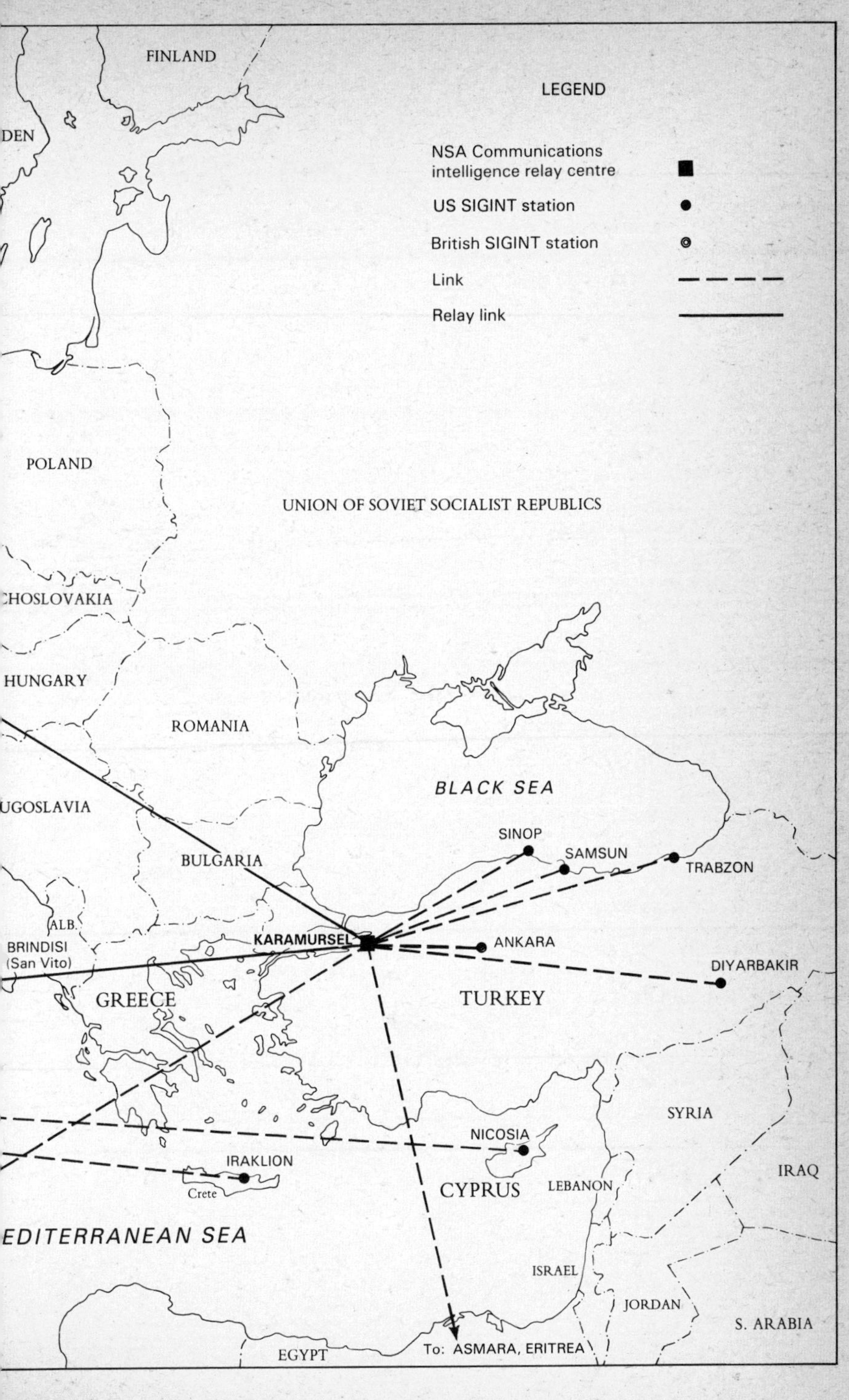

FINLAND
LEGEND
NSA Communications intelligence relay centre
US SIGINT station
British SIGINT station
Link
Relay link
DEN
POLAND
UNION OF SOVIET SOCIALIST REPUBLICS
CHOSLOVAKIA
HUNGARY
ROMANIA
BLACK SEA
UGOSLAVIA
SINOP
SAMSUN
TRABZON
BULGARIA
ALB.
KARAMURSEL
ANKARA
BRINDISI
(San Vito)
DIYARBAKIR
GREECE
TURKEY
SYRIA
NICOSIA
IRAKLION
IRAQ
Crete
CYPRUS
LEBANON
EDITERRANEAN SEA
ISRAEL
JORDAN
S. ARABIA
EGYPT
To: ASMARA, ERITREA

weber' design devised by German scientists during the Second World War, Chicksands can listen in any and every direction. The design was later developed and refined for the US Navy and Air Force. Edzell's Sigint antenna system, installed in 1960, was an earlier Navy-developed type of Wullenweber (probably a 'Flare 7', made by RCA).

During 1976, I was able to interview three former US Air Force Security Service employees about intelligence targets under surveillance from Chicksands and other British Sigint bases. One was Winslow Peck, a former USAFSS analyst from Turkey who, disillusioned like so many during the Vietnam War, had become one of the few insiders to explain something of the Pandora's Box world of Sigint to their fellow Americans, which he did in a 1973 interview with *Ramparts* magazine. Jeff Katz came to England in the late 1960s as a USAF master sergeant to work at Chicksands, and stayed on, working as a journalist and photographer. Jim Haynes, an intercept operator at Kirknewton, also stayed on at the end of his service in Scotland to bestow a considerable cultural legacy on the UK, including setting up Edinburgh's famous Traverse Theatre and the now-defunct London magazine, *IT*.

All say firmly that their stations were involved in monitoring far more than the communications of the Soviet Long Range Air Force. According to Peck:

> A lot of monitoring of France is done from Germany, also Chicksands. Chicksands does everybody in Europe. There is a lot of overlap. Brindisi [San Vito] does just about everybody in Europe in overlap also.

In his interview with *Ramparts*, he had said he had learned that:

> In England . . . our Chicksands installation monitors all their communications and the NSA unit in our Embassy in London monitors the low level stuff . . . These allies can't maintain security even if they want to. They're all working with the machines we gave them.

In August 1976, after being given further information by Peck, former Labour MP Tom Litterick accused the United States of 'economic espionage'.[5] Peck had explained how sanitised Sigint economic information about overseas competitors was passed to US corporations by NSA Special Security Officers.

Entering Chicksands' Building 600 through double security fences and a turnstile where green and purple clearance badges are checked, the visitor first encounters a Sigint in-joke – a copy of the Geneva International Telecommunications Convention pasted up on the wall.

The Convention, to which both the United Kingdom and the United States are signatories, binds treaty states to safeguard the privacy of international communications.

One step further is a 'guest DF' room, occupied from time to time by the sole British national working at Chicksands (other than the so-called 'RAF station commander', who is merely a community relations liaison officer and is not given access to operational information). The guest DF operator has the use of the Flare 9's formidable direction-finding powers to help obtain an accurate fix on any transmission intercepted by other British stations on direction-finding and positioning 'nets'. According to the leaked Top Secret annual Australian Joint Intelligence Organisation report for 1974, for example, their facilities are:

> linked with collaborating US, British and Canadian agencies in a worldwide DF network. It allows Australia and the partners to rapidly task the network to meet their various DF requirements . . .

But although Chicksands' intelligence output should, one would suppose, be shared entirely with the UK and other 'partners', British representatives are not required by the layout of Building 600 to venture further into US operational areas than the guest position. In practice, they don't.

Chicksands' independence from scrutiny by NATO allies was confirmed during a 1983 Congressional military construction appropriations[6] hearing. The US Air Force wanted (and got) $6.5 million to extend the 'Electronic Security Center', a costly project because the building 'must provide the required vault-like physical security and accommodate the extensive communications functions found in this special mission support facility'. The committee asked, why couldn't NATO pay for some of this fancy stuff? The answer:

> This facility supports a USAF operational requirement and the information gathered is not shared with NATO nations. Thus it is not eligible for NATO funding.

Further inside the Electronic Security Center are rooms and compartments with interception and direction-finding positions allocated to different mission targets. Signs hang above the heads of co-ordinating 'mission supervisors', which included, in the early 1970s, 'France', 'Czechoslovakia' and 'Civil Aircraft'. One of Chicksands' targets, Jeff Katz recalled, was French diplomatic radio signals. Nevertheless, the number one priority was the Eastern bloc. On each of the three daily shifts, about 200 operators man intercept positions. Their analysis operations are supported by a large IBM computer, which runs automatic morse and telex receivers, requiring little human intervention.

In the late 1970s, Chicksands was expanded to accomodate a new undercover NSA team, working in their own, compartmented-off section of Building 600. The team is disguised as 'DODJOCC' – the Department of Defense Joint Operations Center, Chicksands. The presence of a civilian NSA team implies either that new developments at Chicksands are concerned in monitoring civilian diplomatic or commercial signals, or that the base's capacity for breaking codes and cyphers on-site was being expanded. With over 1,250 military staff alone, Chicksands is the US Air Force's largest non-flying base in Britain. Liaison teams from Chicksands work at Menwith Hill NSA base, and at RAF High Wycombe, the headquarters of Strike Command.

Kirknewton, a smaller station with 300 staff, operated from 1952 until 1966. Kirknewton ignored opposing air forces, however; its major target was commercially-run radio links between major European cities, which then carried all international communications – or all that could be intercepted. In the Sigint community, such targets were known as International Leased Carrier (ILC) circuits. They could carry anything from birthday greetings telegrams to detailed economic or commercial information exchanged by companies, or enciphered diplomatic messages.

Commercial telegram networks between cities such as London, Paris, Moscow, Belgrade and Cairo were intercepted, according to Jim Haynes:

> Machines in intercept rooms, tuned to transmission channels, would spew out 8-ply paper. I worked on one of the plies . . .

At the end of the day, he said, much of that paper would go into the 'burn bag . . . one week I was asked to scan all traffic between Rome and Belgrade, and another week between London and Berlin'. Around the world, thousands of analysts like Haynes worked from NSA 'watch lists' – weekly key-word charts listing people, companies, commodities of interest for the NSA watchers to single out from 'clear' unencrypted traffic. Coded messages were passed on immediately to codebreakers.

Onto the lists would go the names of big companies, and prominent US and foreign citizens. Targeting American citizens' private communications in this manner was in fact illegal under US law, a fact entirely disregarded by NSA and its subsidiary agencies until summoned before the Church Committee intelligence hearings in 1974.

Economic intelligence was another priority at Kirknewton, according to Haynes:

> I had to keep a special watch for commercial traffic, details of commodities, what big companies were selling, like iron, steel and petrol.

'All traffic', he added, was eventually sent on to NSA's Fort Meade headquarters.

Another unusual task for Kirknewton in the early 1960s, according to local Post Office staff, was to supervise the 'hot line' Head of States' direct communications link between Moscow and Washington. NSA evidently shared responsibility for the security of the line, whose main route crossed the Atlantic to Oban in Scotland and passed through Kirknewton *en route* to Moscow.

On 1 August 1966, Kirknewton closed. Its intelligence tasks and some personnel were moved to Menwith Hill Station near Harrogate. The same day, the National Security Agency took over direct control of Menwith Hill from the US Army Security Agency.

Army Security Agency (ASA) staff had then operated the Menwith Hill Field Station for ten years. The station is secretly plugged into the international communications network passing through Britain, by means of the British Telecom (formerly Post Office) microwave radio network. Underground communications cables provide a massive umbilical link between Menwith Hill and Hunters Stones, a high and overcrowded British Telecom microwave relay station five miles to the south (see Figure 6). Inside the closely-guarded 560-acre base are two large operations blocks, now festooned with many satellite tracking dishes.

In the early 1960s Menwith Hill was one of the first sites in the world to receive sophisticated early IBM computers, with which the NSA automated the tiresome, unreliable and labour-intensive 'watch-list' scrutiny of intercepted but unenciphered telex messages. Since then, Menwith Hill has sifted the private international messages, telegrams, and telephone calls of citizens, corporations and governments to select information of political, military or economic value to the United States.

Menwith is the most secret and recondite United States base in Britain. In a country where there are so many US bases that no political embarrassment attaches to the opening of one new facility, every detail of Menwith Hill's operations has been kept an absolute secret. The official cover story is that the all-civilian base is a Department of Defense communications station (as at Chicksands, NSA facilities are always identified as Department of Defense); Chief of Station at Menwith Hill, Albert Dale Braeuninger, said in 1980 that:

> We do radio relays – material comes in from a variety of places and is rerouted. It is a switching operation. We route it sometimes to the UK and sometimes to the US.[7]

The British Ministry of Defence described Menwith Hill as a 'communications relay centre'. Like all good cover stories, this has a strong element of truth to it. The real question is: *whose* communications do they relay, from where and to whom?

In 1980, with *Sunday Times* colleague Linda Melvern, the author traced how, from late 1954, Menwith Hill station had been developed alongside a set of secret links in the British international communications system. Menwith Hill's Sigint speciality is evidently the interception of the International Leased Carrier signals, the international communications links run by civil agencies – the Post Telegraph and Telephone ministries of eastern and western European countries, and US corporations like ITT and RCA.

In the early 1960s, Menwith Hill, like Kirknewton, intercepted these signals if they were sent by radio. Underground telephone or telegraph cable links in the Soviet Union or eastern Europe were beyond interception, of course. From 1974 on, as international communications came to be increasingly dominated by satellites, tracking dishes have proliferated at Menwith Hill. But even before 1974, Menwith Hill never sported any of the giant direction-finding Flare antennae. The reason was simple; the radio masts in the Yorkshire Dales were intercepting fixed radio links from European cities, not ships, aircraft or military control stations whose unknown position had to be determined.

Plumbed in to Menwith Hill from underground cables were taps on international communications circuits passing through the UK. In the early 1960s, London was quickly developing as a major European 'gateway' communications centre, as cable links from eastern and western Europe to Africa and North and South America were routed through the city. For example, plans of a 1963 London-Paris link in the Post Office microwave system, indiscreetly sent to staff of the Council for the Preservation of Rural England, showed that a third connection was made to tap the London-Paris link, at Fairseat radio station in Kent (see Figure 4). The tapping connection finished at the Menwith Hill link station, Hunters Stones.

The extent of the attack on private and commercial communications by the international Sigint agencies may be surprising to those accustomed to viewing them as a thin electronic warning line to fend off war. But in Britain, since the 1920s, GCHQ and its predecessor, the Government Code and Cypher School, have intercepted international cables from the Post Office and commercial carriers by the simple device of sending a daily van to collect copies. This practice was exposed during the 'D Notice Affair' in 1968. During the post-Watergate investigations of the US intelligence agencies, Americans discovered that the NSA had been doing the same.

During the Congressional Watergate investigations, this was repeatedly acknowledged. In a public hearing before the Pike Committee on 6 August 1975, CIA Director William Colby admitted in public that the NSA 'does monitor foreign communications . . . communications that are abroad or go abroad cannot be separated from the traffic that is being monitored'.

Two days later, Lieutenant General Lew Allen, the Director of NSA, appeared before the committee. He refused to testify in public. But in confidential testimony he acknowledged, as the committee's secret report later stated, that:

> NSA systematically intercepts international communications, both voice and cable. Messages to and from American citizens have been picked up in the course of gathering foreign intelligence.[8]

Allen was asked in detail by Pike Committee members about NSA's interception methods. He mentioned two sites in England doing this work, according to a committee source. These were Harrogate (ie Menwith Hill) and an unidentified centre in southern England. This was probably the joint centre with GCHQ at Morwenstow, described below.

Amongst the issues before these investigating committees was an NSA programme called 'Minaret'. This was a programme for targeting the communications of particular individuals in whom agencies like the CIA or FBI were interested. Included on Minaret 'watch lists' at one time or another were actress Jane Fonda, author Dr Benjamin Spock, and many other US radicals. By 1974, the names of 75,000 Americans and an unknown, larger number of foreigners whose messages and phone calls had been intercepted by NSA had been assembled, and was transferred to a major computer system shared between all US intelligence agencies – COINS, the Community On-Line Intelligence System.

NSA's Minaret activity – involving spying on US citizens – had been illegal. During 1975 and 1976, a US Justice Department task force investigated possible legal action against those responsible for this and other NSA activities. The report, classified Top Secret UMBRA, was finished in June 1976, but never acted on. In 1980, under the Freedom of Information Act, US author James Bamford obtained a 'sanitised' copy of the report. It wasn't sanitised enough, and soon after releasing it, anguished intelligence officials sought unsuccessfully to get the report back.

The task force report gave absolute confirmation of the GCHQ-NSA partnership in spying on international commercial communications. 'Minaret intelligence' they reported:

> was obtained *incidentally* in the course of NSA's interception of aural and non-aural (eg, telex) international communications and the receipt of GCHQ-acquired telex and ILC (International Leased Carrier) cable traffic (Shamrock)[9] [emphasis in original].

This activity had contained 'possible violations' of two US laws. Shamrock had been going since the end of the Second World War. Virtually every commercial cable, telegram or telex going in and out of Britain and America had been scooped up, either by GCHQ or NSA. GCHQ had partnered the NSA in one of its most illegal operations. Indeed, the NSA was and is able to escape from laws protecting the privacy of US citizens by letting GCHQ work against these targets. Under Minaret and Shamrock the intelligence axis combined to break US law as well as the canons of privacy everywhere.

Menwith Hill, according to ex-NSA staff and others, is the collection point for much of the 'aural and non-aural' communications intercepted by NSA. Frank Raven, the former head of NSA's 'G' Group, which monitors the non-communist world, has identified the targets of Menwith Hill as 'western Europe, eastern Europe, and the Soviet Union west of the Urals'. Most of the signals intercepted are now forwarded by satellite to Fort Meade (NSA headquarters), rather than attacked on the site.[10] According to a British military officer who visited the centre in the mid 1970s, Menwith intercepted telephone and other communications to and from the United States and Europe; intelligence dossiers assembled from these sources were maintained on computers at the base, and targets included European political leaders.

Questioned about these allegations by the author in 1980 the British Ministry of Defence, remarkably, issued what the Ministry's spokesman said was a 'limited and highly specific denial'. He was asked if Menwith Hill intercepted domestic and/or international telephone and telex calls. The Ministry stated that Menwith Hall did not intercept 'transatlantic incoming or outgoing calls'; nor did it intercept British domestic calls.[11] The interception of traffic to and from Europe, within Europe, or going *through* Britain was, in this instance, virtually admitted by non-denial.

The station's facilities were built up slowly. Although plans were laid in 1954 and land bought in 1955, full construction was not complete until 1960. Delays in the building of the interception centre correspond closely in time with delays in the construction of the Post Office microwave radio station network to which it was connected. At the start of January 1957, an initial team of 7 was designated the 13th US Army Security Agency Field Station. By 1961, there were 510 US Army staff operating the station.

Several underground cables now link Menwith Hill with the Post Office's radio relay network, which carries most British national and international communications. In 1980, then Chief of Menwith Hill Station, Albert Dale Braeuninger, admitted in an interview that:

> we pass information through the UK communications system. Our line is cable . . . We only use the Hunters Stones power as a customer of the Post Office.[12]

The first links between Menwith Hill and Hunters Stones were laid in the early 1960s. The links to the US monitoring station were evidently a critical part of the first Post Office nationwide microwave radio relay network in Britain, codenamed 'Backbone'.

'Confidential' early plans for the Backbone system supplied in the 1950s to the Council for the Preservation of Rural England show that, whilst the Post Office was prepared to relocate several link towers in the system to meet local landowners' or residents' objections, they were not prepared to move Hunters Stones to a less obtrusive location. Indeed, when the Post Office moved other towers to more suitable locations, they had to build Hunters Stones 200 feet higher. They still wouldn't move it. Yet another tower, already in existence ten miles away in Leeds, could have handled all the capacity of the Hunters Stones tower.

The only conclusion that can be drawn from the Post Office's conduct is that the Menwith Hill-Hunters Stones link was a critical part of the planning of their overall system. By the end of 1963, the importance of Hunters Stones became quite evident. Four radio relay links, running to Maidstone, Dundee, York and Lancaster, all converged at the lonely tower, remote from any large cities (see Figure 4). None of these links were in use, then or now, for telephone or television connections, or even for links in the UK east coast defensive radar network.

According to the International Frequency List, a voluminous international list of all radio transmitters, 5,400 telephone channels now go *inward only* to Hunters Stones. The list, compiled from information supplied by the Post Office itself, also shows that Hunters Stones now carries 10,000 ordinary telephone connections, and many TV signals.

1980 saw the discovery of the cables that proved that Menwith Hill was tapped into the British Telecom tower network. Engineers working at an open manhole indicated a two-inch thick cable lying in a specially constructed aluminium tray. This belonged to the Americans, they said, not BT. It was one of two or three which ran to the base. If it was damaged, 'all hell would break loose'.

The Americans' secret cable was not a cable as such, but a waveguide – a pipe for a radio beam capable of carrying more than 32,000 simultaneous telephone calls. Soon after enquiries were made about the purpose of the cables, staff were warned not to speak to reporters, and a literal cover-up took place. Inside the manholes on the underground tunnel carrying the cables from Hunters Stones to Menwith Hill – which already weighed many hundredweight – thick, padlocked metal covers were installed. Two years later another new cable was laid in the underground duct. On this occasion, BT staff tried to seize the camera to prevent a reporter from taking pictures (see Plate 3).

NSA abruptly took over the Menwith Hill and Kirknewton interception stations' tasks in 1966. The takeover reflected a continuing tension between the military agencies – such as the Air Force Security Service and the Army Security Agency – who operated most of NSA's interception stations, and NSA itself. The military agencies generally wanted to concentrate on their possible military opponents, in this case, the Soviet High Command. NSA wanted more priority given to non-military intercepts – in western Europe as much as east. NSA's new computers brought increased effectiveness by automating the process of scanning telegrams for key words and phrases. The capacity of the IBM computer at Menwith Hill is not known, but at NSA headquarters, the world's biggest computer, IBM's Harvest, could then scan 40 million words *every minute* for information of intelligence significance.

Satellite Sigint operations began at Menwith Hill in 1974, when the first of more than eight large satellite communications dishes were installed. Some of the large, 60-foot diameter dishes are inside protective and concealing radomes. Four are not, and their movements and positioning are revealing. They show that Menwith Hill is connected to three kinds of satellites, either to intercept their signals, or to relay signals back to the United States:

- 'Fixed' satellites over the equator. These could be US communications relay, or fixed Sigint satellites.
- Fast travelling, low (90-mile) orbit satellites. These are probably small US 'ferret' Elint satellites carried 'piggyback' on larger satellites.
- Satellites which use a highly elliptical orbit called 'Molniya' – widely used by the Soviet Union. Molniya-type satellites appear to hover for periods of up to 12 hours high over the northern hemisphere, then rapidly traverse to the south and back.

The most interesting of these are the dishes tracking Molniya-orbit satellites. These dishes are either intercepting Soviet civil and military communications satellites, or tracking a specialised US satellite network, called the Satellite Data System (SDS). According to 1981 US Senate hearings, the SDS satellites provide 'over-the-poles communications for many of the national intelligence programs and many other programs'. Although the SDS satellites are one of many systems for sending orders to B-52 bombers flying in Arctic regions, it is likely that most of the satellites' payload is Sigint equipment. If so, Menwith Hill is likely to be the ground receiving terminal. The SDS series – a seventh $100 million SDS satellite was launched in 1981 – are the only US satellites whose orbit pattern is not published.

Although the exact purpose of Menwith Hill's satellite terminals remains obscure, it is likely that they continue the function of intercepting commercial international links in eastern and western Europe, and the USSR. Although such links are seldom used for critical military purposes, they are the most easily tapped source of long-term intelligence. With eight major satellite terminals installed by 1981, Menwith Hill was the largest satellite receiving terminal known in the world.

Western commercial satellites are intercepted by an NSA-sponsored but GCHQ-controlled Composite Signal Organisation Station, Morwenstow. On the high cliffs of Sharpnose Point to the north of Bude, Cornwall, Morwenstow is an audacious reminder that the Sigint agencies scoop up *all* international communications. Morwenstow, now packed out with US-supplied computers and communications terminals, appears to be a secret duplicate of the British Telecom receiving station at Goonhilly Downs, 70 miles to the south.

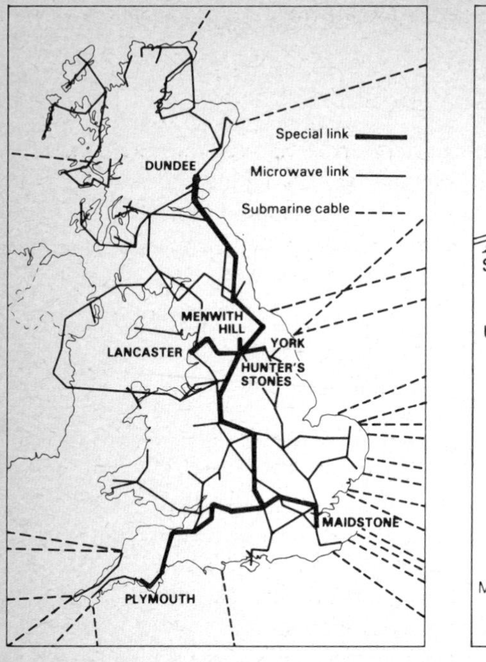


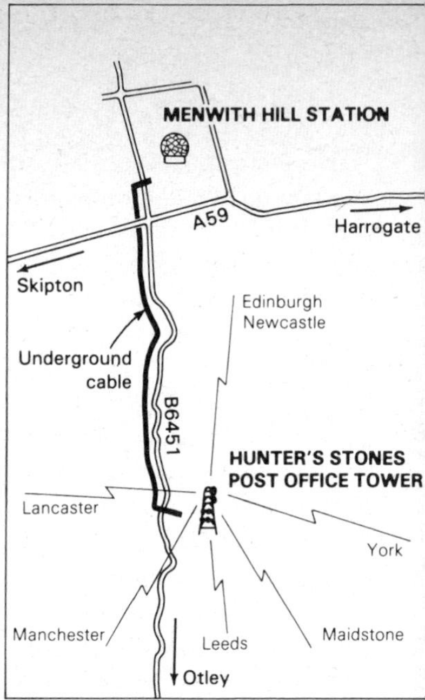


Fig 6. Telephone tapping at Menwith Hill

**Fig 6. Telephone tapping at Menwith Hill**
International diplomatic and military signals are increasingly sent by cable, not radio. At the NSA base at Menwith Hill, a special network of microwave radio connections (shown by bold lines on the map, B) run by British Telecom feed to a radio station at Hunters Stones, near Harrogate. From here, high capacity underground cables (A) run along the B6451 road and cross into the monitoring base. All Britain's international telex, data and telephone connections are secretly tapped by the NSA or its partner, GCHQ.

---

Its two original tracking dishes point in the same direction as those at Goonhilly, to Western Intelsat commercial satellites over the Atlantic and Indian Oceans. The 97-foot dishes are not military equipment. Identical dishes can, however, be found in Hawaii, West Virginia, California, Puerto Rico and at Fucino near Rome. These five stations are all registered, legal civil satellite terminals. Morwenstow is not. What the legal stations send up, Morwenstow pulls back down for computer analysis.

Morwenstow is one of a network of at least three stations spying on Western satellites. Two others, run directly by NSA, are at Sugar Grove, West Virginia, and Yakima, in Washington state. A fourth is likely to be in the west Pacific.

This secret network was planned around 1967. In February that year, GCHQ representatives went to Goonhilly to study the receiving methods there. The news that the intelligence specialists planned to construct their own replica stations leaked out to *The Times*, which reported, with remarkable accuracy:

> Communications specialists from Cheltenham have visited Goonhilly to study the methods used there for handling telephone traffic. This will be the type of messages coming by way of the Bude station.[13]

The Foreign Office endeavoured to cover for NSA and GCHQ by suggesting that the station would provide a satellite link to British embassies. This was untrue.

Morwenstow, a joint UK-US venture, began operations in 1972–3, soon after the new, high-capacity Intelsat III network came into operation. As at Menwith Hill, there are too many voice channels for Sigint workers to be able to monitor every call (and computers which can automatically understand telephone speech in any voice, intonation, language and accent are still in their infancy), but everything 'written' – telex, telegrams, facsimile and data – is scanned. Telephone calls to and from target countries and individual numbers can also be singled out, or listened to at random. Its tapping capacity probably also includes links to the nearby international submarine cable terminal at Widemouth Bay, just south of Bude. A microwave link also connects the Bude communications station to Lands End and Sennen, where all other oceanic cables now land.

It appears that the purse holders at the British Treasury were unconvinced of the intelligence need to monitor Western communications, and resisted GCHQ's application for their share of the Bude project's cost. In a parting letter to Lieutenant General 'Pat' Carter, the retiring Director of NSA in July 1969, GCHQ Director Leonard Hooper explained how he had imputed American needs to get British funds:

> I know that I have leaned shamefully on you, and sometimes taken your name in vain, when I needed approval for something at this end. The aerials at Bude ought to be christened 'Pat' and 'Lou'.[14]

In an official letter to Carter a few days earlier, Hooper had eulogised the special relationship between GCHQ and NSA. He was 'pretty apprehensive' of the new Director, Admiral Noel Gayler, and asked Carter to:

> assure him that we in GCHQ will do our best to assist NSA in continuing its great and important mission under his leadership.

In the personal note, had written rather more effusively:

> Between us, we have ensured that the blankets and sheets are more tightly tucked around the bed in which our two sets of people lie . . . I like it that way.

In contrast to wholly closeted and politically sensitive intercept operations mounted from Morwenstow or Menwith Hill, NSA's fourth British station at Edzell, Tayside has a clearly identified role in the US Naval monitoring system, OSIS – the Ocean Surveillance Information System. Edzell's basic equipment, like Chicksands, is the large circular Flare radio receiving system. But, since 1976, Edzell's scale and importance has grown dramatically as new ocean surveillance satellites have come into operation. Edzell is the eastern Atlantic site in a five-station network – codename 'Classic Wizard' – controlling these new satellites. US military personnel first arrived at Edzell in February 1960. By 1986, there will be 1,089 military personnel at the station.

New computers installed for the Classic Wizard project have modernised the station's high frequency radio monitoring and direction finding facilities. But Edzell, like other US intelligence bases, does not send information to NATO, or even to US units supporting NATO, according to Congressional testimony. When the US Navy applied in 1981 for $1.2 million to expand the 'Ocean Surveillance (Classic Wizard)' Building, they explained that NATO could not be expected to pay because:

> this project . . . is not required for use by or in support of a US unit committed to NATO.[15]

Edzell's Sigint mission was earlier explained indiscreetly in a hearing of the House of Representatives' Armed Services Committee in 1980:

> radio receivers are operated here that can listen for American or foreign broadcasts from all directions.

Edzell's mission is described overtly only as 'Naval Security Group Activity'. Besides the Naval Security Group, a US Marine Sigint 'Company B' works inside the base operations building, in the centre of the Flare antenna. They are likely to be monitoring opposing Soviet marine forces.

US Navy Ocean Surveillance Satellites (NOSS) have been developed since 1971. The first series – 'White Cloud' – became operational in 1976. Each NOSS or White Cloud satellite has three sub-satellites travelling in constellation with it. Elint detectors monitor radar signals received from the oceans, and by comparing the time at which each sub-satellite receives the signals, the position of the emitting ship can be calculated. Military and civil ships can be distinguished by their differing types of radar transmissions.

NOSS/White Cloud satellite constellations were launched in 1976, 1977 and 1980. At a height of about 600 miles, each satellite takes 1 hour and 47 minutes to complete an orbit. White Cloud ground stations and Classic Wizard computers are known to be at Edzell; Winter Harbor, Maine; Adak, Alaska; Guam; and Diego Garcia. The Classic Wizard network provides one ground station in every major ocean area.

Besides radar detectors, the White Cloud satellites also carry infra-red scanners (which can pick up the heat of a ship against a much colder background) and sea state, ice and temperature measuring instruments. A follow-on project, codenamed 'Clipper Bow', was to have emulated the Soviet Union by putting relatively high-power radar ocean surveillance satellites into orbit, but this has now been cancelled. 'Seasat' – a civil satellite project using 'synthetic aperture' high accuracy radar – has gone ahead. Seasat data can be purchased by commercial customers of the US civilian agency, NASA. The radar pictures clearly show shipping. A European Space Agency Seasat terminal has been proposed for Oakhanger, the RAF and USAF satellite ground station in Hampshire.[16]

Britain's second contribution to the Ocean Surveillance Information System is the underwater monitoring station at Brawdy, near Pembroke in west Wales. The Brawdy US Naval Facility, or NAVFAC, started operations in 1973. It is the largest underwater monitoring station in OSIS, reputed to provide the US Navy with almost complete information on the whereabouts of Soviet submarines and shipping in the North Atlantic. Buried around the Welsh coastline, running out into St Brides Bay, and thence hundreds of miles into the Atlantic, are submerged cables which connect rows of underwater listening hydrophones to detectors and computers inside the US base.

Brawdy is part of 'Project Caesar', which began in 1954. The first Caesar stations were sited along the United States coast. Technically, the system is called SOSUS (Sound Surveillance System). SOSUS expanded into the North Atlantic in the early 1960s, when a SOSUS station was installed in Newfoundland – while in Iceland two NAVFACs operated submarine sonar barriers between Greenland, Iceland and the UK.

Brawdy's task is officially described as 'oceanographic research'. There are believed to be 22 such 'Naval Facilities' throughout the world. All do the same job. At the end of 1980, according to official records, 22 US Navy officers, 278 other ranks, and 7 civilians worked at the Brawdy NAVFAC.

SOSUS is based on a remarkable discovery about the behaviour of sound. In the ocean depths, typically at depths of about 2,000 feet, there is a layer of water which holds and protects sounds entering it, carrying them for thousands of miles. It is called the Deep Sound Channel, and it is the key to underwater surveillance from Brawdy. In the Deep Sound Channel sound rays are reflected both from warm surface water and from the freezing depths below. The effect is rather like whispering from one end of an underground car park to the other. Huge ocean tracts 'ring like a bell'.

An unexpected incident focused public attention on Brawdy in 1973 when a miniature submarine, *Pisces III*, was trapped for some days on the seabed west of Ireland. Officially, it had been engaged in 'oceanographic research'; in fact it had been laying SOSUS cables and hydrophones for Brawdy.

Since 1978, more than $20 million has been spent on adding new buildings and equipment at the Brawdy Naval Facility. 80 per cent of this money has been spent on sophisticated electronics and computers. In 1981 $3.6 million was spent enlarging the size of the operations block by 50 per cent. The Terminal Building, where the cables coming in from St Brides Bay are connected, was similarly enlarged. Together these buildings cover more than four acres, all filled with computers and electronics. In 1981 $16 million was spent on 'mission-oriented electronic equipment' for a SOSUS upgrading project.

Inside Brawdy, signals from the listening hydrophones are processed automatically by computer. The noise pattern of a submarine hundreds of miles away can be picked up by adjusting an entire row of hydrophones to act as a single giant listening device. Then the submarine's noise – caused by its propellers, and internal machinery – can be separated from a multitude of other deep sea noises. Like a person's voice, each type of vessel has its own acoustic 'signature', which may be matched to a computer library of such sounds, previously recorded.

Brawdy's part in the worldwide Project Caesar network was publicly confirmed in 1978. In that year, a small item appeared in the US Navy budget mentioning a new Caesar system for Brawdy. The report listed its component parts:

> *CAESAR* Shore Electronics Assembly SDC-2 (Shore Electronics will be installed at US Navy facility, Brawdy, Wales. The associated array and cable will be located in international waters.)[17]

The reference to placing hydrophone arrays in international waters helps to explain the official sensitivity about the Welsh underwater spy station. Like Edzell, Brawdy is described in US hearings as 'not required for use by or in support of a US unit committed to NATO'.

Brawdy's facilities anticipated the developments of new, long-range Soviet submarine-launched ballistic missiles. These Delta-class submarines, each carrying a dozen or more missiles, started operating between 1972 and 1977. The range of earlier missiles had forced submarine carriers close in to the US coastline, where they would be tracked by the ever-listening SOSUS detectors. But the new submarines could fire much further away from the United States. Therefore new SOSUS stations were built in the early 1970s on Hawaii, Guam and at Brawdy, extending coverage of potential Delta-class patrol areas.

Although getting precise information on Soviet missile submarine positions is obviously a gain for American defences, defence specialists have warned that too-effective anti-submarine warfare networks deployed by either side may make nuclear warfare more likely, by undermining nuclear deterrence. Mutual deterrence relies on both sides being assured that, after an attack, they would have enough nuclear missiles left to hit back and inflict unacceptable damage. Submarines at sea were – until the 1970s – regarded as the least vulnerable and most 'survivable' element of nuclear forces. But if one side gains a decisive advantage by technical means, they will no longer be deterred if they think they can attack with near impunity. They might believe that they could launch a disarming first strike – and 'win' a nuclear war. Fearing that the United States might have this capability (even if it were not true), the Soviet Union might be tempted to launch a first strike early in a crisis, to avoid the destruction of their retaliatory forces.

From Brawdy, information on underwater 'contacts' is transmitted to the US Navy's Fleet Ocean Surveillance Information Center. Here, inside the US Naval Headquarters for Europe in Grosvenor Square, intelligence is co-ordinated from all available sources (see Figure 8):

- SOSUS stations at Brawdy, Keflavik and Hofn (Iceland); and an 'acoustic range' in the Azores.

- Classic Wizard Sigint from Edzell and Keflavik, with positioning and oceanographic information from White Cloud satellites.
- Visual, radar or sonar observations by ships, aircraft and submarines of the Sixth Fleet in the Mediterranean, or the Second Fleet in the Atlantic.
- Anti-submarine patrols by US Navy and NATO ASW aircraft.

The London centre, called FOSICEUR, is part of the 'Wimex' (World-wide Military Command and Control System) network. Through an anti-submarine warfare command and control system it is possible to summon up, on a computer display, maps showing the locations of most ships and submarines throughout the world – and particularly those of the Soviet Navy. A second Fleet Ocean Surveillance Information Facility, at Rota in Spain, is the intelligence coordinating centre for the Sixth Fleet. Computers aboard the Sixth Fleet flagship are linked directly both to London and to Rota. 30 ships and 100 aircraft are under Sixth Fleet command.

## Notes

1 New Zealand has no specific Sigint agency, and only one indigenous station. New Zealanders, however, work within Australia's agency, DSD.
2 *New York Times*, 7 September 1960.
3 'Plan for Telecommunications Support of National Security Agency', prepared for Joint Communications–Electronic Committee of the Joint Chiefs of Staff. US National Archives, JCS records, files CCS 334 DCE.
4 The name came from the equipment's open classification number – AN/FLR-9. It formed part of the US Air Force Elint system 466L; a classified codename for the equipment was 'Kinsfolk'.
5 *New Scientist*, 5 August 1976.
6 House of Representatives, Committee on Appropriations, subcommittee on Military Construction, Fiscal Year 1984 Hearings, Part 5, p 320. US Congress, 1983.
7 Duncan Campbell, 'America's Big Ear in Europe', *New Statesman*, 18 July 1980 (reprinted in *Big Brother is listening*, NS Report 2; *New Statesman*, 1981.
8 Pike Report, *op cit*.
9 US Justice Department, *Report on inquiry into CIA-related electronic surveillance activities*, 30 June 1976, p 160; (SC-05078-76: Top Secret Umbra/Handle Via Comint Channels); *See also* James Bamford, *The Puzzle Palace*, pp 331 and 373, Sidgwick and Jackson, 1983.
10 Bamford, *op cit*, p 209.
11 *New Statesman*, 25 July 1980.
12 *New Statesman*, 18 July 1980.
13 *The Times*, 2 February 1967.
14 The letters quoted here are deposited in the George C. Marshall Research Library, Lexington, Virginia; and are also quoted in Bamford, *op cit*, p 333. Lou Tordella was the Deputy Director of NSA at the time, and was closely involved with Shamrock, Minaret and other NSA plans to target individual citizens. Sir Leonard Hooper

refused to comment on the letters when approached by the *Sunday Times* in 1981. He appeared shocked by the public revelation of his personal messages – an ironical situation for the GCHQ Director, who for 36 years had been reading other people's mail.

15 House of Representatives, Committee on Appropriations, subcommittee on Military Construction, Fiscal Year 1982, Part 1, page 1303. US Congress, 1981.

16 *Aviation Week and Space Technology*, 17 October 1977.

17 House of Representatives, Committee on Appropriations, subcommittee on Defense Appropriations, Fiscal Year 1977, Part 5, p 1255. US Congress, 1976.

# PART THREE
# TO THE PRESENT

## 7 *The Electronic Frontier*

Complex electronics, and the collective military system of command, control, communications and intelligence have become a sudden priority in American military development. Existing networks of relay stations, underground and airborne war rooms and warning satellites have now been deemed inadequate. The growing US nuclear arsenal will have been constructed to no avail, policymakers have written, if, during nuclear war, the United States cannot 'prevail'. Winning in the holocaust depends on the generals and political leaders staying in touch with their nuclear forces, and that requires many new projects for 'survivable' lines of command and control.

These key themes of President Reagan's long-term defence policy were contained in a leaked 136-page directive from Defense Secretary Caspar Weinberger, *Fiscal 1984–88 Defense Guidance.* This plan asserted that, in global 'strategic nuclear war':

> The United States must prevail and be able to force the Soviet Union to seek earliest termination of hostilities on terms favourable to the United States.[1]

Against this background, there is also to be a new arena of military conflict – outer space. Weinberger wanted preparations made to 'project force' and 'wage war effectively' in space. Space-based weapons would 'add a new dimension to our military capability', he recommended. Weinberger's proposals have also included a plan to build a new underground war headquarters for the US European Command in Britain.

Inside Britain and the rest of NATO area, US military commanders and their $C^3I$ systems clearly preserve the separate identities of NATO and US forces. Wimex (Worldwide military command and control system) computers, the London Fleet Ocean Surveillance Information Centre and the Anti-Submarine Warfare computers are, for example, located in the London US naval headquarters rather than at NATO command headquarters at Northwood, Middlesex. Throughout NATO, US communications links and command centres are usually separately established and administered from those in NATO. As the previous chapter showed, most US intelligence and communications facilities are ineligible for NATO funds because the information gathered is, in the first instance at least, for US use only.

Northwood, the headquarters of NATO's channel command, is directed by a British admiral. The only other major NATO commands – Supreme Allied Commander, Europe (SACEUR), and Supreme Allied Commander, Atlantic (SACLANT) – are always held by United States officers, each of whom has a US national post. SACEUR is always the US forces' Commander-in-Chief, Europe, while SACLANT is the US Atlantic Commander-in-Chief.

Separate US and NATO communications links are required for controlling nuclear weapons. Permission to fire (or 'release') must come from the President or his substitute, while the *order* to fire, once weapons are released, will normally come independently from NATO or its military commanders. This is not an absolute requirement, however, as the US President can both release nuclear weapons and unilaterally order US military commanders, acting in their national, not NATO capacities, to use them. Neither NATO as a whole, nor its individual European members, have a veto on the use of US nuclear weapons on their territories.

The United States military control system puts the President, as Commander-in-Chief, at the apex of a multi-tiered command structure. In preparing for emergency action during a major conflict, however, US plans speak not so much of the President as the 'National Command Authorities' – a less specific phrase whose exact meaning is secret. But its function is clear: in order to make the US nuclear deterrent 'credible', the authority to fire nuclear weapons in retaliation may be delegated to junior commanders if they have good reason to believe that the higher levels of the National Command Authority have been wiped out.

Officers as low-ranking as majors have, in the past, been given the authority to launch a nuclear strike on their own initiative in some circumstances, according to Daniel Ellsberg, the former US Defense planner who leaked the notorious 'Pentagon papers' about the conduct of the Vietnam war. Ellsberg conducted an official study of emergency command and control arrangements in the Pacific in the mid-1960s. Repeated delegation of authority and emergency orders, he reported, had gone so far as to permit one specific major to launch a local nuclear strike if he believed that his superior military commanders had come under nuclear attack.[2]

A reasonably well-defined line of political succession in the United States sets out who will become National Command Authority and take control of US military forces if the President is killed, or rendered incommunicado during an attack. But the operation of this succession has not always been convincing for US allies, however, as was demonstrated when President Reagan was shot in April 1981. The White House Chief of Staff (and former NATO Supreme Commander in Europe), General Alexander Haig, contested with Vice-President Bush the right of temporary control of the United States of America and its forces.

Below the President and his successors come the Joint Chiefs of Staff, and below them major 'unified' (three-service) or 'specified' commands, who are responsible for a special role or theatre of operations. These include Strategic Air Command, North American Air Defense Command, and the European, Atlantic and Pacific commanders. One step down in the hierarchy are the individual service commanders in the region concerned. In Europe, the US European Command, based at Stuttgart, has three major components:

- US Air Force Europe (USAFE): headquarters at Rhein Main airbase near Frankfurt.
- US Army Europe (USAREUR): headquarters at Heidelberg.
- US Navy Europe (USNAVEUR): headquarters in London.

Wimex (or WWMCCS), the Worldwide Military Command and Control System, is the electronic backbone of this US command and control system. EUCOM, the European Command, and each of its subcommands has a Wimex computer, a Honeywell 6000 series, designed in the 1960s. The computers are intended to pass information between the military commands and on to the National Command Authority.

They have not worked well. As a system for directing US military forces their performance has evidently been poor. As part of the core of the nuclear deterrent system, in whose continued stable operation – at any rate, *pro tem* – the rest of the world has an interest, the Wimex network appears to have been an unmitigated disaster.

The network came into operation between 1975 and 1980. Until July 1977 the network failed, on average, every 35 minutes. An hour's continuous operation was a rarity. At North American Air Defense (NORAD) headquarters, inside Cheyenne Mountain in Colorado, two Wimex-type Honeywell computers finally came into operation in

September 1979. Within nine months, the world had been treated to three separate incidents in which US nuclear forces around the globe accidentally went on war alert. Fighters took off, bombers began to taxi, missile launch preparations were started, command and control aircraft took to the air and civil aircraft were ordered to the ground. During the first alert, on 9 November 1979, the President's National Emergency Airborne Command Post aircraft, 'Air Force One', abruptly took off.

But President Carter was not on board. Neither he nor the Secretary of Defense were told of the alert – even though there might only have been 15 minutes for them to evacuate Washington if the attack had been for real.[3] More than the computers were shown to have failed. Inside the missile silos, missile launch crews knew the alert was not an exercise, and reacted accordingly. One used the few minutes available to phone his wife and tell her to head for Canada. Another strapped on a gun and holster to 'die like a soldier'. Told to insert their launch keys, 13 of 17 crews at the Titan missile base in Kansas failed to carry out their orders.[4]

Sophisticated computer technology appeared to be playing Mephistopheles to the Americans' Faustus, as they sought increased leverage against the Soviet Union by regenerating US nuclear superiority. The loading of a wrong tape onto a US Air Force computer, and the failure seven months later of a $20 microchip, forcibly reminded them and the world that the brink of destruction was never further than a half-hour away.

Over the two previous decades, such worldwide alerts had occurred, so far as is known, only on four occasions; two had been ordered, and two were false:

- An early warning alert in November 1960, when the Thule BMEWS radar tracked reflections from the moon, believing the signals to come from a Soviet missile (the 'Moon alert'; in 1950, there has been a similar incident when Distant Early Warning line radars had tracked a flock of geese, believing them to be Soviet bombers).
- The Cuban missile crisis in September 1962, when US forces were held at 'full readiness'.
- The Middle East war in October 1973, when a global alert was called to counter Soviet preparations to move troops in.
- Late in 1973, a missile launched from Tyuratam was wrongly predicted as likely to impact in California. SAC bombers and missiles were on alert until it landed in the Kamchatka peninsula.

The first NORAD false alert, in November 1979, began when a war game simulation tape, in which the opening move was the launching of a salvo of missiles against B-52 bases from a Soviet submarine in the Pacific, was loaded into the NORAD computers.

Air defence fighters were alerted and took off in Missouri, Oregon and British Columbia. The BMEWS station at Fylingdales was warned; according to an official at the Yorkshire base 'things got very tense'. But they had no radar targets within their 'threat azimuth' – the angles of the horizon at which a Soviet missile would normally be launched to attack Europe or North America. The Pentagon did not announce the alert, and details of the emergency were only given because a Washington reporter, who had witnessed the late stages of the alert in a Virginia Air Traffic Control centre, asked questions.

This November incident was accidental. But it highlighted the gross deficiencies in Wimex computers which were reported only a month later to the US Congress by the General Accounting Office (GAO), the US government budgetary watchdog. By 1980, said the GAO, the Pentagon had spent $1 billion on Wimex in an attempt to get the computers to do the job they were bought for. But the Honeywell computers had not been built to work 'on-line' as required by Wimex, continuously retrieving military information on request. They were heavyweight 'batch' processors, which were at their most efficient when working on only one job at a time. The Wimex system, said the Congressional report[5]:

- Was not reliable.
- Was not responsive to national or local level requirements.
- Could not transfer data and information efficiently.
- *Impaired* a commander's operational back-up capability.

Wimex had been introduced in an attempt to standardise 158 different computer systems, many of them unique, in use in different military commands during the 1960s. This lack of standardisation had prevented the computers 'talking to each other', exchanging information. In the late 1960s, the US had experienced major disasters resulting from command and control failures, which in separate incidents had exposed two US navy intelligence ships, the *Liberty* and the *Pueblo*, to attack by Israeli and North Korean forces.

By the end of the 1970s, Wimex computers had not improved the situation. The Wimex Intercomputer Network (WIN) was unstable and unreliable. In a March 1977 command exercise, codenamed 'Prime Target', the US Joint Chiefs of Staff found that at four out of six Wimex sites, 62 per cent of computer operations went wrong. Yet the WIN network was labelled 'operational', and programmers desperately tried to keep it going by adding new 'patch' computer programs to repair previous errors – often adding new mistakes as they did so.

In November 1978, a US Congressman and three reporters were shot dead in Jonestown, Guyana, after inspecting the Reverend Jones' suicidal cult's settlement. After the disaster in Jonestown, the White House wanted to know what troops and medical supplies might be available from the Florida-based US Readiness Command. Power supplies failed, there was no back-up link to get the information, and Wimex had failed again.

On 3 June 1980, the problem was not the Wimex computer, but a faulty chip in a NORAD communications multiplexer linking it to the outside world. Random numbers went out from the faulty device, indicating a Soviet missile attack. Again, SAC bombers and tankers started their engines, and waited for take-off clearance. The emergency alert extended on this occasion to Fairford, the SAC tanker base in Gloucestershire. In Hawaii, a Pacific Command airborne command post took off.

Three days later, on 6 June, while NORAD technicians were trying to track down the miscreant microchip, they set off another false alarm. NORAD subsequently claimed that this incident was a deliberate action in a search for the faulty part. But they did not warn SAC, who again went on alert. According to defence specialists who read a Pentagon report on the 6 June incident, alert signals on this occasion went to Mildenhall in England, Diyarbakir in Turkey (a tracking radar station), and US headquarters in Frankfurt and Heidelberg.

On each occasion, as US Department of Defense officials pointed out, the alerts were called off in less than ten minutes, after checks of different US reconnaissance systems indicated that there was no attack. With no confrontation taking place, it was unlikely that Soviet forces had time to notice the US alert, still less react. But what if the failure had occurred when military confrontation was occurring, and a real attack might have been expected? Wimex would not help. When the network was tested again in November 1980, in a command exercise codenamed 'Proud Spirit', little had improved. The computers failed to provide data for 12 hours.

In Britain, government ministers received no information about the alerts, and offered none to Parliament. The peak of official complacency on such issues was achieved in January 1980 by a junior minister, Scottish Under-Secretary of State Malcolm Rifkind, who defended the government and the United States for having conducted a nuclear alert about which he knew nothing – and which had not, in fact, taken place. The source of his embarrassment was an erroneous article in the *Scotsman*[6], reporting a 'high-grade nuclear alert' after the Soviet invasion of Afghanistan.

Challenged by one of his Edinburgh constituents about the dangers of these alerts, Rifkind responded:

> I am afraid I cannot agree with you that the decision to put the country on a high grade nuclear alert last week was irresponsible. The whole point of such an action . . . is to ensure that our defence response is fully prepared . . . the values of Western society and of the free world as a whole can only be safeguarded by proper defence provision.

It then took Mr Rifkind another two weeks to discover that there had not been any alert.

Despite the Wimex controversy, NATO European and Atlantic command staff have recently been permitted limited use of some Wimex computers. NATO Atlantic Command staff can now use the computer at Norfolk, subject to 'the development of a security interface to protect national [ie, United States eyes only] information'.[7] Proposals have also been made to allow NATO staff from the Allied Air Forces Central Europe command to use the Wimex computer at Frankfurt, and to provide NATO's European headquarters with its own Wimex-type system. No similar link, however, has been planned to supply data from US naval headquarters to NATO Channel or eastern Atlantic Commands at Northwood. NATO is also developing its own $C^3I$ system called CCIS (Command and Control Information System).

To safeguard against the continuing failure of the unreliable Wimex computers, as well as a possible attack on the data-processing centres or their connecting links, other independent strategic communications systems link the US national command direct to nuclear forces. The communications systems selected for such 'last-ditch' communications are those held to be most 'survivable'; collectively they are known as the Minimum Essential Emergency Communications Network (MEECN). MEECN depends heavily on airborne command posts, the largest of which is the converted jumbo jet reserved for use by the President. Nicknamed (not entirely obviously) 'Kneecap' for its acronym, NEACP (National Emergency Airborne Command Post), the E-4 jumbo jet is normally on ground alert at Andrews Air Force Base, ten miles from the White House and the centre of Washington. It is the cornerstone of the United States government plans for $200 *billion* worth of improvements to their $C^3I$ systems.

MEECN, like all command, control and communications systems, has for the United States authorities one over-riding purpose. That is to transmit a so-called Emergency Action Message to strategic forces. Including the Wimex computer network, there are – according to US Defense Department officials – some 43 ways of sending an Emergency Action message. One of these is to use the ordinary commercial telephone system!

MEECN radio systems include in Britain:

- Low frequency (LF) and very low frequency (VLF) radio; especially used for links to submarines, there are powerful LF transmitters at the Thurso naval radio station and VLF and LF transmitters aboard the Silk Purse EC-135 aircraft (p 241); 'Tacamo' emergency VLF communications aircraft (p 225) are based in the United States and fly out over the Atlantic; the NATO VLF transmitter at Anthorn may be available for US use.
- High Frequency networks include 'Mystic Star' VIP and presidential communications (p 60), at Croughton, Strategic Air Command's 'Giant Talk' at Mildenhall, now being replaced by new $2 million 'Scope Signal III' transmitters and receivers at Barford St John and Croughton; Naval Telecommunications links from Thurso; and 'Cemetery Net'.

'Scope Signal III' at Croughton enables SAC commanders to send confirmation to bombers already airborne to continue on strike missions, and 'will permit':

> under the direction of a single ALERT . . . command, the automatic seizure of up to twelve transmitters at each of twelve worldwide stations within 30 seconds and . . . subsequent voice transmission of Emergency Action Messages[8] . . .

Throughout European Command, Cemetery Net is the normal primary means by which the US sends Emergency Action Messages to nuclear 'field storage sites, delivery units, and mobile and fixed command headquarters'.[9] Cemetery Net high frequency radio links were installed throughout Europe between 1976 and 1982. NATO has its own high-frequency network, codenamed – disturbingly – 'Last Talk'. Cruise missiles will be linked to Regency Net.

Two other networks are available. The older of the two is ECCC-S – the European Command and Control Console System. This is installed at fixed nuclear storage and deployment sites, and is 'essentially used for managing the weapons in peacetime'.[10] It is not mobile. The headquarters of both ECCC-S and Cemetery Net is at Pirmasens,

Germany. The Pentagon's Autovon – US military telephone system – directory indicates a further method for NATO commanders to get permission to fire nuclear weapons: it lists a Pirmasens telephone number – Autovon number 395 8523 – as the 'National Command Authority' centre for Europe.

For the mobile cruise missiles, and other nuclear 'delivery units' which will operate in the field, the back-up nuclear control link will be a UHF (ultra high frequency) satellite terminal, the AN/MSC64. 200 MSC64 terminals were installed in 1981 and 1982, and should by now be installed at each UK nuclear weapons site; MSC64 satellite receivers, part of the Flaming Arrow network, are also fitted to the Launch Control Centers which accompany each flight of 16 cruise missiles.

Emergency action messages are relayed to these ground terminals from 'Afsatcom' (Air Force satcom) satellites – which are not so much satellites in themselves, but relatively low-capacity relay units carried aboard many other satellites, including the Satellite Data System, navigation, and Defense and Navy communications satellites. Afsatcom already provides a direct link between the National Command Authority and all strategic nuclear forces and terminals are installed on Silk Purse aircraft, and, apparently, on the ground at Mildenhall. Afsatcom links bypass normal command structures to get the emergency messages through.

The nuclear 'hot-line' systems – Cemetery Net and Afsatcom – will eventually have British terminals at Greenham Common, Mildenhall, Upper Heyford and Lakenheath. The NATO nuclear command network, SCARS II (SACEUR Status Control, Alerting and Reporting System), provides another link to most nuclear missile or bomber sites.

Besides airborne war rooms, the US 'National Command Authority' has two main locations. In the Pentagon itself, the Joint Chiefs of Staff control operations through the National Military Command Center, on the third floor of the Pentagon building, entirely unprotected against nuclear attack. If a crisis developed into a military threat, staff would move to the 'underground Pentagon' Alternative National Military Command Center, deep below the surface 75 miles north of Washington (see p 49).

Many US bases in Britain are directly involved in providing both routine command and control links, and special connections for the National Command Authority and MEECN. The most obvious British contribution to emergency command and control is the European Command's airborne war room squadron of four EC-135s at Mildenhall, Silk Purse. A three-storey underground bunker at High Wycombe Air Station will, by 1986, also have been converted to serve as a wartime headquarters for US European Command.

The plan to build the new headquarters in High Wycombe was part of Weinberger's 1983–7 *Defense Guidance* document, which directed the Joint Chiefs of Staff:

> To establish a European Command war headquarters in the United Kingdom by 1986 as part of a survivable European command-and-control system.[11]

News of the new war plan appeared in the *Guardian*[12] in December 1982, and triggered off an embarrassed flurry of denials. Initially, High Wycombe was not named, and British officials in Downing Street claimed that the 'central theme' of the report was 'fundamentally incorrect'. Foreign Secretary Francis Pym said he knew nothing about it 'other than what was in the newspaper'.[13] Embarrassed German and American officials denied that the plan meant the United States was abandoning hope of forward defence in Germany.

But the kind of war in Europe that made the peacetime command headquarters at Stuttgart likely to be untenable was spelt out in the document:

> The environment of future warfare is likely to differ greatly from any we have known in the past. Combat against Soviet forces and against Soviet-supplied forces will be of a higher intensity and longer duration, with weapons of much greater accuracy and possibly much higher rates of fire and mobility. It will feature intensive electronic warfare and possibly, chemical, biological and nuclear weapons.

US officials in Washington eventually confirmed that the war headquarters was coming to High Wycombe, and that the then current US defence budget included $13 million for construction work, due to start in July 1983. Congressional appropriations committee documents in 1982 described the High Wycombe bunker as an 'underground building of approximately 20,500 square feet in excellent condition with no sign of moisture or deterioration'. Much of the cost of refurbishment was to strengthen the building and, at a cost of $2.8 million, to help proof it against chemical or biological attack, nuclear radiation, and the electromagnetic pulse of a nuclear explosion. At least $33 million is to be spent on electronic equipment - presumably not including Wimex computers now sited in Stuttgart.

In war, the US European Command staff would divide into those with NATO posts and those with US national responsibilities – primarily 'logistics' staff, responsible for transport and supplies. The NATO staff would go to Casteau, near Mons in Belgium, where a new war headquarters bunker is under construction for SHAPE (Supreme Headquarters Allied Powers Europe). The remainder would move to High Wycombe. Once the bunker there is finished, it will have a peacetime skeleton staff of 24.

After a five-day row, the government admitted that they had given permission for the new High Wycombe headquarters, and Mrs Thatcher acknowledged that:

> We have agreed that in wartime an alternative headquarters for parts of US European Command may be located at Wycombe Air Station. This will be purely a national headquarters . . . USEUCOM is responsible for directing the reinforcement and logistic support of the United States forces in Europe[14] . . .

In June 1983, the United States purchased a £10 million message relay centre to go in the bunker. High Wycombe has also, since 1981, been the home of a USAF computer Squadron, responsible for Theatre Mission Planning – preparing target instructions for cruise missiles. The centre is one of three cruise missile planning centres in Europe, costing $20 million.

Throughout Britain, US forces operate and control their own system of microwave radio stations, providing a grid network into which both fixed and mobile emergency headquarters can be plugged. The early development of this network is described elsewhere, including the US Navy network in Scotland (p 226) and the Air Force system linking US airbases in England to the Continent (p 62). This system is now being reconstructed as a 'Digital European Backbone' (DEB) for US communications.

DEB digital microwave links are all encrypted, preventing signals from being intercepted and understood by others. By the end of 1979, the first phase of DEB was installed in Italy. The backbone was then progressively extended northwards, and reached its northern and western limit in England at Croughton in 1983. DEB's most important connections go to command headquarters and other communications centres, especially satellite terminals. DEB in Britain comprises the southern section of the USAF communications system, running from Croughton via High Wycombe to Swingate, Dover (see Figure 10). It is the most important link from European Command headquarters to US forces in Britain.

More than 100 DEB sites have been built, some 12 of which are interconnection points to other NATO or national communications systems. The main NATO international network is Ace High, a tropo-scatter relay network which has five British Stations in a chain from Sumburgh in the Shetlands to Coldblow Lane, near Maidstone. The Ace High network was built in the early 1960s, primarily in order to link NATO heads of state together in crisis. Two of twelve US/NATO interconnection sites are in the UK, at Mormond Hill north of Aberdeen and Coldblow Lane.

The Navy microwave system in Scotland, linking Thurso naval radio station to the Edzell monitoring station and Mormond Hill, was not included in the early DEB plans, but remains in use. Curiously, the southern portion of this US Navy system – which had provided a link to the former Naval radio station in Londonderry, closed in 1977 – was still installed in 1983 despite government denials.

After a debate about US bases in the House of Lords in July 1983, Defence Minister Lord Belstead claimed that five Scottish microwave relay sites – Craigowl Hill, East Lomond, Kirk O'Shotts, Sergeantlaw and Browncarrick Hill – had been 'handed back by the United States forces long before [1980]'.[15] As so often, the Ministry was in error; had they checked the sites at the time this pronouncement was made, they should have discovered the US still in occupation, with masts and communications shelters still *in situ*. Although two link stations in Northern Ireland had been dismantled, the Scottish sites and communications links may have been held in reserve for future developments in the Clyde area, at Prestwick, Machrihanish, or the Holy Loch.

Current British installations serving US command, control, communications and intelligence networks are shown in Figure 7. These bases provide connections for the world wide military communications

---

OPPOSITE

**Fig 7. The electronic war: Command, Control, Communications and Intelligence facilities in Britain**

$C^3I$ – Command, Control, Communications and Intelligence – is a US-devised acronym intended to convey the growing military importance of control centres and communications links. In the era of nuclear 'war-fighting', such centres take on particular importance as military planners attempt to devise command and control arrangements which may at least partially avoid destruction during a sustained nuclear war. It follows that $C^3I$ centres can climb as high on an enemy's target list as nuclear missile and bomber bases.

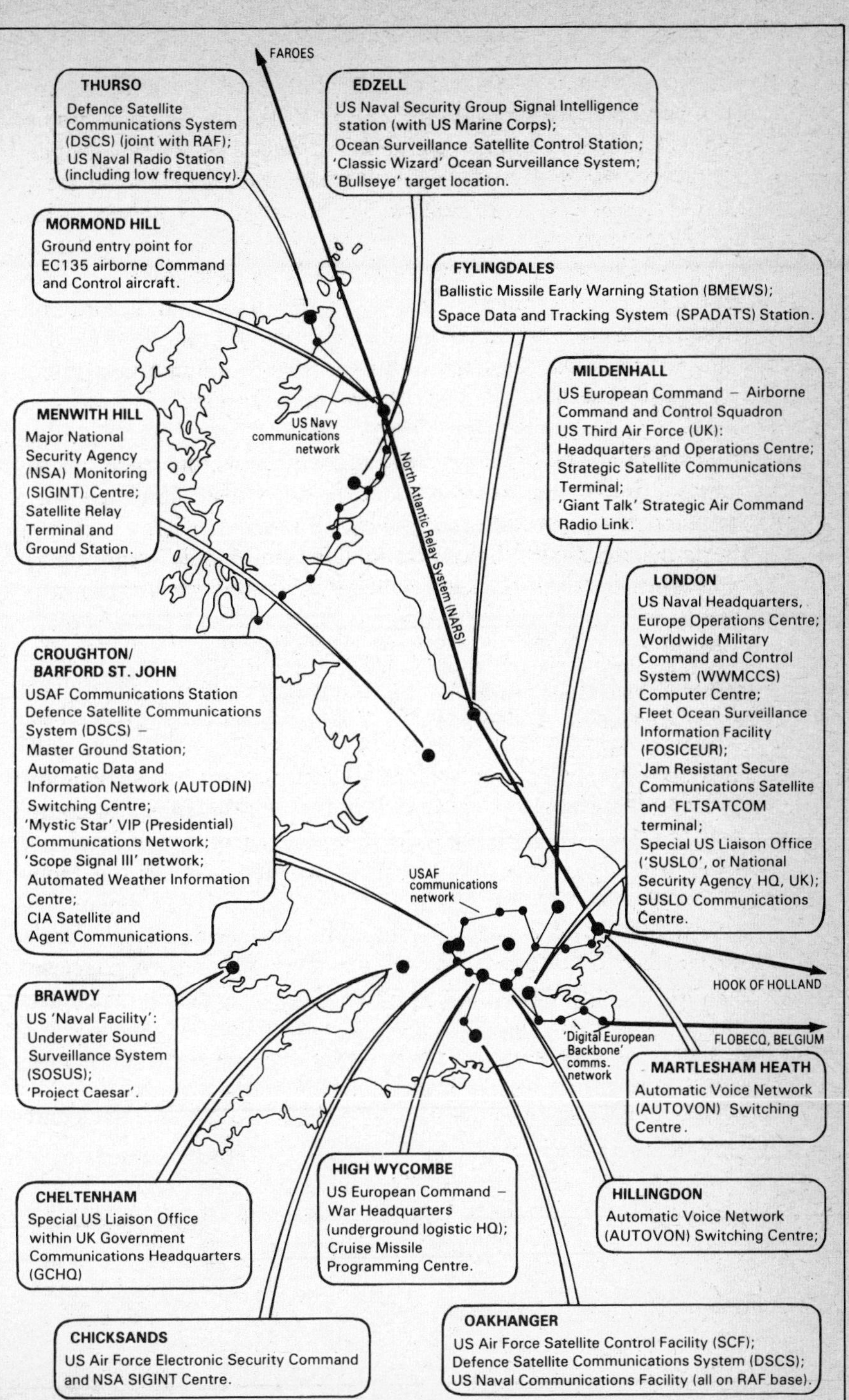


Fig 7. The electronic war: US Command, Control, Communications and Intelligence bases

systems, 'Autovon' (automatic voice switching network) and 'Autodin' (automatic digital network).

Autovon is a telephone system, the US forces' version of STD. Every US base, except the very smallest, has an Autovon dialling access code, which Autovon users in Britain can use to call directly to any official telephone on any US base in Europe. Seventeen major British base exchanges are connected to two Autovon switching centres – Martlesham Heath, an old airfield near Ipswich which is also a tropo-scatter relay terminal (see Project Tea Bag, p 87); and Hillingdon, in the RAF station at Uxbridge, where the Autovon communications equipment is protected inside a former British Army anti-aircraft operations bunker.

Hillingdon is Britain's Autovon 'gateway' connecting the European Autovon system to that in the United States. It is also connected to US bases in Bahrein, Cairo and the Azores. Autovon is a 'major and integral part' of the US Defense Communications System, according to the Department of Defense 'Global Autovon Directory'; its purpose is:

> to provide rapid worldwide command and control communications from the National Command Authority and other high priority subscribers. Its second mission is to provide an acceptable grade of service for operational, intelligence, logistic, administrative and diplomatic users.

To carry out this task, a special group of 1,800 so-called 'subscribers' are singled out and given special telephones and facilities. Additional buttons on such phones, connected directly to more sophisticated exchanges at the Hillingdon and Martlesham Heath centres, allow these subscribers to 'pre-empt' other calls if theirs is more urgent. The top priority is 'Flash' – reserved for the President or events ranging from tasks 'essential to defense and retaliation' to 'catastrophic events of national or international significance'.

In the UK, these more sophisticated telephone connections are available at sites such as the St Mawgan and Machrihanish nuclear weapons stores, and within the hardened 'command operations centers' at all major US Air Force bases.

Despite its sophisticated emergency uses, telephone connections on Autovon are insecure and can be monitored by friend and foe alike. Since 1967, therefore, the US has set up another, smaller, worldwide network of 'scrambled' telephone connections called Autosevocom (Automatic Secure Voice Communications network). Autosevocom has only about 2,000 subscribers, but the system can be used for Top Secret conversations.

Autodin – the 'digital' network – caters for computer data and written messages such as telex. Built in to Autodin are several specialised communications networks – including a replacement for the CRITICOMM intelligence network called the Defense Special Security Communications System. This part of Autodin handles so-called 'SI' or Special Intelligence communications – the output from Sigint stations and other sensitive intelligence sources.

Croughton, the sole British Autodin switching centre, is jointly run by the US Air Force and the Department of Defense's civilian Defense Communications Agency. By 1983, the Pentagon had hoped to introduce new automatic computer–computer links into a new Autodin II system. But this project was abandoned the year before. Instead, the Department of Defense decided to build up two existing computer networks. One is WIN, the Wimex Information Network, linking Wimex computers. The second is Arpanet, an experimental system used by civilian universities and scientific researchers in Britain for more than 10 years.

Croughton is linked to the two other US Autodin centres in Europe, Pirmasens in Germany and Coltano in Italy, and to Andrews Air Force Base near Washington. Lines across the Atlantic are supplied both by communications satellites and the TAT3 transatlantic telephone cable between New Jersey and Widemouth Bay, near Bude. The same cable also carries a link to the Automated Weather Network computer centre sited at Croughton. Croughton is one of four weather information switching centres under the control of the Air Force Global Weather Centre at SAC headquarters in Omaha, where information is collated from international meteorological stations, and civil and military weather satellites. A remote USAF weather station is sited on the Holbeach range in Lincolnshire.

Weather information is critical to planning nuclear or conventional attacks, whether by aircraft or by missiles (the accuracy of a missile warhead is affected by the speed of surface winds). In 1980, the official *Air Force Magazine* described how the facilities in the Automated Weather Network were being expanded to include a 'Pre-[nuclear] strike surveillance reconnaissance system' called PRESSURS. Possibly including covert 'sensors implanted in some way in enemy terrain', PRESSURS would help the Air Force weather service provide commanders with:

> target-by-target probabilities for their weapon system under various weather conditions[16] . . .

Reportedly, some US ballistic missiles carrying large warheads which are particularly sensitive to wind pressure can automatically be re-targeted according to weather conditions and wind speed near their targets.

Arpanet, the international experimental computer network which may partly take over from the abandoned Autodin II system, derives its name from the US Defense Advanced Research Projects Agency which funded the network and linked universities and research institutes to it to provide experimental traffic.

Britain's main Arpanet centre is University College, London. Through their terminal and host computer, groups as diverse as the Royal College of Art, St Bartholomew's Hospital and the Politics Department of Southampton University have linked to similar computer users on the other side of the Atlantic. There was nothing whatsoever military about these projects, of course – it was merely that by providing universities with a cheap system to use, the Advanced Research Projects Agency bought a group of clever and demanding guinea pigs to test ideas for future military computer networks.

Arpa – and latterly the Arpanet computer network – has also been used to military advantage as a quasi-civilian agency to set up international seismic monitoring stations throughout the world. The purpose of the network is to monitor and detect nuclear weapons tests – particularly important after the 1963 Partial Test Ban Treaty (which banned above ground tests by the UK, USA, USSR and other signatories) had come into effect. The London link to Arpanet goes via 'Norsar' – the Norwegian Seismic Array. The array and others like it are particularly useful for intelligence purposes, and can measure the yields of underground nuclear explosions.

In Britain, a small seismic array was set up in 1962 at Eskdalemuir, near Dumfries, at the behest of Arpa. Acting through the US Coastal and Geodetic Survey, the US government presented the equipment for this and 124 other stations around the world free to the countries concerned. One station is at the South Pole – but none were accepted in the Soviet and Chinese blocs. At the time of the gifts, each worth at least £10,000, the Assistant Director of the British Meteorological Office said publicly that he was certain that 'there was nothing behind the offer' except 'to get the science of seismology on a firm footing'.[17]

This was disingenuous. The firm footing the United States sought for seismology was the creation of a sophisticated worldwide network whose prime objective would be to detect nuclear tests. Data went back

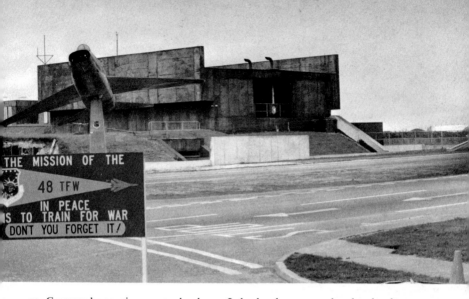

10. Command operations centre bunker at Lakenheath F-111 nuclear bomber base.

11. F-111s dispersed on the Lakenheath flight line.

12. MIG-lookalike 'Aggressor' squadron F-5s guarded by Americans dressed up as Russians on the flight line at Alconbury.

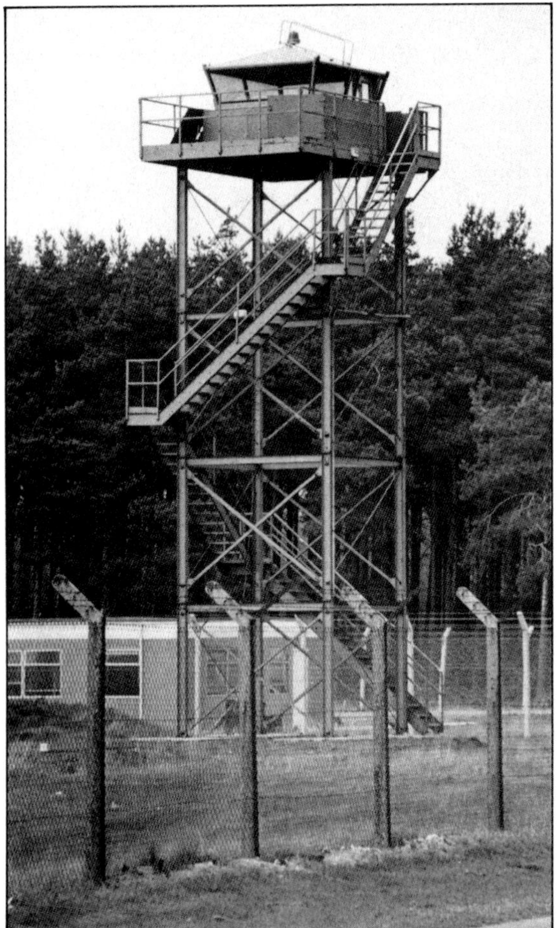

13. A nuclear weapons guard watchtower at Lakenheath.

15. Opposite: American RB-45C Tornado aircraft, photographed at Sculthorpe in 1954, carry RAF markings but without serial numbers. The aircraft were used by mixed British/American crews for still top-secret long-range spy flights over the Soviet Union.

14. US Air Force B-52 bombers are regular visitors to SAC's pre-designated British 'Forward Operating Bases'.

16. EC-135 flying war headquarters for the US European Command, codenamed 'Silk Purse', and stationed at Mildenhall, Suffolk.

17. Interior of a similar EC-135 'Looking Glass' command post used by SAC.

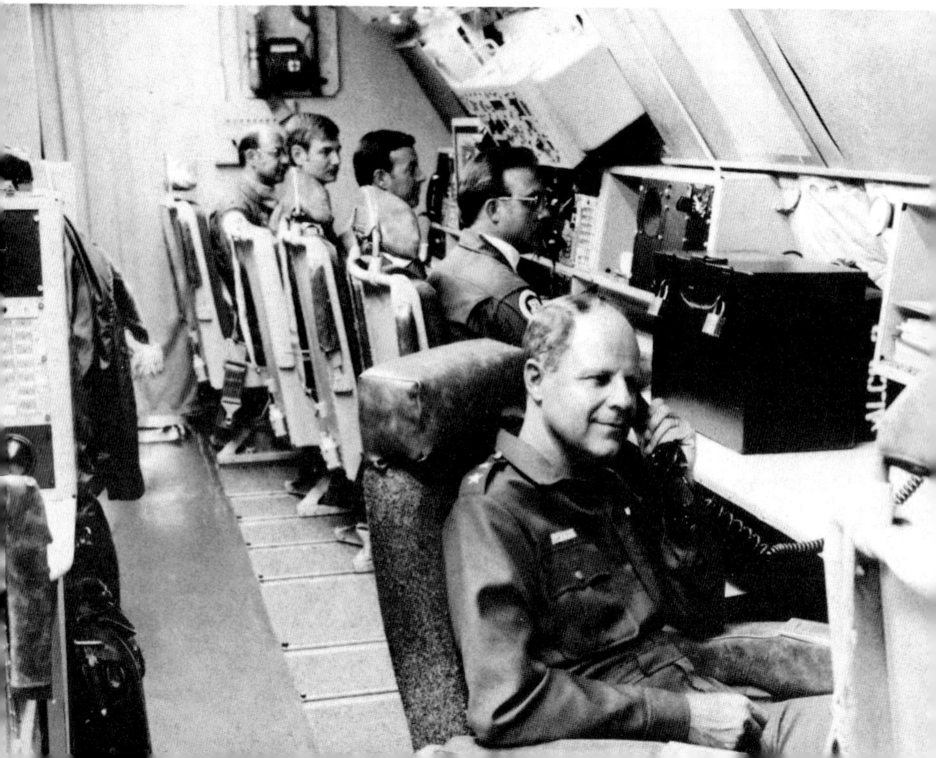

to the United States for this purpose. But the new network did indeed help establish seismology on a compatible international basis, according to seismic scientists. Data from the 125 Worldwide Standard Seismograph Network sites are openly available.

Not available, however, are the results from semi-secret and secret US and British seismic sites whose output is correlated for the US Defense Intelligence Agency by a computer centre at Patrick Air Force Base in Florida – the US Air Force Tactical Applications Centre (AFTAC). AFTAC receives telegraphed and postal data from the British Atomic Weapons Research Establishment at Aldermaston, which has its own nuclear detection network. This network formerly included data from seismic stations in Canada, Australia and India – now handed over to the national governments concerned. Aldermaston's main seismic monitoring field site is now the Blacknest Research Station, near Farnham in Surrey.

Secret data on nuclear test detection is traded between Aldermaston and AFTAC, classified, bizarrely, as 'Atomic Music/Principal', according to US regulations. Data can also come from atmospheric sampling, and from a secret network of 'microbarographs' – sensitive air pressure monitoring devices that can detect the weak remnants of a blast wave from a remote nuclear explosion. The Arpanet computer network has been used to transfer seismic data between Blacknest Research Station, Norsar, AFTAC and other US seismic research centres.

US experimental satellite operations began in Britain in 1960. A quarter-century later, preparations are in hand to make outer space the newest arena of military confrontation, and the United States Air Force has established, for the first time, a military Space Command. The era of peaceful co-operative scientific exploration in space has not yet fully been buried by adventurers of the Buck Rogers sort. But its days are numbered.

On 23 March 1983, President Reagan unexpectedly called for a new US national effort to develop strategic ballistic missile defences. The press, noting the upsurge in US military laser and particle beam research, and the search for 'directed energy weapons' for space warfare, dubbed this the 'Star Wars' speech. The label has stuck; the full-scale technology may never follow, however. But the first steps towards space war have been taken, through the consolidation of tracking networks and control systems around the world to find, analyse and if need be attack in space. Several American bases or facilities in Britain will participate in these developments.

Early ground terminals were set up in the UK to control the plethora of navigation, communication, early warning, Sigint and reconnaissance satellites that went into orbit after the 'Discoverer' satellites were first launched early in 1959. The Discoverer satellites were the joint progency of the CIA and the US Air Force who, soon after, set up the US National Reconnaissance Office (NRO). This agency, which co-ordinates all aircraft and satellite spy missions, is the only US intelligence agency whose very existence still remains secret.

It took the CIA 14 launches before, in mid-August 1960, the first spy-film capsule was recovered in mid-air by a 'snatch' aircraft near Hawaii. That success paved the way for a proliferating spy satellite programme, involving one satellite launch every two weeks during the 1960s. British contributions to the early satellite networks included tracking stations at:

- Winkfield, Berkshire: one of 11 'Minitrack' stations for satellite location, control, and telemetry (data back from the satellite). It has recently been closed.
- Lasham, Hampshire: a similarly-equipped station but run by a military agency, used to improve the reliability of navigation satellites (still in use).
- Kirkbride, Cumberland: planned site for three large MIDAS (Missile Defense and Alarm System) tracking dishes.[18]
- Christchurch, Dorset; Oakhanger, Hampshire; Defford, Worcestershire; experimental satellite communications terminals set up in 1965; Oakhanger has become a US Satellite Control Facility Remote Tracking Station.
- Fylingdales BMEWS station and UK long-range tracking radar at Malvern[19] (Royal Radar Establishment), part of the Space Data and Tracking network (SPADATS), used to monitor all space activity, Soviet as well as American.

Winkfield Radio and Space Research Station, the first to be set up, was operated by staff of the British Department of Scientific and Industrial Research (and latterly the Science Research Council) on contract to the US National Aeronautics and Space Agency. NASA, a civilian US government agency, was ostensibly intended only to deal with civil scientific research satellites. But many space research programmes went into a 'gray area between civilian and military interests'. On these occasions, it was advantageous to the United States if overseas ground stations for quasi-military projects could be obtained by the civil agency.

At Winkfield, a photograph released during the first press visit to the station on 17 January 1961 suggested that it was tracking many unambiguously military satellites. A list on display at the station included 2 CIA Discoverer probes, and military experimental communications satellites such as 'Echo' and 'Courier'. Information received from the satellites was relayed to NASA's Goddard Space Flight Center, and commands could be sent to the satellite on NASA's instructions.

Winkfield was equipped with an accurate tracking antennae system which could precisely locate a satellite from its telemetry signals. The station remained part of the NASA 'Stadan' (Space tracking and data network) until 1982. Two subordinate tracking stations linked to Winkfield were operated at Port Stanley, Falkland Islands and in Singapore. The Winkfield network was also used for British space experiments.

Twenty miles away, at Lasham airfield in Hampshire, a station with less equivocal military purpose was set up in 1961 under the auspices of the Royal Aircraft Establishment, Farnborough. Lasham's first function was as a 'Tranet' station for the US Navy navigation satellite system, Transit. The Transit system was designed to provide highly accurate position 'fixes' to Polaris ballistic missile submarines, then being stationed in the North and Norwegian Seas. Submarine navigators could find their firing position in relation to a Transit Satellite's orbit as they tracked it, using radio signals. First, however, the satellite's orbit had to be known with great accuracy.

The Tranet station at Lasham, and others in Brazil and the United States, supplied this information. US Navy navigation satellites have since become increasingly important in US nuclear target planning, since 'counterforce' disarming attacks on missile silos and similar hard targets require the launch point of the attacking missile to be very accurately known. Missile targeting also required, during the 1960s, that the United States and Soviet Union map each other's territory to a hitherto unknown level of accuracy. For the United States, this vital military task was mostly performed in civilian clothing by series of 'geodetic' satellites launched by NASA.

Lasham is still used as a satellite ground station and test facility by the Space Department of the Royal Aircraft Establishment. Weather satellite pictures are received there by the Ministry of Defence for use at the Meteorological Office in Bracknell.

US–UK collaboration on military satellite communications began in earnest in 1964, with the Interim Defense Communications Satellite Program. IDCSP satellites – single channel relay satellites little larger in

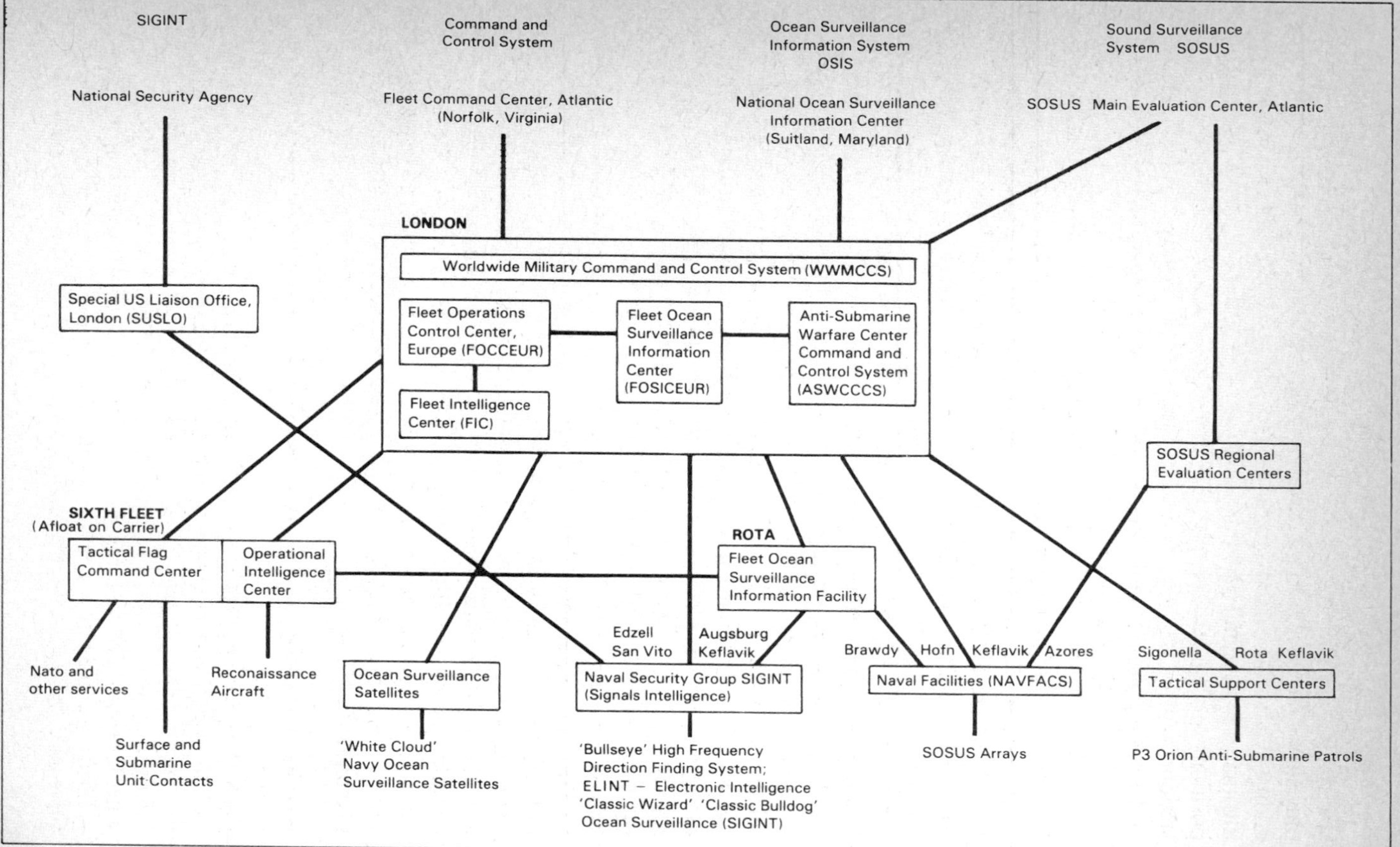


Fig 8. Finding targets; US naval intelligence system

size than a football – were placed in 22,000-mile high orbits, moving only slowly in relation to the earth's surface. The next satellite generation would achieve fixed 'geostationary' orbits over the equator (meaning that the satellite was always available in more or less the same position, and the tracking dish did not need to move). British tracking stations were built at Christchurch, Dorset (then the Signals Research and Development Establishment) and at Oakhanger and Defford to experiment in the use of the IDCSP network.

The US Air Force next launched Defense Satellite Communications System (DSCS) satellites with a capacity to relay over 1,200 simultaneous conversations. Britain ordered two 'Skynet' satellites of similar capacity from US manufacturers, and the IDCSP ground stations were converted to handle Skynet. Oakhanger was designated the Skynet master station, and tracking and control antennae, all compatible with the US DSCS system, were installed. Soon after, a NATO satellite terminal (NATO Satcom) was added to the Oakhanger complex.

The compatibility of the designs proved fortuitous. Skynet was a near-disaster, with four satellites providing less than 5 years total reliable service in 15. DSCS fared little better: the first two satellites did not work well, one of the second pair to be launched failed in 1975, and two other pairs of satellites failed to get into orbit. So DSCS, Skynet and NATO Satcom have sometimes been used interchangeably. When the DSCS satellite over the eastern Pacific suddenly failed in 1976, a NATO Satcom was dispatched around the equator to stand in instead.

Since the last Skynet satellite became unuseable about 1977, British military satellite communications have relied entirely on American DSCS satellites. Under a 1973 memorandum of understanding, Britain and the United States agreed to collaborate in the use of military communications satellites. Subsequently, the United Kingdom became the sole foreign nation to be an authorised user as such of DSCS. In return, the United States gained the use of Skynet and the facilities at Oakhanger.

---

OPPOSITE

**Fig 8. Finding targets: naval intelligence systems**

At US Naval headquarters for Europe, in central London, computers watch the entire Atlantic Ocean and Mediterranean Sea. The Ocean Surveillance Information System combines data from aircraft, ships, satellites and underwater SOSUS arrays. The diagram shows how other British intelligence centres – Edzell and Brawdy – combine in the European section of a worldwide surveillance network.

DSCS satellites are also used by NATO and the US Diplomatic Telecommunications Service, providing links from Washington to overseas embassies. As the Pentagon's main worldwide communications system, DSCS provides high-capacity multi-purpose links. But current DSCS satellites and ground stations are not hardened against nuclear attack or consequent radiation damage. Nor are they hardened against electromagnetic pulse (EMP), a destructive pulse of radio energy which is released at the same time as the flash of a nuclear explosion. A new series, DSCS-3, will come into use during 1984.

Besides providing connections for Autovon, Wimex, and other major US military networks, DSCS satellites carry:

> wideband intelligence information that cannot be transmitted via commercial satellites and . . . bulk-encrypted secure voice/data communications[20]

In Britain, DSCS terminals now are (or appear to be) located at Croughton (a DSCS network control station), Menwith Hill, Thurso, and Oakhanger, near Bordon in Hampshire. Compatible Skynet or NATO terminals are sited at Oakhanger, Defford near Malvern, and Balado Bridge, near Kinross, Fife. Satellite terminals at GCHQ Cheltenham, the British Sigint headquarters, are probably also able to use DSCS when required.

Thurso, a US Navy DSCS terminal installed in 1979, is jointly run by RAF and US Navy personnel; so, evidently, is Oakhanger, according to the local telephone directory, which lists 'US Navy Communication Facilities' at the base. A US Navy Fleet Satellite Communications terminal is also installed on the roof of the US Navy headquarters in central London, with a new 'Jam Resistant Secure Communications' DSCS terminal likely to follow, according to a 1980 report.

Oakhanger is now part of an important and classified new US satellite system. It has also gained an increasingly important role as a general control station for all US military satellites, part of the 'Satellite Control Facility'. Despite Oakhanger's role in the SCF system being openly identified in US Congressional testimony and other public sources, Defence Ministers have recently attempted to deny that the site is an American base at all.[21]

The Satellite Control Facility was set up in 1967 as a worldwide system for controlling satellite operations. All reconnaissance satellites must be instructed when to take pictures, what direction and frequency to monitor for Sigint and Elint purposes, and so on. The SCF is responsible for seeing military satellites safely into orbit, and controlling their operations once they are there. SCF's headquarters is at Sunnyvale, California, the USAF Satellite Test Center.

Oakhanger joined the SCF network between 1974 and 1977. Congressional testimony in 1977[22] listed the Oakhanger control centre among seven sites containing 11 tracking dishes used to control some 40 US and NATO satellites then 'on-orbit'. The other six stations were in Greenland, the Seychelles, Guam, Hawaii, California and New Hampshire.

Oakhanger, apparently codenamed 'Pogo', controls US spy satellite operations through a 60-foot diameter Space-Ground Link System 'wheel and track' antenna dish. According to an unclassified USAF special report on the SCF system:

> All stations are operated under the administration of [US] Air Force site commanders . . . Oakhanger Tracking Station (OTS) is a United Kingdom site . . . OTS is not a complete station . . . and on-orbit satellite support can only be provided when connected to the Command and Data Processing Area at [Sunnyvale] . . .

This link is provided via DSCS satellites. At Sunnyvale, data relayed to and from the satellites is fed to the satellite's Mission Control Center via processing computers called 'bird buffers'.

Oakhanger is getting 'bird buffers' for an unspecified secret mission. In 1982, the US specialist military journal *Defense Electronics* reported that $126.5 million was to be spent during 1983 and 1984 on work including major SCF improvements at Oakhanger, identified as program number 35110F:

> Wideband communications capability for Oakhanger telemetry and commanding station, Data Systems modernisation [and] computer capability for new classified satellite program[23] . . .

Golden Pot, a former US Air Force microwave relay station in Hampshire, was reopened in 1982 as part of this secret program. The relay station now provides a direct high-capacity link between the Oakhanger ground terminal and the Digital European Backbone (DEB) station to the north at High Wycombe.

US Congressional hearings are (for once) silent about the reason for modernising the Oakhanger Satellite Control Facility. But testimony has mentioned one new NSA Sigint satellite system, called 'Ladylove', which required only the refurbishment of two antennae at an unspecified overseas base during 1981 and 1982.

Although most of the Oakhanger satellite facilities have not been secret, the station also incorporated a giant tracking dish over 100 feet in diameter, whose installation or function appears to have had little to do with man-made satellites, and whose existence has never been discussed in public. It is likely to have been part of an exotic, but reputedly abortive, US project to gather signals intelligence by 'moonbounce', listening to Soviet radar and other messages reflected off the moon's surface. The most spectacular experiment of this kind was an NSA station at Sugar Grove, Virginia, where Sigint engineers attempted to construct a $135-million, 600-foot diameter listening dish.[24]

Oakhanger was identified as another 'moonbounce' experimental station in reports from the US Naval Research Laboratory, under whose auspices the 'biggest bug in the world' was constructed at Sugar Grove. The famous British radiotelescope at Jodrell Bank near Manchester has also been used for these unusual experiments. For a few days during the 1960s, civilian scientists were secretly asked to leave their experiments, and the telescope was 'borrowed' by GCHQ and Ministry of Defence technicians to test the Americans' moonbounce plan.

By 1970, however, the CIA had begun developing an alternative giant dish antenna, to be unfurled in space, and which would look down on the Soviet Union from a mere 22,300 miles. The moon would not be necessary. This device was the 'Rhyolite' satellite which, from its geostationary altitude, was capable of 'sucking up like a vacuum cleaner' many terrestrial communications. The first Rhyolite satellite was launched in 1973.

Separate networks of radar and tracking stations monitor the progress of satellites which have been launched by countries other than the United States. By 1986, the US Air Force may have high-flying aircraft equipped with anti-satellite missiles to shoot down low-orbiting satellites. Miniature rockets would steer the anti-satellite weapon into a devastating 8.5 miles-a-second head-on collision with an oncoming satellite. No explosive warhead is needed.

'Spacetrack', a worldwide network of powerful radar stations, tracks potential satellite targets for this system, feeding information to Space Command headquarters inside Cheyenne Mountain, near Colorado Springs. The underground Colorado base is also the headquarters of the North American Air Defense command. Britain participates in Spacetrack by supplying information from the Fylingdales Ballistic Missile Early Warning Station. Until recently a similar and powerful tracking radar at the Royal Signals and Radar Establishment at Malvern, Worcestershire also participated in Spacetrack. The only other Spacetrack radar detectors operating in longitudes between the eastern United States and the Pacific are on Ascension Island, at Diyarbakir in Turkey, and in Thailand.

Fylingdales is thus a part of the space intelligence network, Spadats (Space Data and Tracking System), which maintains a catalogue of everything known in space. Fylingdales is primarily an intelligence station, since its actual role of early warning will only be exercised in nuclear war. When not on exercise, its scanners routinely detect and track Soviet satellite launches or missile tests.

A second British space intelligence station was in operation in East Anglia in 1973, but worked for barely more than a year. This was US Air Force Project 441L, 'Cobra Mist' – an 'over-the-horizon' radar tracking station said to cost £55 million, and constructed to monitor Soviet missile tests. Until its demolition in 1975, Cobra Mist was one of the most powerful, spectacular and large-scale pieces of electronics ever seen in Britain. But it was a failure. Why it was a failure remains secret. When it folded is not: funds were abruptly withdrawn on 29 June 1973, and 90 local staff sacked on a day's notice.

Cobra Mist began test transmissions in March 1971, its powerful radio beam necessitating warnings to mariners and airmen to stay at least three miles offshore when passing the point of Orford Ness, the site of the new station. 189 masts were erected in a semicircular fan covering nearly half a square mile. The masts were arranged to support 18 sloping transmitter arrays, which between them could direct a narrow beam of radio energy, on any frequency and with a peak power of many megawatts, in any compass direction between 15 degrees north-west and 135 degrees south-east. It was perhaps not coincidental that the centre of the fan, with a bearing of about 60 degrees north-west, appeared to point directly at the Plesetsk missile test centre.[25]

Over-the-horizon radar differs from the ordinary sort in that the radar beams do not travel in a straight line, but bounce between the ground and the ionosphere in 'hops' often many hundreds of miles long. The returning radar echo scattered back by a target is usually very weak, requiring the use of extremely powerful transmitters to get a measurable return. Computers were needed to analyse the returning radio signal and find missile or aircraft targets. Reportedly, the Cobra Mist ground station on its own was not enough, but worked in conjunction with satellites and RB-57 reconnaissance aircraft to make synchronised measurements of the paths of the probing radio beams. Its signals may also have been interpreted by an OTH receiving station on the far side of the world, according to the RAF Deputy Director of the project, who explained its purpose as:

> to study in particular the propagation paths through the polar regions to the other side of the world.[26]

News of the establishment of Plesetsk, subsequently the world's busiest space launching centre, only became public in 1966. In 1967, the US signed a secret agreement with Britain to collaborate on the development of the Orford Ness station. Officially a joint USAF-RAF 'long range radio research station', the Ministry of Defence advised reporters informally that Orford Ness was an early warning station which might provide 15 minutes early warning of attack instead of 4.

But Orford Ness was not an early warning station. Fylingdales, which *was* run primarily to detect an attack, reported to the US Aerospace Defense Command. Cobra Mist was run instead by the Sigint specialists of the 81st Radio Research Squadron of the US Air Force Security Service, reporting directly to the National Security Agency. They were assisted by about 200 civilian British and American engineering staff, working on contract from the US corporation RCA.

When the station suddenly closed, the RAF suggested only that 'alternative lines of investigation are more effective ... a further programme at Orford Ness cannot be justified'. The US Air Force contract with RCA was cancelled at a day's notice. Whatever the reason for its abrupt demise, the Soviet Union could not have been unaware of the river of radio energy that had been launched over its territory from the swampy east Suffolk coast. They may well have jammed the OTH radar receiving terminals. Or the US may have found a simpler answer to the problem of monitoring missile tests sites, through the use of better satellites, and new and improved Elint and Sigint stations in Iran, Turkey, and northern Norway.

The deep underground Cheyenne Mountain complex, the control centre for space intelligence, was completed at the same time as the Ballistic Missile Early Warning System. For some time, it was considered invulnerable to H-bomb attack. Inside the mountain, display consoles in the Space Defense Operations Center can predict the future path of any of the thousands of man-made objects in space – most of them just detritus or long-dead satellites and their boosters. The Cheyenne Mountain control centre is being augmented by a new Consolidated Space Operations Center, which will take charge of military space shuttle missions and Satellite Control Facility stations such as Oakhanger. The new Center will start operations in 1985.

Many of the new developments in space are, remarkably, perhaps as much the product of ideology as technology. The new emphasis on fighting in space has been a watchword of Reagan's White House corps of political and military advisers since he was elected. A key figure in promoting space issues since 1981 has been Lieutenant General Daniel O. Graham, a former director of the Defense Intelligence Agency, and a Reagan election campaign adviser. Graham has repeatedly urged his fellow Americans to recall their pioneer frontiersman spirit and 'seize the high frontier [of outer space]'.

The same US 'New Right' lobbyists whose political campaigns helped ease Reagan into the White House, the Heritage Foundation, have generously funded General Graham's 'High Frontier, Inc' campaign. It is a strange combination; there is no *prima facie* reason why the thrust for Star Wars death rays and ballistic missile defence, rather than other sorts of military technology, should have joined born-again Christianity and monetarist dogma on the political slate of the American right.

But it has, and senior military officers have not been slow to take the hint. More Pentagon money than ever before is available for research into space 'battle stations' and high energy lasers. As the $1.4 billion Consolidated Space Operations Center approached completion at Colorado Springs, Space Commander General James V. Hartinger told local leaders that an all-out US Air Force military space programme was merely 'a matter of time'. The new Center was, he said:

> just the beginning if we're really going to fulfill our destiny to be . . . the Guardians of the High Frontier.[27]

## Notes

1 *Stars and Stripes* (US forces newspaper), 18 January 1983; the same *United Press International* report was syndicated in many papers.
2 Information given to the author.
3 *Washington Post*, 14 August 1983.
4 *ibid.*
5 GAO Report LCD80-22, 14 December 1979, 'The World Wide Military Command and Control System – Major changes needed in its automated data processing management and direction.'
6 *Scotsman*, 28 January 1980.
7 House of Representatives, Appropriations Committee (Defense), Fiscal Year 1979, Part 4, p 198. US Congress, 1978.

8 *Nato's Fifteen Nations*, 2, 1980, p 102.
9 Defense Marketing Service, Intelligence Report on EUCOM $C^3$ Systems, 1982. DMS, Greenwich, Connecticut.
10 House of Representatives, Committee on Armed Services, Hearings on Military Posture, Fiscal Year 1981, Book 2, Part 4, p 2329. US Congress, 1980.
11 *New York Times*, 11 December 1982.
12 *Guardian*, 10 December 1982.
13 *The Times*, 11 December 1982.
14 *Hansard*, 15 December 1982.
15 *Hansard*, 6 July 1983; the answer mentioned eight sites, three of which (all in Northern Ireland) had been handed back.
16 *Air Force Magazine*, November 1980.
17 *Glasgow Herald*, 27 February 1964.
18 *New Scientist*, 27 July 1961.
19 *Jane's Weapons Systems*, 1978, p 224. Malvern is believed to have ceased contributing to the SPADATS network after 1979.
20 *Aviation Week and Space Technology*, 17 October 1977.
21 'Oakhanger [and Prestwick] . . . are not American bases', Lord Belstead, speaking in the House of Lords; *Hansard* 3 May 1983.
22 House of Representatives, Committee on Armed Services, subcommittee on Military Posture, FY 1980 Hearings, Book 1, Part 3, p 1275. US Congress, 1979.
23 *Defense Electronics*, October 1982.
24 James Bamford, *The Puzzle Palace*, pp 167–9, Sidgwick and Jackson, 1983.
25 *New Scientist*, 7 November 1974.
26 *Guardian*, 29 April 1971.
27 *Colorado Springs Gazette-Telegraph*, 4 August 1983.

# 8 *Polaris and Poseidon*

New plans for nuclear warfare put the United States Navy in the same position in 1958 as the Air Force had faced in 1948 – that of needing to be relatively close to the USSR to mount an effective attack – and thus endowed the British Isles with a further network of nuclear bases. The range of the first new Polaris missiles – about 1,400 miles – meant that to be in range of their Soviet targets, the submarines would have to patrol in sea areas close by – the Norwegian and Barents Seas, the eastern Mediterranean, and the north-west Pacific. Closer in to the Soviet Union – the Baltic or Black Seas, or the Arctic – would put the submarines too much at risk of detection and destruction. To operate as long as possible in these areas required suitable bases near to the patrol areas, from which the submarines could quickly come and go – much more rapidly than if they had to cross and re-cross the Atlantic on each patrol.

There were United States allies suitably close at hand – Norway in the Atlantic, and Japan in the Pacific. But neither country would accept the presence of nuclear weapons. Although Norway – and later, Japan – were to provide other important bases without which Polaris could not have been effectively operated, they did so without full knowledge of the purpose of navigation and communications stations they accepted. The first submarines would work in and around the Norwegian Sea. So, in searching for new naval bases overseas to operate Polaris submarines, it was inevitable that Britain should, once again, be asked to fill the breach. Thus began the Scottish nuclear missile submarine base, which may still be in use at the end of the century.

Early in 1960, US officials made the first approach to the British government for base facilities. The Clyde and the Gareloch adjacent, were said to be the favoured sites. There were also surveys carried out at Londonderry in Northern Ireland, Stornoway in the Hebrides and Milford Haven in Pembrokeshire. In September 1960 the Cabinet secretly gave the go-ahead for the American submarine base to be sited on the Clyde at a small sea loch and sailing resort west of the Gareloch itself. The new base bore the ironic and inapt name of Holy Loch.

Strategic considerations led the US Navy to acquire its Scottish forward base. But it has also enabled them to lower safety standards compared with the procedures required in United States ports. On at least three occasions, nuclear warheads in Holy Loch Poseidon submarines have been potentially at risk through accident, collision, or fire. Both Polaris and Poseidon warheads have had urgently to be modified to deal with safety and reliability problems. The tensions of ballistic missile submarine operations led, on one occasion, to a riot in nearby Dunoon (p 302). Many US Navy personnel, including those responsible for guarding or operating nuclear warheads on submarines, have used illegal drugs – including while on operational patrols. As many as 1 in 6 of US Navy base staff have been drugtakers.

Turning the Holy Loch over to the United States Navy was another bombs-for-bases deal; yet again the United Kingdom was buying, or hoping to buy, nuclear technology and devices from the United States on cheap, special relationship terms. The trade-off created a further increase in British national vulnerability in crisis or war.

Holy Loch was exchanged for the right to buy Skybolt ballistic missiles, which would be launched by the V bombers. The deal was struck by Prime Minister Macmillan and President Eisenhower during a meeting in March 1960 at the woodland retreat, Camp David in Maryland. Macmillan wanted either Skybolt or Polaris for the UK, but the United States policy favoured the creation of a multinational NATO Polaris nuclear force; it did not want the British to have independent control of their own Polaris missiles.

Buying Skybolt got Macmillan out of one awkward corner in the development of British nuclear weapons; he then was able to cancel the British long-range missile project, Blue Streak. It got him into a further corner when Skybolt was in turn cancelled by the Americans. In the early stages of the Holy Loch negotiations, there was a belated and quite unsuccessful attempt by Macmillan to improve the terms of British control over US nuclear bases. Early leaks to the press, before the Camp David meeting, reported that 'Britain must have some operational control over the submarines'.[1] Macmillan's diary records that he left Camp David having agreed to 'do what he could' for the US Navy. But he then instructed Defence Minister Harold Watkinson, on a subsequent visit, to strike a hard bargain and 'open up the more difficult problem of allowing American submarines . . . to make a base on the

Clyde'. Watkinson apparently managed to 'disassociate the two deals' to seek better terms for Britain – but to little avail.

The need for more stringent terms was reinforced in July 1960, when the RB-47 bomber from Brize Norton was shot down by the Russians on a spy mission over the Barents Sea, while, it was said, it was violating Soviet airspace (p 58). Although the American nuclear horse had long since gazed at open British stable doors, Macmillan nevertheless recorded his intention, after the RB-47 incident concluded a long series of rows over American operations in Britain (and with many brewing for the future), to:

> look carefully again at the precise terms of the agreement for the American bases in order to ensure they were watertight. Accordingly, I asked Eisenhower to arrange for a careful reexamination, to which he agreed.[2]

This was to no avail, for the Prime Minister was soon to be embarrassed yet again over British (non-)control of the US Polaris forces.

The new base was announced to public and Parliament in November 1960, just three months before the first submarines and their tender were due to arrive. Two weeks later, the USS *George Washington* loaded the first-ever consignment of 16 Polaris A1 missiles, and sailed east across the Atlantic from its Charleston, South Carolina base, on the first live patrol. But for the divide within the Labour Party over nuclear weapons, widespread national protest over the announcement of the new base would have made the development of Holy Loch fraught with difficulty. But Opposition leader Hugh Gaitskell refused to endorse a Labour backbench motion opposing the base.

In the streets, however, the Campaign for Nuclear Disarmament, vastly grown in size and impact since its early days, was now a significant feature of the British political scene – sufficient, it was later reported, to cause the US misgivings about coming to Britain, as late as a month before the first missile carrying submarine was due to arrive.

Whatever the military advantages might be, the very idea of missile-firing submarines – operating remote, impersonal and sinister, hidden below the sea – attracted widespread revulsion. Some years later, when an RAF officer revealed British plans to use nuclear depth bombs against Soviet Polaris-type missile submarines, he expressed this feeling eloquently:

> We're not ashamed to be training to attack such a fair target as a submarine which is prepared to attack cities crowded with civilians,

> using imprecisely-aimed nuclear rockets from the apparent safety of the open sea . . .[3]

The same considerations motivated Glasgow Corporation, like the councils of Ayr, Falkirk, and other Scottish towns and districts, to vote against the new base – in Glasgow, by a two-thirds majority. It was hard for Scots living in the densely populated Clyde Valley, less than thirty miles from Holy Loch, and very likely downwind of any nuclear explosion, to avoid the belief that the dangers of accommodating the base in a heavily-populated area might have weighed more heavily on London decision-takers if Polaris submarines could have been accommodated in Reading rather than the remote western outposts of the kingdom that had been sought. Macmillan acknowledged in the Commons that:

> This target [the Holy Loch], like every other target in the country, will be important but no more important, and perhaps a little less important, than the bomber bases . . .
>
> . . . We have to accept the situation that our danger is spread, and that we are all in it.[4]

Government statements stressed that in a crisis the depot ship could and would sail out of the Holy Loch, given time. At the height of the Cuban missile crisis, on 23 October 1962, the depot ship USS *Proteus* did just that, and left the Clyde for an unknown location. But it was nevertheless extremely unlikely that a nuclear attack on Britain would omit an attack on the Clyde and the Holy Loch, even if the submarines and their mother ship appeared to have departed, a point made repeatedly by the Russians themselves.

Even before the official announcement had been made, Soviet officials had been keen to broadcast their concurrence with Scottish fears; Radio Moscow warned in October that 'it is not difficult to imagine how much greater the danger has become for Britain as a result of all this'. The new base was 'fraught with dangerous consequence to its American sponsors and their British allies'. As the *Proteus* arrived off Dunoon a few months later, the station chided that in a crisis, the base 'would attract retaliatory rockets like a magnet'.

The extent of devastation faced by residents of the Clyde Valley as a consequence of the submarine bases (including the British Polaris base later set up at Faslane) was well illustrated in the scenario devised by the Ministry of Defence for the 1980 civil defence exercise, 'Square Leg'. In this attack, no part of Britain was more devastated.

Six hydrogen bombs were anticipated to rain down on the mid-Clyde, embracing the Holy Loch, Faslane, and the Coulport nuclear-missile depot. One attack was an underwater burst in the Clyde which would augment the devastation with floods from water surges, and the extra hazards of 'wet' fallout. Even the erroneously optimistic casualty calculations made by Scottish regional civil defence officials assessed the dead, trapped and severely injured (and thus condemned) at 40 per cent of the entire population of the Strathclyde region, within 24 hours of the attack.

The grim condition of central Scotland in this postulated nuclear war was much worsened by two further nuclear attacks on the US nuclear depth bomb store at Machrihanish, near Campbeltown on the lower Clyde, and on Prestwick, used by the US Air Force Military Air-lift Command. There were also two bombs on Glasgow. The Clyde Valley became a smoking ruin, with 'total or partial destruction of all houses and buildings'.[5]

These risks were also foreseen by the protestors who objected to the plan to allow the Americans to have Holy Loch. They included many Scottish MPs, the Scottish TUC and local councils. In an attempt to forestall protest and criticism, the announcement of the Holy Loch base was accompanied by reassurances about British 'control' of the submarines coming to the UK, and about the safety of their operations. Each of these reassurances was to prove dismally ill-founded.

In rapid succession, British ministerial pronouncements on indigenous control were contradicted in Washington by US officials. At first, Macmillan told MPs that they should realise that:

> It is impossible to make an agreement on all fours with the bomber agreement. The deployment and use in periods of emergency of the submarine depot ship and associated facilities will be a matter of joint consultation between the two governments . . . Wherever these submarines may be, I am confident that no decision to use these missiles will be taken without the fullest possible previous consultation . . .[6]

The same evening, the US State Department spokesman Lincoln White refused to confirm what Macmillan had said about decisions to use the missiles. The statement had 'surprised' the US. 'There might not be time for consultation', they explained, adding that 'no commitment had been made'.

The British government was left in evident and uncomfortable disarray. Foreign Secretary Lord Home told the Commons that indeed

Britain might not be consulted, as this could not be guaranteed 'in case of emergency'.

But Defence Minister Harold Watkinson added a new gloss a day later by announcing that 'our control [of US Polaris submarines] in territorial waters is absolute . . . We have a firm assurance that these missiles would not be fired in any circumstances in United Kingdom territorial waters'. United States officials again refused to confirm this ministerial claim, and attempted to duck the question by explaining that the submarines would normally be on their war stations, far distant from UK territorial waters.

The Defence Minister's credibility suffered further when US Navy officers subsequently explained to the press how they *would* launch at targets 'from Leningrad to Kiev' (in emergency) from the surface of Holy Loch. During the missile-firing salvo, the submarine had to be rolled from side to side as port and starboard missiles were successively ignited.[7]

During the embarrassing week, US and British officials endeavoured to patch up a new phraseology of suitable blandness to be acceptable to public opinion on both sides of the Atlantic. Macmillan explained to the House of Commons:

> As regards facilities in the territory . . . We have exactly the same control in an emergency as exists over United States bomber or missile bases in this country. That is to say there will then be joint consultation regarding the use of these facilities.[8]

There would be the 'fullest possible consultation' with Britain and NATO before launching Polaris, 'because consultation might be impossible in circumstances of a surprise attack on the West . . . we would not wish to insist on prior consultation'.

The Prime Minister evidently had little or no idea of what he was saying; his statement was wrong on many counts:

- Only a week earlier he had said that the understanding on Polaris could not be equated ('on all fours') to the 'bombers' agreement. Now it was 'exactly the same' in its important respects.
- In fact the terms were not the same, but had been devalued from their previous and already hazy form. Use of the airbases was a matter for *joint decision*. With Polaris, this was reduced to 'a matter of *joint consultation*'. And that applied only to the depot ship and Holy Loch facilities – not the submarines and missiles.
- Macmillan was wrong again to characterise the US Thor missiles in East Anglia as being in the same category. Here Britain had dual control, and a clear, full right of veto.

– More interestingly, the British government had put an obvious but thus far suppressed gloss on the meaning of the original airbase agreement; there might not be time for joint consultation, let alone joint decision taking, in many foreseeable circumstances of war.

Macmillan refused to publish the agreement (merely an exchange of notes) concerning Holy Loch. It was evident that far from strengthening British control over US activities, he had again demonstrated its weakness. The UK, it was tacitly admitted, had no knowledge of, or control over, Polaris submarines once they had departed on patrol. US spokesmen explained that what existed was only a 'gentlemen's agreement' and that the argument between Britain and the United States which underlay the row was motivated by US fears that 'a too tightly drawn formal agreement might compel other nations to seek similar agreements.'[9] In fact, most Western nations hosting US bases then or subsequently have sought comparatively much tighter agreements with the US; British politicians have remained uniquely complacent.

Macmillan was also asked whether there were assurances that the submarines would not go on provocative, 'dangerous patrols close to Soviet waters, similar to the RB-47 aircraft.' He ridiculed the idea – to a chorus of 'ministerial laughter', *The Times* reported.

Fifteen years later, it was revealed that the US had repeatedly sent submarines on 'Holystone' intelligence missions into Soviet waters, even as far as Vladivostock harbour (see Chapter 5). Although the revelation of these extraordinarily dangerous missions provoked an outcry in the United States, submarine intelligence activities have been continued. Amongst current top secret US projects are a Sigint (signals intelligence) system codenamed 'Prairie Schooner', and also 'Dark Eyes' – an aptly-named piece of optical spy equipment. Both Fleet Ballistic Missile and ordinary, 'hunter-killer' nuclear submarines were used for Holystone adventures.

The Holy Loch became Fleet Ballistic Missile Submarine Refit Site One, and the first of a series of submarine tenders, the depot ship *Proteus*, reached its new Scottish station early in March 1961. A few days later, the first nuclear submarine, USS *Patrick Henry*, surfaced in the Clyde, after more than two months underwater. The submarine's motto was 'Liberty or Death'. Soon after, the *George Washington* itself, after which the submarine class had been named, arrived after its second underwater patrol.

The Holy Loch unit was named the 14th Submarine Squadron. Its initial strength grew from one to five as submarines of the *George*

*Washington* class were completed. Then it built up to ten. After each submarine patrol was completed, the crew would fly back to the United States, and after maintenance and restocking, a new crew would take over.

The submarines' operational schedule has remained much the same over the years. They can be fully refitted at Holy Loch, but this does not include dismantling to remove and replace the nuclear reactor core. Such extended refits last about two months. Each submarine has two separate captains and crews, identified as the Blue and Gold crews. The crews and some of their supplies fly from Prestwick Airport, near Ayr, at the beginning and end of the underwater tours of duty. Their home base is in Charleston, South Carolina. A second US Poseidon base is now in operation at New London, Connecticut.

The submarine tender on duty in the Holy Loch changes every two to three years as the five tenders available – *Proteus*, *Holland*, *Hunley*, *Simon Lake*, and *Canopus* – rotate between submarine refit sites. Permanently moored in the Loch is a floating dry dock, the USS *Los Alamos*, which was assembled there in 1961 after being floated in sections across the Atlantic. US Navy staff at Holy Loch number 1,800, including the crew of the depot 'mother' ship. Two supply ships, *Betelgeuse* and *Alcor*, ply the Atlantic to bring supplies, including missiles and warheads, to Holy Loch. The depot ships themselves can store 18 missiles on board, two more than on board each submarine. Three tugs, sundry launches and a barge make up a small US flotilla in the Holy Loch. A continuous patrol around the depot ship keeps local sailors or sightseers at a distance.

As the Holy Loch base built up, so did public concern and dissent. The United States openly considered moving out again, as it was faced with what it saw as a three-pronged threat: public protesters from Direct Action groups on the streets, around the shores of Holy Loch, and not infrequently in canoes in the Loch; less public fears for security; and the possibility that an incoming Labour government would send them home anyway. In February 1961, the seeds of doubt in Washington were evidently well embedded and increasingly public; President Kennedy felt obliged to send assurances to the UK that the plan was indeed proceeding.

At Kilmun, on a promontory into the Clyde, the demonstrators set up what we would now know as a peace camp, in February 1961. With canoes and small boats they attempted to block the arrival of the *Proteus*. A month later, the campers attempted to board the ship. At Whitsun, a 2,000 strong march led by Michael Foot made a significant if temporary impact. From May to September there were periodic blockades, and regular and sometimes spectacular canoe sallies into the loch in an attempt to board the submarines or the depot ship. A frogman dived under the ship and scratched his initials on the bottom. In Parliament, the most determined anti-Polaris campaigner, South Ayrshire MP Emrys Hughes, attempted unsuccessfully to introduce a bill to ban Polaris.

In the event, the new Labour government of 1964 banned neither American nor British Polaris submarines. The 14th Submarine Squadron (SUBRON 14) reached its allocated strength of 10 submarines in that year. A new base was opened for a second squadron to operate in the Mediterranean, at Rota near Cadiz in Spain and a third squadron was formed at Guam in the Pacific in the late 1960s. At its peak in 1968, the Polaris force was 41 strong.

On 6 May 1962, in a test codenamed 'Frigate Bird', the USS *Ethan Allan* launched a live nuclear missile against the British nuclear test site at Christmas Island. It detonated successfully; the yield (probably about 1 megaton) was kept secret. Nine months later, *Ethan Allan* came to the Clyde, and was opened for a tour by a press corps awestruck by a close-up view of the machinery of Armageddon. Captain Paul Lacy explained to them that retargeting procedures meant that 'the birds are flexible . . . I could fire one at London'.[10]

The power and range of Polaris missiles was extended successively to 1,800 miles, and then to 2,500 miles, enabling deeper attacks on the Soviet Union or more remote (and hence safer) patrols. The Polaris A3 missile, in use from 1964, substituted a trio of lower yield (about 200 kiloton) warheads for the one megaton bomb carried by the original missiles. Polaris A3 missiles, with similar but British-made warheads, were also purchased for the Royal Navy after the Nassau agreement of 1963.

Polaris A3 was succeeded in turn by Poseidon, with a range said to be in excess of 3,000 miles. Poseidon had a quite different nuclear payload, consisting of up to 14 MIRVed warheads.[11] Miniaturised to fit into a missile not much larger than Polaris had been, each warhead had a yield of 40–50 kT. The number of warheads in an individual missile is traded off against the range it is expected to reach. Depending on the targets allocated to the submarine, and the area of its patrol, each missile may actually carry between 6 and 14 warheads. Also packed in among the Poseidon warheads are 'penetration aids' intended to confuse radar detectors for defensive missiles.

Of considerable strategic importance was a tenfold improvement in the accuracy of Poseidon – the likely error in reaching its target was down to 500–600 yards from 3 miles or worse in Polaris. This changed considerably the military role of the submarines. Warheads with high accuracy and (if need be) lower yield are more suitable for attacks on hardened military targets. This is the essence of the 'counterforce' nuclear strategy which stresses attacks on military targets more than its predecessor public nuclear theory – that of 'countervalue' attacks, where high yield warheads delivered with poor accuracy would nevertheless suffice to destroy large and widely dispersed cities and industrial targets.

Countervalue attacks were the cornerstone of the doctrine of deterrence aptly abbreviated to MAD – for mutually assured destruction. An examination of United States nuclear war plans (in Chapters 1 and 2) indicates that such theoretically refined concepts were public theory rather than private practice, as SAC had from the beginning targeted military and urban-industrial centres together.

In the 1970s, the newly-accurate missiles, and the tenfold increase in the number of warheads they carried, raised anew the consideration of whether the United States, which was years in the lead with MIRV technology, might have reached the dangerous position of being able to contemplate a disarming first strike on the Soviet Union. If all Russian bomber bases and missile forces could reliably be struck by a massive US salvo of missiles, then deterrence did not exist for the United States. Such a situation is destabilising for both sides, as the Soviet perception of their own vulnerability could require them to launch missiles and bombers on receipt of the first early warning sign – or risk losing them altogether.

Starting in 1969, 31 of the Polaris submarines were recalled and refitted with the longer-ranged, MIRVed Poseidon missiles. The first Poseidon submarine came to the Holy Loch in 1971. Although the changeover – which was complete by 1977 – increased by 900 per cent the number of missile warheads supported by the British base, consent to deploy Poseidon to Britain was granted by the government in 1971 in a perfunctory way – with neither an announcement to the House of Commons nor any public debate.

British and American officials made early and determined attempts to convince public opinion that the Polaris submarines would not be a danger to local inhabitants. Within two days of the 1960 Holy Loch announcement, local authorities were summoned to a consultation with government and defence officials, keen to co-opt them into joining the official chorus of reassurance that there was neither hazard of nuclear explosion nor reactor accident from the American submarines.

A Clyde Local Liaison Committee was set up, including local authority members and US Navy and Royal Navy commanders, and it is still responsible for emergency plans in the event of a nuclear accident. The committee's functions consist solely of rubber-stamping official proposals. Chaired by the Royal Navy Commodore in charge of the Clyde, it has no right of consultation over US plans; it does not even have the right of access to details of radiation levels in the area. These are now monitored around the clock by radiation detectors and technical teams at Dunoon and Rhu. When elected councillors attend the Committee once a year, they are never given any information other than that monitoring shows radiation to be within prescribed limits. Council officers fare little better in 6-monthly subcommittee meetings.

A 'Clyde Public Safety Scheme' was devised in February 1961, and incorporated in naval plans for the Clyde, called CLYSO. CLYSO has been updated many times since then. This plan defined the tasks of the Local Liaison Committee, in effect, as public relations to avoid local disquiet over nuclear hazards:

> The Local Liaison Committee is to reassure local opinion following a release of radioactivity from a reactor accident on a nuclear powered submarine . . .[12]

Wherever nuclear submarines went to moor in the Clyde, radiation monitoring teams would follow them on the shore. The description offered of the likely course of a reactor accident was scarcely reassuring:

> The submarine will be converted into a source of radiation . . . initially only Gamma radiation will be able to penetrate the bulkheads and hull of the vessel. As the heat and pressure in the submarine increase, volatile and gaseous fission products are forced out and released to the atmosphere. This 'cloud' of fission products will pour downwind from the submarine . . . and may produce a hazard if inhaled or digested after being deposited on uncovered food and crops . . .
>
> Children should . . . be given priority in any evacuation scheme . . .

If an accident occurred, the Royal Navy would take over the area, notifying the police and local authorities to arrange evacuation, hospitals to receive casualties. They would also issue a press release to the BBC and ITV, which was remarkable for having been totally pre-written. It was cast in soothing and complacent terms, irrespective of the details of any particular accident. It read:

> We have been asked to make the following urgent announcement. There has been a slight accident in the Atomic reactor of a Nuclear Submarine which is at present resulting in *a small release* of radioactive products. There is *no hazard* of an atomic explosion. A *few people* may be asked to move *for a short time*, on the advice of health *experts*, who are *already at work*. There is *no danger* to the general public, but the following precautions are necessary and must be taken in the vicinity to ensure that no harm is suffered by the public in the neighbourhood. [author's emphasis.]

What followed was less reassuring:

> Until further notice no food, which was not in tins or sealed airtight containers, should be eaten and no smoking should take place . . . in the following areas . . .

There is no guarantee that, in the event of an accident or damage to the environment, the United States would pay. The Ministry of Defence will pay claims if British submarine reactors go wrong – under the terms of the Nuclear Installations Act, which limits the amount the reactor owner is liable to pay to a relatively small amount. But CLYSO reveals that with US accidents there is no agreement about liability, only the promise of 'special arrangements' to be devised 'in consultation with the United States authorities'.

Reactor accidents are not a remote or minor contingency. On at least 10 occasions, US Navy vessels have made accidental discharges of radioactivity in coastal waters, according to a 1983 study by the American Fund for Constitutional Government. Nuclear-powered Soviet submarines have been seen to suffer even more serious accidents.

When the base was set up, US naval officers at Holy Loch played their part in the public relations effort, contributing some memorable nonsense in so doing. The first captain of USS *Proteus*, Richard Laning, pronounced on arrival in the Loch that:

> Danger of radiation is practically non-existent. In fact, we could drink the water from one of the primary systems [which circulated cooling water into the submarine reactor core] . . .[13]

Newspaper reports were headlined: 'Polaris ship radiates only goodwill'. It was Captain Laning's good fortune never to be called on subsequently to translate these words into deeds.

After four years of operation in the Holy Loch, the radiation discharged in the self-same cooling water of the Polaris submarines had seriously polluted the Loch and tidal flats around it. The submarines were regularly discharging excess coolant water, in which radioactive isotopes – especially Cobalt-60 – had accumulated, into the Loch. The discovery of unexpectedly high radiation levels was admitted by the Ministry of Defence in August 1965. Their public statements were intentionally couched in reassuring terms, but nevertheless confirmed that a substantial radiation leak had gone undetected until at least four months before. Their statements[14] implied:

- Significant radiation *was* contaminating the shoreline of the loch, with sources above and below the high water mark.
- The strongest radiation sources were emitting about 6 Rads of radiation a year – a more severe dose than would be permitted even for a nuclear reactor worker.

No clean-up was attempted, although the radioactive isotopes would take more than five years to decay even to half of these levels. But 'classified' new orders were given to submarine captains about discharges. Yet such incidents continued, and have been documented at Holy Loch's sister base in the Pacific, Guam. In 1975, the depot ship there dumped highly radioactive reactor cooling water into the Pacific, causing radiation levels at nearby public beaches to rise to over 50 times the allowable dose.

Although such radiation levels pose no risk at all of immediate death or illness, they contribute directly to a local increase in cancer and similar degenerative diseases, such as leukaemia. Because the incidence of cancer can only be linked statistically to radiation exposures, and cannot be legally proven in an individual case, operators of nuclear installations have often been able to escape liability for radiation death and injury in even the most compelling of circumstances. In 1980, a housewife near Dunoon drew attention to the death from leukaemia of her son and other young people resident in the immediate vicinity of the Holy Loch. Naval authorities took no interest in her claim and concern that the US nuclear submarine base had caused or contributed to these deaths; area medical officials declined to investigate any possible connection, relying instead on the continuing assurances of public safety by naval officers.

Although it is fair to assume that the US Navy would not knowingly or intentionally contaminate the Holy Loch basin around which many of their staff also live, the same can not be said for deeper waters of the Atlantic off the British Isles. Many intensely radioactive fluids and solids, including the coolant water used in the submarine reactor, are taken on board the depot ship or its accompanying barge. Periodically the depot ship sails from the Loch on open-sea exercises. During these exercises, say Holy Loch workers, accumulated radioactive effluent and detritus has been dumped at sea off Scotland, or further south – but never within the 12-mile limit. Unlike the procedures for maritime dumping of civil nuclear waste – which in 1983 was terminated after protests by the Greenpeace organisation – there is no public record or official regulation of these dumping activities. (Nor are such acts exclusive to the United States; the Royal Navy has barges permanently moored in the Gareloch in which nuclear waste from British Polaris submarines is collected.) Highly radioactive resin filters are also dumped directly from US submarines – in 1974 one Hawaii-based submarine contaminated its hull during such a dumping operation.

While acknowledging the reality of public concern about radiation hazards brought to the Clyde by the submarines, officials nevertheless deny that any hazard at all can come from the nuclear warheads. It was quite impossible, said the Admiralty at the start, 'to fire a Polaris missile by accident, and special safeguards are provided for the warhead to prevent an accidental nuclear explosion'.

This may be so – but the operation of the submarine missile base has led to repeated and hazardous incidents. One of the most extraordinary, from the US Navy point of view, was the discovery in 1966 that if there had been a war, three-quarters of their Polaris warheads would have failed to explode!

After nuclear tests of the Polaris warhead in 1958, a safety problem had emerged. Some of the warheads might have detonated accidentally during handling or storage. So a new mechanical interlock was fitted to the production version of the Polaris warhead. The new interlock, however, aged rapidly and jammed, preventing the warhead from being detonated under any circumstances. The fault was not discovered until 1966, when tests showed that three in four were probably defective. A new version of the W47 thermonuclear warhead was urgently designed, and tested a few months later. All the submarines then using early model Polaris A1 and A2 missiles were rapidly re-equipped.

For six years, three-quarters of the Polaris missile force thus appeared to have been inoperative. Some might regard this as the truest possible expression of an Act of God. For the US Department of Energy, whose officials revealed the incident whilst campaigning against a comprehensive nuclear test ban in 1978, it had been 'truly catastrophic'.[15]

In November 1970, three US sailors died and 40 were overcome by fumes in a fire aboard the then depot ship USS *Canopus*. Polaris missiles were carried in storage cells on the ship. The stern of the *Canopus* was ablaze, while two Polaris submarines, *Francis Scott Key* and *James F. Polk* were alongside. Their responses were oddly varied. The *Key* cast off immediately, but its companion did not budge. The fire was, however, extinguished before it spread far enough to threaten the missile stores or submarines.

On New Year's Day 1975, the *Washington Post* revealed that the first Poseidon-equipped submarine from the Holy Loch, the USS *Madison*, had collided with a Soviet submarine in the North Sea. Both submarines had surfaced to inspect their scraped hulls after colliding.

In 1981, hidden dangers inside the Poseidon warheads combined with the mishandling of a nuclear missile to produce, reputedly, a 'Bent Spear' incident in the Holy Loch. In a Bent Spear 'incident' (see Chapter 2), nuclear weapons or their components have been at hazard; it is, in official terminology, less serious than an 'accident'. This occurred aboard the tender USS *Holland*, on 2 November 1981, while a Poseidon missile was being transferred from a berthed submarine into one of the storage cells aboard the *Holland*.

According to sailors aboard the tender, the crane operator – either drunk or under the influence of drugs – let slip the missile, which fell uncontrolled for 17 feet. Its fall eventually was arrested by an automatic emergency brake, and the missile swung violently against the side of the mother ship. It was armed with MIRVed Poseidon warheads, which contain a particularly sensitive and unstable conventional explosive, known as LX09. Everyone froze as this happened; according to an eyewitness:

> We all thought we'd be blown away . . .

An alarm warning, ordering an 'alpha' alert state, had crew members running to radiation-protected areas on board the tender and the drydock vessel USS *Los Alamos* moored behind it.[16]

LX09, the explosive inside Poseidon warheads, combines unusually high sensitivity in handling with the property of detonating completely once an explosion begins. If the shock of collision in the Holy Loch incident had detonated any of the explosive, it is virtually certain that the whole of one warhead would have exploded (but conventionally only, without the additional power of a nuclear explosion). Up to a dozen other warheads inside the missile might have followed in turn. A massive conflagration would then have released the extremely toxic plutonium cores as dust and fragments into the atmosphere, with devastating consequences for the area around the base.

In 1979, the US Congressional General Accounting Office examined the likely consequences of nuclear weapons being destroyed like this in storage or transit. They suggested that dispersal of particles of plutonium from the weapon's nuclear core would be the chief hazard, and might create:

> a radiological cigar-shaped cloud extending from the accident scene for about 28 miles, with a maximum width of 2.5 miles . . .

Given the prevailing wind, such an accident could have created a radiological disaster area in much of the city of Glasgow, and across all of the lower Clyde.

No report was made about the accident, when it was over, to local police officers or members of the Clyde Local Liaison Committee. At first, newspaper reporters were deceived about the event; an elaboration of the story to the effect that the missile had fallen 'in the water' was denied by US Navy 'public affairs' officials who failed to acknowledge that there had been a missile incident of any kind. But gossip by US sailors in nearby Dunoon soon confirmed essential details, and a major public row in Scotland was the result.

US Navy officials in London refused even to confirm the presence of nuclear weapons on board the Poseidon submarines, and would not say how serious the incident had been. According to the US base commander, the fall was caused by a 'mechanical malfunction', not a drugged operator. There had not been an alert, he claimed, although 'personnel assigned were required to report to duty stations to correct the problem'. Under pressure, the US Navy admitted that the missile had indeed struck the ship, hitting the storage cell.

At the time of this accident, the US Navy were in the middle of a programme to replace the LX09 high explosive inside the warheads. LX09 was a plastic explosive of particularly high power, one of a number developed in the 1950s and 1960s to enable nuclear warheads to be dramatically miniaturised and built into new weapons. It is inevitable that explosives of high energy such as LX09 should be more unstable than conventional substances like TNT. LX09, however, was one of the worst. Tests by the US Lawrence Livermore nuclear weapons laboratory in the early 1970s uncovered 'erratic behavior when fabricated into parts for nuclear weapons'. It was described as 'drastically unstable'. A 1975 Livermore report warned that LX09:

> displays some very undesirable properties . . . the reaction levels are quite high. LX09 exhibits both low threshold velocity for reaction, and rapid build-up to violent reaction. *Any accidental mechanical ignition has a large probability of building up to a violent deflagration or detonation'* [author's emphasis].

In such tests as the 'drop weight', it was found that small samples of LX09 were likely to detonate if a 6- or 12-pound weight was dropped on them from a height any greater than 13 inches.

On 30 March 1977, LX09 was believed to be responsible for a major explosion at the US nuclear weapons assembly factory – Pantex, in Amarillo, Texas. Three men died. Further handling of LX09 at the plant was banned forthwith.

An official US Department of Energy investigation of that disaster, which caused $2.5 million worth of damage and distributed wreckage up to 320 feet from the explosion, would have remained secret but for lawsuits brought by relatives of the dead men. The investigators had concluded that the explosion had occurred during machining of LX09 components for warheads. An unformed 'billet' of the plastic explosive had been placed in the chuck of a lathe, and tapped into place with a rubber mallet. It detonated, setting off a chain reaction in that section of the plant.

Soon after the explosion, the US Navy began to recall all five thousand w68 Poseidon warheads to the Pantex plant for refitting with a new and less sensitive explosive. This news was kept secret for at least three years. But it was officially admitted in a 1981 Congressional hearing that the Poseidon warhead problem 'had to do with the particular high explosive that was used in that system'. Subsequently, military officials attempted to deny that the problem was the safety of LX09; they said it was replaced because one of its ingredients tended to leak out and contaminate other components in the warhead, leading to possible failure to explode when required. Officials claimed that it was merely 'coincidence' that the replacement work had begun the year after the LX09 explosion.

Unlike the earlier rush to replace the defective Polaris warheads, the Poseidon replacement programme went at a leisurely pace. The replacement of LX09 was scheduled to be completed during 1984. Despite protests by members of Congress about the continued use of LX09, the US Department of Defense refused a 1981 request to accelerate the refitting programme. In any case, the risks involved in handling the missiles during refits are confined to overseas bases, according to official regulations. These specify that procedures used by the US Navy in the Holy Loch are banned in the United States itself. Parts of Dunoon and other settlements around the Holy Loch are in a blast danger area, Congressional testimony has revealed. During a 1977 discussion on the development of new submarine bases on the US east coast, Admiral Kelln of the Department of Defense agreed that – as far as the United States itself was concerned – 'you need a rather unpopulated area' to meet safety regulations. He added:

> One good statistic to remember is that the blast safety zone required around a tender with four Poseidon submarines alongside is in excess of 9,000 feet. That is about a 3 mile diameter clear zone around it . . . one looks for that, plus accommodating a dry dock which has its blast safety zone . . .[17]

It was apparently not permissible at such United States ports as New London, Connecticut, for industrial development – let alone housing – to be sited in the 'clear zone' near a submarine tender. Yet at the Holy Loch site, two lochside settlements (Kilmun and Sandbank) and parts of Dunoon itself are well within the danger area.

In a written submission accompanying his testimony, the US Navy representatives confirmed local observations that four Poseidon submarines are often berthed alongside the Holy Loch tender. At Holy Loch, there were ten Poseidon SSBNs (nuclear missile submarines) assigned, and 'approximately three or four SSBNs may be alongside the tender conducting refits at any given time'.

Nor is this the only normal explosive safety rule disregarded where foreign bases and citizens are concerned. Before refit work can be done in United States naval shipyards, according to further testimony to the same Congressional committee:

> [The] Department of Defense required unloading of missiles before an SSBN submarine enters . . . This requirement . . . does not apply to the sites abroad, which are *remotely located* [author's emphasis][18]

The committee was told that it was both quicker and cheaper to use the overseas sites for refit work because the irksome safety requirements did not apply. At the time there were three such Fleet Ballistic Missile sites – Guam, Rota and the Holy Loch. Now only Holy Loch is still in operation.

The safety hazards at Holy Loch drew attention and concern in the House of Commons after the Poseidon accident. Some 78 Labour, Liberal and Plaid Cymru MPs signed a parliamentary motion asking for an enquiry; their motion:

> noted that the United States authorities have already considered the withdrawal of nuclear submarines from the Holy Loch and urges that this now be done, without further delay, in order to provide safety and peace of mind for residents of the Clyde estuary and to make a small but positive step towards improving international security.

The role of drugs in the Poseidon missile incident caused particular concern to the MPs. The US Navy continued to deny that drugs were involved. But on 3 January 1982, an administrative court martial was held to hear charges against an operator involved in the incident of being 'unfit for duty' through the use of drugs. Strong evidence suggests that drug abuse in this and other parts of the US Navy had reached epidemic proportions:

- Illegal drugs have been imported into Britain by Poseidon nuclear missile submarine.
- In January 1982, Naval Investigative Service special agents raided the SOSUS underwater listening stations in Brawdy, Wales, and Antigua in the Carribean. Of 281 men at Brawdy, most with Top Secret clearances, 46 were charged with drugs offences. More were probably users, as official Defense Department studies suggested that nearly 50 per cent of enlisted sailors were on drugs.[19]
- A 'sniffer' dog is kept by the US Navy at Holy Loch, and taken aboard the tender and submarines 'about once per week', according to a local vet. A special Naval Investigative Staff office is sited in Dunoon, separate from the base.

A local journalist on the Clyde, Stuart Hoggard, was offered a stunning cocktail mixture of cocaine, LSD, mescalin, marijuana, 'uppers' and 'downers' by US Navy men in hotels and cafés in nearby Gourock in 1972. Sailors from the *Canopus* depot ship jokingly called it the 'Cannabis'. The US Navy Public Affairs Office denied then, as now, that there was a Navy drugs 'problem' or any access to illegal drugs by sailors on the base. Any drug offenders, they promised the local community, were invariably dishonourably discharged and sent home.

This statement was proven untrue in 1981 when a former US Navy civilian employee at the base discovered court martial papers of drug cases left on a local rubbish dump. He sent the papers to the *New Statesman.*

A radio operator who also acted as nuclear weapons guard with the Blue crew of the missile submarine USS *Casimir Pulaski* was found to have set off from the submarine's US base at New London with marijuana stashed in his locker. He was not discharged or sent home;

his Top Secret security clearance was reduced to Secret. But a subsequent report on his conduct described him as 'totally irresponsible when not accounted for daily by direct supervision'. He was then 'disqualified for assignment to nuclear weapons position'.

Another man was a fireman aboard the *Holland.* He had taken amphetamines, cocaine and LSD to a Dunoon bar, and sold the amphetamines to a second US Navy sailor and the acid and coke to a third. The fireman told the court that he had 'possibly 12 hits . . . at least 10' of acid with him. He received confinement and hard labour, but no discharge. He had been at the Holy Loch, evidently heavily involved with hard drugs, for over three years.

The prospect of nuclear submarine crews as well as missile handling staff enjoying hallucinogenic trips while in charge of a cargo of missile-borne megadeath is about as chilling a vision as one can imagine. Yet they do 'trip' with Polaris, one submariner revealed:

> You can't sample [marijuana] on a sub, they'd smell it. I do uppers most of the time, but as a special treat, like when I'm on watch, I'll do a little mescalin. It's really a buzz to know that you're cruising the Arctic with Polaris missiles that could wipe out half of Russia – man, that's a real trip.[20]

Whatever the condition of their sailors, missile submarines do not operate alone. A mobile underwater missile force poses unique problems of communication and navigation.

To operate Polaris reliably as a nuclear fighting force, the US Navy had not only to create the submarines and bases like Holy Loch. They had to provide new networks of communications and navigation transmitters, a satellite navigation system, and deploy new intelligence networks into Polaris operating areas to protect them from hostile hunter-killer submarines and other enemy forces. An extensive network of new US bases in the North Atlantic dates from this period.

Radio signals do not travel far through sea water. So in order to receive orders, the submarine has either to surface and raise an antenna – with consequent risk of detection – or use very low frequency (VLF) radio signals, which can penetrate at least 10–15 metres into the ocean. The submarine can raise a buoy to this depth from the deeps. Or, when travelling near the surface at speed, thin, silvered wire, a half-kilometre long, can be trailed behind.

VLF radio transmitters are not simple to construct. They are gigantic affairs, with a curtain of wires suspended from masts perhaps 300 metres above ground, and fed with as much as a megawatt of electric power. A network of US Navy VLF transmitters can provide worldwide coverage from relatively few locations. The main Atlantic transmitter which would send firing orders to Poseidon submarines is in Cutler, Maine.

To cover against possible nuclear attack on these vulnerable fixed targets, the Navy also operate a squadron of TACAMO aircraft – C-130 Hercules specially converted as mobile VLF transmitters. Once airborne, an aerial wire ten kilometres long is winched out behind and below the aircraft, and signals can then be sent. TACAMO is part of the US plan to keep in touch with nuclear forces even under heavy nuclear attack, the so-called Minimum Essential Emergency Communications System (MEECN; see Chapter 7). TACAMO aircraft are normally based in the United States and are seen intermittently at British bases.

There are three VLF transmitters in Britain, all operated for the Royal Navy by British Telecom: Rugby near Northampton, Criggion in Shropshire, and Anthorn on the Solway Firth. They share common frequencies, callsigns, and a mission to get the message of doom through to Britain's own Polaris fleet from their Northwood HQ. It is probable – although the subject is naturally highly classified – that these facilities are also available to the United States in emergency, after national requirements have been fulfilled.

One of the trio, Anthorn, was built at NATO expense in 1961, before Britain had decided to purchase the Polaris system itself. A sister VLF station was built for NATO at the same time straddling a fjord at Novika in northern Norway. The timing of these two VLF projects suggests a connection with Polaris, but the Norwegian transmitter has been claimed only to communicate with conventional submarines in the NATO northern fleet.

Another important link to Poseidon submarines is provided by the naval communications station at Thurso, near Wick in north-east Scotland, which opened in July 1962. Thurso, like its erstwhile sister station in Londonderry, Northern Ireland (closed in 1977), is equipped with powerful low-frequency transmitters. The two stations had registered a lowest frequency of 40.75 kHz with international authorities; such signals will penetrate at least 5 metres into the sea, allowing a submerged submarine to stay concealed while receiving orders. The Thurso station has two sites, east and west of the Scottish town. At the transmitter site, West Murkle, a network of acres of copper wires, dug into the soil, boosts the power of its signals.

The new missile fleet was to be protected against Soviet naval countermeasures by an extensive intelligence network covering their entire deployment area. Two vast new Sigint stations covering northern waters were built at Edzell in Scotland, and Keflavik in Iceland. Operating together with a third station (now closed) at Bremerhaven, the US Navy could expect to detect and locate any unknown radio signals in the Polaris deployment area. Many opponents of Polaris, who noted that the construction of Edzell's vast circular array of Sigint aerials paralleled the deployment of Polaris, claimed wrongly that it too was a VLF communications station.

Ironically, following this, the erroneous description of Edzell as a Polaris VLF station has often been repeated in Russian magazine articles and propaganda writing. But in fact its role was more subtle, but no less important.

In 1969, the US Navy network in Scotland was welded together by a new high-capacity microwave radio network, making it independent of the British Post Office. Eleven new radio relay facilities[21] were built across Scotland and Northern Ireland, linking the Thurso and Londonderry stations. Also connected were the Edzell Sigint station, a radio station at Kinnabar, and the US Air Force North Atlantic Relay System station at Mormond Hill, near Peterhead. Other links direct to the United States were rented on transatlantic telephone cables.

Of equal importance to missile-carrying submarines as reliable communications is an accurate navigation system. The accuracy with which an underwater-launched missile can strike its target is only as good as the accuracy with which the submarine knows its own position, in order to programme the missile's guidance system. Before a missile can be launched, the navigator must know where the submarine is, which direction it is pointing in, and which way is up. Otherwise the missile will lose its course, and target.

On board the submarine, a host of navigation systems link into a central computer. Gyroscopes provide an inertial navigation system of

---

OPPOSITE

**Fig 9. Militarising the ocean: the Polaris build-up**

When the Soviet Union began to acquire its own nuclear bomber force, Britain became the far eastern flank of US defensive and early warning systems like BMEWS and the DEW (Distant Early Warning) line. Giant long-range 'troposcatter' links of the North Atlantic Relay System connected radar stations and the underwater SOSUS network to the mainland United States. In anticipation of the deployment of Polaris submarines in 1961, new radio and navigation stations, monitoring networks and naval surveillance covered the Norwegian and North Seas.

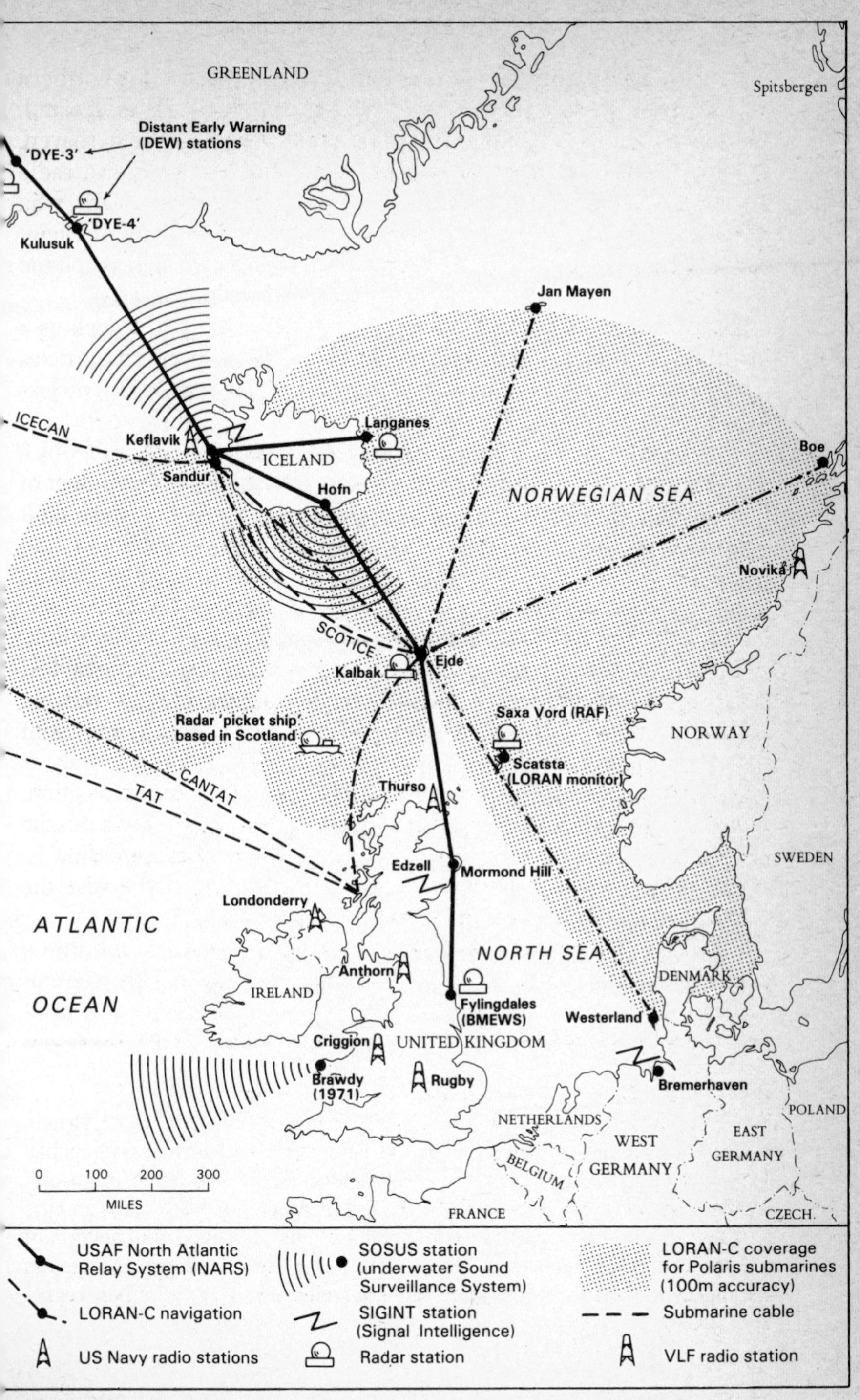

ig 9. Militarising the North Atlantic; the Polaris buildup

high accuracy, but this can nevertheless drift by as much as a mile a day. Conventional celestial navigation is possible, but requires raising the periscope, risking detection by radar. Radio signals from beacon stations on land are the main addition to these systems. But the reception of navigation radio signals underwater poses the same difficulty as for orthodox communications.

The first new radio navigation system was LORAN-C (for LOng RAnge Navigation). By receiving signals simultaneously from three or more LORAN transmitters, a submarine could tell its position. In each of the main Polaris deployment areas – the Norwegian Sea, the Mediterranean, and the north-west Pacific, LORAN-C networks were installed between 1959 and 1963.

The north Atlantic stations – in Iceland, the Faroes, Norway's Jan Mayen Island and Norway itself – are shown in Figure 9. Over most of the North Sea and Norwegian waters, a submarine can fix its position to within 100 metres. In Norway, the construction of the LORAN-C stations was particularly sensitive, and in time became the focus of an intense public row. Norway does not permit foreign military bases or nuclear weapons on its soil in peacetime. (See Chapter 11.) Neither ministers nor Parliament were told, before approving the construction of the two stations, that the system was essential to Polaris submarines and the operation of their missiles. Eventually, government officials were told that LORAN was required to give 'accurate calculations of the condition of the bottom and depths . . . in the northern ocean areas, with a view to deploying Polaris submarines from this area'. During these surveys, sonar beacons were fixed to the seabed. Their signals provide another means by which the submarines can locate their position accurately.

Britain's contribution to the LORAN-C system is a monitoring station at Scatsta in the Sullom Voe inlet in the Shetlands. Although the Scatsta station does not transmit navigation signals, it is critical to maintaining the accuracy of the LORAN-C network. The station, like all the non-Norwegian LORAN stations, is run by the civilian US Coastguard. Although there is no longer any secrecy about its role in Polaris and Poseidon submarine navigation, the Coastguard service was originally given charge of the network in order to conceal from Norway and other nations the urgent military significance of LORAN-C.

In 1977, the Norwegian Parliament appointed a special Commission of Enquiry to examine whether it had been misled into approving the construction of the LORAN-C stations, and another navigation system, 'Omega', built a few years later. Although Commission members found that the decisions had not violated normal procedure, the issue of such 'infrastructure' for nuclear weapons became much more politically sensitive.

Soon after this report, the US Navy wanted to modify the LORAN stations to incorporate a new emergency communications system to transmit messages to the missile submarines. The system, called 'Clarinet Pilgrim', would be invisible to ordinary LORAN navigation receivers, but could be interpreted by special receivers on the submarines. They would be another, 'survivable' method of sending emergency firing orders to the submarines. Because of the sensitivity of the nuclear weapons issue in Norway in particular, Clarinet Pilgrim was eventually only installed in the Poseidon operating areas of the Pacific, and not in the Atlantic.

Satellite navigation systems started operating in 1963, and provided much more accurate position fixes. Given favourable conditions, a single overhead 'pass' of a Transit navigation satellite, received by an aerial floated to the surface, could determine a submarine's position anywhere to an accuracy of 150 metres. The satellites transmit continuously, providing both a tracking signal and mathematical information on its position in space, from which the ground station's position can be found.

For the Transit system to work properly, the satellites have to be tracked accurately from a worldwide network of ground stations. Any variation in the satellite orbit is noted, and used to correct data transmitted down by the satellite. Transit's special tracking network – Tranet – included an earth station at Lasham, Hants, operated by the Royal Aircraft Establishment. The station was paid for by the US Navy. The satellites were also tracked at a second and ostensibly civilian British station, Winkfield near Bracknell, Berkshire (see pp 194–5).

All US military navigation systems – LORAN-C, Omega, and Transit – have subsequently been made available for civilian use. Except for Transit, the US always drew attention away from their role in nuclear warfare by stressing civilian and wider military applications. The stratagem of disguising critical military developments as civilian in character has often been applied, particularly in order to obtain base rights in Western or non-aligned countries which wish to be disassociated from US nuclear forces. In time, as described in Chapter 11, these secret elements of nuclear infrastructure have been the focus of critical public debate in countries as far apart as Norway and New Zealand.

The British debate over the Holy Loch in the 1960s left a permanent mark, and singled the base out as a particularly critical target for those concerned with nuclear disarmament. This was reflected in a manifesto commitment of the 1974 Labour government, which promised 'to seek the removal of the Polaris bases'. This commitment had been the outcome of a fierce battle between left and right wings in the party. It was dumped shortly after the 1974 election, although not before the NATO and US Supreme Commander Atlantic (SACLANT) had, with his British deputy, attacked the British government at a press conference at SACLANT's Norfolk headquarters. Closure of Holy Loch, claimed Admiral Ralph Cousins, would create 'real dangers' leading to a 'serious weakening of the deterrent position'. The Holy Loch was 'absolutely vital'; there were 'no credible alternatives'.

A year previously, the US had in fact enlarged the South Carolina depot at Charleston, and announced that some Poseidon submarines would be withdrawn from advanced overseas bases – possibly including Holy Loch. The US Navy had privately continued to plan its withdrawal from Holy Loch; in 1977 the US Congress were told that the US Chief of Naval Operations had ordered a study to find 'permanent sites for relocation of Poseidon SSBNs' from both Rota and Holy Loch.

But the Labour government did not pursue its policy of ousting the Americans from Holy Loch; casting the issue into the melting pot of waiting eternally for successful multilateral disarmament negotiations, Defence Secretary Roy Mason told the House of Commons in March 1974 that:

> I must warn the House and my party that it will be a little time before I can start the multilateral discussions which will be necessary . . .

The issue was thus adjourned, *sine die.*

In the event both Rota and Guam have been closed, and the Poseidon submarine force reduced to 19 in number (of the remainder 10 are retired and 12 have been converted to Trident-I missiles). In contrast to the British stance, the Spanish government took a firm line over Rota. Under the terms of the 1976 US-Spanish defence agreement, the United States agreed to pay the Spanish government $1,200 million for the use of the bases, and to close Rota as a submarine base and withdraw all nuclear weapons by July 1979.

The 4,000 mile range of the new Trident-I missile has removed the necessity for forward bases. In 1983, however, the Holy Loch depot ship USS *Hunley* moved temporarily to moorings in deeper water, provoking brief local fears that it might be used anew to support and service the larger-draught Trident-II submarines. There were also fresh press reports that the United States did intend to withdraw its remaining Poseidon force from the Holy Loch to US east coast ports by 1990. But the US Navy then made it clear that if it was leaving Scotland, it would go of its own accord and at a time of its own choosing. To underscore the point, the Navy have applied for $10 million in 1984 to build a new unloading pier and warehouses in Dunoon. The Poseidon base, said US Navy headquarters in London, would still be in operation 'at least until the end of the century'.[22]

## Notes

1 *Daily Herald*, 18 February 1960.
2 Harold Macmillan, *Pointing the way, 1959–1961* (Volume 5 of Memoirs); Macmillan, 1965.
3 *Sunday Times*, 2 May 1976.
4 *Hansard*, 1 November 1960.
5 Strathclyde Regional Council, *Exercise 'Square Leg'*, Assumed situation at H+24 hours (RESTRICTED); October 1980.
6 *Hansard*, 1 November 1960.
7 *Daily Express*, 4 March 1961.
8 *Hansard*, 8 November 1960.
9 *Daily Mail*, 3 November 1960.
10 *Daily Herald*, 1 March 1963.
11 MIRV stands for Multiple Independently Targetable Re-entry Vehicles.
12 CLYSO Volume 5, Section 08, para 14 (1968 edition).
13 *Daily Telegraph*, 4 March 1961.
14 *Scotsman*, 28 August 1965.
15 *Washington Post*, 4 December 1978.
16 See *New Statesman*, 27 November 1981.
17 US Congress, House of Representatives, Military Construction Appropriations for 1978 (Hearings before a subcommittee of the Committee on Appropriations), Part 1, p 823. US Congress, 1977.
18 *ibid*, Part 3, p 663.
19 *Norfolk Virginian-Pilot*, 1 January 1982. Norfolk, Virginia, is the site of the US Atlantic Fleet Headquarters.
20 *New Statesman*, 27 November 1981.
21 Latheron; Clochandighter, Aberdeen; Inverbervie; Kinnabar; Craigowl Hill; East Lomond; Kirk O'Shotts; Sergeantlaw; Browncarrick Hill; Slievenorra; Dungiven.
22 *Guardian*, 16 December 1982.

# 9 *Air Power*

'Nowhere in the world,' according to the US Third Air Force's *Welcome to England* booklet for arriving service personnel, 'has a foreign operating environment been more congenial to Air Force operations than that in the United Kingdom. In few places could there be less doubt about dependability in time of crisis . . . The acceptability of Americans and their mission to the British people', it adds, 'has been remarkable . . . The Third Air Force welcomes you'.

The Third Air Force, and other USAF units under its supervision, is now being welcomed into Britain in increasing numbers. Over one-fifth of the US Air Force's total strength abroad is already in Britain. Now, the mid-1970s air-force strength of 20,000 people and 300 aircraft has grown by a third. The scale of US Air Force operations in Britain thus continues to dwarf those of other American military services. A new Third Air Force commanding general, William P. Acker, arrived at the Mildenhall headquarters in July 1983 to take command of 26,000 of the USAF military. Another 3,600 personnel and 6,000 dependants are already in the pipeline to move over to Britain.

The numbers will rise again if ground-launched cruise missiles are deployed to Molesworth as well as Greenham Common – both until recently reserve bases. At present, nearly 400 US Air Force aircraft are normally based in Britain. In war or crisis, the number of bases and aircraft in Britain would treble as squadron after squadron of US-based reserves crossed the Atlantic. Nearly half of the military aircraft in Europe – 40 per cent of US and NATO strength – would use British bases.

The eight main airbases are the most prominent aspect of American forces in Britain. Unlike the many US communications and intelligence facilities, command centres and reserve bases here, the giant airbases are well known to many members of the public. Despite making bullseye targets for any attacker, however, these forces do not contribute in any direct way to British air defences. On the contrary, they impose a substantial additional burden on Royal Air Force defence fighters, which are already stretched in defending their own airbases and have not been regarded, for 25 years, as capable of protecting British cities from air attack.

Britain asks no rent for US use of British bases. Construction costs of runways and new facilities are shared between NATO, including Britain, and the United States. Building costs are allocated according to the purpose of each base. If a unit is allocated to NATO, the common NATO funds will pay for many facilities to be built to an agreed standard, including runways and shelters. Exceptionally, if new facilities are for bilateral UK–US use, then costs will be split directly between the two countries. The US has to pay entirely for the many British-based units which are operated for the unilateral purposes of the United States, and not committed to NATO. Most of the building work is supervised by the Department of the Environment, and costs are reimbursed by the US government. Although operating costs are normally all paid by the Pentagon, some tasks – such as air defence missile units around the main bases, or guarding cruise missile convoys – are the financial responsibility of the RAF.

The Americans sometimes appear bemused by the easy ride they have in Britain, compared with other overseas territories. Their 'Welcome' booklet notes:

> When the Air Force returned to Britain in 1948 . . . there was not even a written agreement. When the arrangement was formalised, it included many advantages to the Air Force and its personnel . . .

Not that most US personnel need notice which country they are in if they don't want to. Inside the big bases, currency and commodities, living and leisure are exclusively all-American. Visitors there are invariably struck by the cultural isolation the Yanks can achieve with the aid of imports of all kinds.

The American airmen seem unembarrassed about behaving in accordance with caricatures of presumed national stereotypes. Luxury is cheap and abundant, as many visitors' accounts describe:

> In the officers' mess at Mildenhall, a champagne brunch is laid on. For just over a pound, an officer can get an averagely huge American breakfast . . . It is 8 am. Few officers are up yet but one, a young pilot clad in a very zippy flying suit festooned with bright badges, flashes, emblems, decals, numbers and bars, sits at a table covered with fine linen eating a giant cream puff with a silver fork. He has champagne there and three

other types of cream cake and, as he quaffs away at both, he is deeply absorbed in the pages of a child's comic . . .[1]

To the *New York Times*, the Public Affairs commander at Mildenhall, Lt Col Alan Schreihofer, explained in 1977 that:

A young airman can live as if he is in the middle of Kansas . . .[2]

'Public affairs' officers like Schreihofer are attached to every US base of any size, with a mission to win acceptance of the American military presence. Much of their work is public relations in the local community. Community attitudes are often deeply riven between the tolerance of traders and easily flattered self-important local officials, and opponents of the bases who have been moved to hostility by intrusion, noise, unruly behaviour, simple antagonism toward foreigners, or the looming chill of war that they bring. In good times, officers like Schreihofer sponsor local PR 'liaison committees' of no formal standing, and arrange open days and social events. On more difficult occasions, they fend off the awkward questions of opponents with bland and anodyne approved statements about military activities. All military establishments have created a symbolic public vocabulary in which offence is defence; but the American language, especially since Vietnam, has become particularly rich in this newspeak.

Off the base are the 'natives' and the local 'economy'. On the base there are pizza parlours and Mexican chilli take-aways, bowling alleys and pool halls, with Britain – even the Britain of Kentucky Fried Chicken and McDonald hamburgers – known to many only as a remote abstraction beyond the fences and barbed wire.

To the observer outside those fences, a major airbase is a strange, different, alien and menacing world. From hills to the west, one can overlook a base like Lakenheath in Suffolk – which with around 80 F-111 bombers and 5,000 personnel is the largest US airbase in Europe. There are laid out below a huge area of runways and buildings, teeming with many activities: rows of aircraft, spare fuel tanks, practice bombs, and squads of technical vehicles. Around them move security police station wagon patrols, jet fuel bowsers, and busy squads of technicians. A control tower with blue tinted windows and a revolving radar scanner watch over the scene.

This activity surrounds more silent and still areas in the centre of the site. Beyond and behind additional fences, guards and watchtowers are the grey, streamlined profiles of the Quick Reaction Alert F-111 aircraft – bombed up and ready to go on nuclear missions at short notice. In

1981, the US Congress was informed that the Quick Reaction Alert F-111s at Lakenheath and Upper Heyford are, as would be expected, permanently nuclear-armed.

The F-111 can carry three nuclear bombs – two on pylons under the wings and a third inside the bomb bay. Three types of bombs can be carried: the usual, and most modern, is the B61. Weighing just 765 lbs, this nuclear weapon offers the pilot the option of four selectable yields, from around the Hiroshima size of 10 kilotons, up to 300 kT or more. It can be lowered to the target by parachute, tossed towards it, or just plain dropped. To choose the desired destructive power, all that is neccessary is to turn a dial. The United States has an estimated 3,000-strong stockpile of B61s. Many of them are deployed in Europe as multi-purpose tactical nuclear weapons. Nerve gas bombs will join this arsenal of sensitive F-111 weapons held in Britain late in 1985, if current US defence plans go ahead.

At Lakenheath and Upper Heyford, nuclear weapons are stored in munitions 'igloos' inside double fenced 'Special Ammunition Stores'. The so-called 'igloos' are large, earth-covered concrete sheds. Although not especially strongly fortified, like all the important base facilities they are resistant to air attack. The wing 'Combat Operations Center' and base headquarters have walls two feet thick, blast shields, and air filters to remove radiation and biological or chemical agents. In 1983, a new, semi-sunken $3 million 'hardened logistics facility' was being constructed beside other bunkers close to Lakenheath's main entrance.

Targets for the F-111s include Warsaw Pact airbases, major road and rail centres and other transport centres, supply depots, staging areas and troop concentrations. This swing-wing bomber was designed to be able to take off from very short, rough strips only 3,000 feet long. Folding back its wings into a supersonic delta, the F-111 has a top speed over Mach 2.5 – two and a half times the speed of sound. It is heavily equipped with electronics, of which the most important is a low-level, terrain-following radar.

Non-nuclear weapons carried on the F-111 are complex and expensive, and now include television- and laser-guided bombs and missiles. Their sophistication offers pilots much-desired higher 'kill probabilities' each time a bomb is released. In 1982, many of the more modern Lakenheath F-111s had their bomb-bays re-equipped with 'Pave Tack' – a new system for steering these 'smart' bombs and missiles onto their target. A rotating sensor head below the aircraft shines a laser beam on the selected target; the aircraft's central computer keeps the laser pointing at the target after the bomb has been dropped, or 'tossed'. The laser beam is not exactly harmless – its use is forbidden on exercises in Britain where ground personnel might look into the beam – but it is less than lethal, unlike the bomb or missile which homes in on laser light reflected from the target. Pave Tack can also bring arcade games to life by letting an F-111 navigator steer a TV or infra-red guided bomb to its target by keeping it lined up in view as the bomb or missile homes in.

Fitted into the F-111 airframe are six separate electronic radar detectors and jammers intended to confuse and disrupt defending fighters, their missiles, and their ground radar controllers. If, despite these sophistications, a bomber is pursued by missiles, metal foil 'chaff' can be released into the jet exhaust to throw off homing mechanisms by creating many new, phoney targets. Terrain-following radar and jamming equipment is packed into the aircraft's long, pointed nose, giving rise to its nickname of 'Aardvark' – an African groundhog.

So with comparative ease, the F-111s can fly their low-level attack routes to the east. Hogging the ground to avoid radar detection and missile attack, F-111s are intended to be able to penetrate deeply into Soviet territory, in all weather conditions. They would fly low, and fast.

Rehearsing for their war missions, the pilots of the many F-111s at Lakenheath and Upper Heyford fly about 15,000 sorties every year. Most of these are low-level training flights, across Britain to ranges in northern Scotland and eastern England, or abroad – to Aviano Air Force Base in northern Italy or the giant NATO range in Sardinia, Decimomannu. In Britain there are eight RAF-run coastal ranges used by F-111s, plus an inland range in Wales and a joint British/US electronic warfare centre at Spadeadam in Cumbria.

The eight ranges include two in northern Scotland – Tain in Ross and Cromarty and Rosehearty near Aberdeen; five in England – Cowden, Donna Nook, Theddlethorpe, Wainfleet, and Holbeach; and Jurby Head, on the Isle of Man. At the ranges, barges or old ships are moored offshore as bombing targets. Dropping to a height of 200 feet, and flying at 500 miles an hour, lightweight simulated bombs are released and the crew's performance scored. Near to each range, local residents suffer heavily from the noise of continual low flying.

At some ranges, like Rosehearty, the F-111s practise the special manoeuvre of toss-bombing. In this fashion an aircraft flying as low as 50 feet above ground will suddenly fly upwards, releasing a bomb as it does so. The bomb rises in a ballistic arc before falling to ground, giving the pilot time to get away before nuclear detonation. But toss-bombing was temporarily banned in February 1980 after an F-111 tossed one some way off target, and on to a local farm. The bomb, said junior Defence Minister Geoffrey Pattie at the time, was 'basically inert'. In fact, it wasn't inert at all, but contained a pyrotechnic charge intended to release a smoke trail marker when the bomb struck the ground.

Off Cape Wrath in north-western Scotland, a Royal Navy range is another practice zone, as an *Observer* correspondent visiting the Lakenheath F-111s was told in 1983:

> They go up there [Cape Wrath], bomb the shit out of some little island off the coast of Scotland, using smoke bombs . . . I've seen the pictures. It's really neat.[3]

Spadeadam, a remote Cumbrian valley, contains simulated Warsaw Pact surface-to-air missile radars, provided by the US Air Force. Formerly Britain's rocket test centre for the aborted Blue Streak project, Spadeadam is jointly run by the USAF and an RAF Signals Unit. It is a small-scale version of the huge 'Red Flag' war-games theatre at the Nellis Air Force Base in Nevada, where whole tracts of US government land are laid out with simulated Warsaw Pact radars, anti-aircraft missiles and army targets.

Complementing this land simulation in the air is an inaptly named 'Aggressor Squadron' of Northrop F-5 fighters. The title is a characteristic misnomer, as the role of these fighters is to play at being Soviet air defenders. The MiG-21 and the F-5 have many common characteristics. The 'Aggressors' are painted in standard Soviet camouflage schemes. In Soviet air force style, large squadron numbers are painted on aircraft noses. Since 1977, the US Air Force in Britain has had its own Aggressor Squadron, based at Alconbury near Huntingdon.

Pilots of Alconbury's 527th Tactical Fighter Training Aggressor Squadron are encouraged to study and follow Soviet aerial combat tactics. Their badges and helmets sport the Red Star. RAF, NATO and USAF units come to Alconbury, or to the squadron's detachment at NATO's large Sardinia range, to take on the Aggressors. The F-5s may fly defensive patrols around a target area, and are then guided to intercept and attack their opponents' aircraft which are attempting to penetrate to the target. The result can be a spectacular dogfight, which is closely watched on radar, and taped for later appraisal. A large part of the airspace over the Wash is designated an Aerial Combat zone for these rehearsals – which at first often spilled out, dangerously, into the way of Air Anglia's local civilian flights.

The Aggressor squadrons – a third is now in the Philippines – were born as much of commercial convenience as military requirements. In 1975, the US Air Force was suddenly faced with a large surplus of F-5s, which had been intended to go to the South Vietnamese air force, before that country's military collapse. Nominated the 'Freedom Fighter', the aircraft had been designed by the Northrop Corporation as a cheap and cheerful aircraft exclusively for foreign military sales. Lacking the sophisticated facilities of purpose-designed United States Air Force combat aircraft, Pentagon officials conceived the idea of getting the F-5s to play enemy. In attacks on North Vietnam a few years before, USAF and US Navy pilots had found their prior dogfight training against orthodox US pilots and tactics unsatisfactory. Most pilots shot down were on their first few raids.

More complex war games with the US are featured in periodic exercises codenamed 'Mallet Blow' or 'Osex'. Suitable units of both American and British forces join combating 'Blue' and 'Orange' sides. In Mallet Blow the enemy has marched across Scotland and northern England as far as Manchester. Bombers and fighters support the gallant defenders still holding out in Yorkshire by attacking a simulated motor rifle regiment, a convoy bridge and a simulated airfield at Otterburn, simultaneously avoiding the anti-aircraft missile defences at Spadeadam, defending aircraft, and enduring the jamming of their communications by a secret RAF jamming squadron. Up to four times annually, Mallet Blow planners bring over 30 air raids and 150 low level attackers a day to northern England. 'Disturbance,' said an MOD press release for the June 1982 Mallet Blow 'will be unavoidable . . . over northern England and southern Scotland'. Classified exercise plans revealed that pilots could only be restrained from flying overland at up to supersonic speed by allowing them a high speed zone at sea.

In another series of exercises, 'Border Flag', the Spadeadam electronic warfare range is electronically attacked by 'Wild Weasel' Phantom aircraft from Germany, equipped with high-power jammers.

US Air Force Phantom, A-10 and F-111 squadron commanders, like their RAF counterparts with low-level targets to penetrate, are continually seeking areas where they may practice skimming virtually at grass-burning height over fields and mountains. Between ranges like Spadeadam, and for general flying training, the Ministry of Defence has independently authorised US and British pilots to use a series of low-flying routes – which were entirely secret until 1977, when an increasing toll of accidents and complaints forced the Ministry to publish their instructions to military aircraft, giving details of the low-flying 'tactical route' between the already designated low-flying ranges. It runs from Poole in Dorset, across Wales, the Irish Sea, to Cumbria – where one branch continues to the Isle of Lewis, while another extends across central Scotland and curves down to the Wash.

In October 1981, on behalf of the Ministry of Defence, the Board of Trade decreed that most of the Scottish Highlands should become a special day and night low-flying training area for F-111s and RAF Tornados, using all-weather low-flying equipment. Four days a week, the area is sealed off for military training. Other planes are forbidden to enter it because the military pilots may not necessarily be able to see where they are going. Within the 'Highlands Restricted Area', which encompasses the Isle of Skye and all but a few coastal stretches of the remote and beautiful Highland countryside, military pilots may fly between 300 and 400 feet above ground.

Besides noise and disturbance, intensive low flying puts aircraft, pilots and those below them at risk. The F-111, whose complex electronic systems are difficult to maintain, has a particularly poor safety reputation. As the largest and heaviest aircraft regularly flying at low level across Britain, and responsible for many well-publicised crashes, the F-111 is not a popular sight overhead in many parts of the country. F-111 losses have increased, rather than decreased, over time. Five were lost in the first six years they have been in Britain. Then three crashed in 1977; in December that year one falling aircraft missed a school in Newmarket by only a few hundred yards. Another was lost in 1978. With a second wing operational at Upper Heyford, losses in 1979 rose to seven, one crashing at Harlton, south-west of Cambridge. There, US Air Force Security Police guards arrived to cordon off the site even before local police arrived.

In 1980, one aircraft crashed near the start of the low-level 'tactical route' west of Bournemouth. Another hit the deck near Thetford in 1981. In 1982, F-111s from Lakenheath crashed three times in Scotland – twice in the Highlands low-flying area and once in Fife – and once in Turkey. With another downed off the Norfolk coast in 1983, more than one-eighth of the F-111 force now based in Britain had gone down by September 1983 – a total of 23 aircraft.

Seven main US Air Force operating bases in Britain have facilities and equipment which match the scope, if not quite the scale, of Lakenheath. Each base, its equipment and aircraft is worth between £1,000 and £2,000 million.

After the massive developments in Britain in the 1950s, and the hectic arrivals from France in the 1960s, there were few changes in the US Air Force structure in Britain until late in the 1970s. From 1977, numbers began to climb as new squadrons or aircraft types arrived: extra F-111s to Lakenheath, the Aggressors to Alconbury, tankers to Fairford, A-10s at Woodbridge. The key tasks of the major bases are outlined below.

- Long-range bombing – Lakenheath and Upper Heyford.
- Ground attack to support troops – Bentwaters and Woodbridge.
- Air refuelling – Mildenhall and Fairford.
- Transport – Mildenhall.
- Rescue – Woodbridge.
- Reconnaissance – strategic at Mildenhall, tactical at Alconbury.
- Emergency airborne command and control – Mildenhall.
- Fighter training – Alconbury.

Mildenhall, near Bury St Edmunds in Suffolk, has an eclectic range of functions. It is the headquarters of the Third Air Force; a transport base, passenger terminal and refuelling tanker centre; and host to the exotic electronic spy planes of the National Security Agency and Strategic Air Command. It also is the base for Silk Purse, the airborne war control centres of the US European Command.

Mildenhall became the headquarters of the US Third Air Force and took over command of most British USAF units in 1972, with the responsibility of supporting the rest. But no combat aircraft are based at Mildenhall.

The largest flying unit there is the 513th Tactical Airlift Wing, successor to the Troop Carrier Wing which General de Gaulle evicted from Normandy in 1967, but except for the four Silk Purse EC-135s – airborne war rooms based on the commercial Boeing 707 jetliner – the airlift wing has no aircraft of its own. It is a 'host' unit whose function is to look after temporary-duty aircraft from the United States stationed in the UK. At any one time, staff at Mildenhall are looking after about 30 temporary-duty planes – 16 C-130 Hercules transport planes, and usually a slightly smaller number of KC-135 refuelling tankers of the European Tanker Task Force – although the Task Force's strength can double during large-scale exercises.

Silk Purse, despite its oddly-chosen codename, is the most portentous of the Mildenhall missions. Since 1961, the United States has vested its capability to 'ride out' a nuclear attack, respond and sustain a nuclear war by putting commanders and war control centres aloft. These plans include provisions for the President, for whom a rather

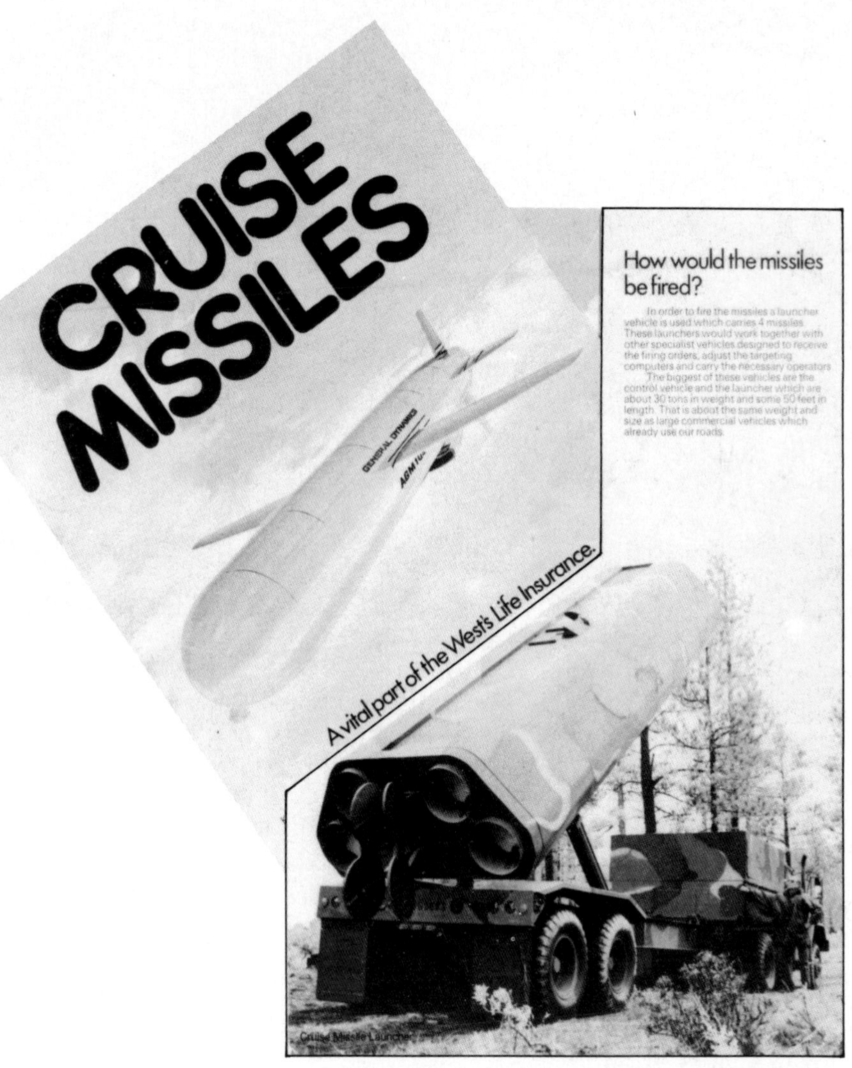

CRUISE MISSILES
GENERAL DYNAMICS
A vital part of the West's Life Insurance.
How would the missiles be fired?
In order to fire the missiles a launcher vehicle is used which carries 4 missiles. These launchers would work together with other specialist vehicles designed to receive the firing orders, adjust the targeting computers and carry the necessary operators.
The biggest of these vehicles are the control vehicle and the launcher which are about 30 tons in weight and some 50 feet in length. That is about the same weight and size as large commercial vehicles which already use our roads.
Cruise Missile Launcher


18. 'Cruise Missiles—A Vital Part of the West's Life Insurance'; £8,500 Ministry of Defence propaganda pamphlet for residents around Greenham Common incorporates cardboard cutaway cruise missile launcher.

19. Above: Cruise missile silos at Greenham Common. Each silo holds one 'flight' of sixteen missiles.

20. Left: British soldiers guarding Greenham Common against peace demonstrations.

21. Opposite above: A major US Air Force ammunition storage dump at Welford, Berkshire. High explosive bombs are stored in the open.

22. Opposite below: Nuclear weapons store at RAF Waddington, near Lincoln—a 'Colocated Operations Base' for wartime US Air Force use.

23. British surface-to-air missiles at West Raynham in East Anglia. Britain has to provide air defences for US airbases.

24. Poseidon missile submarine at its tender in the Holy Loch.

larger Advanced Airborne National Command Post was recently refitted inside a jumbo jet. Around the world, seven units like Mildenhall's 10th Airborne Command and Control Squadron operate the windowless EC-135 jets. The squadrons are dotted across the globe: in Hawaii for the Pacific commander, at Norfolk, Virginia for the Atlantic commander; and at several sites in the United States for the President and SAC. The SAC fleet and its 'Looking Glass' command post is airborne 24 hours a day. Three aircraft share the daily duty in 8-hour shifts.

A Silk Purse control group, some 54 strong, is part of US European Command headquarters in Stuttgart, and includes officers of all three armed services. They provide the operating staff for the four Mildenhall EC-135s. The Silk Purse command centres probably provide a safer alternative to underground control posts – even the massively hardened control posts in the United States.

The Silk Purse fleet can communicate directly with US Air Force relay satellites orbiting over the poles. These satellites, called AFSATCOM, effectively provide a hot line to all parts of the US nuclear arsenal – submarines, bombers and missiles – and to other command centres. Wherever it goes in Europe, Silk Purse has a network of communications centres, called Ground Entry Points, which allow the aircraft to plug in to the US and NATO communications network on land. Mormond Hill, a US and NATO communications station which dominates north-eastern Aberdeenshire, is one such terminal. The entire hill is strewn with giant antennae – for the American North Atlantic Relay System, NATO's command network, called 'Ace High', and British Telecom links to the North Sea oil and gas platforms.

When Air Force One, the President's personal command post, visits Europe (which happens about once a year) it will plug directly into the same network. 'Night Watch' is this aircraft's official codename; refuelled, it can direct nuclear battle from on high for three days without landing. AWACS, the airborne warning and control aircraft, are another user of the skyborne switchboard system, for which three more ground entry points are being built in Britain by the RAF, as far apart as Cornwall and northern Scotland.

Siemens, the German computer manufacturers, are also installing a new command, control and communications sytem called 'Eifel' at all the main US bases in Britain. Eifel will feed intelligence and orders to and from the ground command posts, AWACS, other surveillance planes, and the Silk Purse commanders.

Mildenhall has an additional powerful transmitter array sited in the north-west of the base. This is part of SAC's high frequency 'positive control' network for B-52 bombers, Giant Talk.

Like any large international civil airport, Mildenhall has a passenger air terminal, customs and baggage facilities, and a large sign offering a 'Welcome to Britain' to visitors who step off the passenger transports run by the USAF Military Airlift Command. Thousands of passengers come through every year. These transport facilities are also shared with and used by many US Navy and Army aircraft, to whom Mildenhall is the main UK base for regular courier flights that dot about Britain and Europe.

During large exercises, such as the Reforger series of reinforcement rehearsals (see also p 269), Mildenhall may handle nearly 200 flights of giant Starlifter (C-141) and Galaxy (C-5) transporters, at rates of a dozen a day. The locally based Hercules provide tactical transport from Europe to the flanks of NATO in Turkey and Norway.

For transport and airlift operations, an alternative to Mildenhall is the civil airport at Prestwick near Ayr, where both the Navy and Air Force maintain permanent transport units, and an Armed Forces Courier Depot. (Although a civil base, Prestwick is also the site of a British Royal Navy anti-submarine warfare helicopter squadron.)

Mildenhall has periodically been used as a base for the world's most sophisticated and most notorious spy planes – the U-2 and the SR-71, both regularly used illegally to overfly hostile and neutral territory gathering photographic and electronic intelligence. U-2s and SR-71s, as noted in Chapter 5, have come to Britain and operated from Upper Heyford, Lakenheath and Mildenhall in ones and twos since the start of the U-2 programme in 1956. Mildenhall is one of four main forward locations for these aircraft. U-2s regularly use the British base at Akrotiri in Cyprus. These high-flying spy planes are detached from Beale Air Force Base in California, the headquarters of SAC's 9th Strategic Reconnaissance Wing. Between 1975 and 1981, SR-71s and U-2s visited Mildenhall on 39 occasions.

Their intermittent presence has now become permanent, after the British government agreed to the construction of first one, then two of the special hangars needed for permanent SR-71 operations. The first hangar was built during 1979 and 1980 and an SR-71 arrived with a permanent accompanying staff from California. A second hangar was added in January 1983, and Mildenhall gained a permanent complement of two SR-71s. Soon after, U-2 operations moved to Alconbury, where a new reconnaissance squadron has been set up. The purpose of the new, permanent SR-71 presence in Europe is officially held by the

US to 'simplify logistic support' and help integration into NATO's reconnaissance programme. As late as September 1980, US Air Force officials continued to deny that the spy planes were 'based' in Britain, and did so that month whilst a Thames Television crew were filming on the airbase; to their deep embarrassment, U-2R number 10332 glided out of low clouds to land shortly afterwards. The TV crew filmed the landing and watched as, in less than two minutes, it was hurried out of sight into a hangar then reserved for it.[4]

Mildenhall sports two other spy planes, both RC-135s, adapted Boeing 707-like aircraft which carry millions of dollars worth of specialised Elint equipment. Long, proboscis-like noses conceal radar detectors; large flattened fuselage panels below and behind the cockpit are believed to contain side-look radar which can be used at a suitable altitude to obtain reconnaissance images of ground targets at least 50 and possibly 200 miles from the aircraft's path. The RC-135s come from the Offutt Air Force Base in Nebraska, the headquarters of SAC. Another RC-135 detachment normally operates from Hellenikon airbase, near Athens. The aircraft and their crews ultimately come under the control of the NSA intelligence agency. Details of the five intelligence planes at Mildenhall are not included in 'fact sheets' handed out by the US Air Force headquarters in Britain. But the official *Air Force* magazine, published in Washington, lists the 66-person 6988th Electronic Security Squadron – the Elint operators of the RC-135s at Mildenhall.

The RC-135s may not now penetrate Soviet airspace as they fly along Warsaw Pact borders in central Europe and the Baltic, but they aim to provoke. A 1980 interview in the *Air Force* magazine quoted the Chief of Strategic Air Command on this matter:

> it is possible to operate these systems in a way that induces the 'other fellow' to react in a way that tells us things we want to know . . .

More succinctly, this activity is privately described by Air Force intelligence specialists as 'provocative penetration'. As it depends on triggering an adversary's defensive and retaliatory systems it can be a highly-dangerous method of acquiring information.

Although such sensitive aircraft as U-2s are carefully kept from public view as much as possible, they have not been made invisible to the community of methodical and vigilant aircraft-spotting enthusiasts around Britain's major airbases. They are easily able to chart the build-up of spy planes in Britain, and enumerate those that are here. They have also detected evidence of at least two US Air Force covert operations, for which US officials are not prepared to offer any satisfactory explanation. On 16 January 1982, an RC-135V passing through Mildenhall en route from Nebraska to Athens was seen to have five small red silhouettes of Soviet Sukhoi aircraft painted on its nose. This is normally a pilot's badge of having achieved a 'kill' and shot down another aircraft. In the case of the unarmed RC-135, it is unlikely to have that highly-alarming meaning. But it is not likely to mean less than that the aircraft had been challenged by Soviet Air Force interceptors whilst in their airspace, and got away with it.

On another occasion, 3 and 4 July 1982, another RC-135 was seen which had been repainted with a false fin number. The manoeuvre was easily spotted as the disguised aircraft, an RC-135U marked 14848, was carelessly parked beside the genuine number 14848, a slightly different RC-135V version. Again no explanation for this gambit is available from the US Air Force. Strategic Air Command headquarters would only say that they did not comment on 'operational matters'. Detecting such implied clandestine activity may be more difficult in future as American national insignia are now missing from the all-black SR-71s operating from Mildenhall.[5]

Mildenhall's 306th Strategic Wing – including the spy force of SR-71 'Blackbirds' and U-2s – is organised from Germany by SAC's 7th Air Division, at the Command's European headquarters, Ramstein Air Force Base, near Frankfurt. Refuelling tankers – KC-135s – are the 306th Strategic Wing's second responsibility at Mildenhall. Fifteen tankers normally form the core of the European Tanker Task Force. They come from United States bases on short-duty tours, and operate across Britain and Europe to support bombers, transports and the spy planes.

Because of special fuel requirements, the SR-71s can refuel only from special tankers (KC-135Q) carrying a unique jet fuel, JP7. Unlike most aviation fuels, JP7 has been designed not to be inflammable, as far as possible. Since SR-71s leak copiously, this was vital. Large pools of fuel gather wherever they are left parked; their special hangars are often awash with fuel, creating an alarming fire hazard. The leaks cannot be stopped since the SR-71 was designed without internal fuel tanks, and holds fuel only within its outside skin. The same skin is so regularly strongly heated – parts of the SR-71 become orange or even white-hot during supersonic flight – that it is impossible to avoid it springing leaks.

In war, the first task of the European Tanker Task Force would be to attend to the needs of their F-111 'chicks' – the sobriquet applied to aircraft which come to suck in fuel below the KC-135s. So when the F-111 strength in Britain was doubled as 84 new F-111s were deployed to Lakenheath early in 1977, the tanker force had to double in size too. Secret preparations to take the new tankers began almost immediately at Greenham Common, the USAF support base near Newbury which had been on stand-by status since SAC and its B-47s had left in 1964. In 1977 and 1978, over £1 million was spent on resurfacing the runway, and renewing the underground fuel pipeline to the base and other facilities. In February 1978, the news leaked out that Greenham Common was about to come back into fulltime military service.

But, for once, cosily pre-conceived plans agreed between US and British defence officials were to run into serious and effective opposition. After the base had closed in the 60s, the Defence Ministry had repeatedly reassured local planners and MPs that there was no intention of permanently reactivating the airfield in peacetime. More than 2,000 new houses, schools, and other community buildings had been constructed within two miles of the runway, and directly in its path. Now, it was proposed to place there a working force of more than a dozen aircraft with a reputation for ferocious noisiness. The Greenham Common tanker plan ran immediately into trouble.

Within two weeks 16,000 local residents had signed a petition against the base. The campaign created an ironic contrast with the events three years later, when comparatively few local residents joined the protest against cruise missiles. The 1978 campaign was wholly environmental, and was backed by left and true-blue right and MPs alike. They succeeded. The firm determination of the Defence Ministry and the US Air Force wavered, the Greenham Common decision became impermanent, and an extensive survey of alternative sites was announced in Parliament. The Americans resisted a Defence Ministry proposal to resite the tankers at Waddington, near Lincoln, a V bomber centre which was running down and had already been earmarked as a US wartime base. They were only really interested in two airfields, which both already had the requisite 10,000 foot of strengthened runways. These were the two other former SAC airfields now back in RAF hands – Brize Norton near Oxford, and Fairford near Cirencester.

Fairford they didn't much care for, as it had few useable support facilities, and there would be a likely $38 million bill to get it back in working order. But to get Brize Norton would mean ousting the RAF from a modern base they had converted to become their main long-distance transport centre. Two months after the row began, the MOD affected to notice that prohibited airspace around the Aldermaston atomic weapons research centre was extremely close to Greenham. For this reason, they said, it would now be rejected. Fairford was selected instead – and the environmental battle began anew.

On this occasion, however, the Leader of the Conservative Party, Mrs Margaret Thatcher, moved in to dismantle her side of the opposition to the deployment. She instructed local MPs to lay off fighting for their constituents' rights, writing that there was 'no way in which a future Conservative government would wish to change the decision over the use of Fairford'. Shadow Attorney-General Sir Michael Havers abruptly pulled out of a £2,000 commitment to represent the Fairford villagers' case in public. The Cotswold District council pronounced itself 'totally opposed' but gave way gracefully. It had no choice, as the Ministry of Defence is free to ignore planning and other regulations as it sees fit, on its own behalf or that of the US. Nevertheless, the Ministry promised the council that no more than 15 tankers would come to Fairford, and that flying would normally be confined to daylight hours.

SAC bases thus came back to Britain in September 1979, with 1,100 personnel, 1,900 dependents and a $35 million construction bill. By March 1981 there were 15 tankers of the 11th Strategic Group based at Fairford. Like those transports and tankers already at Mildenhall, the aircraft rotate from the United States on 30-day visits. Smaller groups are based elsewhere in Europe – half a dozen at Zaragoza in Spain, and two in Iceland.

Secret plans have been made to use Fairford for US Middle Eastern operations including possible tanker and bomber support for the Rapid Deployment intervention force. This was confirmed by secret testimony in the US Congress in 1980. Published details of the plan, which were censored before being released, mentioned:

> a viable plan . . . that is secret. It is classified . . .[6]

Although details had been struck out before publication, the Middle East context was betrayed in the succeeding question when an Air Force witness observed that the distance from Fairford to the Persian Gulf was 3,700 nautical miles. The proposal has since become reality, three of the 11th Strategic Group's tankers having moved out to the Saudi Arabian capital, Riyadh, to back up US AWACs in flying over the Arabian peninsula.

Fairford was the seventh USAF Main Operating Base in Britain. During the first of the false war alerts sent out from North American air defence headquarters on 3 June 1980, Fairford was alerted and its aircraft scrambled. The Ministry of Defence later admitted only that crews ran to their planes and engines were started. But Fairford villagers say they saw the planes take off in rapid succession on full power. It was this sudden commotion that provoked several of them to telephone the base to ask what was happening. The base switchboard cut off the calls, responding only that:

> It's an emergency . . .

Vultures, Pirates, Avengers and Buzzards are the self-applied nicknames given to four Thunderbolt squadrons at Bentwaters airbase near Ipswich, a US Air Force base since 1951. Over one hundred A-10 Thunderbolts are now stationed at Bentwaters and its next-door alter ego, Woodbridge. The A-10 is probably the first modern aircraft designed to be shot at, keep on flying and bombing, and get shot at some more. A slow, heavily-armoured and massively-laden craft, it is almost a flying tank. Crews nickname it the 'Warthog'.

Six squadrons of A-10s – officially a total of 108 aircraft, although the real total is always higher – are now based at Bentwaters/Woodbridge. The number may increase when and if a proposed seventh squadron moves into Woodbridge. Protruding from the front of the Warthog is a heavyweight cannon, which fires uranium bullets more than an inch in diameter, 70 every second. Not in any sense nuclear weapons themselves, the bullets in the Warthog's Gatling gun are a by-product of nuclear refining to make weapons. When the valued and rare $U^{235}$ isotope of uranium is extracted from natural ore to make weapons or reactor fuel, 'depleted' uranium remains. An ample stockpile of depleted uranium from the weapons programme has been the raw material stockpile for the A-10's special ammunition.

Far heavier than the orthodox lead composition, uranium bullets carry extra momentum and energy to their target. Striking metal shielding, the impact may melt both bullet and armour, letting fly deadly spalls of molten fragments within the target tank or vehicle. Up to 18 cluster bombs or missiles can also be carried on pylons under the A-10's wings, including a TV-guided missile, Maverick, or 90 gallons of napalm. In front of the pilot, a television screen allows him to guide a Maverick on its one-way journey to an explosive end. Whilst unleashing this arsenal, the pilot himself sits in a half-ton bath of titanium armour shield to protect him from ground fire. Fuel tanks, engines, and the ammunition store are all armoured. There are two engines, mounted high, two control systems, and two tails. Survivability is the purpose of the design.

In war, the Vultures, Pirates and the rest would work from forward operating bases in Germany, and – so long as the battle remained non-nuclear – regard their Ipswich home as a safe haven for rest and repair. At peace, eight aircraft are usually positioned at each of four German air bases – Alhorn, Norvenich, Sembach and Leipheim. The aircraft involved rotate from England to Germany. Scattered from north to south, the German forward bases allow the planes to get back into fighting as quickly as possible – making perhaps 6–8 attacks a day. Badly damaged planes would be patched up to get back to Bentwaters/Woodbridge – or if need be, just cannibalised. Damage from close-range gunfire or missiles is a certainty, and the A-10 carries no sudden turn of speed or fancy electronics to throw off a homing SAM missile.

Another new British base has been pressed into USAF service to keep the A-10s flying: Kemble, near Cirencester, was the home of the RAF Red Arrow display team until March 1983. Before the Red Arrows moved out the base was offered to the US as a 'going concern' repair depot. The offer was accepted, and the USAF contracted to take over the RAF workforce to maintain A-10s at Kemble, saving the many days and vast costs otherwise incurred by flying the aircraft back to Sacramento, California. USAF officials also stressed, in Congressional testimony, that it would provide them with:

> an excellent expansion base for wartime battlefield damage repair[7]

At the time of writing, the Kemble maintenance depot was the only genuinely joint US/British airbase in the UK, with administration shared between the two air forces. However, it is set to grow. Besides the A-10 Thunderbolts, Kemble is to repair 'selected special purpose vehicles'. This role might expand to include cruise missile transporter/launchers and control centres, as current US plans for the Ground Launched Cruise Missiles call for a central repair Facility/Depot. On plans issued by the manufacturers, General Dynamics, a suitable location for the facility is shown in central England.[8] US planners stressed to Congress that Kemble had 'excellent facilities and a massive amount of hangar space'.

Although the construction of a new cruise missile maintenance depot is unlikely to start until 1985 or 1986, another new US Air Force project was lined up to go to Kemble in April 1983. The Ministry of Defence notified the local council that it intended to lengthen the runway there. As usual, the Ministry did not venture to describe to local residents or officials the purpose of the runway extension, which was to carry large US Air Force transport aircraft. But the purpose of the initiative was openly explained in March at the same time to the US House of Representatives' Military Appropriations subcommittee. Kemble would become a giant warehouse for wartime aircraft spares, a project called the 'European Distribution System' (EDS). A Memorandum of Understanding had been negotiated with the United States at least two months before details of the runway lengthening project became known in the area.

The EDS project was a product of the US Air Force's 'think tank', the Rand Corporation. Rand scientists claimed that without a large stockpile of parts and a good transport system, some 300 aircraft – or one in six of the wartime American strength in Europe – would be grounded on every day of the war. The answer they proposed was new warehouses in Prestwick, Scotland and Germany and a squadron of 18 new transport aircraft.

The contemporary conduct of US-British military relations was well illustrated by the sudden abandonment of the original plan for the EDS system to go to Prestwick, in April 1983. The last organisation to find out about the Prestwick plan was, apparently, the British government. Documents submitted to the US Congress show that the decision to move in to Prestwick had been taken in Washington and the building plans were half complete before the British government was asked to agree.[9]

In the autumn of 1982, Air Force officials surveyed Prestwick Airport and planned the construction of a 20,000 square foot 'Forward Storage Warehouse' for the EDS system. Design work and surveying began on 9 November 1982. The warehouse would cost $1.82 million to build. Airport officials at Prestwick knew about the project, and brief details were reported in the *Scotsman* newspaper. On 6 January 1983, an official application for funds was submitted to the US Congress. Construction would begin at the start of November.

By the start of January 1983, one-third of a projected $145,000 had been spent designing the new warehouse. The US Air Force admitted to the *Scotsman* that they had not yet asked for permission to increase their use of Prestwick. The new warehouse would, according to the application for funds, 'insure logistic requirements to support an additional 300 to 600 sorties in Europe per day' and 'in peacetime . . . provide an increased level of force readiness'.

In March 1983, when Kemble became available, the Air Force apparently began to reconsider going to Prestwick. But the application for funds went ahead for a Congressional Armed Forces Committee budget hearing on 26 April. At the end of March, the *New Statesman* reported that the US Air Force had applied for funds to develop the Prestwick warehouse. In Parliament, South Ayrshire MP George Foulkes then asked the Minister of Defence 'what discussions have taken place with the United States . . . about extensions of the use of Prestwick Airport?' 'None,' was the reply. But at Prestwick, the airport manager confirmed details of the US warehouse plan.[10]

Three weeks later, the Ministry of Defence seemed unperturbed as they maintained that they had never heard about the plan. The Scottish Secretary of State, George Younger, denounced reports of the US plans as 'irresponsible and very misleading'. In a statement telexed to newspapers by the Scottish Office, he asserted that 'there are no plans to build a warehouse or any other US facility at Prestwick', adding:

> I can assure you that there is no question of any American military facilities being built in this country without the knowledge or approval of our government . . .

Scottish Office officials had clearly not researched the issue carefully on behalf of the Secretary of State. The same day, US Congressional officials affirmed that the budget application was still in force. Told that Mr Younger had denied knowledge of the scheme they were astonished: 'He didn't know?' It was assumed, they added, that the host government's approval had been obtained before funds were sought. But the budget application was abruptly withdrawn by an embarrassed US Department of Defense. Whether it was public embarrassment over the offhand way in which British government permission for US military expansion was taken for granted that killed the project, or whether it was merely the new attractiveness of the rival site at Kemble, is not known. But the affair illuminated some dark crevasses of the US military planning process in Britain.

Half the globe, from North Pole to South, and from Burma to the mid-Atlantic, is the operating area of another US unit in Britain, the 67th Aerospace Rescue and Recovery Squadron, based at Woodbridge. The squadron operates specially converted long-range Hercules transports, which were originally fitted with a unique STARS (Surface To Air Recovery System), intended to snatch downed airmen out of the waves or desert sands as the rescue craft flew overhead.

The crashed pilot would use a helium-filled balloon to suspend a cable attached to his harness. With two diverging scissor probes extended forward like an insect's feelers, the HC-130 rescue Hercules would fly at the wire, which the probes would grab and direct into a winch. In case the pilot missed the balloon cable, fender wires in front of the wings prevented it from entangling the propeller. If all went well, the rescued victim would be pulled aboard through the rear cargo door of the Hercules.

The STARS system has since been abandoned for air-sea rescue purposes in favour of more orthodox helicopter recovery methods, and the probes and fender wires have been removed from the Woodbridge aircraft. STARS apparatus is still fitted to other Hercules operating periodically in Britain – the MC-130ES, codenamed 'Combat Talon' – which are regular visitors to Mildenhall, and to the US support bases at Sculthorpe and Wethersfield. These planes are used by the 10th Special Forces Group, and its detachments in Germany. The MC-130ES specialise in 'covert infiltration and exfiltration'; more bluntly, smuggling spies and their supplies in and out of hostile territory, during peace as well as war (see pp 137–42).

Woodbridge's Hercules, despite the removal of STARS, are nonetheless distinctive aircraft, with a humped back containing direction-finding apparatus to home in on rescue beacons, and, on each wing, refuelling 'drogues' for accompanying rescue helicopters. There are usually six Hercules transports at Woodbridge, and these are backed up by six helicopters. These long-range search and rescue helicopters are Sikorsky 'Super Jolly Green Giants', a type extensively used in Vietnam.

Just over one-half of the 67th Rescue Squadron's aircraft are at Woodbridge; the others are detached to Keflavik in Iceland, Zaragoza in northern Spain, and Ramstein in Germany – which is the US rescue control centre for Europe. There is also a designated 'operating location' for the Hercules at Pensacola Naval Air Station in Florida – which, USAF officials in Britain have suggested, may be used to recover capsules of film jettisoned earthwards from spy satellites.[11] This may not be entirely accurate, since the satellite capsule recovery apparatus is slightly different from the STARS system once used at Woodbridge. Capsules are normally recovered over the Pacific Ocean by Aircraft based in Hawaii.

As a former base for the nuclear-equipped F-4 Phantoms, Woodbridge airbase has a prominent and substantial nuclear weapons store on common land in the Rendlesham Forest, Sutton Common. The nuclear store is guarded by layers of barbed wire and rolls of barbed tape, surmounted by a high, modern watchtower and floodlit at night.

The base's current complement of Warthogs and rescue aircraft do not carry nuclear weapons, so there is no means of estimating whether or not nuclear bombs are still in store. But as the A-10s go forward to Germany in crisis or war, there would be room for new, nuclear-capable units to move in from the United States. This type of deployment was rehearsed in April 1982, when under the rubric of 'Coronet Wrangler', a squadron of nuclear-capable F-16s arrived from Nevada.

For the first time since 1969, the United States plans to start the manufacture of nerve gas weapons. These include bombs bound for Britain. However, late in September 1983, the US Congress unexpectedly withdrew a $115 million authorization to the Pentagon to begin manufacturing VX nerve gas. A new plant had been constructed at Pine Bluff, Arkansas in 1981, but production has still not been approved.

US nerve gas artillery shells are already held in little-known stockpiles in Europe – notably the Fishbach US Army depot in south-west Germany, a few yards from the French border. But their condition is said to be poor, and they are in danger of leaking through age or corrosion. In some seven chemical depots in the United States itself, more than a thousand leaking nerve gas weapons are already a serious safety hazard.

The new VX weapons are 'binary'. In a binary nerve gas bomb, two stable and relatively non-toxic chemicals are stored separately. Whilst an aircraft or shell is flying towards its target, a mixing process is activated, and the nerve gas produced.

First off the Arkansas production line will be artillery shells, closely followed by 'Bigeye' bombs. Britain is the chosen site for Bigeye deployment, according to a study by the Pentagon's Defense Science Board. The study's secret findings were revealed to Reuters reporters in December 1981 by US Deputy Assistant Army Secretary Amoretta Hoeber. Her remarks caused a storm. The Pentagon made a flimsy attempt to contradict her, while Defence Secretary John Nott said that the US had not yet asked about bringing nerve gas to Britain, and he was not expecting to be asked.

According to the original Reuters report[12]:

> The Pentagon want to deploy a large new arsenal of nerve gas in Britain, as part of a multibillion dollar build-up for possible chemical war in Europe . . .

The Defense Science Board, of whose task force Ms Hoeber was a member, had:

PEACE .... Is Our Profession

Fairford and Mildenhall:
Strategic Air Command (SAC)

Mildenhall:
513th Tactical Airlift Wing

Mildenhall:
306th Strategic Wing

Greenham Common:
Air Base Group

USAF Europe:
50th Tactical Fighter Wing

Welford:
Ammunition Supply Squadron

Chicksands:
6950th Security Group

Fig 10. US military crests

> wanted new nerve gas bombs to be deployed on US airbases in Britain partly because of concern that West Germany would not accept deployment of new chemical weapons ... The most compelling reason for basing the bombs in Britain was the need to strike deep into the Soviet Army's rear echelons with the deadly gas if necessary ...

This type of mission is planned for the F-111s at Upper Heyford and Lakenheath. Consequently, these will be the most likely places for initial nerve gas stores in Britain.

In March 1981, the British Defence Ministry promised that any US 'request to base chemical weapons in this country ... would be the subject of specific negotiations'. But John Nott's predecessor, Francis Pym, repeatedly stated his view that offensive chemical weapons should be available to Britain and its NATO allies. Recent propaganda campaigns from the United States have stressed the alleged Soviet use of lethal chemical weapons in Cambodia and Afghanistan, in a flimsy, unsubstantiated and ill-disguised attempt by the Reagan administration to overcome European and Congressional resistance to the administration's own nerve gas programme.

The US Air Force still hopes to buy 4,500 new Bigeye bombs by 1985. Pentagon officials say there is a 'pressing need' for a long-lasting chemical bomb to drop far behind enemy lines. Once mixed, VX has the consistency of a heavy oil and sticks to leaves, grass, and other matter. Colourless and odourless, it remains active for up to three weeks. It is an extremely potent chemical. A tiny one-milligram drop absorbed through the skin is sufficient to kill rapidly. The nerve gases are so called because they disable the nervous system, producing convulsion, vomiting, defecation, and ultimately paralysis and respiratory failure.

Both the Soviet Union and United States have said that they will respond 'in kind' if attacked with chemical weapons by an adversary. All US bases in Britain are prepared for a chemical attack, and NBC (Nuclear-Biological-Chemical) defence exercises are held regularly. All exposed personnel wear complete, protective NBC suits and gas masks. If, under chemical attack, everyone dons protective clothing in time, the main effect of nerve gas on military personnel is merely to make military operations cumbersome, difficult and more dangerous. But no plans have been made to protect civilians from likely chemical targets, an 'immoral' feature that was stressed in 1983 during a last-ditch attempt to block production of nerve gas in Arkansas, by the State's Senator David Pryor:

> Nerve gas doesn't kill soldiers, it kills civilians.

## Table 6

### US Air Force in Britain – 1984

| *Main Operating Bases* | |
|---|---|
| Mildenhall | Headquarters, US 3rd Air Force |
| | 513rd Tactical Airlift Wing (part of Military Airlift Command): |
| | Bravo Squadron: |
| | About 16 C-130 Hercules transport aircraft |
| | About 15 KC-135 refuelling tankers |
| | 10th Airborne Command and Control Squadron: |
| | 4 EC-135H airborne command aircraft for US European Command (Silk Purse) |
| | Also a Military Air Terminal, and a US Naval Air Facility |
| | 306th Strategic Wing (part of Strategic Air Command, with headquarters at Rhein-Main, Germany): |
| | 2 RC-135 electronic intelligence aircraft (from 55th Strategic Reconnaissance Wing, Offutt Air Force Base, Nebraska (SAC headquarters)) |
| | 6988th Electronic Security Squadron: |
| | Sigint and Elint specialists fly in RC-135S |
| | Detachment, 9th Strategic Reconnaissance Wing (from Beale Air Force Base, California): |
| | 2 SR71 (and until 1983, 1 U-2) spy planes |
| Lakenheath | 48th Tactical Fighter Wing: |
| | 492, 493, 494, and 495th Tactical Fighter Squadrons |
| | 78–84[13] F-111F nuclear bombers – continuous alert |
| Upper Heyford | 20th Tactical Fighter Wing: |
| | 55, 77, and 79th Tactical Fighter Squadrons: |
| | 66–77[14] F-111E nuclear bombers – continuous alert |
| | 42nd Electronic Combat Squadron (from 1984): |
| | 12 EF-111 electronic jamming aircraft, converted from F-111A bombers |
| Bentwaters | 81st Tactical Fighter Wing: |
| | 92, 509, 510, 511 Tactical Fighter Squadrons: |
| | 72 A-10 Thunderbolt II ground attack aircraft for NATO central front |
| Woodbridge | 81st Tactical Fighter Wing: |
| | 78, 91 Tactical Fighter Squadrons: |
| | 36 A-10 Thunderbolt II ground attack aircraft for NATO central front |

| | |
|---|---|
| | 67th Aerospace Rescue and Recovery Squadron (part of Military Airlift Command):<br>6 Hercules rescue aircraft (HC-130)<br>6 Super Jolly Green Giant rescue helicopters (HH-53) |
| Alconbury | 10th Tactical Reconnaissance Wing:<br>1st Tactical Reconnaissance Squadron:<br>20 RF-4C Phantom reconnaissance fighters<br>527th Tactical Fighter Training Aggressor Squadron:<br>18 F-5E fighters, disguised as Soviet MiG fighters<br>17th Reconnaissance Wing:<br>95th Reconnaissance Squadron (from 1984):<br>8–20 TR-1 (formerly U-2) for reconnaissance and Precision Location Strike System |
| Fairford | 11th Strategic Group:<br>18 KC-135 refuelling tankers |
| Greenham Common | 501st Tactical Missile Wing:<br>96 Ground Launched Cruise Missiles in six mobile flights of 16<br>7273rd Air Base Group |
| Molesworth | Tactical Missile Wing from December 1986:<br>64 Ground Launched Cruise Missiles in four mobile flights of 16<br>Currently Defense Mapping Agency European Chart Depot and Defense Property Disposal Service Centre |

### *Stand-by Operating Bases*

| *Base* | *Existing and likely deployment* |
|---|---|
| Sculthorpe | Stand-by operating base – subsidiary to Lakenheath<br>7519 Combat Support Squadron:<br>Used for staging transport aircraft to Middle East<br>F-105 Thunderchiefs from Oklahoma and Texas – visited 1978<br>A-7 Corsairs from Ohio – visited 1983<br>Special Forces MC-130E 'Combat Talon' covert operations aircraft, with supporting units |
| Wethersfield | Stand-by operating base – subsidiary to Alconbury<br>66th Combat Support Group<br>819 Civil Engineering Squadron (Heavy Repair) – 'Red Horse' – runway repair engineers<br>Special Forces MC-130E 'Combat Talon' covert operations aircraft, with supporting units |

### *Colocated Operating Bases*

| *Base* | *Likely or observed deployment* |
|---|---|
| Abingdon | Unknown; full munitions stores built |
| Bedford | Unknown; probably F-111 bombers |
| Benson | Unknown |
| Boscombe Down | F-111 bombers from New Mexico – visited 1980, 1983 |
| Coltishall | RF-4 Phantoms from South Carolina and Alabama – visited 1976, 1983 |
| Cranwell | Unknown |
| Finningley | F-4 Phantoms from Illinois and the District of Columbia – visited 1982, 1983 |
| Leeming | F-4 Phantoms from Missouri – visited 1982 |
| Odiham | Unknown |
| Waddington | A-7 Corsairs from Iowa and South Dakota – visited 1979 |
| Wittering | A-7 Corsairs from Oklahoma, South Carolina, Pennsylvania, New Mexico and Ohio – visited 1978, 1981, 1983 |

### *Forward Operating Bases (Strategic Air Command)*

| *Base* | *Likely or observed deployment* |
|---|---|
| Brize Norton | B-2 bombers from California and Texas – visited 1980, 1981, 1983 |
| Fairford | B-52 bombers from California and Texas – visited 1980, 1981, 1982 |
| Marham | B-52 bombers from California and Texas – visited 1980, 1981 |
| Upper Heyford | B-52 bombers from Texas – visited 1979, 1980, 1981 |

(Upper Heyford and Fairford are both Main Operating Bases for US Air Force Europe (see above).)

## Notes

1 *Now!* magazine, 23 November 1979.
2 *New York Times*, 16 December 1977.
3 *Observer*, 6 March 1983.
4 Shown on *TV Eye*, 30 October 1980.
5 *Aviation Week and Space Technology*, 31 January 1983.
6 House of Representatives, Committee on Appropriations, subcommittee on Military Construction, Fiscal Year 1981, Part 5, p 92. US Congress, 1980.
7 House of Representatives, Committee on Appropriations, subcommittee on Military Construction, Fiscal Year 1984, Part 5, p 273, US Congress, 1983.
8 *BGM 109 – Ground Launched Cruise Missiles for Theatre Nuclear Force Modernisation*, presentational pamphlet; General Dynamics, Convair Division, circa 1981.

9 House of Representatives, Committee on Appropriations, subcommittee on Military Construction, Fiscal Year 1984, Part 2, pp 733–6. Project number 10941H. US Congress, 1983.

10 *Scotsman*, 1 April 1983.

11 *New Statesman*, 31 October 1980.

12 US newspapers carried the original report. A version appeared in the *Guardian*, 30 December 1981.

13 Official US Air Force statements of F-111 strength at Lakenheath claim a total of 78 aircraft; however, aircraft spotters have enumerated 84 aircraft allocated to the 48th Tactical Fighter Wing, as at November 1983.

14 As 13; the US Air Force says that 66 F-111s are officially allocated to the 20th Tactical Fighter Wing, but aircraft observed total 77. One F-111 crashed during December 1983, making an observed total of 160 aircraft (USAF 144).

# 10 *Reinforcement*

Official silence about reinforcement plans is one way in which public opinion in western European countries is misled about relative NATO and Warsaw Pact strengths. When 'balances' of forces in Europe are drawn up, the Soviet Union's entire strength (other than that facing China) is included. But American forces not already deployed in Europe are usually forgotten in these calculations. This is a serious omission, as detailed plans are naturally in existence for NATO land, sea, and air forces to be massively reinforced, and for the number of major US airfields in Europe to more than quintuple, in the event of war.

In Britain, there would be a significant boost for US forces. The Third Air Force's current strength of three tactical fighter and bomber wings on seven main bases would rise to perhaps 10 wings on 21 bases. Four airbases would be available to accommodate, if need be, three wings of B-52 bombers, to be used either for conventional or nuclear bombing or minelaying in Europe.

Precise details of reinforcement plans are secret. But the Ministry of Defence admitted to the author in 1980 that a memorandum of understanding had been signed with the United States in 1974, giving permission for special arrangements to be made for units normally based in the United States to take over ten RAF airfields as 'Colocated Operating Bases' (COBs). Other, long-standing arrangements permit Strategic Air Command to return with its B-52 or FB-111 bombers to four British 'Forward Operating Bases' (FOBs). Three British reserve airbases – Sculthorpe, Wethersfield and Greenham Common – are already in US hands as 'Stand-by Operating Bases'.

Although these arrangements make a substantial difference to real comparative strengths of NATO and Warsaw Pact forces in any projected confrontation, the only details normally vouchsafed to the public about these plans concerns the stand-by bases.

Fallacious and misleadingly constructed 'balances' have also been used to justify the deployment of NATO's planned 464 new cruise and Pershing missiles between 1983 and 1987 – 160 of them in Britain. NATO's presentation in support of cruise has depended on carefully selected and massaged figures. It is argued that NATO has no land-based medium-range nuclear missiles actually sited in Europe, and that such missiles are needed so that nuclear weapons, east and west, balance in every category. As described further in Chapter 11, this is a specious and dishonest argument. The qualifications to this 'balance' are precise, and carefully selected to stress a disparity in 'medium' range missiles that is in fact nothing new.

Historically, NATO chose to put its missiles at sea. It is therefore neither new nor shocking that Soviet forces have the upper hand in *land-based* medium-range missiles. They always had, even when the United States had 105 Jupiter and Thor missiles stationed in Britain, Italy and Turkey. The United States has major reserves of long-range strike aircraft on carriers, and reinforcements in the United States. When these carefully forgotten factors are reinserted in 'balance' tables, the disparity of forces diminishes or even reverses (depending on who does the arithmetic).

Even without emergency reinforcement, the US Air Force will enormously increase its peacetime establishment in the United Kingdom during the mid 1980s. New units which will become established in Britain in this period include:

- Greenham Common – 501st Tactical Missile Wing with 96 cruise missiles and 1,700 personnel; first operational at the end of 1983.
- Molesworth – a second Tactical Missile Wing, with 64 cruise missiles; planned to be operational at the end of 1986.
- High Wycombe – Theater Mission Planning Squadron detachment to compute target routes for cruise missiles.
- Alconbury – new 19th Reconnaissance Wing with at least one squadron of TR-1 (formerly U-2) spy planes, and 1,350 personnel; TR-1 force will then be trebled in size by 1988; also new support facilities for Molesworth cruise missiles.
- Upper Heyford – new 42nd Electronic Combat Squadron of 12 'Electric Fox' EF-111s begins operations during 1984.
- Kemble – warehouse for new European Distribution System, with 450 personnel in Germany and Britain.
- At least fifteen new hospital bases for all three US services all over England.

At the same time, at least $15 million has been spent on constructing US facilities at the 'Colocated Operating Bases'. During 1984, the US

Air Force is planning to spend $11 million constructing fuel and ammunition facilities at Finningley airfield in Lincolnshire – in peacetime an RAF training base. US facilities constructed at British COBs already include 18 shelters for F-111s at Boscombe Down near Salisbury, 'full' ammunition stores at RAF Abingdon, and other stores at RAF Wittering and RAF Waddington near Lincoln.

COBs are the largest of half a dozen different systems for US Air Force reinforcement or 'augmentation' in Europe. The COB plan was partly developed in response to the removal of US Air Force bases from France after 1967, and the then new NATO strategy of 'flexible response' to an attack. Under flexible response, NATO forces had to develop a greater capacity to keep fighting with conventional weapons, instead of simply providing an annihilatory 'tripwire' nuclear response to a conventional attack.

In the late 1960s, the US Air Force selected 73 airbases belonging to its European allies from which US forces might operate in war. Their idea was simple – moving into an existing allied airbase was vastly cheaper than developing standby airfields from scratch. In 1981, the head of the Air Force's military construction programme, General Clifton D. Wright, told a congressional committee that the advantage of COBs were that they provided 'the Air Force [with] a series of strategically located air bases for a relatively small dollar investment'. Other officials stressed that they were 'very cost-effective'. According to the Commander of the US Air Force in Europe (USAFE), General Charles A. Gabriel, they also had the advantage, for US fliers if not local residents, of providing multiple 'additional high-value targets around which the enemy must plan'.[1] They were, he said:

> the biggest bargain in Europe . . .

In Britain, these additional 'high-value targets' were to be found in 1980 in and around Lincolnshire at Finningley, Leeming, Waddington, and Wittering at Coltishall in Norfolk, and west of London at Odiham, Abingdon, Brize Norton, Benson, and Boscombe Down.

In 1983, two new COBs were added, at the Bedford Royal Aircraft Establishment and at Cranwell, the RAF college in Lincolnshire. RAF Brize Norton, the RAF transport headquarters and former SAC base, was at the same time removed from the COB list.

Details of the current 11 COBs are given in Table 6. Two other bases in Britain, Sculthorpe and Greenham Common, have also been designated as COBs, although they are already in American hands. All the others are peacetime RAF establishments which would, in war, be jointly or solely used by the US. At each base, a British 'sponsor unit' has to plan to support the US unit which will arrive in war, and to provide them with fuel and ammunition.

The British government is supposed to know which United States-based units will come in to the COBs in war, but neither the Ministry of Defence nor the US Air Force will reveal this information. By 1979, out of 73 COBs originally sought, the United States had obtained the use of 53 airbases, in 10 countries.

For each base in Britain, a specially written technical agreement specifies how the US unit and their British 'sponsors' will share facilities. US Air Force logistics and other experts then visit the base and draw up a 'joint support plan', describing how British or United States forces will keep the base supplied and working. After this, 'minimum essential facilities' for American use should be constructed at the base, including communications links, fuel and liquid oxygen storage, munitions dumps, and the preparation of operations and intelligence centres.

The US Air Force has been very keen on getting COBs, but Congressional budget committees have refused to provide them with funds. Between 1979 and 1983, USAF asked for nearly $100 million for developing the bases, and got a mere $3.6 million. Members of Congress thought that the NATO countries concerned, or NATO itself, should pay for 'minimum essential facilities' in their own territory. Because of delay and squabbling about funds, only 9 colocated bases had minimum facilities installed by 1983. These nine bases appear to include, in the UK, Abingdon and Boscombe Down.

Even at the few COBs where the Pentagon got permission and money to develop facilities, they have been accused of mismanagement by the Congressional financial watchdog, the General Accounting Office (GAO). A GAO report in March 1983 attacked the Air Force for 'misspending' $240 million on nonessential but costly projects like aircraft and fuel truck shelters on just a few bases, instead of getting runways and other facilities in working order at the dispersed COBs. In 1983, the US Air Force asked for $44 million to spend on COBs, including Finningley. They want to spend $300 million on construction at the bases by 1989. Then, the entire network would be operational.

Although none of the COBs are permanently staffed by US personnel, US communications are already installed linking the bases to the worldwide Autovon and Autodin communications systems. Radio communications networks are also pre-positioned in operations centres which have been put aside for US use. In storage are 'starter' kits of aircraft spares, bombs and ammunition. These are known as War Readiness Spares Kits.

Munitions to be stored in advance at the COBs are supposed to be 'low-risk . . . because security must be provided by host nation personnel'. This would appear to preclude pre-positioning of complex missiles or nuclear weapons at most COBs. But several of the COBs allocated to the United States Air Force in Britain are current or former RAF V-bomber or tactical nuclear bases (Finningley, Wittering, Coltishall, Waddington), and have Special Storage Areas for nuclear weapons. Since RAF nuclear weapons are currently stored at Waddington and Coltishall, sufficient secure storage space would be available to US forces. However, US law would require United States 'custodial' guard detachments to take charge if US nuclear weapons were to be stored there.

US-based aircraft which would come to the British COBs include F-4 Phantoms, A-7 Corsairs, F-16s and more F-111 bombers. All are nuclear-capable. F-111 reinforcements, in particular, would significantly increase the US nuclear striking force in Britain. One of the earliest reserve US nuclear bases to be developed in Britain was Boscombe Down, where 18 new concrete 'hardened aircraft shelters' (HAS) for F-111s were built between 1978 and 1980. Soon after the shelters were complete, the first F-111s arrived from Cannon Air Force base in New Mexico to check out their new British home. The deployment exercise, called 'Coronet Hammer', was the first time the F-111 reinforcements had come to Britain.

Boscombe Down, with its evident nuclear mission, was the only reserve base to be included in the extensive HAS network which has been built at all main US bases – at Lakenheath and Upper Heyford for F-111s, at Alconbury for Phantoms, and at Woodbridge and Bentwaters for the A-10s. New shelters for the TR-1 spy planes are planned at Alconbury, but their 103-foot wing span has created unusual engineering headaches for the shelter designers.

Resembling giant concrete World War Two Nissen huts, each aircraft shelter is a custom-designed home for a single aircraft. Each has reinforced concrete layered over a steel core, and is intended to withstand a direct hit from a 500 lb conventional bomb. The HAS are scattered almost at random at the main bases, so that a systematic conventional bombing attack on weak points in symmetrical lines of shelters is impossible.

Exercises like Coronet Hammer at Boscombe Down are the only indication that local residents may get of the role that each COB will have in war. Such exercises have been held increasingly frequently since the late 1970s. One series, called 'Crested Cap,' tests plans to reinforce US forces by bringing in 'dual-based' US Forces. 'Dual' basing allows part of a wing of aircraft allocated to a particular European base to be stationed more cheaply in the United States. They visit their second base for regular exercises. Alconbury is one British base known to have been a dual base. After two of its three RF-4 Phantom reconnaissance squadrons were withdrawn in 1976, they remained dual based at Shaw Air Force base in South Carolina.

Most dual bases are on the Continent, so Britain tends to host only the 'Coronet-' series of exercises, which are tests of the COB system. For example, in June 1982 'Coronet Brave' brought F-4s from Illinois's Air National Guard reserves to RAF Finningley, and 'Coronet Cactus' took the F-4s of Missouri Air National Guard to RAF Leeming. Table 6 identifies the US aircraft which have used the British COBS, and which are likely to come back as 'augmentation' in war.

On the basis of the exercises and other information set out in Table 6, it appears that two wings of F-111 bombers, two wings of F-4 Phantoms, one wing of RF-4 reconnaissance fighters, and two wings of A-7 Corsairs could come to Britain in crisis. The purpose of the four other colocated British bases is unknown, but is likely to include more of the same. Britain is therefore likely to host a large proportion of the 1,500 fighter aircraft planned as 'augmentation' for European forces. Including Strategic Air Command bomber forces moving to British forward bases, and extra transport aircraft, more than 1,000 US aircraft may be packed into a crowded island already densely populated with 'high-value targets'.

Some of the Colocated Operating Bases and the units going to them have not been guaranteed to be allocated to NATO forces in war. Depending on whether the US aircraft are definitely 'assigned' or merely tentatively 'earmarked' for NATO, they may stay under US control – or not come at all if the US Air Force wants to send them elsewhere. Any units assigned to NATO come under direct NATO command when allied governments agree to a procedure called CHOP – Change of Operational Control. All the US aircraft planned to come to Britain would be allocated to the two Allied Tactical Air Forces in Germany, and would not assist British air defence. Instead, COB aircraft coming to Britain would carry out tactical nuclear strikes, reconnaissance, battlefield attacks and provide air transport across Europe.

Other arrangements to bring reinforcement aircraft to Europe include Stand-by Dispersal Bases, 'Aircraft Cross Servicing' and 'Forward operating bases'. The least complicated arrangement is 'Aircraft Cross Servicing'. NATO standard facilities, suitable for most US aircraft, are installed at RAF bases – allowing the *ad hoc* use of further bases by tactical aircraft.

Major new developments in all-out electronic warfare are taking place at Alconbury, and on the F-111 bases at Upper Heyford and Lakenheath. The new breed of updated U-2 spy planes – TR-1s – have rolled off a reopened U-2 production line in California since the summer of 1981. The first TR-1 came to Alconbury early in 1983. Some 35 are being built, most intended for use in Europe. The first TR-1 squadron, part of SAC's 19th Reconnaissance Wing, began operations at Alconbury early in 1983. Its arrival brought to an end the secretive and intermittent U-2 visits to Mildenhall during the previous decade.

TR1s, despite their cosmetic new title, are spy planes. They can carry Elint detectors, side-looking radar, and photographic or infra-red, heat-sensitive cameras. During one high-altitude TR-1 flight, its cameras and radar detectors can scan and record military activity across a 100-mile wide strip, more than 3,000 miles long.

A new feature of the TR-1 is a 'real time' radio link to the ground. Two TR-1 ground stations have been set up in Europe to receive reconnaissance data direct from the TR-1s, enabling battle commanders, in effect, to watch war as it happens, 15 miles below the spy plane. The main job of the force, however, is to pinpoint and target missiles and aircraft onto defensive radar installations in eastern Europe. Its payload for this is 1.7 tonnes of electronics and radar detectors – chiefly the Precision Location Strike System (PLSS).

PLSS was first tested in Britain in May 1975, when five U-2s came for three months to the stand-by base at Wethersfield. The deployment was instantly controversial. On this occasion, the incumbent British (Labour) government showed, unusually, some nervousness about hosting the U-2s. Before they arrived from California, they were repainted from 'sinister black', without US markings, to a light grey warplane camouflage pattern – with (US) national markings.

British official nervousness was not ill-placed. On 29 May 1975, one of the fleet crashed at Winterberg, West Germany, perilously close to the border, and drawing unwelcome attention to the U-2 deployment in Britain. US and British governments then claimed that the U-2s had come to test a 'precision navigation system'. This was an ingenious half-truth. The aircraft were indeed testing a precision navigation system, which would determine accurately their position in three dimensions, relative to fixed points on the European battlefield. Knowing their own position, PLSS should locate radar targets to be attacked with equal accuracy.

The Precision Location Strike System, then called the Precision *Emitter* Location Strike System, relies on at least four aircraft being airborne at once. It is the eyes and ears of an automatic airborne battlefield, which seeks out targets electronically and rapidly directs aircraft, missiles or drones to destroy them.

Sensors in the TR-1's wing pods and electronics bays receive signals from dozens, even hundreds, of Warsaw Pact radars. By measuring the difference in the time of arrival of each separate electronic pulse from these far-off radars, their position on the ground can be accurately mapped by computer. Flying above 65,000 feet, PLSS may monitor ground activity at least 350 miles away.

During 1980, the British government agreed to the deployment of the new electronic war squadrons: TR-1s to Alconbury, and EF-111s to Upper Heyford. The plans were only revealed to Parliament more than a year later – by the traditional low-key means of a planted question. The prepared answer gave more details of financial benefits to the local economy in each area than of military construction, or details of how the aircraft would help NATO's military plans.

At Upper Heyford, the base was to be extended by 30 acres to accomodate 18 new hardened aircraft shelters, and provide facilities for twelve EF-111s. Protestors at the base's peace camp discovered that Oxford County Council had already agreed to sell the necessary land five years before – in 1978. During 1982 and 1983, this major enhancement of another US nuclear base in Britain brought attention and extensive non-violent protest to Upper Heyford. Two major rallies during 1982 led up to a well-publicised four-day attempt to blockade the base the next summer. A heavily reinforced local police force responded by arresting waves of hundreds of demonstrators *en masse* for obstructing the entrances to the base.

The 42nd Electronic Combat Squadron began operations early in 1984. The 'Electric Fox' EF-111s ('E' for electronic) are extensively rebuilt F-111s, and display the many unusual bulges characteristic of electronic warfare craft. Their most characteristic feature is the high-powered jamming array, ALQ99, which sits atop the aircraft's tail fin. Below the fuselage and on the wings, a bulging 'canoe' and electronic pods hold yet more jammers.

Electric Foxes, and similar 'Wild Weasel' jammer-equipped Phantoms in Germany, are intended to blind long-range air defence radars to prevent ground controllers finding and destroying invading aircraft. In the abstract language of the Pentagon, they produce:

> a decrease in the number of engagements of our aircraft by enemy threat systems; this reduces the attrition of our aircraft . . .

So fewer F-111s bombers will get shot down. The jammers can work in three ways. They may fly close in to a defended zone, so as to use maximum power against a few dangerous radars, or they can orbit safely behind the lines, jamming from there. Their most likely role, however, is to fly as a 'penetration escort' alongside attacking F-111s, jamming enemy radars as they pass *en route.*

The fin-mounted ALQ99 jammer is formidably powerful, and may threaten air safety in western Europe if operated at full power, according to US Air Force planners:

> We turned one EF-111A on full force near Vandenberg, California and wiped out every radar up to Seattle [800 miles away]. We can't do that in the crowded airspace of western Europe . . . it will be a problem training with the aircraft.[3]

Strategic Air Command, Military Airlift Command, the US Navy and Marine Corps all have plans for emergency operations in Britain. The Ministry of Defence admitted to the author in 1980 that rights to use four British bases – Brize Norton, Upper Heyford, Marham and Fairford – had been retained by Strategic Air Command after B-47 bombers withdrew in 1964. In 1980 too, the incoming Conservative government gave permission for B-52s to begin frequent deployments to the UK. Usually coming in threes, there have been at least four B-52 exercises a year in the UK since exercise 'Open Gate' began at Marham in April 1980.

Allocated to British forward bases until the end of 1983 were three 72-strong wings of B-52 'D' model Stratofortresses. This ubiquitous eight-engined jet bomber first took to the air in prototype form in 1952. More than 700 B-52s were built during the 1950s and early 1960s, succeeding B-47s in Britain and elsewhere as the mainstay of the US strategic bomber force. Many B-52s later took part in the notorious Christmastime raids on Hanoi and other North Vietnamese cities – 'Linebacker', in 1972/73 – with at least 17 being shot down in action.

B-52DS are no longer part of the US strategic nuclear bombing force's continuous alert, this being the task of later 'G' and 'H' models. The three wings which have regularly come to Britain are the 22nd Bomb Wing from March Air Force Base in California, and the 7th and

96th Bomb Wings from Dyess and Carswell Air Force bases in Texas. In the first days of war in Europe, their role would be conventional bombing on the central front, long-range mining of Baltic ports and similar targets, and possibly anti-shipping patrols.

Until 1982, the later B-52 'G' and 'H' models, or SAC's other bomber force of FB-111s (a long-range strategic version of the ordinary swing-wing F-111) did not come to Britain except to participate in bombing competitions against the RAF. But B-52Gs are now replacing the earlier type, which is being taken out of service. However, the peacetime location of the FB-111 force, at two bases in the extreme north-east of the United States – at Pease, New Hampshire and Plattsburgh, New York State – strongly suggests that these 60 strategic bombers are likely candidates to be deployed to the British forward bases if time is available. The relatively short range of the FB-111s (compared with B-52s) means that they need mid-ocean refuelling if they set off on an intercontinental nuclear bombing raid from their peacetime bases. At Plattsburgh, the 509th Bomb Wing is the successor to the unit which A-bombed Hiroshima and Nagasaki.

Probably for reasons of security and public policy, FB-111s have never exercised moving forward to Britain, from which Soviet targets would be more quickly and conveniently reached. To do so would publicly and awkwardly undermine the calculations of 'long-range land-based theatre nuclear forces' which were constructed as a public justification for the deployment of cruise missiles. In many alliance documents, for example the fiscal year 1982 Annual Report by the US Department of Defense, Soviet long-range air forces are credited with 390 long-range nuclear bombers; against this NATO is said only to have 226, including 56 RAF Vulcans, by then growing long in the tooth. But 190 F-111 and 60 FB-111 bombers stationed, in peacetime, in the United States are discounted. If these aircraft move forward, as the majority are planned to do, to COBs and FOBs in Britain and Europe, this balance is reversed in favour of the West.

The US Navy has no known reserve bases in Britain, but is able to use Machrihanish and other RAF bases such as Kinloss and St Mawgan as operating locations for P-3 Orion anti-submarine aircraft. Machrihanish was upgraded as a NATO transport and maritime airfield between 1960 and 1962. In a second phase of development, some £11 million has been spent at Machrihanish since 1979 on a fast refuelling facility, and new lighting, hardstanding (aircraft parking area) and perimeter tracks. Although no aircraft are normally stationed on the airfield – at the end of the remote Mull of Kintyre – it was acknowledged by the Ministry of Defence in a 1979 memorandum concerning developments at Stornoway to be 'fully committed to our contingency plans'.

Both Machrihanish and the new NATO airbase at Stornoway will be forward operating bases for RAF Tornado aircraft. But a major task at Stornoway is evidently to provide a staging base for 'Reforger'[4] reinforcements from the United States. MoD officials also acknowledge that Stornoway, when developed, will become an operating location for American P-3 Orion aircraft from Keflavik and bases in the US.

Although public statements about Stornoway by government officials have tended to stress an air defence role, greater stress was placed on its importance as a staging post for US maritime and transport aircraft by the then Defence Under-Secretary Geoffrey Pattie, in a 1981 lecture to the Air League.[5] Pattie stated that the RAF's ability to attack surface shipping was already an area of 'over-investment' and that this RAF role was 'not absolutely essential'; NATO forces were already 'more than a match for the Soviets at every stage of the conflict'. The critical reason for the £40 million construction programme at Stornoway, he said, was that it was:

> needed to provide cover for transatlantic sea and air lanes and to provide a staging post for flights from North America . . .

For this and related reasons, virtually all of the cost of developing Stornoway has been met by NATO's 'infrastructure' funds, which normally only pays for such basic essential joint facilities as fuel pipelines and stores. This stress on US reinforcement operations confirmed an explanation given earlier to the Western Isles Island Council. A senior RAF officer, Air Commodore Chesworth, explained to the council in 1979 that:

> NATO strategy relies on . . . emergency reinforcement. The majority of these reinforcements would come from the United States and their timely arrival in Europe depends on safe passage across the Atlantic . . . The scale of this reinforcement is enormous . . .

Once reinforcement was ordered, he explained:

> the aircraft inflow to the UK from the west is likely to give an arrival rate almost as high as the 1976 summer average . . . In addition there are the Marine Amphibious Forces which each have their own air wing.

Many units would require staging facilities in the UK, and these were already anticipated to be chock-a-block with US aircraft moving through:

> Currently we plan to use all suitably equipped airfields to capacity – including, for example, Prestwick, Turnhouse, Manchester Ringway, Blackpool and Liverpool Speke, to name but a few.[6] Stornoway's enhanced facilities would afford us the much needed additional staging facilities.

Defence Under-Secretary Geoffrey Pattie was less than sanguine about the military consequence of these moves for Stornoway, or indeed the other civil airports listed, in a published 1979 letter to Islands MP Donald Stewart:

> One has to admit that the airfield's present status as a forward operating base means that it must be reckoned a military target already (though I submit of a lesser order than many other places in the UK).

Both the precision with which many of the civil airfields to be used by the US Military Airlift Command were identified, and the public admission that Stornoway could (implicitly) be a nuclear target were unusual features of the highly-charged debate about the new development. However, the targeting of Scottish and northern English civil airfields likely to be used in US reinforcement operations was a notable feature of the 1980 civil defence exercise, *Square Leg*. During other exercises, the huge C-5 Galaxy transports have landed in Britain at Glasgow, Prestwick, and Liverpool civil airports, as well as at the RAF bases, Leuchars and Farnborough.

Development of the Stornoway base went ahead against virtually unanimous local opposition, a vigorous 'Keep NATO Out' protest campaign and despite a finding against the Ministry of Defence in a 1981 planning enquiry appointed by the Secretary of State for Scotland, George Younger. Younger then overruled the enquiry's conclusion – whose scope he had limited to 'local planning aspects' only – for reasons of 'national interest'.

Besides using Stornoway, Machrihanish and other bases for Anti-Submarine Warfare (ASW) aircraft, the US Navy has made plans to bring strike aircraft from its carriers ashore if the ships in the NATO-allocated Carrier Striking Force Atlantic come under heavy attack or are sunk. A plan, codenamed 'Invictus', to bring long-range A-6 Intruders ashore in Norway, was discovered by researchers at the Oslo Peace Research Institute, but no similar plan involving Britain has been revealed. In Norway there is also a plan for a standby Marine Air Base for US Marine Corps units, which may operate on the northern flank of NATO in north Norway. Again, although no Marine Corps bases appear to have been earmarked in the UK, occasional deployment has been noted. For example, in the autumn 1982 NATO exercise 'Northern Wedding', Marine Corps Harrier 'jump-jets' used the Anglesey airbase of Valley as a staging post. St Mawgan and Lyneham (Wiltshire) have also been used for Marine Corps exercises.

US Navy facilities in Britain hold stocks of nuclear weapons (as do the Air Force), in circumstances, apparently, of uncertain security. A US Navy controlled nuclear weapons store at Machrihanish, described as a 'Naval Aviation Weapons Facility' was built in 1967. Like its southern counterpart at St Mawgan (where a nuclear store was built in 1965) a communications centre at Machrihanish is directly linked to US Navy Headquarters in London so that orders to release nuclear weapons to NATO maritime aircraft may expeditiously be issued.

Both nuclear stores are central repositories for nuclear depth bombs to be used by British, Canadian, Dutch and American anti-submarine aircraft operating in the North Sea and North Atlantic. They hold B57 nuclear depth bombs, slim 15-inch diameter cylinders probably similar in internal design to the Little Boy weapon that was used on Hiroshima. Designed specially for use against submarines, they can be set to explode with a variety of nuclear yields, above, on, or below the surface. About 1,000 of the B57 depth bombs were produced for use by anti-submarine aircraft and helicopters, and from aircraft carriers. B57 bombs were first delivered to the US Navy in 1964.

Set on low-lying land near Campbeltown, the Machrihanish nuclear weapons store butts onto the local golf course (the village is a minor holiday centre). With high guardtowers surmounting the double fences of the nuclear store, it resembles nothing better than the 'Stalag' German prisoner-of-war camps popularised in postwar British films. Inside are rows of small, garage-like storage buildings, divided by high earth walls.

Machrihanish and St Mawgan between them hold most, if not all, of the land-based European reserve of US nuclear depth bombs (other possible NDB sites are Sigonella in Italy, and Keflavik). Because of its remoteness, Machrihanish was undoubtedly the site singled out for criticism in a 1973 survey of the security of US nuclear weapons in Europe.[7] Facilities at over 100 'special ammunition sites' holding the then 7,000 US tactical nuclear weapons in Europe were surveyed by a team led by two US Senators. The report commented that:

> Nuclear depth bombs are stored in a desolate area and are vulnerable to attack . . .

The same report discovered even more alarming security dangers than the remoteness of Machrihanish; at one unidentified European site, atom bombs had been stored in the basement of a barracks office block. The basement door was open and unguarded when a Senate investigator visited.[8] A guard was posted for the first time on the day that the Senators arrived!

US Defense officials rapidly responded to the criticism by reducing the number of weapons stores by over 20 per cent and speeding up plans to introduce more sophisticated tamper-proofing systems known as Permissive Action Links (PAL) into the bombs. The bomb's built-in PAL should prevent stolen nuclear weapons from being used without knowledge of special activation codes. Some modern versions of PAL cause the weapons to destruct in a conventional explosion if interfered with.

But, ten years later, little has changed. Although the total number of US tactical weapons in Europe has fallen to 6,000, there are still 108 nuclear weapons stores – 49 US-only and 59 NATO-guarded – scattered across Europe, from the Scottish Highlands to Turkish Armenia. At most of the NATO depots security is said in some reports to be 'terrible'. None of the improvements planned a decade before, such as special electronic movement detectors mounted on or between the two fences, have yet been implemented at most NATO nuclear stores. In exercises, US Special Forces teams have invaded nuclear stores and succeeded in getting possession of a bomb within half an hour. One such exercise, called 'Rising Star', was held on 5 and 6 May 1982, to test what the United States would do if terrorists seized a nuclear weapon in transit in Western Europe.

Although US guards inside the inner perimeter fence of NATO nuclear stores are ordered to shoot to kill if their zone is breached by intruders, the US Defense Secretary's chief nuclear adviser, Dr Richard L. Wagner, acknowledged in a 1983 interview that stealing a US nuclear weapon could be accomplished by a terrorist group with 'relative ease'.[9] It would, however, be much more difficult to set it off. Other specialists commented at the same time that NATO nuclear sites were:

> highly vulnerable to hostage-taking or a high publicity siege. Either would yield tremendous pressure in the United States and abroad to withdraw nuclear weapons from Europe.

If warned in time, US guards could cause the weapons to self-destruct. But in extreme emergency, the interview report explained:

> the bunker could be blown up, destroying the warheads and releasing alpha radiation, but not setting off a nuclear explosion. [This] expedient would cause heavy casualties and destruction within six miles of a site. Although most of the sites are relatively isolated, a few are close to heavily populated areas.[10]

A 1978 CIA report suggested that there was by then 'moderate likelihood' of terrorist attacks on nuclear weapons in storage or transit. In the same year, a US reporter posed as a building contractor, and successfully obtained blueprints of nuclear weapons stores which were being modernised. Having signed applications to visit the sites with the names 'Baader' and 'Meinhoff' (after the German 'Red Army Faction') he was able to visit several SAC nuclear stores and see half a dozen H-bombs at close quarters.

Responding to the threat that independent terrorists – or for that matter, a government outside the Warsaw or NATO pacts – might attempt to steal nuclear weapons, the US Energy and Defense departments have set up Nuclear Emergency Search Teams (NEST). The risk that nuclear weapons might also be stolen from NATO countries' depots led to the formation in the late 70s of a small, five-strong European team – ONEST – which is believed to be located at a US base in Britain.[11] ONEST's job would be to find a stolen nuclear weapon by detecting the radiation emitted from its nuclear core.

US government experts expect that a stolen or fabricated terrorist nuclear weapon would be used in a blackmail plot against a city or major industrial or military installation. Some targets of especially high risk, such as Washington itself and Manhattan, have been surveyed by NEST teams to map in advance legal sources of radiation in hospitals and laboratories which might otherwise provide false leads for their detectors during an emergency search for a clandestine nuclear bomb. Washington was surveyed by NEST for sources shortly before the US Bicentennial celebrations in 1976. By 1983, more than 70 terrorist nuclear threats had been made against US cities.[12]

In 1982, the European ONEST team was issued with extra equipment to help find stolen nuclear weapons using specialised neutron- and gamma-radiation detectors. They already had over 40 detectors which could be carried in suitcases. The team also got a truck-mounted detector, ten roadblock monitors and two helicopter pods of particularly high sensitivity. The US-based NEST teams in Washington and Las Vegas are equipped with undercover vans which can be used to close in on a radiation source suspected to be a bomb.

US facilities at Machrihanish have recently expanded to accommodate new US Navy units, ironically including the naval special forces (SEALS), which is part of the US special forces (see Chapter 5). Some 37 strong, the SEALS unit has the use of special operations aircraft and vessels.

To support reinforcement and emergency operations, extensive US conventional munitions supplies and army stocks are stored at ten British sites. The US Third Air Force's main British depot is at Welford, near Newbury. Another depot is leased nearby at Bicester. Largest of the US Army depots in Britain is the five-square-mile Burtonwood store near Warrington with its subsidiary munitions store at Caerwent. Since 1978, this store has been augmented by another ammunition depot leased from the British army – Bramley, near Basingstoke. For amphibious operations and landings, the US Army has a further 'Marine Fleet' depot network in southern England, centred on the British Army military port in the Solent, Marchwood. There are two subsidiary depots, at Hythe and Poole – also a British Royal Marines base.

Sophisticated new underwater mines to seal off the Greenland–Iceland–UK gap for Soviet submarines, and to block operations in other strategic areas in the north Atlantic, have recently been moved into two further storage depots – Machrihanish and the nearby NATO depot, Glen Douglas near Arrochar. About 1980, a detachment of the US Navy's 'Mobile Mine Assembly Group' was set up at Machrihanish with a job described unrevealingly as 'maintenance and assembly of underwater mines for NATO use'. By 1983, the second detachment had been set up in Glen Douglas to supervise further stores of underwater mines.

Although naval officials are unwilling to explain the exact purpose of the new units, their creation ties in closely with the development of a US robot underwater mine called Captor. Captor 'will kill more submarines per dollar than any other ASW system', it was reported in congressional hearings in 1978. A Captor minefield can provide a relatively quick, cheap way of building a submarine barrier. Inside each Captor mine is an advanced homing torpedo, with the ability to distinguish between the sounds made by friendly and hostile submarines and surface vessels. When it detects a hostile submarine within range – at least 6 miles – the torpedo is released to home in on the target. If it misses the first time, the torpedo can swerve back for further attacks. Theoretically, 500 such Captor mines could 'choke' the Greenland–Iceland–UK gap altogether, blocking the passage of submarines. The only other easy Soviet outlet from Murmansk or the Baltic to the Atlantic, the English Channel, can easily be blocked by other anti-submarine forces.

Captor mines can be dropped by any of the NATO anti-submarine aircraft, or by B-52s deployed to British bases. Laying the minefield would have to be done quickly in crisis or war, explaining the need for forward bases such as those in Scotland. If the mines were activated and the Captor barrier breached by penetrating submarines, they could be relaid by further B-52 or P-3 Orion flights from Machrihanish.

At Glen Douglas, the NATO storage depot is intended for loading ships rather than aircraft. An ammunition-loading pier and pipeline fuel terminal is adjacent to the depot in Loch Long, a deep-water inlet from the Clyde. Glen Douglas is also one of two British depots which hold about 40,000 tons of US Navy conventional shells, depth charges, missiles and rockets, pre-positioned for use during battles in the Norwegian Sea. Broughton Moor Royal Naval Ammunition Depot, near Whitehaven, is the second site for these stocks. It is wholly British-run, but its storage capacity is leased exclusively to the US Navy.

Although no US-only fuel stores have been built in Britain other than at airfields, US forces are naturally a major customer for fuel supplies. All major US airbases are connected to the 1,200 mile underground pipeline network run by the British Pipeline Agency Ltd, as agents for the Department of Energy and Ministry of Defence. A basic network across England, connecting refineries, underground fuel stores, and airfields in the east, was created during the Second World War, and has been considerably extended since using funds from NATO's infrastructure programme. Mildenhall, for example, receives all of its JP4 aviation fuel through a direct pipeline from the British Pipeline Agency (BPA) depot in Thetford, Norfolk.

Both BPA and NATO or Royal Navy POL (Petrol-Oil-Lubricants) stores are designated US Defense Fuel Supply Points by the Pentagon. These include five refineries producing oil and fuel for US use (a list is given in Table 7). A US fuel 'quality assurance' supervisor is stationed at the BPA depot in Sandy, Bedfordshire, to check pipelined supplies to US airbases in East Anglia. Three NATO fuel depots on the Clyde estuary – Faslane, Loch Striven, and Campbeltown – are designated US Defense Logistics Agency bulk fuel supply centres.

Welford, the extensive Berkshire ammunition depot, cost the US government $5 million to build and has been storing reserve stocks for USAF units in Britain since 1955. In some 95 buildings, it provides three quarters of a million square feet of covered storage for weapons – bombs, missiles and ammunition. Although Welford would be the obvious site for any UK reserve nuclear stocks, neither physical inspection nor internal USAF information indicates that there is a nuclear 'Special Ammunition Store' at the base. Welford's 7551st Ammunition Supply Squadron is subordinate to the nearby Greenham Common airbase. Its crest of crossed missiles on a starry background boasts characteristically, if ghoulishly, 'Yes we can'.

Frequent road convoys of ammunition trucks to Welford have aroused considerable concern throughout Berkshire – the rail siding used for munitions shipments into the base closed during the 1960s. Two seaports are regularly used to ferry US Air Force explosives in and out of Britain: Barry Docks, near Newport, and Felixstowe in Suffolk, where permanent US Army staff operate a Military Transportation Terminal for the UK. At times, the heavy convoys transporting explosives between Welford and these ports have attracted stringent criticism from residents in nearby villages along the eight-mile route from the M4 motorway to the base.

Shipments have occasionally reached major proportions. In June 1975, 500 lorries travelled between Barry and Welford carrying ammunition, with groups of 5–9 lorries moving through local villages at 'all hours of the day and night', according to the area's Conservative MP.[13] On 15 September 1981, the USAF practice of hiring unmarked and unguarded civilian lorries to make such trips came to particular public attention. A British Road Services lorry loaded with 20 tonnes of 'Rockeye' cluster bombs caught fire on the M4 near Swindon that afternoon, and fifteen miles of the motorway was sealed off.

The lorry had been in a convoy of three; BRS subsequently said their lorries were regularly used for such shipments. The lorries travelled unguarded, and government spokesmen said they were more concerned about the terrorist threat of hijacking than about a risk to public safety from explosions. Such loads were 'not dangerous', they claimed. A joint USAF/RAF enquiry was promised, but no report was published. However, in 1982, to alleviate complaints of environmental damage around the base, the Department of the Environment began work on a £2 million link road directly connecting the Welford ammunition store to the M4.

Welford had aroused less parochial concern in the summer of 1972, when some of an estimated 5,000 tons of bombs from Welford were spotted leaving Britain, believed headed for the Vietnam War.[14] A local councillor in Sheerness, Kent, had discovered that under the tarpaulins of a sudden stream of private lorry convoys going through the town that midsummer were cases of green and yellow-striped 200 lb bombs. Their ostensible destination was Zeebrugge, but there was little doubt in some quarters that the ultimate destination was Thailand. Arriving some weeks later, they would have sustained the B-52s in their mass bombing campaign against North Vietnam, then reaching a peak.

Few new military preparations could seem as repugnant as current American plans for an extensive new network of hospitals, pre-positioned for war in Europe, in countries identified, like the UK, as the 'communications zone' – a buffer region in military planning between the United States and the front line. In Britain alone, facilities for at least 15 hospitals will have been installed by the mid-to-late 1980s. Augmenting the build-up in stores, equipment and aircraft, the hospitals are intended to help sustain military operations by catering for at least 8,000 casualties.

Each hospital will have a minimum of 500 beds, and its facilities will only be brought into operation during a war. In that event, the hospitals will only be available to US service personnel. Details of this new initiative in US defence planning emerged slowly during 1982 and 1983. In June 1981, the Reagan government had created considerable concern in the United States when the Department of Defense asked US hospitals to keep a proportion of their beds free at all times to receive 'decontaminated' service casualties from a tactical war in Europe.[15] There was considerable opposition there to the proposal that health facilities should be left idle for wartime use only, rather than be used for peacetime health care.

But soon after, this policy was extended to the UK. In a country where public hospitals were and are being closed down by the dozen, where senior physicians have warned of the lethal consequences of cutting the health service, the US Air Force have begun pre-positioning full-scale hospitals reserved solely for war. At first, only one site was mentioned in public. Then details emerged of a dozen more. None of the hospital bases mentioned here have ever been announced by the Ministry of Defence. During 1982 and 1983, Ministry officials were unaware of the hospital network plan, and denied that these new US bases were planned.

An official US publication, *Air Force* magazine, revealed in May 1981 that the first 'wartime medical complex' was to be installed at Little Rissington, an RAF base in Gloucestershire, then recently out of service. 'The initial installation will be a medical war-readiness storage facility', the magazine reported. 'A 500-bed wartime hospital and 500-bed aeromedical staging unit will be added later.' Beds and supplies began to be moved in early in 1983, and Little Rissington is now a war hospital under the care and supervision of the 7020th Air Base Group at near-by Fairford.

In congressional testimony in 1983, details emerged of a second hospital for the US Navy, costing about £30 million. This would be sited at Locking, a former RAF airfield near Weston-super-Mare. Some $6 million was to be spent on the buildings for a 'pre-positioned fleet hospital' by 1986. The hospital and its equipment will cost a further $26 million. British Defence Ministry officials, asked about the testimony, insisted wrongly that there were definitely 'no plans for a US Forces base at Locking'.

Then further details of the consolidated plan emerged during US Defense Appopriations hearings. There would be over forty 500 or 1,000 bed hospitals in Europe, including at least fifteen in Britain. The Ministry of Defence had already agreed, it was reported, to 2 Navy sites and 4 Army sites, and were to be asked by the US Air Force for the right to instal 8 more. They were:

- US Air Force: Upwood, Bicester, Nocton Hall, Kemble, Bordon, Newton, Waterbeach, Feltwell.
- US Army: Cosford, Colerne, Bulford, Tidworth.
- US Navy: Locking; one other site agreed but not identified.

A sixteenth potential UK site, Lindholme near Scunthorpe, has been mentioned as a planned US hospital in press reports.[16]

Besides these stockpiled units, there are major hospitals already in operation at several US airbases, including Upper Heyford and Lakenheath. In war, medical staff from Upper Heyford would evacuate to the Bicester hospital instead of staying on in the high-priority target area of Upper Heyford itself. Bicester's wartime field hospital role was rehearsed in the 1981 Reforger exercise. Wounded casualties were flown into Upper Heyford from Germany, and later evacuated to the United States.

Repairing airfield runways rather than wounded personnel is the function of another new Air Force unit recently arrived in East Anglia. Identified by the overdone acronym 'Red Horse' – for Rapid Emergency Deployable Heavy Operational Repair Squadron, Engineering – a 400-strong team was set up at the Wethersfield USAF 'stand-by' base in 1979. The Red Horse civil engineering squadron will repair bomb and crater damage on runways, in order to get airbases functioning again hours rather than days after an attack. Each airfield has stocks of aluminium mats, fill-in aggregate, concrete slabs and even plastic sheets, ready to cover bomb craters with a smooth new usable surface.

The Wethersfield unit is mobile, and is intended to keep all main and some colocated airbases going, even in the event of 'massive' Warsaw Pact air attacks. In 1982, Pentagon officials proposed augmenting Red Horse with a US-based reinforcement team – to be called 'Prime Beef'.

Both Wethersfield and the other East Anglian stand-by base, Sculthorpe, are in regular use by US special forces during the annual Flintlock exercises. It seems likely therefore that these two centres would be used as rear support bases for some of the exotic behind-the-lines operations proposed by the Special Operations Task Force Europe (SOTFE), and described in Chapter 5. SOTFE's specially converted helicopters and transports such as the MC-130E 'Combat Talon' are regular visitors to the two bases.

Sculthorpe is also included in the Colocated Operating Base network, and appears to be allocated to A-7 Corsairs. The growing pace of war rehearsal intensified in April 1983 when the largest ever 'Coronet' practice reinforcement seen in Britain took place at Sculthorpe. In exercise 'Coronet Castle' 24 Corsairs from Ohio's Air National Guard reserves flew across the Atlantic to Sculthorpe.

Between exercises, Sculthorpe has been a scrapyard for old aircraft being returned to the US government after finishing service with overseas air forces who have received US military assistance.

Despite the hundreds of aircraft coming to and through Britain in war, defending the US base network in Britain is a matter left entirely to the meagre resources of the RAF. Only Alconbury's Aggressor squadron, when not playing at being the Russian enemy, has aircraft suitable for this role (they appear to be suitable for little else). But even this USAF contribution to regional air defence will be concerned with the North Sea, rather than the UK mainland. In wartime, the surprisingly large percentage of USAF personnel in Britain who are Security Police – guarding US bases and installations in peacetime – would also be responsible for ground defence. In 1981, there were 1,848 Security Police at eleven British bases. In war, another 1,800 Security Police reinforcements could be mobilised from the United States.

In peacetime, the Security Police seek intelligence on what they regard as threats to any US base or its personnel. This includes the peace camps and protest demonstrations which have become an almost permanent feature of life at many bases. Investigating both on-base threats – such as crime rackets and drug dealers – and off-base threats –

such as CND and other local protest organisations – is the work of the Air Force Office of Special Investigations (AFOSI), which has its 62nd District based at Wethersfield. AFOSI detective and security detachments are stationed at Mildenhall, Lakenheath, Bentwaters, Upper Heyford, Alconbury, Chicksands, and at the Grosvenor Square naval and intelligence headquarters in London.

AFOSI and Security Police officials are conscious of the danger and impropriety involved in mounting freelance intelligence-gathering operations against 'native' British groups who are not breaking the law. They prefer to obtain this intelligence through the informers and surveillance activities of local police Special Branch officers, with whom liaison is close. Publicly, they do not like to comment on the protests outside their gates, arguing that it is a matter for the British government and not – one way or the other – for them. Security off the base is left as far as possible to the Ministry of Defence and local police. US commanders are well aware of the hostile reaction that would follow if US personnel were seen to manhandle protestors in the same fashion as do the British army or police.

In wartime, US airbase defences would be extended five kilometres[17] (three miles) outside the normal perimeter fences. Secret plans have been made at each base to establish defensive positions covering possible infiltration routes and sites suitable for stand-off attacks by enemy paratroopers or special forces (Soviet *Speznaz* units). This defensive zone will always include nearby British villages and housing. Details have not been given as to whether it is planned to move local residents out from the US defence zone.

Despite these plans, a budget-conscious Congress was critical in 1981 of the US Air Force's failure to get more ground defence provided by host nations such as Britain and Germany. They were told by General Lew Allen, the US Air Force Chief of Staff, that a 'current diplomatic initiative' was being pursued for 'increased host nation support'. On 11 February 1981, a new swap of British resources for cut-price nuclear weapons – in this case Trident – was agreed with the United States in a memorandum of understanding on Rapier, the anti-aircraft missile made by British Aerospace.

Redolent of the undercover way in which, fifteen years earlier, Britain had traded off Diego Garcia and the islanders' rights to live there for a reduction in research and development charges for Polaris submarines and missiles, so this time part of the RAF Regiment was hired out to the United States in return for a reduction in Trident R & D surcharges. Under the 1981 agreement, the RAF will maintain and operate Rapier batteries around major US airfields. The missiles, (which cost $350 million) and their maintenance costs, are paid for by the United States. Explaining the arrangement in 1983, Deputy Assistant Secretary of Defense Robert A. Stone told the Congress that schemes like the Rapier deal were a bonus for the US:

> Under the terms of NATO, air base defense is normally considered a national responsibility . . . to get the British or the Germans . . . to contribute toward the defense of an American airbase in those countries seems like a beneficial deal to the US, and that is why we are pursuing arrangements of this sort.

The arrangement whereby the US hired foreign troops to defend its bases was unique, and was criticised. The arrangement partly arose because of infighting between the US Army and Air Force over who should run the Rapier system, and other in-fighting on behalf of commercial interests. Defense Secretary Harold Brown had first ordered a discontented US Air Force staff to buy Rapier from Britain in August 1980 (they had committed themselves to another manufacturer). Then the plan lapsed. Criticism of this 'mercenary' departure for US defence policy was resisted on the reasonable grounds that the hired British troops were 'not sent there by some potentate 3,000 miles away, but rather they are protecting their own turf'.

Rapier missiles, however, only provide short-range defence, primarily against low-flying aircraft. Area defence of the British Isles is still the RAF's job alone, as has repeatedly been acknowledged. After British air defences had taken a simulated pounding in a 1980 exercise, 'Elder Forest', the RAF newspaper *RAF News* reported pressure on the Ministry of Defence to get US Air Force aircraft to participate in British air defences. But the RAF Under-Secretary Geoffrey Pattie explained that:

> No United States aircraft are currently assigned to the air defence of the UK . . .

At about the same time in 1980, as a result of the Rapier deal controversy, General Allen described air defence arrangements in Britain in some detail to several Congressional committees. To the House of Representatives Committee on the Armed Services, he explained:

> The British do provide area air defense. That is clearly their responsibility. They have the interceptors and the longer range systems that provide area defense . . . The airbases are vulnerable to the long-range aircraft being introduced by the Soviets into the Warsaw Pact countries.

In a hearing of the House's Appropriations Committee Allen was asked what arrangements the US could make to provide local 'point' defence of its British bases:

> *Q:* If the Air Force chooses to, could the Air Force provide whatever weapons system it desired and man it with Air Force personnel?
> *General Allen:* The Air Force, sir, can do anything –

Asked if anything in 'the agreement we have on the use of these [UK] bases' constrained him, Allen replied:

> That in general has not been the limitation that has concerned us the most . . .

The wartime threat to British air defences was described at length by the Ministry of Defence itself in 1975 evidence to the House of Commons Defence and External Affairs Committee. In a memorandum[18], the Ministry explained that 'The UK represents a complex military and civil target system containing many key points':

> The most likely targets in the UK (Air Defence Region) during a conventional phase of hostilities are RAF and USAF bases . . .

Also included were 'control and reporting centres and air defence radars' and:

> facilities for the movement of reinforcements and maritime targets including the mining of approaches to UK ports and naval bases.

Commenting five years later on the effect on the British Isles 'target system' of the cruise missile deployment, Air Under Secretary John Peters told the House of Commons Defence Committee that:

> The stationing of ground-launched cruise missile forces will not make that much difference . . . We have been for so many years, in effect, the base for NATO's long-range theatre nuclear force. The US F-111s and our own Vulcans are our present force and, in effect, the cruise missiles will be replacing these.

On these public occasions, Defence Ministry officials have not objected to discussing likely British targets for conventional attack. When asked about the likely pattern of a nuclear attack, however, they invariably go silent, as such unpleasant, terminal matters should not be set out too plainly before a vulnerable, nervous and unprotectable public.

Yet the pattern and priorities of an enemy's nuclear attack is certain to follow the same highly-predictable course as a conventional bombardment. The target priorities are set out in the Ministry's own memorandum, referred to above.

Inevitably, those who plan to make nuclear war are also best placed to envisage how an enemy may plan. For each US base, such as Lakenheath, there is a counterpart in the east, where thousands of personnel also have their sinews stretched for the mission of war. Certain Soviet pilots and navigators are no doubt familiar with the massive airbase nestling in the Suffolk hills, and other key segments of the UK 'target system'. Like their counterparts at Lakenheath, they will have studied satellite reconnaissance photographs and air target plans, and noted the best routes past missile batteries and interceptor bases. Their nuclear weapons specialists have already precomputed the optimum height and yield for a nuclear detonation which will flatten that remote Suffolk airbase and all its facilities.

OVERLEAF

**Fig 11. Present and planned US military bases and facilities in Britain**

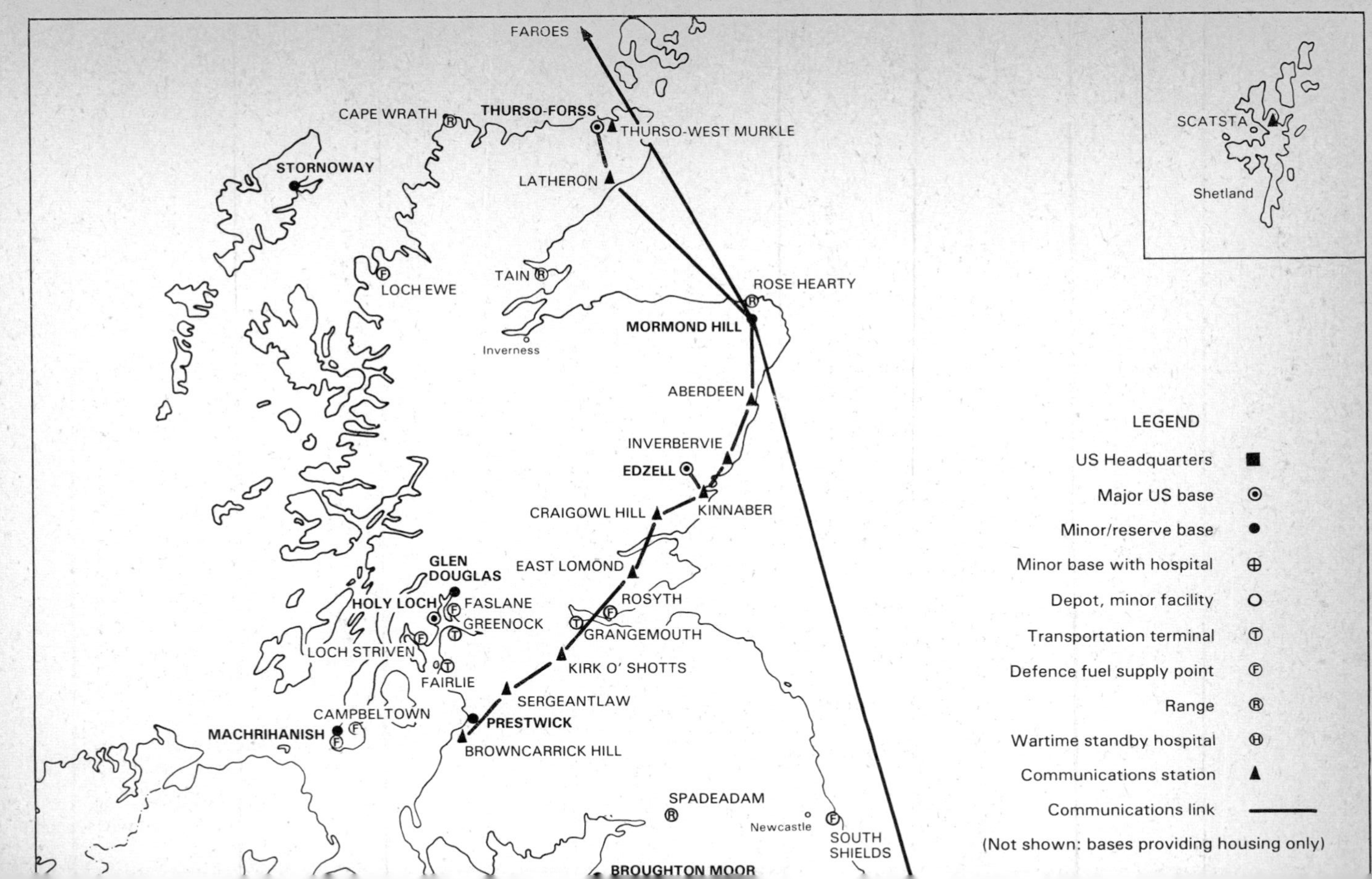
FAROES
CAPE WRATH
THURSO-FORSS
THURSO-WEST MURKLE
STORNOWAY
LATHERON
LOCH EWE
TAIN
ROSE HEARTY
MORMOND HILL
Inverness
ABERDEEN
INVERBERVIE
EDZELL
KINNABER
CRAIGOWL HILL
EAST LOMOND
GLEN DOUGLAS
HOLY LOCH
FASLANE
GREENOCK
ROSYTH
GRANGEMOUTH
LOCH STRIVEN
FAIRLIE
KIRK O' SHOTTS
SERGEANTLAW
CAMPBELTOWN
PRESTWICK
MACHRIHANISH
BROWNCARRICK HILL
SPADEADAM
Newcastle
SOUTH SHIELDS
BROUGHTON MOOR
SCATSTA
Shetland
LEGEND
US Headquarters
Major US base
Minor/reserve base
Minor base with hospital
Depot, minor facility
Transportation terminal
Defence fuel supply point
Range
Wartime standby hospital
Communications station
Communications link
(Not shown: bases providing housing only)

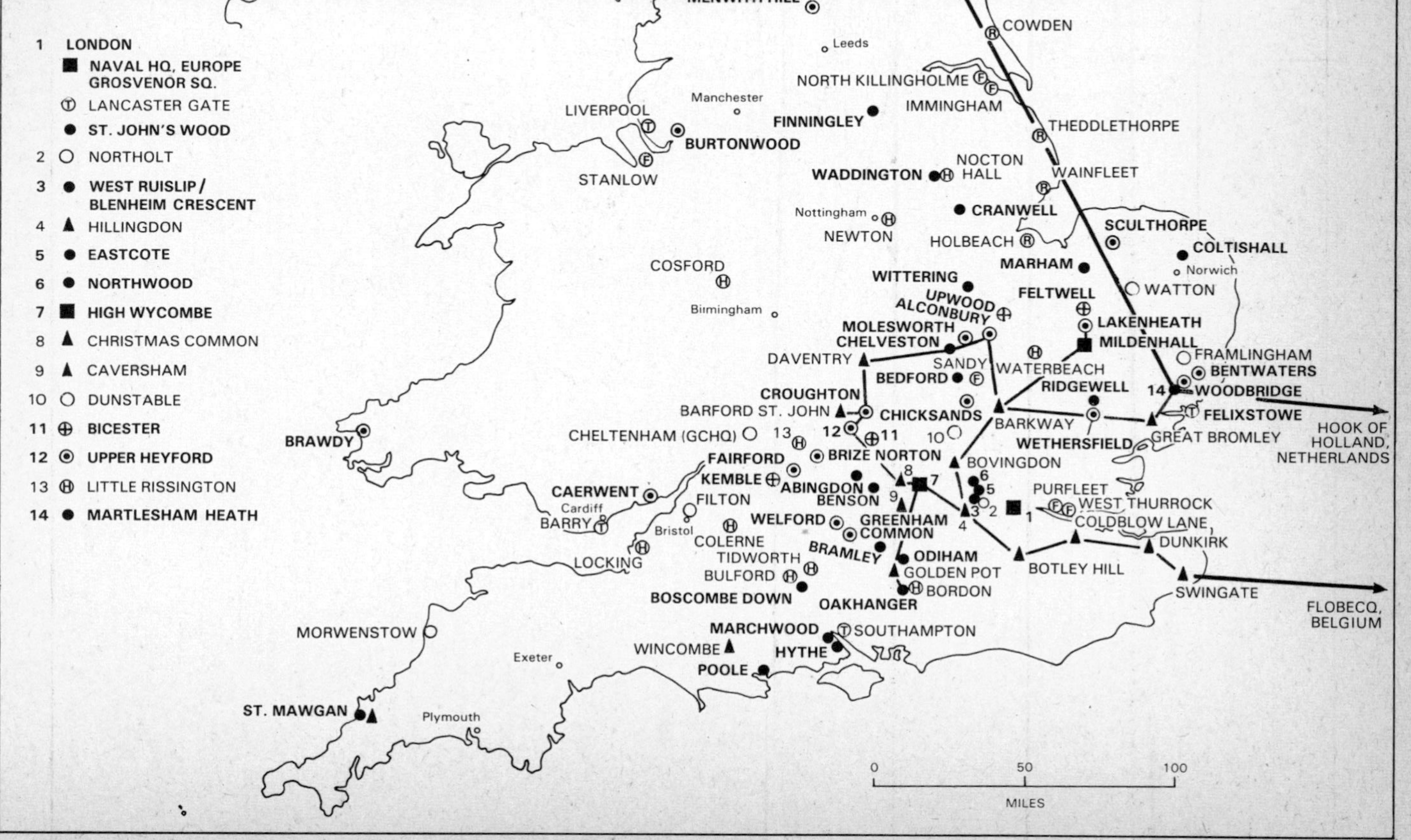


Fig 11. Present and planned US military bases and facilities in Britian, 1984

## Table 7

### The present: US military bases and facilities in Britain

This table is a complete list of all known or planned US military bases and facilities in Britain, with brief descriptions. The table includes all the sites acknowledged as 'US bases and facilities in the UK', in the list published in 1983 by the Ministry of Defence. Sites not included in this list are marked by an asterisk; sources are given in the footnotes, as far as possible, confirming their use by US forces.

### *Headquarters, administration and command and control centres*

| | |
|---|---|
| Mildenhall | US European Command airborne command and control squadron in 'Silk Purse' aircraft; USAF Third Air Force headquarters and operations centre. |
| High Wycombe | US European Command war headquarters under construction in underground facility. Also USAF school, administrative offices and housing for Upper Heyford, and communications centre. Cruise missile computer programming unit planned but not deployed. |
| Grosvenor Square, London | US Naval Headquarters Europe, and US eastern Atlantic naval commander, in command of US Sixth Fleet; with Worldwide Military Command and Control System computer centre; Fleet Ocean Surveillance Information Center (FOSIC) intelligence centre; Naval Communications Unit. |
| Eastcote/Lime Grove, Ruislip | US Navy administrative offices, annexe to Grosvenor Square HQ; Naval Intelligence staff and Naval Investigative Service European regional office; regional Navy contracting center; school; and US Department of Defense schools HQ. |
| Northwood | US Navy element attached to headquarters of NATO Commander in Chief, Eastern Atlantic; headquarters under overall command of US/NATO Commander in Chief Atlantic, based in Norfolk, Virginia. |
| West Ruislip | US Navy stores. |
| Ruislip – Blenheim Crescent[19]* | Third Air Force headquarters unit and offices. |
| London | US Air Force Europe administrative offices – includes Office of Scientific Research. |
| St John's Wood, London* | Marine Barracks (US Naval headquarters and Embassy military security force). |

***Airbases***

| | |
|---|---|
| Alconbury | Main operating base; see Table 5 for detailed functions. |
| Bentwaters | " |
| Fairford | " |
| Greenham Common | " |
| Lakenheath | " |
| Mildenhall | " |
| Upper Heyford | " |
| Woodbridge | " |
| Sculthorpe | Standby operating base; see Table 6 for detailed functions. |
| Wethersfield | " |
| Molesworth | Designated as the second main operating base for cruise missiles, to begin operations in December 1986. |
| Abingdon | Colocated operating base (COB); facilities, fuel, munitions and equipment stockpiles prepared for use by aircraft normally based in US. Construction on some bases financed by USAF, other facilities paid for by NATO. See Table 6 for likely wartime use. |
| Bedford | " |
| Benson | " |
| Boscombe Down | " |
| Coltishall | " |
| Cranwell | " |
| Finningley | " |
| Leeming | " |
| Odiham | " |
| Waddington | " |
| Wittering | " |
| Marham* | Forward operating base (FOB); advance facilities and right of use provided to Strategic Air Command bombers normally based in US.[20] |
| Upper Heyford | " |
| Fairford | " |
| Brize Norton* | " |
| Prestwick[21]* | USAF Military Airlift Command staging facility; US Naval Air Transportation Co-ordinating Office; US Armed Forces Courier Station, responsible for storage and handling of secret documents in transit. Major development of Prestwick as a USAF warehouse centre was planned late in 1982, but |

| | |
|---|---|
| | abandoned in 1983 after embarrassment over lack of consultation with UK government. |
| Northolt[22]* | RAF base jointly used by US headquarters staff for communications flights. |
| Machrihanish | Used by US Navy and NATO anti-submarine warfare aircraft. |
| Stornoway[23]* | When new NATO facilities are complete, will be used by US Navy and NATO anti-submarine warfare aircraft. |
| ***Naval base*** | |
| Holy Loch | Poseidon submarine base; Submarine Squadron 14 (10 submarines); Ballistic Missile Submarine Refit Site one; submarine tender, dry dock, barges and support vessels permanently moored in Loch. Offices and stores ashore; new pier planned, 1984. |
| ***Intelligence centres*** | |
| Menwith Hill | Major US National Security Agency signals intelligence (Sigint) station and satellite terminal; plugged into British national communications network to intercept international links, and exchange intelligence with British agency, GCHQ. |
| Chicksands | USAF Electronic Security Command, 6950th Security Group, operates long-range radio interception and direction-finding station. Main target is Warsaw Pact air forces. Also includes undercover NSA unit – 'Department of Defence Joint Operations Center Chicksands' – with civilian targets, including western European government signals. Site prominent through presence of giant circular 'Flare 9' antenna. |
| Edzell | US Naval Security Group Sigint station, co-ordinates ocean surveillance in north Atlantic and Norwegian Sea areas. Recently extended as regional ground control station for US Navy Ocean Surveillance satellites; satellite terminals and Sigint facilities built in late 1970s. Prominent 'Flare' electronic eavesdropping antenna, of earlier design to that at Chicksands. |
| Brawdy | US Naval facility (NAVFAC). Like two dozen other such NAVFACs, Brawdy's announced public purpose – oceanographic research – is the approved cover story for Project Caesar – the underwater Sound Surveillance System for plotting submarine and surface vessel movements. |

| | |
|---|---|
| Fylingdales | BMEWS radar station operated jointly by US Strategic Air Command detachment and RAF. Includes NARS communications relay station. Also supports the USAF Space Data and Tracking System (SPADATS). |
| London | Special US Liaison Office (SUSLO) inside Grosvenor Square Naval HQ; with SUSLO communications centre. |
| Cheltenham* | Liaison office (SUSLO) and US detachments at British Sigint agency, GCHQ. |
| Morwenstow* | US detachment from National Security Agency stationed at GCHQ satellite interception terminal. Morwenstow appears to monitor international commercial satellite links in worldwide eavesdropping programme devised by NSA. |

***Communications centres***

| | |
|---|---|
| Croughton | Defence Satellite Communications System terminal; USAF aeronautical radio station; automated weather information centre; includes CIA satellite and agent communications, and Presidential emergency radio communications system. |
| Barford St John | Transmitter annexe for Croughton. |
| Thurso – West Murkle | US Naval Radio Station receivers; includes Defence Satellite Communications System (DSCS) terminal, jointly operated by RAF. |
| Thurso – Forss | US Naval Radio Station transmitters; includes low frequency transmitters, part of Minimum Essential Emergency Communications Network (MEECN) – link to strategic nuclear forces. |
| Oakhanger[24]* | USAF Satellite Control Facility – part of worldwide network controlling operations of US military satellites; satellite communications terminal for RAF, USAF, and NATO SATCOM; also US Naval Communications Facility. |
| Hillingdon (Uxbridge) | AUTOVON (Automatic Voice Network) switching centre (underground). |
| Martlesham Heath | AUTOVON switching centre. |
| Mormond Hill | North Atlantic Relay System long range communications centre, and US Navy microwave relay station (site shared with similar NATO and British Telecom systems). |
| St Mawgan | USAF radio communications station. |
| Wincombe | " |
| Great Bromley | USAF microwave communications relay station. |

| | |
|---|---|
| Barkway | " |
| Chelveston | " |
| Daventry | " |
| Christmas Common | " |
| Golden Pot | NATO/USAF microwave communication relay station. |
| Bovingdon | USAF microwave communications relay station. |
| Botley Hill Farm | " |
| Coldblow Lane | " |
| Dunkirk | " |
| Swingate (Dover) | " |
| Latheron | US Navy microwave communications relay station. |
| Aberdeen | " |
| Inverbervie | " |
| Kinnaber | " |
| Craigowl Hill* | US Navy microwave communications relay station.[25] |
| East Lomond* | " |
| Kirk O'Shotts* | " |
| Sergeantlaw* | " |
| Browncarrick Hill* | " |
| Scatsta, Sullom Voe[26]* | US Coastguard LORAN-C monitor station. |

### *Stores and depots*

| | |
|---|---|
| Burtonwood | Vast US Army 'POMCUS' (Prepositioned military core unit stocks) equipment depot has 2 million square feet for equipment storage and covers 5 square miles. Base employs 600 civil and military staff. Army store replaced US Air Force depot in 1968. |
| Caerwent | US Army munitions depot and ammunition maintenance facility, stores 25,000 tons of munitions in 400 buildings for US Army European 'theatre reserve stocks'. Part of 60th Ordnance Group, subordinate to Burtonwood. |
| Bramley | US Army ammunition depot (operated by British forces solely on behalf of US), leased since 1978. |
| Welford | US Third Air Force central UK munitions depot, run by USAF Ammunition Supply Squadron. |
| Bicester | US Air Force depot. |
| Chilwell | Proposed US Army vehicle depot. |
| Glen Douglas | NATO and US Navy ammunition depot. US Navy Mobile Mine Assembly Group detachment 4 maintains stocks of mines for use by NATO and US. |
| Broughton Moor | US Navy ammunition depot (operated by British forces solely on behalf of US). Stores 20,000 tons of |

| | |
|---|---|
| | munitions – half of US Navy stock pre-positioned for use in Norwegian Sea. |
| Hythe | US Army Marine Fleet HQ; centre for amphibious military operations set up in 1974. |
| Marchwood | US Army Marine Fleet Store (at British army military port). |
| Poole | US Army Marine Fleet Store. |
| St Mawgan | US Naval Aviation Weapons Facility; stores nuclear weapons (depth bombs) for use by US, British, Dutch and Canadian anti-submarine warfare forces; set up January 1965. |
| Machrihanish | US Naval Aviation Weapons Facility nuclear weapons store set up July 1967. Also Naval Special Warfare Unit 2 – covert underwater or seaborne infiltration and sabotage teams; and Mobile Mine Assembly Group detachment 2. Used by US Navy P-3 Orion anti-submarine warfare aircraft. |
| Kemble | Joint USAF/RAF maintenance depot for A-10 aircraft. Proposed major warehouse for European Distribution System of wartime aircraft spares. |
| Filton* | Depot maintenance of F-111 strike aircraft by British Aircraft Corporation under contract to USAF. |
| Dunstable | US Navy Exchange (equivalent to Air Force 'PX' warehouse; distribution centre for supplies to US Navy bases in UK. |
| Upwood | USAF storage depot. |
| Ridgewell | USAF storage depot (said to be unused). |
| Watton | USAF storage depot (said to be closing). |
| Framlingham | USAF storage depot. |
| Feltwell | USAF depot and equipment laboratory for Lakenheath. |

### *Wartime hospitals*[27]

| | |
|---|---|
| Little Rissington | USAF 500-bed contingency hospital (additional 500-bed aeromedical evacuation unit also planned). |
| Bicester | USAF 500-bed contingency hospital. |
| Bordon* | " |
| Feltwell | " |
| Kemble | " |
| Newton* | " |
| Nocton Hall* | " |
| Upwood | " |
| Waterbeach* | " |
| Bulford* | US Army 500-bed general hospital. |

| | |
|---|---|
| Colerne* | " |
| Cosford* | " |
| Tidworth* | " |
| Locking* | US Navy 500-bed fleet hospital. |

***Transportation terminals***

| | |
|---|---|
| Liverpool* | US Army UK transportation terminal (manned).[28] |
| Felixstowe | US Army transportation terminal (manned). Major US military logistics centre, handles munitions, equipment, food supplies (35,000 tons a year) and personnel movements. |
| Greenock[29]* | Normally unmanned US Army transportation terminal; also US Navy warehouse. |
| Barry* | US Army transportation terminal (manned); used for shipments to Caerwent and Welford. |
| Grangemouth* | Normally unmanned US Army transportation terminal. |
| Southampton* | " |
| London | " |
| Fairlie | NATO anchorage and pierhead used for shipments to Holy Loch; to be replaced by pier at Holy Loch itself.[30] |

***Defense Fuel Support Points***[31]

| | |
|---|---|
| Loch Ewe* | DFSP |
| Loch Striven* | " |
| Faslane* | " |
| Machrihanish | " |
| Rosyth* | " |
| Rosneath* | " |
| Campbeltown* | " |
| South Shields* | " |
| North Killingholme* | " |
| Immingham* | " |
| Stanlow* | " |
| Purfleet* | " |
| West Thurrock* | " |
| Sandy* | Quality Assurance Resident fuel supplies. |

***Air to ground bombing and electronic warfare ranges***

| | |
|---|---|
| Spadeadam | Joint USAF/RAF electronic warfare range; with simulated Warsaw Pact surface-to-air missile radars. |
| Rosehearty[32]* | Air-to-ground bombing range |
| Cape Wrath* | " |

| | |
|---|---|
| Tain* | " |
| Jurby* | " |
| Cowden* | " |
| Donna Nook* | " |
| Holbeach* | " |
| Wainfleet* | " |
| Theddlethorpe* | " |

***Family Housing Annexes*[33]***

| | |
|---|---|
| Rosehearty | Grampian |
| Monkton | Ayrshire |
| Dunoon | Strathclyde |
| West Raynham | Norfolk |
| Thetford | Norfolk |
| Tuddenham | Norfolk |
| Bircham Newton | Norfolk |
| Brandon | Suffolk |
| Bury St Edmunds | Suffolk |
| Freckenham | Suffolk |
| Isleham | Suffolk |
| Grundisburgh | Suffolk |
| Haverhill | Suffolk |
| Ipswich | Suffolk |
| Kesgrave | Suffolk |
| Melton | Suffolk |
| Newmarket | Suffolk |
| Red Lodge | Suffolk |
| Shepherds Grove | Suffolk |
| Trimley St Martin | Suffolk |
| Stilton | Cambridgeshire |
| Brampton | Cambridgeshire |
| Wantage | Oxfordshire |
| Ardley | Oxfordshire |
| Gaydon | Warwickshire |
| Bishops Green | Berkshire |
| Blackbushe | Hampshire |
| St Columb | Cornwall |
| Carpenders Park | Herefordshire |
| West Drayton | Middlesex |

**TOTAL: 135 US military bases and facilities in Britain installed or planned (1984); made up of 25 major US bases or military headquarters, 35 minor or reserve bases, and 75 facilities used by US forces.**[34]

**Major US bases include 3 headquarters, 11 airbases (one, Mildenhall,**

**also a headquarters), 1 naval base, 2 communications centres, 5 intelligence centres, and 4 stores and depots.**

**Minor or reserve US bases include 4 administrative centres and 1 barracks, 14 minor or reserve airbases, 5 communications centres, 12 stores or depots, and 1 transportation terminal.**

**US facilities include the use of 3 airbases, 2 intelligence centres, 23 communications stations, 1 navigation station, 5 stores, 7 transportation terminals, 13 fuel supply points, 10 aircraft weapons ranges, and at least 14 contingency military hospitals.**

**There are 5 confirmed US nuclear weapons stores in the United Kingdom (Lakenheath, Upper Heyford, Holy Loch (afloat in the submarine tender), Machrihanish and St Mawgan. Two further bases (Woodbridge and Alconbury) have storage facilities which appear to be suitable for peacetime nuclear weapons storage.**

**Including 30 detached US Air Force housing annexes, 164 sites listed here are currently used, or planned to be used, by US military forces in the United Kingdom.**

## Notes

1 *Aviation Week and Space Technology*, 7 June 1982.
2 In one sense, the new name is more accurate. The 'U' of the original U2 was intended to imply that the plane was a knockabout Utility model for transport and research.
3 *Aviation Week and Space Technology*, 7 June 1982.
4 'Reforger' stands for Return of Forces to Germany; the major US plan which would move up to a million reinforcements from the United States to the central front in Germany.
5 *New Statesman*, 11 December 1981.
6 The others are, probably: Inverness/Dalcross; Aberdeen/Dyce; Glasgow/Abbotsinch; Newcastle; Leeds/Bradford; Machrihanish.
7 *US Security Issues in Europe: Burden sharing, MBFR, and nuclear weapons*; staff report to US Senate Subcommittee on US Security Agreements and Commitments Abroad, US Congress, 1973.
8 *Philadelphia Inquirer*, 3 January 1983.
9 *ibid.*
10 The reporter's account was reproduced in the *Guardian*, 6 May 1978.
11 *Flight*, 8 August 1981.
12 *US News and World Report*, 22 February 1983.
13 *Hansard*, 24 June 1975.
14 *New Statesman*, 30 June 1972.
15 *Guardian*, 11 June 1981.

16 *Daily Telegraph*, 19 June 1982.

17 Testimony by General Lew Allen, Air Force Chief of Staff, to the House of Representatives Committee on Appropriations; Department of Defense Appropriations for 1982, Part 2, p 222. US Congress, 1981.

18 Ministry of Defence memorandum SCOE 77/1.

19 USAF offices in Ruislip and the US Marine Barracks in St John's Wood are listed in telephone and postcode directories. The 'London administrative office' is listed in the *USAF Installations Directory*.

20 The presence in the UK of Strategic Air Command Forward Operating Bases for B-52 (or FB-111) bombers was admitted by the Ministry of Defence in response to a question from the author in October 1980. Arrangements are different from the US NATO Colocated Operating Base system because SAC units are not allocated to NATO. Two FOBs are already USAF main operating bases.

21 All three US military units at Prestwick are listed in the Clyde Coast public telephone directory. The US Air Force Europe 'Terminal Facilities Guide' (USAFE Manual 75–2) identifies Prestwick as an operating location of Military Airlift Command. This unit 'contracts all Terminal Facilities through British Airports Authority' and 'handles aircraft and military contracted flights'.

22 Northolt is in use 'to present' as a centre for base and HQ flights, according to an officially supported report on the 'US Third Air Force – a short history', by S. J. Bond, *Air Britain*, February 1975. Continuing use is confirmed by aircraft spotters' reports.

23 NATO facilities in Stornoway were still under construction in 1983.

24 See pp 198–200.

25 These five US Navy relay stations in central and southern Scotland originally formed part of a chain connecting Scotland to the Londonderry Naval Communications Station – which was closed in 1977. Defence ministers claimed in parliament in 1983 that these stations had been handed back to Britain by the US Navy before 1980. This is untrue; checks at these locations in 1983, found that the stations were still installed, unlike the Northern Irish stations, which had indeed been dismantled.

26 US Coastguard LORAN-C site at Sullom Voe is listed in local telephone directory, and in international navigational publications.

27 US military hospitals at Little Rissington and Locking were installed during 1983/84. Plans for Locking and UK hospitals other than Little Rissington were revealed in March 1983 US congressional hearings, which were published after the Ministry of Defence had provided its 1983 list of US bases. The USAF hospitals at Upwood, Bicester and Nocton Hall, and the US Army hospitals at Colerne, Cosford, Bulford, and Tidworth are to be installed during 1984/85. The remaining USAF hospitals may be installed during 1986. At least one further US Navy fleet hospital, out of nine to come to Europe, will be installed in Britain.

28 Although unacknowledged by Ministry of Defence lists, telephone and telex directories list the US Army 'Liverpool Port Operations' office at Nautilus House, Liverpool 2. The US Air Force also controls an installation at 'Liverpool Port', according to the *USAF Installations Directory* (*Worldwide*), Air Force Pamphlet 87–13, unclassified, (US Department of Defense, Washington, 1979). It is a separate item in a list of 'installations arranged alphabetically by major installations'.

29 Greenock, Grangemouth, Barry, Glasgow, Southampton; from *DoD's Traffic Manager*, published by Headquarters, Military Traffic Management Command; Department of Defense, *circa* 1980.

30 US use of facilities at Fairlie was described in US congressional hearings in March 1983.

31 US Defense Logistics Agency Defense Fuel Supply Points (DFSP) in Britain are listed in Department of Defense Manual 4140.17M (Supplement 1, June 1982).

32 Ministry of Defence press releases have repeatedly described US Air Force use of RAF ranges in press releases detailing exercises such as 'Mallet Blow'. A detachment of Bentwaters airbase personnel have housing quarters at Rosehearty. See also Note 3.

33 This list contains only sites used only for housing, and which are not listed elsewhere in the table. Details of all US Air Force owned or leased property in Britain is contained in the *USAF Installations Directory* (*Worldwide*).

34 Definitions used in Table 7 and Figure 11:
*Major US base:* More than 100 permanent personnel of, or working for, US military forces;
*Minor/reserve base:* 10–100 permanent personnel of, or working for, US military forces; or planned site for deployment of more than 100 military personnel in crisis or war;
*US facility:* Any other base or facility, whether manned or unmanned, reserved for or normally used by US military forces (including joint use).

# PART FOUR
# THE ISSUES

## *11 US Bases: The Issues*

This book has explored the history and present scope of American military activities conducted in or affecting the United Kingdom. From the American point of view, the UK is host to a relatively small but nonetheless significant part of its overseas military establishment – which amounts to some 359 major bases[1] and about 1,200 other facilities. Two or three dozen major bases and a hundred other facilities are Britain's contribution to this network – a contribution that has never been charted in detail, certainly not by the British government, whose continuing ignorance of US activities – whether wilful or unwitting – is a national scandal.

Underlying this investigation is the obvious premise that matters should not remain as they are at present. Whether the bases eventually stay or go, only the most pusillanimous of public officials could accept the inadequacies of the present relationship as they affect British political control of the use of foreign military bases, the legal status of 'visiting' military forces, or the lack of information provided in Britain about the development and use of US bases and facilities.

Like their allies throughout the world, Americans are divided in their attitude to overseas defence and security commitments. Although there is near-unity of support for the conduct of ideological and political warfare against communism, the same wide consensus is not available to support US military engagement in Europe, the Middle East or the third world, or to back the defence budget needed for America's role as 'global policeman'. As European wealth has grown since the war, the feeling in some US quarters that the United States is being 'taken for a ride' has grown correspondingly. Other Americans do not understand why western Europeans, whom they see as living directly in the shadow of Soviet power, are so enthusiastic in pursuit of détente, arms control agreements and nuclear disarmament.

Attitudes in Britain and western Europe are similarly split – quite sharply – between those who regard an American involvement in

Europe as essential to safety, and those who see it as the chief danger. There is a true ideological gulf across the Atlantic, a gulf that is well recognised and repeatedly debated inside the NATO alliance. But NATO has not been able, by its nature, to deal with this by any radical realignment. NATO's attitude is historically conditioned both by continually having to plan to counter the most pessimistic military analysis of the Soviet threat, and by the dominating position of the United States.

This wide divergence of opinion is reflected by general public attitudes in Britain to US bases. There is fear in the centre and left that American forces in Europe are here to pursue a continuing Cold War of Soviet 'containment', thus ill-advisedly importing an ugly external clash of extreme rival ideologies, both of them rejected by western European liberal social democracies. Whilst public attitudes to NATO are generally favourable, there is, paradoxically, evident and substantial public mistrust of the judgement or competence of the United States authorities. This distrust of US competence or leadership has been most marked under the Reagan administration.

The alternative, official view on US bases, and the view of the centre and right, is that US forces are here at American risk for the sake of European lives and property – and that they should, perhaps, be free to come on whatever terms they wish. The official rationale for 'The United States Forces in the United Kingdom' was set out, for the first time, in the Defence Estimates in 1983. A concise one page 'essay' explained:

> There has been an American military presence in the United Kingdom for an almost unbroken period of 40 years ... American forces have remained in this country ever since [1948] as a major symbol of the United States' commitment to defend Europe[2] ... their presence in Europe in substantial numbers is essential if deterrence is to be effective.

The official response to the argument that Britain takes on greatly enhanced significance as a nuclear target because of American nuclear and other bases is that:

> [Although] some maintain that the presence of American forces in our country increases our chance of becoming a target in war ... to argue thus is to miss two crucial points: first, that in any conceivable conflict affecting Western Europe, the facts of geography and the United Kingdom's strategic importance would alone be enough to make this country a target for attack; and secondly that the solidarity of the NATO alliance, and its strategy of deterrence, are themselves our surest guarantee against war ...

> So far from putting the United Kingdom at greater risk, the presence here of United States forces is a vital element in ensuring that war does not break out.

These are important arguments, but they are badly flawed – chiefly because the Ministry of Defence has not evaluated the effects of alternative defence strategies which it may not wish to adopt. These crucial considerations – and in particular the special dangers of the cruise and Pershing missile 'modernisation' programme – are analysed below. But whichever long-term view is taken, the present operational, administrative and legal status of US forces in Britain is quite unacceptable.

Repeatedly, the British government has misled the public, or been in manifest ignorance itself, about US military activities or intentions. These failings of information or administration are almost entirely the product of British inadequacies, rather than American mischief. It would be a true political innocent in Whitehall or Westminster who ever expected United States military commanders to act other than in consonance with the long-term national interests of the United States, or tell the British more than they had to rather than as little as they could get away with.

Despite rhetoric to the contrary, the British people and their national interest have been treated with evident disdain in transatlantic dealings by the United States. Mrs Thatcher's government appears to have taken the view that almost anything goes, so far as the deployment of US forces is concerned. But the Conservatives are in a deeply contradictory position. On the issue of British sovereignty, they found war with Argentina necessary over the Falkland Islands. For the sake of sovereignty and independence, £10 billion is to be spent on Trident missiles and submarines – so that Britain shall have its own, completely independent, non-negotiable (at the Geneva arms reduction talks) national nuclear deterrent. Yet, where the risks for and restraints on British independence created by the presence of foreign military bases on our soil are concerned, British sovereignty is regarded both as negotiable and almost irrelevant.

Mrs Thatcher's government made, in 1983, a fleeting attempt to restore some of the rights and sovereignty the British government should have had, and which previous administrations gave away. But she and her ministers found that an expedient alternative to this difficult political task was to exaggerate the extent of British control over American activities, citing previous Labour governments' acceptance of the *status quo* as if that implied that matters were automatically satisfactory.

Perhaps only British administrators could have created a 'special relationship' like this one. If it had happened in America, paradoxically, these difficulties would never have arisen. The existence of foreign military bases on American territory would be an affront to national pride, and a slur on the capability of US armed forces. American Congressmen would not have stood idly by while Washington civil servants handed away territory *en masse* at no charge, sanctioned the imposition of a foreign legal code, and capped the whole by permitting a foreign nation – ally or not – the right to start a war from US territory without guaranteeing even as much as a by-your-leave.

The most serious abrogation of British sovereignty now bound into the special relationship is the 'understanding' – or lack of it – about the 'emergency' use of US bases in Britain. This is 'a matter for joint decision' – a form of words capable of highly elastic meaning. But there are problems in peacetime too.

British legal authority over US bases and their personnel is as inadequate as its military control in crisis or war. The US Air Force acknowledges that, legally, they have had an easy ride, with 'not even a formalised agreement' at first. The presence of foreign military forces in Britain has produced unwelcome incidents of crime and disorder for local communities. But an intense public relations campaign by US authorities has improved the image of US forces. In the 1950s, arriving servicemen were bombarded with advice about how not to offend the Brits. The worst thing they could do, they were told, was to make rude remarks about politicians or the Royal Family.

In the 1980s, US forces in Britain still arouse xenophobic 'Yanks go home' sentiments in ample measure – but Americans in Britain are probably rather less badly-behaved and better tolerated by local communities than are British Army units in Germany, Norway and other NATO territories. US forces in Britain enjoy a greater degree of immunity from legal proceedings than in Germany or other NATO states. The London Agreement on the Status of Forces, signed in June 1951, required host NATO governments to provide bases and facilities and support services as required, and allowed foreign troops stationed abroad to carry arms and police their own camps. Members of foreign 'visiting' forces were declared to be immune from prosecution or the risk of civil proceedings in a 'receiving state' if they were in the process of carrying out 'official duties'.

This led to formal UK legislation in 1952, in the form of the Visiting Forces Act, which exempted all US service personnel being tried for any offence in British courts, if the offence (or non-criminal injury or damage) 'arose out of and in the course of duty as a member of [US forces]'. Off-duty offences were also exempt if they involved only American property or only Americans were victims of crimes against the person. The sweeping legal powers and immunities available to US forces in Britain through this Act are not widely known, even in legal circles. Magistrates and judges who have attempted unsuccessfully to deal with US servicemen have been angered and dismayed to discover that the Visiting Forces Act can make British courts powerless even when serious crimes are committed against British citizens, and damages cannot be claimed by victims of such American crimes.

Thus, an American serviceman on guard duty who shot a British visitor or demonstrator, whether accidentally or deliberately, could not be charged and brought before a British court unless the US authorities agreed. British police can arrest American offenders, but have to hand them over to US military police – who are at liberty not to charge them, and to remove offenders from the country.

Although it would be difficult for US commanding officers to argue that serious crimes or assaults committed off-base arose in the course of official duty, they have often done so in respect of motoring offences. To magistrates involved in these cases, it was 'very wrong that such a situation should exist'.[3] The scope of this problem is considerable – US servicemen have been involved in over 1,500 driving accidents every year, up to 100 of which are 'serious'.

Sporadically, public antagonism towards US bases has increased as a result of high-handed or deranged behaviour by US servicemen. British civilians have periodically been held at gunpoint inside and outside US bases. October 1952 was a particularly bad month, during which US police set up illegal roadblocks around Upper Heyford, a farmer was held up at gunpoint in country lanes near Chicksands, and three civilian workers at Heathrow were held at gunpoint by US guards for over an hour. In February 1954, a US guard at Northolt shot at and wounded an eighteen-year-old British maintenance worker on the base. There were more than a dozen reported cases of this kind during the decade. In February 1957, future Conservative Attorney-General Michael Havers prosecuted two 'trigger-happy' armed American airmen for illegally imprisoning a British fireman at Sculthorpe. But no one is known to have been killed by over-zealous guards.

Casualties have occurred in other mishaps, however. In June 1958, a twenty-one-year old Master Sergeant at Manston in Kent went berserk and killed two US airmen, wounded three more, killed one RAF policeman and wounded six British civilians before killing himself in Broadstairs. Another hazard was created the same month, by a mechanic from Alconbury who took off unauthorised in a B-45 bomber. He crashed almost immediately, blocking the main London to Edinburgh railway nearby.[4] In May 1969, a mentally-ill USAF sergeant at Mildenhall, Paul Meyer, followed suit and took off in a C-130 Hercules. He came down a few hours later in the English Channel.

In October 1958, at Sculthorpe, nuclear weapons technician Master Sergeant Leander Cunningham locked himself in a tower with a revolver and threatened to kill himself. Four year later, it was claimed that he had threatened to take others with him by attempting to detonate an A-bomb.[5] Britain's most notorious case of US military disorder was a major riot in Dunoon in 1973. Nearly 100 US sailors rampaged through the town waving knives and giving Black Power salutes, damaging 22 shops and stabbing one youth.[6]

But in more serious cases – 'negligent homicides' – offenders have been removed from British jurisdiction. Also in Dunoon, a US Navy sailor at the Holy Loch base ran down a mother and baby, killing the baby and maiming the mother. The baby's killer was not tried in Scottish courts, at the US Navy's insistence. He was fined $100 (then about £35) for the offences.[7] In another 'negligent homicide' case in August 1979, a US marine at St Mawgan in Cornwall was given a trivial fine. He had crashed into and killed a seventeen-year-old youth. The US Navy interrupted an inquest on the dead youth, and prohibited the local coroner, Mr Alan Harvey, from continuing. Six months after blocking the inquest, the US Navy held a court martial in London and fined the marine $1.[8]

US servicemen who have run down and killed Britons have been able to evade civil liability to pay damages as well as criminal punishment from British courts. The parents of a twenty-four-year-old man killed near Northolt were told by Mr Justice Winn that an American serviceman was 'wholly responsible' for their son's death – but they did not have any hope of getting damages. He had left the country.

The Visiting Forces Act and accompanying orders give US military authorities the power to compel British witnesses to attend US hearings. To the astonishment of magistrates at Stockport, Cheshire, US officers at Burtonwood used their subpoena powers to abduct two girls aged 15 and 16 to appear as witnesses at a court martial – refusing to allow parents or guardians to accompany them.

Challenged by MPs that the abduction had been illegal, Home Secretary David Maxwell-Fyffe told the House of Commons in 1952 that any British civilian who refused to comply with a US military subpoena was liable to be jailed under the (British) Army and Air Force Acts.[9]

In crisis or war, before sending reinforcement troops to Europe, the United States plans to obtain more extensive powers from NATO governments. The text of an Emergency Status of Forces (SOF) Agreement, which would be negotiated with NATO governments before reinforcements arrived, was among secret US documents leaked in 1980. Once signed, the emergency agreement would give local US commanders the right to deploy nuclear weapons and military forces as they pleased, and the right to 'quell' local disorder by any 'unilateral' means necessary. Members of US forces would be exempt from all national laws in all circumstances. The United Kingdom was uniquely exempt in that an emergency wartime SOF agreement was not required. The reason for this apparent discrepancy is simple – the Visiting Forces Act and other agreements already provide the US in Britain in peace with the powers it would seek elsewhere in NATO in war.

Defending the presence of US bases in the 1980s, government ministers have revived an old argument in their favour – that they contribute to the economy. This is a sad, cheap and irrelevant argument. If the purpose of having American bases in Britain is in fact to help a few local tradesmen make money, then let the government say so and abandon its high flown rhetoric of deterrence and instead maximise their profit from beer, petrol, and sweets. If so, the Ministry of Defence should be instructed to extort hundreds of millions of dollars out of the United States for the use of military bases. The United Kingdom should do rather well, and the Ministry would have a new and positive incentive to determine how many bases and facilities there are in Britain.

The government has not done this, accepting that if the special relationship and historical and cultural ties with the United States do mean anything, they mean that if the Americans are invited here, it is not for the money. It might be reasonable to ask for the market value rental of the land concerned, but no more. This is simply not the issue. For those who wish the bases removed it would be cheap prostitution of principle and a dereliction of national safety to change one's opinion if the price was right. Those who support the American presence may perhaps wish to avail themselves of accessory financial advantage, but to argue that US cash buys their support merely weakens their other and more compelling arguments.

Yet the Prime Minister and Defence Ministers are attempting to offset popular concern about cruise missiles by using an economic carrot.[10] The Ministry of Defence claimed in its 1983 essay on US bases that US 'expenditure directly benefits local economies by providing employment and income for British contractors and workers'. During a well-publicised visit to Lakenheath in February 1983, Armed Forces Minister Peter Blaker claimed that 'Britain's economy benefited to the tune of more than £500 million last year because of the presence of United States Air Force bases here'.[11]

According to US Air Force figures, the Ministry of Defence is wrong again. For 1982, for example, USAF say that the correct figure is £347 million ($524 million). But only some £70 million actually went to the government (as repayments to the Property Services Agency), and in the end a pittance of about £5 million was in fact paid to public funds; the balance is passed on to building subcontractors.

The erroneous figure of £500 million appears to originate in the 1983 Defence Estimates, which specify that construction projects in the UK in 1982 cost £70 million, and that *total* projected US spending in the UK in 1983/84 would be £430 million. These figures may have been meaninglessly added together. The Ministry of Defence also claims that:

> At least 25,000 workers are employed either directly or indirectly to meet [US] needs.

This employment claim is erroneous, misleading, and blatantly contradicted by actual figures released by the US Department of Defense. According to the Pentagon's worldwide breakdown of military employment, the US Armed Forces in Britain employ 856 people directly, and 1,198 indirectly – a total of 2,054 jobs, not 25,000![12]

Where are the missing 23,000 workers? It can only be assumed that the figure given does not in fact refer to persons employed, even indirectly, by US forces, but is merely an estimate of the number of jobs in the British economy which may be sustained by the claimed financial input. But any economic activity generates 'knock-on' employment, and American military bases are actually comparatively poor local economic wealth generators.

Further, all land used for US bases is held by the British government and provided rent-free. Thus, when the US has wished to expand its bases (as for example at Upper Heyford), the British government has to pay for the land it needs. Between 1973 and 1982, $70 million (£45 million) was spent buying new land for US bases.[13] The 1983 Defence Estimates explained:

> In some cases, such as the provision of surplus defence land for operational and other facilities, [UK] support is free of charge . . .

Of course, the specially-bought new land at Upper Heyford cannot be described as 'surplus'.

So as far as the British Exchequer is concerned, US bases are a net financial burden. During the nine months from 1972 to 1983, US Forces' repayment receipts amounted to $400 million; of this, the British government directly received only $28 million for design and management services supplied. Against this, the UK paid $70 million for new land for US bases, leaving a deficit of $42 million – about £25 million, depending on exchange rates.

Further British costs arise through subventions to NATO infrastructure funds, which pay for specific facilities on US bases in Britain and Europe. Over the last nine years British expenditure on NATO infrastructure totalled £1.4 *billion*. It is apparent that United States repayments to the British government are tiny in comparison to costs incurred in military infrastructure development. The 1983 Defence Estimates, as published, carefully did not assert that US repayments or local expenditure were a net benefit to the British economy – although ministers have known no such restraint. Overall, defence activities incur an annual net loss to the British balance of payments of about £1 billion.

Throughout this book, there have been many other examples of the laxity of British administration of US forces in Britain. The introduction examined how, through ignorance or incompetence, the Ministry of Defence has been unable to identify the full extent of US military facilities in Britain, and has repeatedly misrepresented their extent. These errors are created by loose or non-existent official reporting procedures, which were demonstrated by the development plans at High Wycombe (p 186), Prestwick (p 249), and Little Rissington (p 278).

These matters are important topics for discussion, but they are not the crucial issue in determining whether US bases, individually or collectively, should go or stay.

That issue turns on whether we dare risk continuing the 'coupling' to

United States foreign policy and strategic interests that cruise missiles, as well as the existing forces, are intended to create. If so, we remain inescapably joined as handmaiden to America in international affairs – urging as well as supporting a highly confrontational foreign policy. That is clearly a satisfactory situation for the British government at the time of writing. But western European peoples' attitudes, as well as national geo-political interests, have always been different to those of the United States. However much Mrs Thatcher would care to convert political attitudes in Britain to the American pattern, Britain cannot cross the Atlantic to join the Union and pass sovereignty to Washington.

Sovereignty is critical in the context of 'dual control' of cruise missiles. In the cruise missile debate, the demand for a British right of veto – which is what dual control must mean – has become a prominent political issue. But even before the issue was promoted by the SDP late in 1982, opinion polls consistently found that only a few per cent of the population were content to leave the control of cruise missiles in US hands.

No one disputes that, as matters stand, the only document which grants Britain any rights in the matter is the 1952 Churchill–Truman communiqué. The communiqué is the sole document governing the use of American bases in Britain in emergency; no British or American official or politician has ever suggested that any supporting memorandum of understanding or other clarifying or implementing document exists. It stands alone.

But the communiqué is *not* an agreement; it merely 'reaffirms' an 'understanding'. What it means, therefore, is what both sides think that 'understanding' means. In practice, since they are American weapons and American bases, what matters is what Americans think it means.

Mrs Thatcher has claimed that the document confers dual control and a right of veto on the United Kingdom. She is wrong to say this; indeed, she is probably more aware of the inadequacies of the understanding than any Prime Minister since Harold Macmillan.

She is wrong because, in the first place, such an interpretation runs counter to the obvious logic of the situation, historically, militarily, technically and politically. Secondly, no United States official has ever supported her view that Britain has an unqualified veto. Even if these officials were unreasonably quarrelling with Mrs Thatcher, which they are not, it would not matter. If they do not believe that the understanding embodies 'dual control' and a British right of veto, then what the

British Prime Minister thinks does not matter a whit. Britain has no available, effective means of physical restraint on US actions.

This issue is of critical importance, and merits careful and detailed examination. What did the 1952 understanding seek to achieve? What was its background? What do American leaders and military officers, on whose shoulders its implementation rests, think it requires of them? What has actually happened in crisis?

In 1948, the *Modus Vivendi* had ceded Britain's right to consent before the bomb was used anywhere. This had been a key objective of the American side in those 1948 talks. In December 1950, Prime Minister Attlee visited President Truman, concerned about possible US use of atomic bombs in Korea. The issue was the potential use of the atomic bomb anywhere, not specifically from bases in England. But Attlee did not get the agreement he sought.

The US policy continued to be 'no veto', but the special relationship required consultation. At the end of their meeting on 7 December 1950, Truman told Attlee that:

> he would not consider the use of the bomb without consulting the United Kingdom. The Prime Minister asked whether this agreement should be put in writing, and the President replied no, that it would not be in writing, that if a man's word wasn't any good it wasn't made any better by writing it down. The Prime Minister expressed his thanks.[14]

Dean Acheson, the US Secretary of State, was quite clear that while consultation might be in order, it would only be allowable if time was available. The US was willing to talk about consultation, he wrote in 1971, but prior agreement (the *sine qua non* of a 'veto') was not:

> To require the agreement of the British before this [the atom bomb] would be used was a silly thing to do because it might have to be used at once.[15]

In his own words, Acheson 'unachieved' the near agreement that Attlee had obtained from Truman on the issue.

The present-day understanding was first drafted by the British Ambassador in Washington, Oliver Franks, in October 1951. His draft subsequently formed the basis of the critical 9 January 1952 communiqué, agreed by Churchill and Truman after a meeting on board the Presidential yacht *Williamsburg*:

> Under arrangements made for the common defence, the United States has the use of certain bases in the United Kingdom.
>
> We reaffirm the understanding [this referred to the Attlee–Truman

> discussion, although Attlee and Truman had in fact focused on wider issues] that the use of these bases in an emergency would be a matter for joint decision by His Majesty's Government and the United States Government in the light of the circumstances prevailing at the time.

The communiqué is described as a reaffirmation of an earlier understanding, and the continued acceptance of that understanding is apparently reaffirmed by successive heads of state, as Defence Secretary Michael Heseltine explained in May 1983:

> That agreement is ratified and reaffirmed every time a British Prime Minister or the President of the United States changes, and each of them personally examines the agreement and reaffirms their satisfaction with it. [All Prime Ministers have] reaffirmed this agreement ... The agreement has existed since 1951 [*sic*]. It exists now, tonight[16] ...

Heseltine also stated on the same occasion that the understanding had been subsequently construed by both parties to apply to US 'weapons' – such as Polaris or Poseidon submarines and cruise missiles – as well as bases. 'The reaffirmation does mention bases and weapons ... The Prime Minister has made that quite clear', he said. This is the only known modification to the (agreed) implied terms of the understanding.

The 'agreement' on the use of the bases is therefore just an 'understanding', albeit given an undue solemnity by a process of repeated reaffirmation. What did the original parties to the understanding think they had negotiated, and what was its status?

Luke Battle, who was at the time the special assistant to Secretary of State Acheson, explained the US negotiating position at length to BBC reporter David Henshaw in 1983, in the course of a well-researched examination of this issue by the BBC2 current affairs series, *Brass Tacks*.

> At the time it was made [it] did not seem as earthshaking as people are making it now. The agreement was as precise as anyone could make it – as precise as we wanted it to be – but there was still a little ambiguity there that served everybody's interests and everybody's needs.[17]

Did it provide Britain with a veto, or 'dual control', the former State Department official was asked:

> No, absolutely not. It meant in each, every instance that everybody wanted it to be in full consultation, in full harmony with the other. But veto ... no.

Battle's understanding of the matter is confirmed by public official statements of the US position made soon after Churchill's visit. Three weeks after Churchill left, Acheson's Assistant Secretary of State, Jack McFall, told the Congress that:

> The talks were not in any sense negotiations toward final and binding decisions on the part of either government.[18]

Acheson added later that the talks 'were not agreements in the international political sense'. Nor did the then British Ambassador who attended the talks, Roger Makins (now Lord Sherfield), think that Churchill had agreed a veto:

> I think binding agreements dealing with matters of national security are very difficult to come by and not perhaps wholly to be relied on.[19]

What each side intended is obvious, and has not really changed over the three decades. The United States would not grant a veto on its use of nuclear bases. But the special relationship with Britain, and, later on, the ties of the NATO alliance, did imply and require that, if circumstances permitted, the United States should consult its allies about proposed military actions.

But how do two sides in a consultative discussion reach a 'joint decision', if they do not agree? Should the outcome by default be no action, or should one side prevail regardless? Eugene Zuckert, the US Air Force Assistant Secretary who represented the USAF in the negotiations, says that:

> A 'joint decision' would mean that a one-one tie would be construed in favour of the Americans. It was not a veto. I couldn't imagine that we would think there was a veto on our actions. I just don't believe that, as part of our own concepts of sovereignty, we could concede [a veto on the use of US forces] to another.[20]
>
> Who's to say what will happen at a time of crisis. I think that agreement would be implied rather than sought expressly . . .
>
> Certainly the 1952 agreement does not give Great Britain joint control over American nuclear weapons. There's a great difference . . . between an informal – relatively informal – agreement that there will be consultations, and a situation in which there is a *de facto* veto.

The formula of the 1952 communiqué has often been repeated in Britain, but seldom – until recently – in the United States. The statement was always intended primarily for a domestic British audience. No US President, Secretary of State or of Defense has ever said that it contained a veto. Many have said the opposite. Dean Acheson pointed out in 1950 to President Truman that:

> No commitment of any sort to anyone limited his duty and power under the law to authorise the use of the atomic weapon if he believed it necessary in the defence of the country.[21]

Acheson's successor as Secretary of State was a fierce Cold War warrior, John Foster Dulles, whose view in 1958 on any potential British or allied veto was unequivocal:

> There could be no question of a veto on the use of nuclear weapons being exercised by other countries . . . No Government could legally cast a veto against a decision of another government taken for its own defence.[22]

The withdrawal of US nuclear forces from France to Britain a year later was clear evidence that the kind of firm veto on US plans that General de Gaulle had sought was not then (or now) granted to the United Kingdom government.

Robert McNamara, who was Secretary of Defense for Presidents Kennedy and Johnson for seven years, said in 1983 that he did not think Britain had a veto in American eyes:

> I don't conceive of it as a veto . . . I think 'consultation' means a discussion . . . with the party having the authority – in this case the US – making the final decision . . .
>
> I doubt very much that there was any understanding that Britain had a veto. I say that simply because I think that it would have been thought quite contrary to the appropriate relationship among allies.[23]

One of McNamara's Assistant Defense Secretaries, Paul Warnke – who headed the US Arms Control and Disarmament Agency under President Carter – had an almost identical view as to whether the understanding amounted to a veto:

> If you mean that at a time of crisis you could be quite confident that American nuclear weapons could not be launched from your territory without your agreement with it, then I think you would be deluding yourself . . .[24]

He was extremely doubtful as to whether most of his colleagues at the time in the Pentagon even knew of any special arrangement with the British. Warnke was asked what the phrase 'joint decision' actually meant:

> I haven't the slightest idea . . . No piece of paper, no matter how well intentioned, is going to make any real difference at a time of crisis. The person . . . the country that physically controls the weapon is going to make the decision . . .

> At the time of genuine emergency, I don't think any piece of paper, and certainly not an informal, relatively loosely worded piece of paper [like the communiqué], is the equivalent of a twin key system.

In other words, said Warnke:

> The 'joint control' would be effective until it counted.

President Nixon's Defense Secretary, James Schlesinger, offered a slightly more generous interpretation in 1983; it was 'close' to a veto:

> I think that, as a practical matter, it comes close to being a veto . . . The intention is of course that there be intimate consultation at any time . . . if there is time available.[25]

Since Schlesinger's time in office in the 1970s, the issue has moved into the limelight in Britain. As the row over 'dual control' grew in 1982 and 1983, Mrs Thatcher and Defence Secretary Michael Heseltine stuck resolutely to the position that the existing agreement was entirely satisfactory, and that no change was needed. But in the spring of 1983, Mrs Thatcher – evidently embarrassed by her poor position on the issue in the pre-election period and by the growing unhappiness in the Conservative Party – did attempt, secretly and unsuccessfully, to get something better from the Americans.

At first, Mrs Thatcher tried to move the United States' public position by direct action; she asserted, unilaterally, that the agreement was indeed 'joint control', knowing that on this occasion US officials would not dare to correct the Prime Minister. In a February 1983 press conference, following a meeting with Italian Prime Minister Fanfani, she explained exuberantly:

> The arrangements we have made for the new missiles are the same as those of long ago between Mr Churchill and Mr Truman. They are arrangements for joint decision – not merely joint consultation – but joint decision. I am satisfied that those arrangements would be effective. A joint decision on the use of the bases or the missiles would of course be dual control.[26]

'Got it?', she asked her questioner, 'Good! Excellent! Worth asking the question!'.

Soon after this, however, it became clear that Mrs Thatcher was trying to alter the substance of the UK–US understanding to conform with what she had previously said. British diplomats in Washington met with Pentagon officials from March to May 1983, in an attempt to negotiate a new deal. By the time of the planned Western summit meeting in Williamsburg, Virginia, she wanted to get the United States on the record with, according to the *New York Times*:

> An 'absolutely unambiguous' statement, pledging that the missiles would never be used without British consent, or [the addition of] a clause to that effect to the 1952 agreement.[27]

United States Assistant Defense Secretary Richard Perle confirmed at the time that negotiations with Britain were taking place. But he did not think that it was 'necessary to change existing procedures governing US weapons systems stationed in Britain'.[28]

Mrs Thatcher repeated her claim about dual control in Parliament two weeks before the summit, asserting that the existing agreement:

> [means] that no nuclear weapon would be fired or launched from British territory without the agreement of the Prime Minister. That is categorical.[29]

But the sovereignty that Attlee had lost and could not recover, that Churchill and Macmillan had failed to retake, Mrs Thatcher could not restore. She, like Sir Winston Churchill 30 years before, met her Williamsburg.

In a television interview two days before the summit, President Reagan went as far as he dared. He remained ambiguous, and his comments were characteristically blurred. Reagan was asked by a British correspondent to say who was 'ultimately in control' of US nuclear weapons.

> We will . . . I don't think either one of us will do anything independent of the other . . . er, this constitutes a sort of veto power, doesn't it? But, er, we have an understanding about this and would never act unilaterally with any of our allies on this.[30]

Continuing Mrs Thatcher's diplomacy by other means, the BBC pressed Reagan's Defense Secretary Caspar Weinberger at the same time to discover if there had been a change in position. Weinberger was asked, was the understanding with the United States now construed to give Britain a veto? He evaded a direct answer:

> The agreement should speak for itself to the extent that it can be discussed publicly. You've read the [1952] communiqué from the British government and I would simply stand on that . . . These matters of the release of nuclear weapons are obviously sensitive. The agreement . . . has been in effect for a long time . . . I don't think I would serve any

> purpose nor would it be very helpful to you in trying to elaborate on words that are in fact perfectly clear.[31]

Did this mean that the missiles would not be launched without the agreement of the British Government?

> I can't read any other way to interpret the phrase joint decision . . .

But did *that* mean dual control and a full veto? Weinberger avoided saying that there was, in fact, still no veto:

> Let's just stand directly on the words of the communiqué which has been in effect [all these years] . . .

Reportedly, Britain had been offered the chance of dual control of cruise missiles, but had turned the offer down. In February 1983, Michael Heseltine claimed that the only terms on which dual control had been available were if Britain agreed to purchase the entire missile system from the United States at an estimated cost of £1 billion.[32]

True dual control differs from a political veto in that there must be a second technical 'finger on the trigger' – the physical control of firing, or the sending of a firing order – at some level. A political veto – even if Britain had such a right – can only be exercised through the US President or National Command Authority. Dual control systems provide for the veto to be exercised at a much lower level, and for it to be effective without question.

Dual US-NATO or US-British control exists now for many US nuclear weapons, including short-range missiles, artillery shells, air-dropped bombs and depth charges. The previous generation of medium-range missiles sited in Britain – Thor – was indeed fitted with dual locks with which to activate the firing control panel. Launch Control Centres for cruise missiles similarly contain duplicated launch controls, but both controls are US-manned.

But it would not be difficult to modify US command and control arrangements to give Britain or other allies a dual key, without necessarily requiring British officers to join the missile launch crews. The US Permissive Action Link (PAL) system prevents nuclear weapons being readied for use until authorised by or on behalf of the National Command Authority. A PAL code has to be transmitted to the missile crew, over command and control systems such as 'Cemetery Net'. Firing orders are issued subsequently, authenticated by another code or a prearranged top secret password.

US control of PAL codes and the allied control of firing is the existing basis of dual key systems in Europe; the system could be applied in reverse, requiring Britain to pass PAL codes to US missile commanders to authorise a US request to launch the missiles. This is only one of many possible technical means of implementing a right of veto. The key point is that even a watertight international treaty can be circumvented if the political will is there; there would be no point in arguing the niceties of international law after a nuclear exchange. Unless the technical means to implement a veto are there, even the most tightly-drafted document is of no avail.

As explained above, the communiqué is far from tightly drafted; according to US officials concerned:

- It is not 'final and binding'.
- It is not an 'agreement in the international political sense'.
- Failure to reach an agreed joint decision 'would be construed in favour of the United States'.
- It is heavily qualified by the phrase 'in the light of the circumstances prevailing at the time'.

Similar problems over the use of nuclear weapons have arisen elsewhere in NATO; especially in Germany, where one nation may launch the nuclear weapons of a second from the territory of a third. NATO as a whole has drawn up guidelines on the use of nuclear weapons, which in effect promise other NATO allies the same rights as the United Kingdom – amounting to consultation if time is available. Curiously, although the NATO guidelines have the same general effect as the 1952 communiqué, they are never mentioned in Britain, as though reserved for others in NATO not enjoying a special relationship.

In the NATO context, the NATO Supreme Allied Commander Europe, General Andrew J. Goodpaster, told the US Congress in 1973 that the only and ultimate authority controlling US nuclear weapons was the President of the United States.[33]

NATO first published instructions on the employment of nuclear weapons in 1962. The 'Athens guidelines' and their subsequent amendments do not affect the substance of the analysis of 'the circumstances in which the Alliance might be compelled to have recourse to nuclear weapons'; they assess the 'degree to which consultation on [nuclear weapons] use might be possible'. In the event of a nuclear attack on a member state, according to the communiqué following the May 1962 Athens meeting, there was provision for immediate, automatic response even without consultation among the membership. In the case of a conventional attack, however, the nuclear weapon states would consult with their allies before using nuclear weapons, if time permitted.[34]

In subsequent discussions on NATO's flexible response policy, the guidelines were amended to cater for a range of pre-defined contingencies, and to give as far as possible the final say to the countries most directly involved. But the ultimate position remained that:

> The United States President retains the right to use American nuclear weapons without prior consultation.[35]

Following the Athens meeting, it became of some importance to test out the physical and political procedures by which NATO members would actually consult in crisis – when every national seat of government and military headquarters might be under conventional attack, with the threat of nuclear attack to follow. A special series of exercises to test decision taking – 'Fallex' (Fall [Autumn] Exercise) – followed, one being held that September and annually thereafter. In the 1970s, Fallex exercises were replaced by the 'Wintex' (Winter Exercise) series. These have all been command-post exercises, involving no actual troop movements, in which national heads of state participate – or are played by surrogate senior officials or ministers.

The basic scenario seldom varies. On some pretext, the Soviet Union attacks – usually in Germany, sometimes also on the northern or southern flanks. The outcome of the exercises, as players such as the former Chiefs of the Defence Staff, Lords Mountbatten and Carver, have described, has also not varied. After about ten days, Wintex leads to nuclear war.

Formally, the joint decision-taking arrangements between Britain and the United States have 'not been activated' in any crisis to date, Armed Forces Minister Peter Blaker told Parliament in March 1983.[36] But there have been a number of occasions in which the Anglo-American crisis consultation procedures have been tested.

As Chapter 2 showed, eight years after the communiqué, there was no arrangement even to notify the United Kingdom that US forces had been placed on alert. The arrangement then created provided for a message to be passed to the Defence Ministry via US Naval Headquarters in London. That precise arrangement had evidently lapsed by 1973, when the British Ambassador in Washington was the first recipient of a warning of a US alert during the Yom Kippur war. Evidently, there is no London–Washington 'hot-line', although there have been hot-lines from both London and Washington to Moscow since the mid-1960s.

President Kennedy's conduct of the Cuban missile crisis in 1962 was cited by Harold Macmillan in his autobiography as evidence that the special relationship worked. Macmillan attacked his critics of the time for being in 'ignorance of what really happened', when they accused the United States of having risked total war for a quarrel that did not concern Europe, and of having failed to consult their allies in Britain.

But Macmillan's own blow-by-blow account shows that as the crisis deepened, President Kennedy and his officials first ceased to seek advice, then rejected any that was offered and – in the last desperate thirty-six hours of the crisis – cut off communications altogether. In his final phone call to Macmillan, on Friday 26 October 1962, Kennedy promised, as the moment of confrontation approached:

> I will also keep in touch with you tomorrow at this time or . . . send you a message unless we get something immediate . . . We will not take any further action until I have talked to you in any case. I will send you a message if there is anything new, in any case, I'll talk to you on the phone before we do anything of a drastic nature[37] . . .

But Kennedy did not do this. Instead, he launched his final démarche to Khrushchev on Sunday morning two days later neither consulting or even informing the Prime Minister. The final humiliation for Macmillan and the British Cabinet occurred after they met in crisis session on Sunday morning, 28 October 1962. They drafted a British démarche supporting the last known position of the Americans (which was by then out of date), sent it off to the Russians at noon, and went to lunch. Then, Macmillan himself records:

> News came (*by radio*) that the Russians had given in [author's emphasis]

On the next occasion the United States deliberately raised its global defence alert status (Defence readiness condition, or 'Defcon'), Britain was not consulted, or its position even considered. On Friday 25 October 1973, at about 5 am London time, with no warning or discussion with any allies, US nuclear alert forces were ordered to Defcon 2 – one step short of full war alert – and the remainder to Defcon 3, slightly lower readiness. Nuclear strike forces, including the F-111 bombers at Upper Heyford were on alert by 7 am; the entire available force was then on 'Quick Reaction Alert'.

The crisis had been provoked by Israeli actions in the Yom Kippur war. After US Secretary of State Henry Kissinger had negotiated an

Egyptian-Israeli ceasefire, the Israeli army had moved in regardless to encircle the Egyptian Third Army, threatening to annihilate them. On the afternoon of 24 October, it was apparent to the United States from Sigint and other intelligence that Soviet military intervention to save the Egyptians was only hours away. At least 85 ships, and 40,000 airlift troops, possibly with nuclear weapons available, were being readied. That evening, the Soviet Union delivered a blunt and still-secret ultimatum to the US President, confirming that they were on the point of unilaterally intervening in the war.

The United States response to the Soviet Union was decided on within three hours, and the Defcon alert ordered. For a few hours thereafter, US officials refused to communicate with the Soviet Union in order to allow time for Soviet Sigint sources and reconnaissance satellites to detect the American alert. It was deliberate brinkmanship. But during these hours, the United States sought no consultation with its allies. Five hours after calling the alert, President Nixon sent a message to the Soviet Ambassador – a carefully drafted response to the earlier Soviet threat that left no doubt about the United States' intent to escalate the conflict if the Soviets proceeded as planned.

> Mr General Secretary:
>
> ... We must view your suggestion of unilateral action as a matter of gravest concern, involving incalculable consequences ...
>
> In the spirit of our agreements [ie, the 1973 Agreement on the Prevention of Nuclear War], this is the time for action ... in harmony and with cool heads ...
>
> Unilateral action ... would produce incalculable consequences which would be in the interest of neither of our countries and which would end all we have striven so hard to achieve.[38]

The nuclear threat could scarcely have been made more explicit. To make sure the point struck home, Kissinger appeared at a press conference at noon the same day (25 October 1973) and reminded the world that the United States and the Soviet Union:

> possess, each of us, nuclear arsenals capable of annihilating humanity. We, both of us, have a special duty to see to it that confrontations are kept within bounds that do not threaten civilized life ... The issues that divide the world do not justify the unparalleled catastrophe that a nuclear war would represent.[39]

A message about the alert was sent to the British Ambassador, Defense Secretary James Schlesinger said later – but not to any other NATO ally. By the time most European statesmen heard of the alert, it was public knowledge in the United States. Early morning radio and TV bulletins showed bombers on alert, warships setting off, and soldiers being recalled from leave. 'Because of the speed of the crisis,' Schlesinger has claimed, 'timely consultation was made more difficult.'

In fact, timely consultation was not attempted, even during the five hours after calling the nuclear alert when the United States was deliberately marking time. But the alert was merely a 'signal', said Schlesinger, and the United States:

> felt that all the allies would back up that signal. That is quite different from the actual use of force. If there were the use of force contemplated, I believe that consultations would have been extremely intimate.[40]

The distinction made between a threat of force as a 'signal' and the actual use of force is more subtle than it seems. The United States did not intend a general nuclear response at any stage, yet alerted all its strategic nuclear forces. But if the Soviet Union had not taken the United States seriously, it would not have responded, as it did, by backing down. But what if the Soviet Union had decided to call what Schlesinger now portrays as a bluff? In a 1982 study of the political utility of nuclear weapons in this crisis, the Harvard journal *International Security* asked what would have occurred if the Soviets had proceeded regardless to intervene against Israel. Would the Israelis have counter-attacked against the Soviets, or the Soviet Air Force against the United States Sixth Fleet in the Mediterranean?

> Where would the conflict have ended? Given that the United States already had introduced the possibility, perhaps likelihood, that the confrontation would escalate to the nuclear level, would not the Soviets have chosen to initiate the use of nuclear weapons, thus gaining whatever advantage might reside in the side that strikes first?[41]

In the British view, there has historically been little dispute that 'the circumstances . . . at the time' might leave them uninformed and unconsulted. But they have seldom considered that eventuality arising – as it always has – out of circumstances other than a nuclear attack on a NATO state. Churchill, who publicly remained highly equivocal about the terms on which US airbases had been reintroduced, acknowledged in 1955:

> I suppose an immediate, destructive, surprise and treacherous attack . . . might possibly be acted upon by our allies in the United States . . . without further or prior consultation.

Macmillan, who styled the understanding 'a loose arrangement', was embarrassed when US State Department officials refuted his claim that the firing of Polaris missiles was subject to British sanction. He acknowledged afterwards that:

> Consultation might obviously be impossible in circumstances of a surprise attack upon the West. He would, indeed, not wish to insist on prior consultation in such circumstances.[42]

Francis Pym, when Defence Secretary in 1980, told the Americans that Britain wanted 'a degree of say' before cruise missiles were fired. But he nevertheless acknowledged that everything might happen too late:

> If you get a situation, and you know, with only minutes' notice, well you're in a very dangerous situation anyway.[43]

American history is peppered with examples of threats to use nuclear weapons, many of them secret. They began in 1946 with the crisis in Iran, according to a detailed and well-documented study by Daniel Ellsberg.[44] There followed Korea, in 1950 and 1953; French Indo-China, 1954; the Lebanon crisis, 1958; Taiwan Straits, 1958; Laos, 1961; Berlin, 1961; Cuba, 1962; and Vietnam, repeatedly between 1968 and 1972. In 1980, US forces again went on Defcon alert without warning, during the abortive attempt to rescue the US embassy hostages from Iran.

The poverty or absence of consultation with allies on each and every occasion is poor testimony to the United States' intent to honour its pledges. The history of US nuclear crisis management can thus engender little confidence in Europe that, despite promises and good intentions in peacetime, allies would be likely to be let in on the life-and-death decisions before nuclear war.

That is why the 'dual key' principle, and the political control of foreign military forces, is of inestimable importance. In the critical hours or minutes of many sorts of nuclear crisis that can be envisaged, Her Majesty's Government would also have dire need of 'signals'. If the crisis arose from threatened US or Soviet regional nuclear escalation outside Europe, Britain should be able to signal convincingly that she was not a party to the conflict – by diplomacy and by having previously let it be known that US forces in Britain could effectively be restrained by dual key means.

British and American foreign policy interests have diverged often and widely enough in the past for this type of contingency to be no idle fear. It is simply not good enough for Britain to be lectured by US generals on its duty to 'hang in there' as allies, wherever the United States may choose to go. Far too much is at stake.

Most NATO allies are much more guarded in their military relations with the United States than is Britain. In NATO, only a slim majority – 8 of 15 – permit the United States to station nuclear weapons on their territory. Seven do not allow the US to have nuclear bases – of whom five (Norway, Denmark, France, Luxembourg and Portugal) do not permit any foreign military bases to be established in their territory (except, *pro tem* in the case of Portugal, for the Azores). One ally – Canada – has already opted for unilateral nuclear disarmament, and has nearly completed the process (retaining only defensive and near-obsolescent low-yield anti-aircraft nuclear missiles). Iceland, although it has US bases, has no national military forces at all. Two NATO allies, France and Spain, have expelled US nuclear bases, and a third, Greece, has announced the termination of all US bases during 1989 – which will put Britain in a minority among American allies, as far as US nuclear weapons are concerned.

Only five of fourteen European NATO countries have agreed to the deployment of US cruise and Pershing missiles, and of these two – the Netherlands and Belgium – still retain such reluctance to go ahead that deployment of cruise missiles in these countries was, at the time of writing, still in doubt. The majority of northern NATO countries have rejected US bases or nuclear weapons, whilst a majority of the Mediterranean states have negotiated stiff and costly terms for their retention.

After the fall of the dictatorship in Spain, the new socialist government negotiated a 'Treaty of Friendship and Cooperation' with the United States in 1976, which replaced a 1953 Treaty with the Franco regime. The treaty allowed the US to continue using three airbases, the naval port at Rota and other minor facilities, subject to the withdrawal of all US nuclear weapons, and the closure within three years of the Poseidon submarine base at Rota. Rota was duly closed at the start of 1979, and the submarine facilities were dismantled during the following six months. Spain also received $1,200 million from the United States over five years in the form of military credits and grants. The treaty made the circumstances in which US bases were used subject to 'mutual agreement' – a phrase which obviously embodies as much ambiguity as the undertaking to make a 'joint decision' with Britain.

However, both Greece and Turkey *have* obtained considerable control over the use of US bases, as well as receiving substantial payments and military aid from the United States after renegotiating their joint defence treaties in 1983 and 1980 respectively. Greek and Turkish relations with the US and NATO had a stormy history in the 1970s. Greece withdrew from NATO altogether between 1974 and 1980, following the Turkish invasion of Cyprus. US bases were not removed at the same time, however, but continued to operate on a bilateral basis. In 1976, parallel agreements for US bases in and military and economic aid to Greece and Turkey were proposed, from which Turkey would receive $1 billion and Greece $700 million. But because of the US arms embargo to Turkey, these agreements were never ratified.

During the mid- and late-1970s, US bases in Turkey were put under complete Turkish control or closed. A new US-Turkish 'Agreement for Cooperation on Defense and Economy' was signed in March 1980, which formally confined the use of the Turkish bases to 'obligations arising out of the North Atlantic Treaty', and gave Turkey complete control over US activities. All US bases became Turkish Armed Forces Installations at which US units were authorised to take part in 'joint defence' activities.

The effect of the restriction on operations to NATO purposes is partly annulled by provisions contained in a series of unpublished 'supplementary agreements'. These allow Turkish officials to reach a further and secret 'mutual agreement' which could permit US forces to operate outside the NATO area. However, the supplementary agreements also gave the Turks the apparently untrammelled right to see US intelligence data gathered from bases in Turkey: 'all intelligence information, including raw data, produced at intelligence collection installations . . . shall be shared by the two governments . . .'.[45] Turkey was promised $450-million worth of military equipment and development aid in 1981. By 1983 this had become $650 million a year; Pentagon officials proposed to give Turkey nearly $1 billion in aid in 1984/85.

Greece began renegotiating the use of US bases in 1981. Andreas Papandreou's Pan-Hellenic Socialist Party, Pasok, came to power the same year but an agreement was not reached until 1983. Its terms provide a useful example of what ought to be sought and achieved in Britain by anyone who wishes some respect for national sovereignty to be regained. As the agreement is ultimately ambiguous about whether the bases go or stay, it is also a useful model for those who might wish to use US disengagement from Britain as a trigger to regional disarmament. The agreement, initialled in Athens on 15 July 1983, gives Greece several important rights:

- US bases in Greece will be closed from the start of 1989, with a period allowed for dismantlement (termination of the US lease is not completely automatic; the US says that the treaty terms permit them to renew their use of the bases).
- Greece has the right to control all US military activities from the bases, which are under Greek command. They are intended only to be used for NATO purposes. In the event of US unilateral action outside NATO (ie, in the Middle East), or in 'extreme emergency', Greece can order the suspension of the use of the bases.
- The exemption of US forces from Greek law was withdrawn, and Greek authorities can decide in each case whether the offence should be tried in Greek courts or by US courts martial. Greece had never been a party to the 1951 NATO Status of Forces Agreement.

Greece has also obtained an undertaking that their American bases will only be used for defensive purposes – and a promise of substantial military assistance funds starting in 1984 with a payment of $500 million.

In 1983, Portugal began renegotiating its lease to the United States of bases in the Azores – chiefly a refuelling airbase at Lajes, often used for flights to the Middle East, and a SOSUS underwater tracking facility. In 1979, a four-year renewal of the lease on the Azores base cost the US $140 million; $80 million of this went to pay for development projects in the Azores. In February 1983, when the Azores agreement expired, it was not renewed by Portugal's socialist government although US forces remained temporarily *in situ* whilst new terms were considered.

In Europe, therefore, the United States pays a total of about $1,500 million (£1,000 million) a year to Greece, Turkey, Spain and Portugal for the use of bases.

In the Pacific, neither Australia nor Japan permit US nuclear weapons on their territory. Australia only accomodates – amid considerable controversy – US support facilities including a number of satellite control, communications and relay stations, rather than actual troops or weapons. However the Australian satellite communications bases are extremely important in the operation of US early warning and intelligence satellites.[46]

The terms on which US bases are tolerated – or not – by other countries and especially by NATO allies, make a remarkable comparison with the 'open house' policy of non-supervision and official complacency in Britain. It does not follow, as argued above, that Britain should enter a formal claim for Pentagon payola – although if we did, it would certainly yield a handsome profit of hundreds of millions of dollars. But it is certainly grotesque that a country that claims the rights and privileges of a special relationship with the United States has in fact neither gained special privileges nor ever asserted its rights. It is absurd that no treaty has ever specified formal controls or conditions of use for US bases in Britain – as is done in the vast majority of NATO states. The NATO treaty covers some of the issues, but is deficient in that the United States has wide interests in 'unilateral' non-NATO military operations.

Nor can the British government claim that cultural and political ties have been so good that such a treaty has been unnecessary. As documented above, Britain does not have a formal veto on the use of US nuclear weapons and US officials say they would never grant one. There is no general control over the use of US bases, and Britain has *not* been consulted in the critical stages of international crises. US servicemen have evaded British criminal responsibility and civil liability – not always, but sufficiently often to arouse judicial and political concern. American bases in Britain are under sole US control, despite the flimsy 'RAF' designation of their titles.

Seen in this context, the special relationship is meaningful only as a delusion collectively entertained by the British political establishment. If the Anglo-American special relationship is to have military form, it should be characterised by clear and well-understood terms, and not by the contemporary woolly and ill-defined ambiguities of non-regulation which now surround US bases. The only country generally laxer in its treatment of US forces is West Germany – whose government is still constrained by the terms of surrender to the occupying allies, a rather different position from the UK.

The most contentious contemporary issue concerning US bases is the deployment of cruise missiles. NATO governments agreed to the stationing of 572 cruise and Pershing missiles in Europe in December 1979. Like many other nuclear forces, the new NATO missiles are primarily symbolic. The role for which they were intended is complex, and not easily explained. In consequence, many of the arguments used in public debate about cruise missiles – from both sides – have been false.

Government spokesmen usually assert that NATO has to have the new missiles because the Soviet Union began to deploy SS-20 missiles in the late-1970s and thus gained a new and dangerous advantage in land-based medium-range missiles. This is a fallacy; the Soviet Union had always had such an advantage, and from the mid-1960s to the mid-1970s had at least 600 SS-4 and SS-5 missiles – most of them aimed at Europe, tipped with 1-Megaton H-bomb warheads. When these missiles first arrived, in the late-1950s, the US deployed Thor and Jupiter missiles to Britain, Italy and Turkey. These were later to be replaced by a NATO multilateral nuclear force (MLF), but this plan foundered. In place of the aborted MLF, the United States allocated an eventual total of 400 Poseidon missile warheads to SACEUR, and insisted (in the Nassau Agreement) that Britain do likewise with its 192 Polaris warheads.

Thus in the 1960s, NATO sensibly chose to put its medium-range nuclear missiles at sea, where they were much less vulnerable to attack. When the plan to 'modernise' NATO forces by means of cruise and Pershing missiles was revealed in 1979, NATO governments cast the missile balance in terms of land-based missiles only. Since this 'balance' dishonestly concealed the fact that NATO's medium-range European missiles were at sea, the resulting figures unsurprisingly disclosed that the USSR had an advantage in land-based missiles. This advantage was by then nearly 20 years old.

The real trigger for the 1979 NATO decision was not the SS-20s, but fears expressed by some German politicians that they could no longer rely on the United States to use its strategic nuclear arsenal in defence of Europe. Instead, the US might fight a limited nuclear war in Europe in which both American and Soviet territory would remain a sanctuary.

For this reason, many popular arguments *against* cruise missiles are also misconceived. Europeans, not Americans, first asked for the missiles. They are not intended to help fight a nuclear war limited to Europe; in theory, they are supposed to enhance deterrence by ensuring that a nuclear war is *not* limited to Europe. Nor are cruise missiles (unlike the new Pershing ballistic missiles in Germany) likely to be of major assistance in carrying out a US disarming first strike against the Soviet Union.

NATO's rationale for cruise stems from the alliance doctrine of flexible response, which argues that deterrence is sustained at several levels, and that war – even nuclear war – can be fought at one level, while deterrence continues to operate at a higher level.

For example, a war in Europe might start conventionally but one side initiates the use of 'tactical' nuclear weapons – to start with, only in the battle area. Escalation may then lead to tactical nuclear targets in 'rear' areas in Germany and Poland being attacked. But the Soviet Union, the United States, and the more remote NATO countries are not attacked with nuclear weapons. Although nuclear deterrence has failed at one level, strategic weapons continue to deter both major powers from starting an all-out war by attacking targets far behind the battle area.

This is the concept of the 'ladder of deterrence' – the Soviet Union is deterred from attacking NATO Europe by the knowledge and belief that the United States has the capability and the will to launch a strategic nuclear attack (and accept the consequences). But after the US and USSR began to negotiate parity in strategic weapons in the SALT agreements, some politicians raised fears that the US deterrent was, for Europe, no longer credible. In effect, SALT had created a strategic stalemate. West German Chancellor Helmut Schmidt reflected these fears when he suggested in 1977 that SALT had indeed neutralised the US strategic arsenal. By implication, the ladder of deterrence had lost its top rung, and the Soviet Union might believe that it could fight in Europe without fear of strategic attack from the United States.

The 'ladder of deterrence' theory and flexible response plan have often been criticised by senior military and defence officials, who point out that NATO exercises have not uncovered any way in which a limited nuclear war could stay limited. And if full-scale nuclear warfare is likely to be triggered by the use of battlefield nuclear weapons, then it follows that there is no need for the new 'intermediate' nuclear forces. It also follows that NATO is extremely foolish to rely on the early and 'limited' use of nuclear weapons to counter a conventional attack.

NATO's High Level Group – part of the Nuclear Planning Group – began working on 'Theatre Nuclear Force' (TNF) modernisation in May 1977. Among other objectives, they sought high 'visibility' for the new weapons. Despite the increased risk of destruction, it was argued in the High Level Group that the new missiles should be based on land so as to reassure the European public that they were protected. This was indeed an ironical misperception.

In theory, the new TNF missiles would 'couple' the US strategic deterrent to European defences. Their presence on land meant that, unlike submarines or ships, the US could not withdraw or redeploy the forces in crisis. Since they could strike the Soviet Union directly, their effect was 'strategic'. In practice, the very visibility that nuclear specialists argued would reassure Europeans of their safety became the trigger for and focus of a massive and adverse public reaction across Europe.

To urge the new missiles on Parliaments and publics, NATO created a second specialist team – the 'Special Group' – which contrived to link the deployment of cruise and Pershing missiles to disarmament proposals. The coupling of modernisation to disarmament proposals became known as the NATO 'twin track' decision. Once European governments had accepted in outline the need for the new weapons, American nuclear specialists moved in with specific proposals for cruise missiles and long-range Pershing ballistic missiles. The High Level Group report suggested that 200 missiles would be the minimum necessary for coupling to operate successfully; 600 would be the maximum if NATO were not to be seen as engaging in unilateral escalation and promoting an arms race.

A 572-strong 'mix' of 108 Pershing II missiles and 464 Ground Launched Cruise Missiles (GLCM, pronounced 'glickim') was finally chosen. A timetable for deployment was announced, with the rider that the numbers installed would be reduced if disarmament negotiations with the Soviet Union were successful. At this point, the myth that the new missiles were a simple response to the SS-20s was fully born. Since much nuclear weapons policy is about signalling anyway, this myth has since 1979 virtually become the truth by being repeated sufficiently often.

A second NATO misrepresentation – that the missiles are merely a 'modernisation' of existing forces – has collapsed. In 1976, the Institute of Strategic Studies' *Strategic Survey* noted that the US Air Force was studying the potential use of GLCM to replace F-111 bombers in Britain. When the 'modernisation' decision was announced, NATO's existing long-range nuclear strike force – British Vulcan and US F-111 bombers – were described as either obsolescent or ageing. The suggestion that the new robot GLCMs would replace the manned F-111 bombers was given further credibility when proposals to site the missiles at the existing F-111 bases at Lakenheath and Upper Heyford were publicised in 1979 and 1980. But by 1983, it became quite apparent that cruise missiles were going to augment, not replace, the manned nuclear bombers.[47]

Six cruise missile bases are planned, two of them in Britain. Base number one is Greenham Common (96 missiles) which first became operational by the start of 1984. Comiso, Sicily (112 missiles) is the second, whose construction has been delayed to follow Greenham. Florennes, Belgium (48 missiles) is site three, followed by Wunscheim, West Germany (96 missiles); Woensdrecht, Netherlands (48 missiles); and Molesworth, Cambridgeshire (64 missiles). Molesworth is planned to be operational by the end of 1986. Before construction starts at Molesworth, a third British base, Alconbury, will be developed as the cruise missile support centre for Molesworth. Targeting instructions for the GLCMs will be prepared by the Theater Mission Planning Squadron detachment at a fourth British base, High Wycombe.

With the slogan 'Poised to deter, quick to react' reflecting the fact that at least one flight of 16 nuclear-armed missiles on the base would be permanently on 'QRA' (Quick Reaction Alert) and ready to fire, the 501st Tactical Missile Wing of the US Air Force was set up at Greenham Common in 1983. Missile crews began to arrive in July, fresh from training in Arizona. By the end of October, construction of six hardened drive in/drive out GLCM shelters was nearly complete, in anticipation of the arrival of the first missiles a few weeks later. Greenham Common's 'Interim Operational Capability', with one flight of 16 missiles ready to fire, was achieved at the end of December.

Each of the six shelters houses the main vehicles for one 16-missile flight: four transporter-erector-launchers (TELs), each carrying four GLCMs, and two accompanying launch control centres (LCCs). Each shelter is said to be hardened to the astonishing degree of resisting blast of 2,000 lb per square inch.[48] This is as hard as ICBM missile silos in the United States, and would be sufficient to resist the blast from a 10-Megaton bomb detonated 1 mile away. Officially, the shelters are claimed merely to be designed to resist a direct hit by a 500 lb conventional high explosive bomb.

In time of tension, it is claimed, the missiles 'will be moved away from their bases to secret locations' in the countryside. The British government has suggested that the radius of potential dispersal is of the order of 200 miles – but this is likely to be a deliberate overestimate. The convoys which accompany each flight of 16 missiles include more than 20 vehicles and 70 personnel. They are hardly speedy, or inconspicuous! The Ministry of Defence appears to have accepted that a devastating wide-area nuclear attack could be launched against almost all of southern England by the Soviet Union, in an attempt to destroy the dispersed cruise missiles. Former RAF Under-Secretary Geoffrey Pattie claimed however that such a strike would need 'more than 1000 Megatons worth of H-bombs'.[49]

A much more serious danger is that the dispersal of cruise missiles will be the signal that starts a strategic nuclear war. Cruise missiles are intended to offer an unambiguous strategic nuclear threat to Soviet territory. It is unlikely that the dispersal of the missiles and their cumbersome supporting convoys could be accomplished in complete secrecy. Dispersal has to imply, to an adversary, preparation to fire – and once the Soviet Union had detected preparations to move the missiles out, the Soviet leadership would inevitably come under pressure to pre-empt a Western strike by striking first themselves. The mobility of cruise missiles is a dangerous disadvantage, creating terrifying instability in time of crisis.

This problem has evidently been recognised, since each flight of missiles is being housed in extremely heavily blast-hardened shelters. This gives the lie to the Ministry of Defence claim that the missiles would be dispersed 'in time of tension' before war, even conventional war. If this were true, there would be no need to build any shelters for the 80 missiles not on Quick Reaction Alert. In war, it is likely that the only sense in which cruise missiles can be considered mobile is that they have wheels.

British-based GLCMs will probably be targeted on airfields, nuclear weapons and ammunition stores, and command and communications centres in the Warsaw Pact. The targets are similar to those allocated to F-111 bombers. There is considerable doubt about whether the Tercom guidance system fitted to cruise missiles is effective, and tests on both cruise and Pershing II missiles have shown them to be very unreliable. But since the missiles' function is to a large degree symbolic, this does not matter as much as might seem. Challenged by the US General Accounting Office over the technical inadequacies of cruise missiles in 1980, the Pentagon responded that the 'success of NATO's efforts' should be 'measured by focussing on the political and strategic significance of the missiles' and not, by implication, on whether they were likely to work or not!

In 1983, Pentagon plans which might involve another cruise missile base in Britain were disclosed.[50] The new Ground-Launched Anti-Ship System (GLASS) cruise missiles might be deployed at the NATO base at Stornoway in the Hebrides, in order to attack Soviet naval ships in the Iceland–UK gap. GLASS missiles would not normally be armed with a nuclear warhead, but would carry a 900 lb conventional charge. Soon after this report, US officials began an on-the-ground survey of Stornoway's suitability for GLASS missiles.

---

OPPOSITE

**Fig 12. Inside a cruise missile bunker**

Despite the public stress laid on the mobility of cruise missiles, at least 16 missiles at each base are always on Quick Reaction Alert, ready to drive out and fire from mobile missile launchers on fifteen minutes' notice. The crew live in adjacent underground quarters.

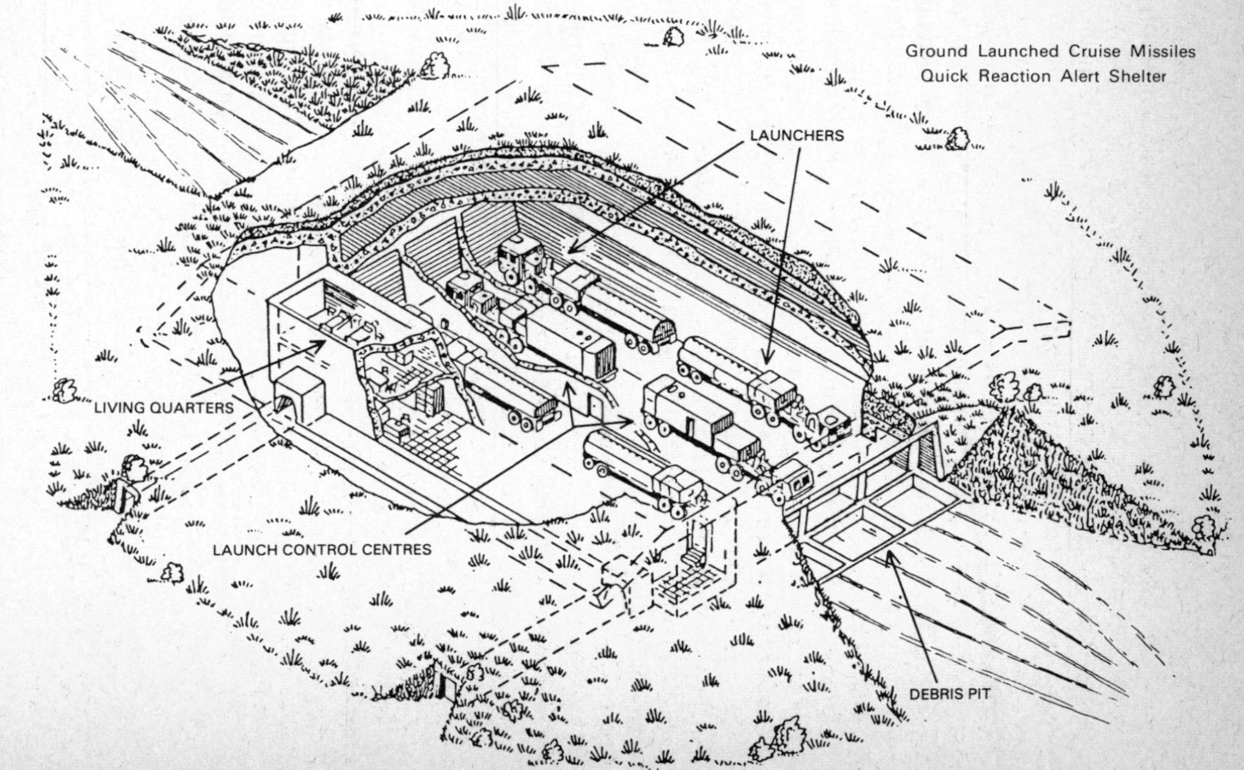


Fig 12. Inside a cruise missile bunker

This book is intended to provide an informative account of the US-British military relationship rather than an exhaustive analysis of each possible future option for defence policy. But such analysis must necessarily be underpinned by a full understanding of the US role in Britain. At the time of writing, it is apparent that no substantive change in British government policy towards the United States is likely for several years. Detailed prescriptions are therefore for the future.

Above, it has been argued that the terms on which US bases operate in Britain are quite inconsistent with and contrary to the British government's avowed respect for and concern with national sovereignty. The present agreements and terms ought not to stand in any circumstances. Meanwhile, a future government, less belligerent than that of Mrs Thatcher, may wish to examine what improvements in national and European security might be gained by US withdrawal.

A key issue in such a debate is the question of Soviet intentions. Does the Soviet Union wish, as a matter of policy, to conquer or politically dominate western Europe in the foreseeable future? May it not perhaps have enough on its plate already – with confrontation in Poland and Afghanistan, and belligerents encircling it from west to east? The United States has already launched a covert war of harassment against Soviet forces in Afghanistan. Soviet policies in satellite and border territories are repugnant – but are the Soviets engaged in imperialism, as the US claims, or merely trying to maintain their ugly but protective *cordon sanitaire* set up after the Second World War?

In the writing and speeches of President Reagan and his advisers, there has been more than a whiff of warmaking in the air. His administration simply denies the right of the Soviet Union – styled as the 'evil empire' – to exist. Right-wing foreign policy advisers are once again dreaming of the spontaneous collapse of the Soviet Union, as the CIA schemers did in the 1950s with their great visions of wars of liberation. This time, the war of liberation is economic, as the US drives the arms race upwards, forcing the Soviet Union to divert scarce resources to follow suit. US policymakers would like to make the effects of the arms race on the Soviet Union as severe as possible by economically isolating it, but have run into opposition from both US farmers and European governments. The ultimate objective of the US policy of economic coercion was clearly set out in a 1983 article in the influential US journal, *Foreign Affairs*.

> In the last analysis, we shall triumph when the people of the Soviet Empire decide they have lived in subjection and misery long enough and

take steps to achieve the freedom to which they too aspire. The Polish people have already taken the first giant step.

This type of dangerous outburst, which is indicative of the views of many in the Reagan administration, should be seen as a warning to Europeans to clearly separate their foreign and defence policies from those of the United States.

Looking around NATO, there are many models available for partial or complete US withdrawal. None involve becoming a Soviet satellite, as defenders of the *status quo* habitually claim. Each NATO ally has undertaken the duty of mutual defence which is the principal object of the NATO treaty, and many are happier doing this without US nuclear bases – or any foreign bases at all – on their territory. So if NATO and British membership thereof remain intact for the duration, there are still ample precedents for the withdrawal of US bases.

Britain is also engaged with the United States for bilateral, non-NATO purposes. The Ministry of Defence has argued that it is immaterial whether US bases are stated to be in use for NATO or US purposes. Most other NATO countries sharply distinguish between military co-operation within the scope of the North Atlantic Treaty, and that which is unilateral to the United States. Challenged in 1983 that intelligence bases like Chicksands, Edzell or Brawdy do not support NATO, the Ministry claimed that it was 'unrealistic to make a distinction' between NATO purposes and other unilateral or bilateral purposes: 'The US is

---

OVERLEAF

**Fig. 13. Target Britain: British and Soviet views**

A: British view: US bases are nuclear targets in British civil defence exercises.

In the September 1980 civil defence exercise 'Square Leg', Ministry of Defence planners anticipated the possible course of a large scale nuclear attack on the UK, involving over 200 Megatons of nuclear weapons. Many targets (A) were US bases or shared facilities.

B: Soviet view: US bases singled out in Soviet 'Foreign Military Review' article.

In a May 1980 article in the Soviet journal *Foreign Military Review*, a Soviet Colonel, V. Leskov, offered a brief (and crude) 'strategic survey' of Great Britain. Heavy stress was laid on the presence of US Armed Forces, who it was noted had 'constructed . . . a significant quantity of military facilities'. The map (B) shows the American bases which were specifically identified in Leskov's article and accompanying map. The map also showed numerous British airfields.

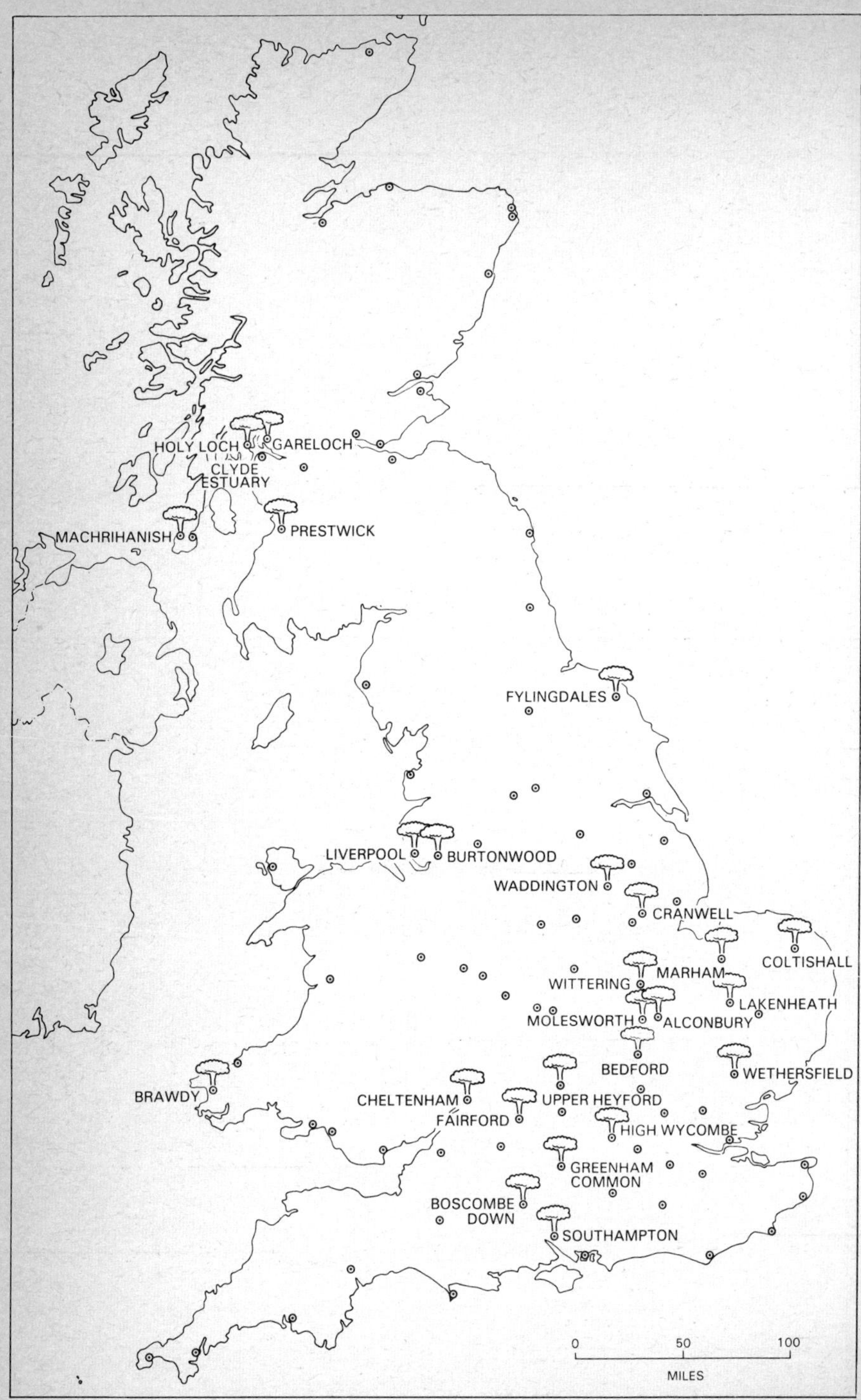


Fig 13a. Target Britain: a British view

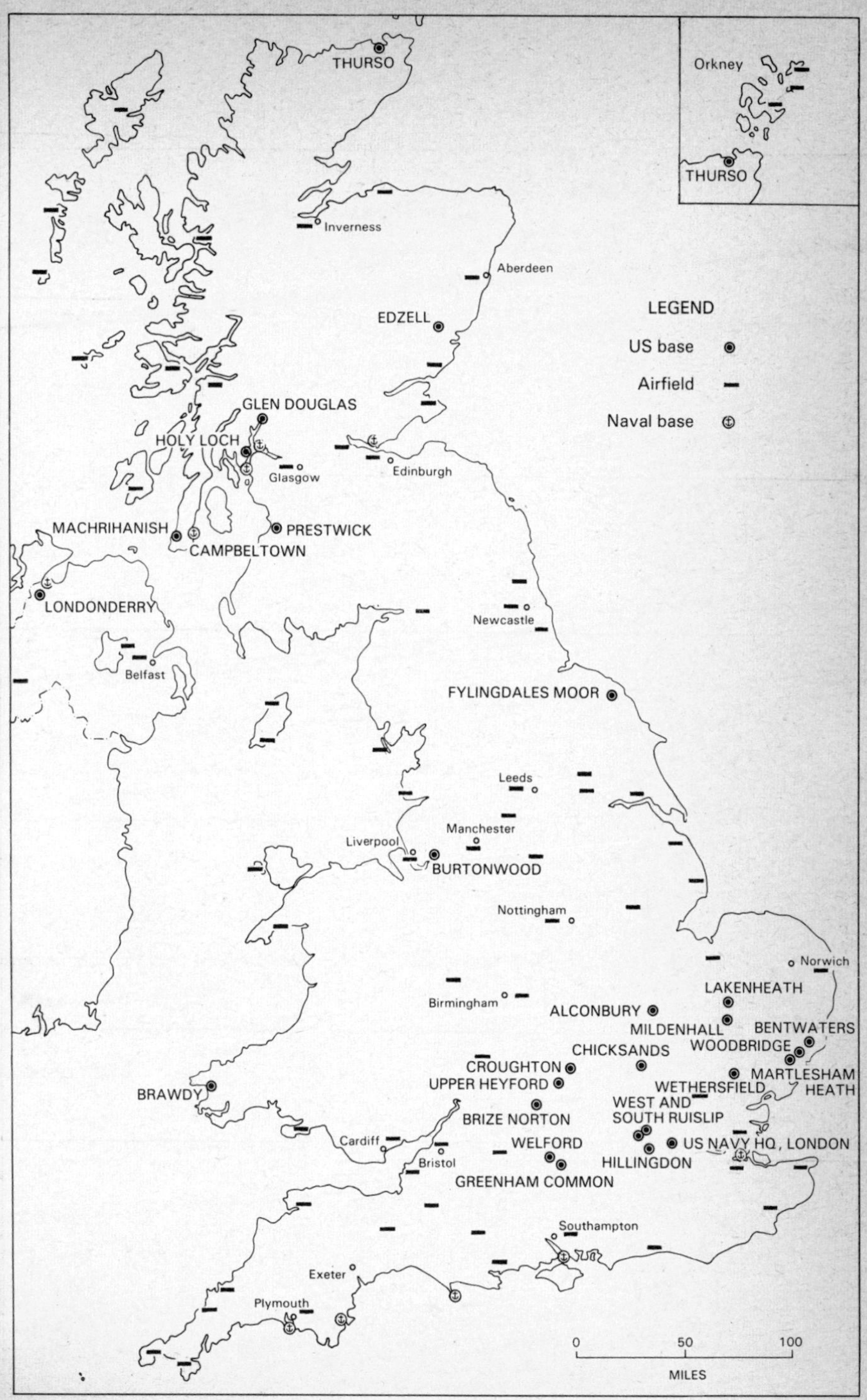
THURSO
Orkney
THURSO
Inverness
Aberdeen
EDZELL
LEGEND
US base
Airfield
Naval base
GLEN DOUGLAS
HOLY LOCH
Glasgow
Edinburgh
MACHRIHANISH
PRESTWICK
CAMPBELTOWN
LONDONDERRY
Newcastle
Belfast
FYLINGDALES MOOR
Leeds
Manchester
Liverpool
BURTONWOOD
Nottingham
Norwich
LAKENHEATH
Birmingham
ALCONBURY
MILDENHALL
BENTWATERS
WOODBRIDGE
CHICKSANDS
CROUGHTON
MARTLESHAM
HEATH
UPPER HEYFORD
WETHERSFIELD
BRAWDY
WEST AND
SOUTH RUISLIP
BRIZE NORTON
Cardiff
WELFORD
US NAVY HQ, LONDON
Bristol
HILLINGDON
GREENHAM COMMON
Southampton
Exeter
Plymouth
0
50
100
MILES

Fig 13b. Target Britain: a Soviet view

here in the interests of collective security, otherwise they would not be here at all'.

The greatest risks of continuing engagement with the US stem from the high and increasing levels of nuclear armaments, and the American pursuit of a confrontational foreign policy. US policymakers have discussed the idea of a nuclear war limited to Europe too frequently for many Europeans to trust entirely to US good intentions. US disengagement would enhance British security in the first instance simply by removing many major targets of likely attack, and some possible centres of confrontation in crisis. A strategy of US disengagement from Britain and Europe should be intended to provoke reciprocal steps from the Soviet Union and the Warsaw Pact, so moving towards greater European security at vastly reduced levels of confrontation.

Britain receives no direct defence assistance from US forces. On the contrary (see Chapter 9), US bases are a burden on British defences – and national vulnerability in nuclear war has long been multiplied by the presence of the bases. This is exemplified by the two 'target lists' illustrated in Figure 13. One list shows the US targets which were subject to nuclear attack in the 1980 military and home defence exercise, 'Square Leg'. The Square Leg list was drawn up by Ministry of Defence planners. The second map comes from an article in a Soviet military journal. The Soviet map gave special prominence to a few key American facilities, and included almost every British airfield in existence. Removing major US nuclear bases would naturally reduce the number of likely nuclear targets in Britain. But this may only be a marginal gain if there is no consequent change to foreign and defence policy.

Should US disengagement be a unilateral or multilateral strategy? Britain can improve its national security by unilateral US disengagement, which need not be conditional on reciprocal moves from the east. Even if disengagement were not reciprocated (in which case the resulting military situation would be far less attractive), the argument for limiting damage in war by diminished risk of nuclear destruction would still be persuasive. On the other hand, a total absence of reciprocity and goodwill by members of the Warsaw Pact in such circumstances would necessarily be taken as evidence of hostile intent, leading to a lack of support for total withdrawal. A strategy of unilateral disengagement which is not reciprocated in a reasonable manner by the Soviet bloc is unlikely to enjoy popular support through to its completion.

The key counterargument against US withdrawal for damage limiting purposes has been put by the Ministry of Defence. They assert that the UK must face 'facts of geography' and is of 'intrinsic strategic importance'. As phrased, this is not an argument of great consequence. Every single country in a zone of possible confrontation has facts of geography and an intrinsic strategic importance to confront. The United Kingdom is not unique in this regard, and there are many states – such as Iceland, Norway, Romania or Poland – where the facts of geography are a great deal tougher to live with than in Britain.

The 'facts of geography' are that Britain is an island, and that we stand close to Europe but facing America and the Atlantic. The fact of being an island provides an intrinsic natural defence against invasion, which has long been a feature of British history. That is also a fact of intrinsic strategic importance. The MOD argument is ultimately tautologous, as the Ministry has not thought through the consequences of US withdrawal. So long as Britain supports US military forces, its role as a forward US base and the first stop between the United States and Europe is a substantial fact of geography – and one of military importance. If US forces were removed, and replaced by a posture of armed neutrality or a Western European defence union, Britain's critical position vanishes. Instead of being the middle ground, Britain becomes the rear. It loses its importance as a transit centre, strategic stockpile – or unsinkable aircraft carrier.

Ultimately, it is undeniable that one or other belligerent in the late stage of a nuclear conflict might choose to destroy the industrial or military assets of non-belligerents to deny them to an opponent, or to ensure that minor or neutral powers were as badly damaged as the great ones and unable to dominate a postwar world. There is no defence against this sort of attack, just as nuclear deterrence offers no protection against irrationality, accident, or vengeance. The only sure protection is nuclear disarmament and the disengagement of foreign military forces.

The whole edifice of nuclear deterrence theory is erected on an assumption of rationality. Deterrence cannot operate once an opponent becomes irrational. Nuclear weapons have given madmen or the mindless and vengeful an almost unhindered opportunity to destroy the world, and that opportunity will remain while nuclear arsenals are at their present level.

A posture of determined and armed neutrality is the best and only line of defence in such a situation. Belligerents should be assured that they or their adversaries would have to fight to seize ports, airports, or other military assets in a general war. Ultimately, the defenders should prepare for and advertise widely a 'scorched earth' policy of destroying industrial or logistic facilities themselves by preplanned conventional demolition, in order to avoid seizure. Such a policy would be the most effective way of avoiding nuclear attack on assets of strategic importance – so long as each belligerent remains convinced that if the other attempts to capture neutral assets, they will be destroyed first.

The second Whitehall argument against US withdrawal is that deterrence is, in effect, a seamless robe – if the need for nuclear weapons is accepted, then Britain should accept all types of nuclear weapons and bases that may be required, without discrimination. For those who reject nuclear deterrence and nuclear weapons altogether, this does not matter, and their position against US bases is clear. But deterrence is not a seamless robe. The 1983 Labour election manifesto erred badly on this matter, by offering an unequivocal assurance that Polaris would be removed, while equivocating on US nuclear bases by means of references to consultation with European allies and sister socialist parties before considering removing the bases.

Not only did this line cut across the opinions of the electorate – who did not want cruise missiles or US nuclear bases, but accepted British nuclear weapons – it also attacked the relatively rational part of the deterrent system. However morally unattractive Polaris may be as a city-busting strike force, it combines two important features. For those who either wish nuclear deterrence at minimum force levels, or wish to retain some nuclear weapons until reciprocation is evident during unilateral disarmament, Polaris is more than an ample minimum nuclear force. For those who wish to be assured that nuclear disarmament would eventually be complete, the finite lifetime of the Polaris system provides that assurance, technically instead of politically.

US disengagement from Britain would take some time. The type of defence policy that then might be followed has been charted in recent debates, most notably by the Alternative Defence Commission.[51] Their study examined the new possibilities of defensive deterrence, without nuclear arms, and the military skills of territorial defence by conventional means – as well as less conventional strategies of civilian resistance. Another option is the formation, or re-formation, of a Western European defence union.

A more conservative position would be to consider retaining some but not all US facilities in Britain, removing the forces considered most destabilising. This would be an alternative to the 'all-or-nothing' strategy promoted by the government, which is neither credible nor followed by NATO allies. We could have some – although the balance would have to be tested to see whether any particular alteration achieved greater security at lower levels of confrontation.

Another alternative for Britain would be to emulate de Gaulle and ask the US to agree firm new terms, or leave. Such minimum new terms should include:

- Altering the legal status of US forces to ensure that British courts always had jurisdiction when necessary.
- Making each base or facility the subject of an administrative agreement, available to the public and Parliament.
- British control over and authorisation of all US unilateral (non-NATO) military operations, when permitted.
- Agreement on joint plans for use of the bases in war – and an absolute, physically-enforceable veto on the use of nuclear weapons.

From a pro-NATO but anti-nuclear perspective, it is necessary to pay attention to issues of infrastructure – the fact that far more bases are involved in the use of nuclear weapons, for example by providing or supporting navigation, communications, or command and control systems, than the mere handful on which the nuclear weapons and their carriers are located.

Those are the alternatives. But would the United States leave if they were asked to go? They would – but not without a fight. Officially, USAF officials say that:

> If we were asked to leave, we'd leave. But the government doesn't subscribe to that philosophy. We feel welcome here.[52]

In France in 1960 and 1966, the US did leave as ordered. Nevertheless, many in Britain fear that if the US were now to be ordered out of its British bases, the official response would not stop short of military obstruction and CIA plots to 'destabilise' the British government. This fear has been particularly frequently expressed in the writings and speeches of Tony Benn and his colleagues.

There can be no doubt that the United States has the capacity militarily to intervene in Britain, but not against the opposition of British military forces. However, in joint military exercises on Salisbury Plain with British units, US airborne troops have rehearsed suppressing dissent and rebellion in make-believe Western states. Politically, however, US military intervention in the UK must be inconceivable except in a situation of near civil war, when US forces might portray themselves as acting in support of a lawful power. Covert action against a radical British government judged to be seriously likely to upset US interests is much more probable, on the basis of precedents established elsewhere in western Europe. But covert action in such circumstances would merely be an accompaniment to a much greater volume of overt political and financial harassment.

Times change. As many in western Europe have expressed their unease at the pace of US nuclear rearmament and the arrival of the new NATO missiles, events in the Pacific having been going in the opposite direction. Japan was atom-bombed in 1945. In 1983, Japanese premier Yasuhiro Nakasone called for Japan now to become 'America's unsinkable aircraft carrier'.

Times change. 200 years ago, the American Revolution proved the new country's strength by expelling the British. Since the Second World War, British politicians and civil servants have nurtured the Anglo-American special relationship in an endeavour to prove the old country's strength. Failing, they have proved their weakness.

## Notes

1 *New York Times*, 24 July 1983.
2 In fact, US forces had, at the time of writing, been stationed in Britain for an *unbroken* period of 42 years, not 40 years.
3 Private communication to the author from members of the Bench near the US base at Fairford, Gloucestershire.
4 *Sunday Telegraph*, 25 May 1969.
5 *ibid.*
6 *International Herald Tribune*, 15 October 1973; *Daily Telegraph* 16 October and 24 December 1973.
7 *Scottish Daily Express*, 30 November 1965.
8 *Cornwall Courier*, 9 August 1979; *Cornish Guardian*, 10 January 1980.
9 *Hansard*, 11 December 1952; *Daily Express*, 13 November 1952.
10 *Hansard*, 17 November 1981 (Mrs Thatcher), and 3 February 1982 (Peter Blaker, Defence Minister).
11 *Royal Air Force News*, 10 February 1982.
12 Figures given for September 1979, from *Department of Defense Personnel Strengths*, DOD Table 309A/B/C, US Department of Defense, Washington Headquarters Services, Directorate for Information, Operations and Reports, Washington, February/March 1980. By 1983, the US Air Force was employing 1,400 UK civilians, a slight increase.
13 House of Representatives, Committee on Appropriations, subcommittee on Military Construction, Fiscal Year 1984, Part 5, p. 254.
14 *Foreign Relations of the United States*, 1950, Vol VII, p 1462.
15 *Listener*, 8 April 1971.
16 *Brass Tacks*, 30 May 1983; further reported by David Henshaw in the *Listener*, 2 June 1983.

17 *ibid.*
18 *Listener, ibid.*
19 *Brass Tacks, ibid.*
20 *ibid.*
21 From Acheson's autobiography, *Present at the creation*, quoted in Margaret Gowing, *Independence and deterrence*, Volume 1, p 314, Macmillan, 1974.
22 *The Times*, 20 November 1957.
23 *Brass Tacks, ibid.*
24 *ibid.*
25 *ibid.*
26 BBC television news, 26 February 1983; *Guardian*, 27 February 1983.
27 *New York Times*, 14 April 1983.
28 *Guardian*, 18 April 1983.
29 *Hansard*, 12 May 1983.
30 BBC television news, 27 May 1983.
31 *Brass Tacks*, 30 May 1983.
32 *Sunday Times*, 16 February 1982.
33 United States Senate, Committee on Foreign Relations, report on *US Security issues in Europe: Burden sharing and offset, MBFR, and nuclear weapons*, US Congress, 1973.
34 For details see Paul Buteux, *The politics of nuclear consultation in NATO 1965–1980*, Cambridge University Press, 1983, esp. pp 102–5; *US Security issues in Europe, ibid.*
35 *Brass Tacks, ibid.*
36 *Hansard*, 1 March 1983.
37 Harold Macmillan, Autobiography, Vol VI, pp 187–219, Macmillan, 1963.
38 Richard M. Nixon, *The memoirs of Richard Nixon*, Vol II, p 495, Grosset and Dunlap (New York), 1978.
39 Barry M. Blackman and Douglas M. Hart, 'The Political utility of nuclear weapons', *International Security*, Summer 1982, pp 132–156.
40 *Brass Tacks, ibid.*
41 *International Security, ibid.*
42 *Hansard*, 7 November 1955.
43 *TV Eye*, 30 October 1980.
44 Nuclear Armaments – An interview with Dr Daniel Ellsberg, Conservation Press, 1980. (Box 201, 2526 Shattuck Avenue, Berkeley, California 94704).
45 *New Statesman*, 20 June 1980.
46 A detailed account of US bases and facilities in Australia is given by Des Ball, *A suitable piece of real estate*, Hale and Ironmonger, Sydney, 1980.
47 *Guardian*, 18 March 1983.
48 *The modernisation of NATO's long-range theater nuclear forces*, Report to the US House of Representatives, subcommittee on Europe and the Middle East of the Committee on Foreign Affairs, Congressional Research Service, Library of Congress, December 1980; p 22.
49 *Hansard*, 6 March 1981.
50 *Aviation Week*, 28 February 1983.
51 *Defence without the bomb*, Report of the Alternative Defence Commission, Taylor and Francis, 1983.
52 *Daily Express*, 18 March 1982.

# Index and glossary